T0366955

The Secret War between the Wars

MI5 in the 1920s and 1930s

History of British Intelligence

ISSN 1756-5685

Series Editor
Peter Martland

With the recent opening of government archives to public scrutiny, it is at last possible to study the vital role that intelligence has played in forming and executing policy in modern history. This new series aims to be the leading forum for work in the area. Proposals are welcomed, and should be sent in the first instance to the publisher at the address below.

Boydell and Brewer Ltd, PO Box 9, Woodbridge, Suffolk IP12 3DF, UK

The Secret War between the Wars

MI5 in the 1920s and 1930s

Kevin Quinlan

THE BOYDELL PRESS

First published 2014
The Boydell Press, Woodbridge
Paperback edition 2022

ISBN 978-1-84383-938-5 hardback
ISBN 978-1-78327-709-4 paperback

The Boydell Press is an imprint of Boydell & Brewer Ltd
PO Box 9, Woodbridge, Suffolk IP12 3DF, UK
and of Boydell & Brewer Inc.
668 Mt Hope Avenue, Rochester, NY 14620-2731, USA
website: www.boydellandbrewer.com

A catalogue record for this book is available
from the British Library

The publisher has no responsibility for the continued existence
or accuracy of URLs for external or third-party internet websites
referred to in this book, and does not guarantee that any content
on such websites is, or will remain, accurate or appropriate

This publication is printed on acid-free paper

FOR MY MOTHER AND FATHER

It was his profession, which was that of intelligence officer. It was a profession he enjoyed, and which mercifully provided him with colleagues equally obscure in character and origin. It also provided him with what he had once loved best in life: academic excursions into the mystery of human behaviour, disciplined by the practical application of his own deductions.

John le Carré, *Call for the Dead*, 1961

Contents

Illustrations

Foreword

Intelligence remains the only profession in which a fictional character (James Bond) remains many times better known than any real practitioner, alive or dead. The tradecraft used by intelligence agencies tends to be thought of as the province of Bond and the spy novelist rather than the serious scholar. References to 'invisible ink', for example, are vanishingly rare in the many scholarly studies of twentieth-century international relations published by university presses. It was not always thus. Robert Boyle of 'Boyle's Law', one of the key figures in the seventeenth-century scientific revolution and a founder of the Royal Society, invented the term 'invisible ink' and devoted much research to the way reagents make messages written in it 'confess their secrets'. As Professor Kristie Makrakis has argued, the fact that until 2012 the CIA refused to declassify files on the use of invisible ink in the First World War (the oldest classified documents in the US National Archives) is evidence of their continued relevance to intelligence tradecraft. The simplest methods of transmitting secrets are still sometimes the best.

As Kevin Quinlan argues persuasively, 'The most successful intelligence gathering has depended upon good tradecraft.' His path-breaking (and often colourful) analysis of the interwar development of MI5 tradecraft opens up new and important perspectives on counter-espionage, counter-subversion and the British response to Soviet Communism, Italian Fascism and German Nazism. *The Secret War between the Wars* also has major implications for our understanding of the role of intelligence in both the Second World War and the Cold War. MI5 tradecraft was essential to the success of probably the most effective strategic deception in the history of warfare: the 'Double-Cross System' which fed Hitler and his high command with an unprecedented volume of high-grade disinformation.

Soviet tradecraft also had major successes. The sophistication of the intelligence tradecraft deployed against Moscow's wartime allies enabled it to capture probably the single biggest secret in the history of espionage: the plans of the first US atomic bomb, on which the Soviet Union modelled its own. Superior tradecraft also allowed Soviet intelligence to profit from the sometimes woeful lack of security in Western embassies in Moscow. When an FBI expert carried out the first, long overdue, electronic sweep of the US embassy in 1944, he found 120 hidden microphones in the first 24 hours. Thereafter, according to an eye-witness, 'they kept turning up, in the legs of any new tables or chairs which were delivered, in the plaster of walls, any and everywhere'. The major contribution of US and UK intelligence during the Cuban Missile Crisis, the most dangerous point of the Cold War, would have been impossible without much improved Western tradecraft in operations against the Soviet Union.

As well as being a very good read, *The Secret War between the Wars* makes a powerful case for giving much greater recognition to the role of tradecraft in assessing the past role and influence of intelligence agencies.

Christopher Andrew
Emeritus Professor of Modern and Contemporary History,
University of Cambridge
Former Official Historian of the British Security Service (MI5)

Acknowledgements and Disclaimer

This book represents the labour of many people. I would like to thank Professors Peter Hennessey and Keith Jeffery, my doctoral examiners, for their thoughtful commentary on the dissertation underpinning this work, and for being among the first to urge me to turn it into a book. I alone, of course, take responsibility for any errors contained herein, but what follows certainly would have been more flawed without comments and contributions made by Ms Gill Bennett OBE, Mr Hayden Peake and Dr Michael Warner. I would like to thank Michael Middeke, Megan Milan, Rosie Pearce and Boydell & Brewer Press, as well as editor Dr Peter Martland, for their confidence in this project. I also extend thanks to Dr Amy E. Davis for her editorial contributions. During years of research, the staff at the Reading Room of the National Archives made work incomparably easier than it otherwise might have been: Julie Ash and Emily Ward deserve mention. I regularly attended the University of Cambridge Intelligence Seminar from 2004 to 2008, and this book benefitted substantially from insights provided by current and former government officials who spoke in confidence about their experiences. Thanks to all. A special note of gratitude goes to seminar members Dr Johnny Chavkin and Dr Adam Shelley, for their constructive criticism on previous drafts, and to Thomas Giles, Benjamin Hutchinson and Dr Dina Rezk, all of whom provided welcomed diversion and hospitality after long hours of research. I am particularly grateful to Dr Calder Walton for reviewing multiple iterations of this book and acting as a sounding board throughout this project, as well as to his family for looking after me during my time in the UK. This book could not have been written without Professor Christopher Andrew, my supervisor and mentor. My gratitude to you cannot be overstated. Thank you. My deep appreciation goes to my wife, Esha, for her patience and sustenance as this book came to publication. Above all, I would like to thank my sister and especially my parents, whose warm encouragement and support have made it all possible.

This book contains no classified information and relies entirely on publicly available information, predominately the records available at The National Archives, UK, but also published memoirs and academic studies. The University of Cambridge Intelligence Seminar, arguably the preeminent seminar of its kind in the world, is convened by the former official historian of the Security Service (MI5), Professor Christopher Andrew. The information discussed in the Seminar is unclassified but the forum operates under the Chatham House Rule, which stipulates that the information obtained may be used but that speakers and participants may not be identified. For more information on the Seminar, please see http://www.hist.cam.ac.uk/seminars/seminars-list/intelligence. The analysis and research within this book were conducted during the period 2004–2008 for my doctoral dissertation at the University of Cambridge. The views and opinions expressed herein by the author do not represent the policies or position of any government, including the United States Government or any of its constituent Departments or Agencies, and are the sole responsibility of the author.

Kevin Quinlan

Abbreviations and Acronyms

ARCOS	All Russian Cooperative Society
BUF	British Union of Fascists
C	Chief of SIS
CHEKA	Extraordinary Commission for Combating Counter-Revolution and Sabotage (Bolshevik intelligence and security service, 1917–1922)
CIA	Central Intelligence Agency (US)
CID	Committee for Imperial Defence
CID	Criminal Investigation Department (Metropolitan Police)
CIGS	Chief of the Imperial General Staff
COMINTERN	Communist International (Third Congress)
CPGB	Communist Party of Great Britain
DI	Directorate of Intelligence (UK)
DDG	Deputy-Director General (Security Service)
DG	Director-General (Security Service)
DNI	Director of Naval Intelligence (UK)
FBI	Federal Bureau of Investigation (US)
FO	Foreign Office
FPA	Federated Press of America
GC&CS	Government Code and Cypher School
GCHQ	Government Communications Headquarters (successor to GC&CS)
GPO	General Post Office
GPU	Soviet intelligence and security service (within NKVD, 1922–1923)
GRU	Soviet military intelligence (successor to the Fourth Department)
HO	Home Office
HOW	Home Office Warrant
HUMINT	Human intelligence
IIB	Industrial Intelligence Bureau
IKKI	Executive Committee of the Comintern
INO	Foreign department of Cheka/OGPU/NKVD (1920–1941)
ISOS	Intelligence Section Oliver Strachey (SIGINT)

JIC	Joint Intelligence Committee
KGB	Soviet intelligence and security service
LAI	League Against Imperialism
MI1(b)	War Office Cryptographic Department
MI1(c)	Secret Intelligence Service (First World War and immediate post-First World War designation)
MI5	Security Service (First World War and 1920s designation, still in common usage)
MI6	Secret Intelligence Service (First and Second World War designation)
MI8	Wireless Censorship (First World War)
MI9	Postal Censorship (First World War)
MI9c	Testing Department – Postal Censorship (First World War)
MO5(g)	Security Service (First World War designation)
MPSB	Metropolitan Police Special Branch (Scotland Yard)
NARKOMINDEL	Soviet Commissariat for Foreign Affairs
NMM	National Minority Movement
NKVD	People's Commissariat for Internal Affairs (incorporated state security, 1922–1923, 1934–1943)
OMS	Organisation for the Maintenance of Supplies
OMS	Comintern International Liaison Department
OGPU	Soviet intelligence and security service (1923–1934)
PCO	Passport Control Officer
PUS	Permanent Under-Secretary
RILU	Red International of Labour Unions
SIGINT	Signals Intelligence
SIS	Secret Intelligence Service
SOE	Special Operations Executive
STC	Supply and Transport Committee
STO	Supply and Transport Organisation
SSB	Secret Service Bureau
SSC	Secret Service Committee
TUC	Trades Union Congress

Notes on Style and References

This text generally follows the rules set by the Modern Humanities Research Association (MHRA) *Style Guide* (2002). Footnotes are given as follows: abbreviated archive name (NA); record collection (NA KV); series (NA KV1); file number and title (NA KV1/1 MI5 File); serial and document name (either by document heading or description, or by minute entry, depending on which more clearly identifies the document) (NA KV1/1 MI5 File, s.1a, 'document name'); and the author or author's designation, followed by the document's date (NA KV1/1 MI5 File, s.1a, 'document name', by John Bull (A.1.), 1 January 1919). In longer documents, such as summary reports, page numbers are also given. In subsequent citations the file title or document name may be shortened. Not all information is available for each document, but in every case sufficient detail is provided for the document to be easily located by future researchers.

The style of the documents quoted has not been altered, so subjects of investigation in MI5 documents, for example, appear in CAPITAL letters. Similarly, where the quoted passages retain full stops in abbreviations ('M.I.5.'), the main text drops them ('MI5'). The @ symbol in MI5 documents denotes aliases. This dissertation generally uses the designation 'MI5' instead of the Security Service, and uses the abbreviation SIS instead of the Secret Intelligence Service, or MI6. Furthermore, whereas some quoted passages may refer to MI5 and SIS in the plural (e.g. MI5 or SIS 'were'), the main text employs the singular (MI5 or SIS 'was'). The term British 'security services' does not refer to *the* Security Service, but to both MI5 and the Metropolitan Police Special Branch (MPSB). For the sake of simplicity, military ranks are generally not given, and honorific titles (e.g. knighthoods) for recurring individuals are only given at an individual's first appearance in the text. Titles awarded chronologically later than the individual's first appearance in the text are given parenthetically. Again for simplicity's sake, reference made to generic agents and officers uses the masculine gender despite the fact that there have been many female agents and officers – including the ones who appear in this book.

Some of the information below was obtained in forums governed by the Chatham House Rule, which reads, 'When a meeting, or part thereof, is held under the Chatham House Rule, participants are free to use the information received, but neither the identity nor the affiliation of the speaker(s), nor that

of any other participant, may be revealed.' 'Private information' refers to information obtained in conversations with five current or former American and
British intelligence officers. To respect their privacy, the identities of these individuals remain confidential.

Preface

The spies' American neighbours were stunned when the FBI arrested them as part of a roundup of Russian operatives in 2010. One young neighbour was incredulous: "'They couldn't have been spies,' she said jokingly. "Look what she did with the hydrangeas."'[1] Two matters stand out about the case. The Russian spies had been planted in the suburban soil of the United States to report home on news that could just as easily, in most cases, have been pulled from the internet. And then, too, they were astonishingly well trained and equipped for what seems so frivolous an enterprise. As the *New York Times* reported, the group 'had everything it needed for world-class espionage: excellent training, cutting-edge gadgetry, deep knowledge of American culture and meticulously constructed cover stories.'[2] And that is why the hydrangeas were important. Whether the Russian denizens of that particular house were simply avid gardeners or had been trained in the ways of American suburban horticulture, they looked like they belonged. It takes craft for a spy to blend in. Without that craft, there is no espionage.

Espionage is said to be more art than science.[3] And as the world's second oldest profession, it is an ancient and practised art. The tricks of its trade are so well established that, as one British veteran claims, 'There are no new ways of collecting intelligence.'[4] Another old Asia hand notes that although the tools have grown more sophisticated, the principles of espionage are essentially the same today as they were between the World Wars. He explains that 'The steamship is to the navy as tradecraft is to espionage.' Whether in a calm sea or stormy sea, the principle is the same: the boat must get from Point A to Point B. In order to do this, the captain must know the vessel, just as the officer must know the agent.[5] For all the technical developments that have aided intelligence collection over the last century, one basic element remains the same: people. The psychology of agent handling, including an understanding of human motivations and an ability to manipulate and even control, has been a fundamental part of tradecraft. 'As long as emotional needs and frailties exist, so will spies,' one former KGB officer has written.[6]

Sources and methods remain the most closely guarded secrets of intelligence services, for these form the base of all espionage. In human intelligence (HUMINT), *sources* are agents and informants, and *methods* refer to their recruitment and handling. It is these skills of recruiting and especially running agents in the field that we call *tradecraft*, and it is tradecraft that makes the systematic collection and, consequently, analysis of intelligence possible.[7] Yet tradecraft is commonly regarded as either scholarly antiquarianism or the stuff of movies. Almost no academic book on international relations considers it, even though the methods used by spies have provided intelligence in support many of the major foreign policy initiatives of the twentieth and twenty-first centuries.[8]

The most successful intelligence gathering has depended upon good tradecraft. During the Cold War, Soviet spies succeeded in stealing what were practically the complete plans of the first atomic bomb only because the USSR's tradecraft was superior to the security systems that the United States had instituted to protect atomic secrets.[9] Before the Cuban Missile Crisis, human intelligence enabled the imagery analysts at the Central Intelligence Agency (CIA) to interpret U2 spy-plane photographs of Soviet missile bases in Cuba because the tradecraft of double agent Oleg Penkovsky and his British handlers allowed secrets to travel from one set of hands to another without detection.[10]

The early twenty-first-century fight against terrorism has brought renewed interest in intelligence and made it the subject of unprecedented public debate.[11] The 11 September 2001 terrorist attacks and the controversy regarding intelligence on weapons of mass destruction (WMD) in Iraq have brought intelligence into the public consciousness with great immediacy; its successes and failures are all examined and scrutinised.[12]

Yet much about these contemporary crises is not novel. To understand the challenges faced today it may be worth heeding Winston Churchill's claim that 'the further back one looks, the further forward one can see'.[13] The period between the two World Wars may prove an illuminating comparison for understanding the forces shaping today's international relations. At that time, the world's dominant power – Britain – found itself sapped and indebted after the First World War. As London contended with austerity, the success of the Russian Revolution threatened to reorder existing civil and economic norms – it threatened to destroy capitalism and imperialism, two of Britain's guiding principles of administration for previous centuries. That is to say, revolutionary powers – first the Soviet Union and then Nazi Germany – sought to challenge the patterns of governance and trade favouring the dominant power. Not at first able to confront Britain as a 'peer competitor', to borrow today's language, Moscow challenged London in less conventional and more covert ways. In turn, Britain vigorously fought to block those subversives at home and abroad who would see its ideological demise.

With this context in mind, it is noteworthy that the former head of the CIA's Strategic Assessments Group wrote in the aftermath of 9/11:

> To gain an appreciation of what may be in store for the United States [and Britain, too], it is useful to compare the present stage of terrorism to the days of evolving communism in the 1920s and 1930s. The useful historical metaphor is not an ossified Soviet Union but the early days of largely autonomous, independently operated and financed cells. Those cells organized local labour movements, fostered radical political causes, acted with global reach, and attracted the sympathies of otherwise moderate citizens.[14]

Even as the Soviet Union under Stalin turned inward and away from plans to foment worldwide revolution, it continued to plot the disintegration of the capitalist world order and the unravelling of the British Empire more specifically. Despite the manifold differences that exist between the contemporary struggle against terrorism and the communist espionage and subversion that followed the Bolshevik revolution, much of the problem for the West is similar – an ideologically driven enemy operating in secret cells, blending in with the local population and determined to destroy the status quo. British security and intelligence services faced a similar enemy then as now: conspiracies held together by ideology and 'a state of mind rather than a state'.[15]

Conspiracy was a defining characteristic of Bolshevism, an ingrained feature of the revolutionary mentality. It was a trait inherited by the Comintern and often expressed by national communist parties.[16] Bolshevism's most fervent believers professed a universal ideology that they hoped to institute through subversion when it faced political rejection, and the communists leveraged a *myth-image* of communist utopia to gain recruits.[17] Acts of conspiracy – such as clandestine agitation, propaganda and recruitment – required secretive methods. Equally, for opponents of communist subversion, secret agents and moles became the primary method of countering these conspiracies.[18]

Tradecraft has the odd distinction of being misunderstood in opposite ways. On the one hand, it is seen as a world of brilliant minds, exciting technology and fierce cunning. At its literary best, that is the world of George Smiley. Some, however, treat tradecraft as parody, seeing, whatever its value, 'a secret world of fantasy and flimflammery'.[19] Even at the inaugural lunch in 1946 for the Central Intelligence Group, the forerunner of the CIA, President Harry Truman presented guests with black cloaks, black hats and wooden daggers, stuck a fake moustache on Admiral William Leahy (Chief of Staff to the Commander in Chief), and pronounced the new intelligence head Sydney Souers the 'Director of Centralized Snooping'.[20] Yet secrecy is often the point of this world, for hiding reality by using false identities (*covers* and *legends*) is a fundamental aspect of clandestine operations with potentially fatal consequences. Hardly nonsense, tradecraft ensures the protection of sources and the collection of intelligence despite the security structures in place to guard it.

Still, tradecraft needs explanation. Former Director of Central Intelligence Allan Dulles noted, 'Clandestine intelligence collection is chiefly a matter of circumventing obstacles in order to reach an objective.' That objective is access to secret information.[21] Its clandestine retrieval depends on tradecraft, defined as 'the particular methods an intelligence officer uses to operate and communicate with sources without being detected by the opposing intelligence service'.[22] The tradecraft used by officers or other spies to obtain information from an agent includes methods of communication, meeting arrangements, source protection and the recruitment and handling of those sent out into the field. Tradecraft is not a monolithic phenomenon, but a variety of clandestine methods used to secure information from a human source. It is the *how* of HUMINT.

Introduction

The Architecture of British Intelligence

I NVISIBLE inks. Hollow heels. Hidden briefcase compartments. Microdot photography. All seemingly the stuff of spy thrillers, born of the imagination of writers such as Ian Fleming. But all are actual historical examples of espionage methods. Spies cannot conjure the tools of their craft out of thin air. No single person in the field can develop the technology required for a fake rock to store and transmit secret information to spies' hand-held devices, as a senior British official recently acknowledged was one method used by British intelligence in Russia until discovered by Russian security officials.[1] A considerable administrative apparatus stands behind intelligence operatives to develop new technologies, coordinate operations and compile, categorise and analyse the information they gather. Indeed, it could be argued that the greatest weapon for early British intelligence was not the knife or the gun, as might be supposed, but rather the filing cabinet. So although bureaucracy is not the most scintillating focus for a study of intelligence, it was the establishment of a bureaucracy that brought intelligence into the modern era.

Britain emerged from the First World War victorious but in tatters. A postwar recession set in and cuts were made across government, and the intelligence services were no exception. These cuts to MI5's budget and staff left the service a shadow of its wartime self. Yet the basic features and methods that had existed before Britain entered the Great War continued to underpin intelligence operations. The organisation of British counter-intelligence was actually developed in the years immediately preceding the war with the founding of the Secret Service Bureau (SSB). Its core components were a Preventive Branch (security) and a Detective Branch (investigations).[2] Effectively 'distinct but inseparable members of a single organism', they were joined by the Administrative Branch, which was carved off from the Preventative Branch soon after the war began.[3] Together, these comprised the tripartite soul of Britain's counter-espionage apparatus.

Many years later, one practitioner observed that 'counterintelligence consists of two matching halves, security and counterespionage'. Security 'consists basically of establishing passive or static defences against all hostile and concealed acts, regardless of who carries them out'. Counter-espionage, on the other hand, 'requires the identification of a specific adversary, a knowledge of the specific operations that he is conducting, and a countering of those operations by penetrating and manipulating them so that their thrust is turned back against the aggressor'.[4] It is a perfect description of MI5's early years of operations.

Although no legislation created MI5 itself, the service depended on a system of legislative procedures, security measures and record keeping methods without which effective agent operations would have been practically impossible.[5] Counter-espionage without legislation and security structures would have been like a body without a skeleton; without records it would have been like a body with no head.[6]

The Foundations of British Counter-Espionage

Registries and warrants formed the foundation of counter-espionage, both at home and abroad. Over the course of the First World War, operations, security measures and record keeping developed a sequential and reciprocal relationship. A year after its founding in 1909, the SSB split into the domestic department under Sir Vernon Kell, later becoming MI5 (and then the Security Service) and the foreign department under Sir Mansfield Cumming, which later became MI6 (and then the Secret Intelligence Service, SIS).[7] Kell, with the encouragement of the new Home Secretary, Winston Churchill, soon implemented the two counter-espionage weapons that would underpin MI5's operations well into the future: the Precautionary Index and the Home Office Warrant (HOW), the latter of which is still used in the early twenty-first century. The registration of foreigners ('aliens') at ports and hotels allowed the government to trace or actively shadow their movements throughout the country. The establishment of port security and immigration controls during the war had been a major innovation in counter-intelligence, one that was strengthened by the introduction of standardised passports.[8] The Precautionary Index and the Central Registry, its successor during the First World War, and the accompanying MI5 Black List, kept progressively more detailed accounts of suspected spies and undesirable foreigners. As a corollary, Churchill proposed that 'a warrant might be issued in the time of emergency authorising' censorship of the correspondence of those on the list.[9] The Index became a vital step in building cases against suspects and a necessary precondition for HOWs, which granted the right to open and censor the correspondence (and later to wiretap the telephone calls and premises) of those individuals and organisations believed to pose a threat to national security.

Legislation such as the Official Secrets Act (OSA) of 1911 supported the collection of intelligence. The 'unalterable' principles of preventive work, as described by one MI5 postwar summary report, consisted of identification, classification and control.[10] OSA 1911 prohibited drawing pictures, taking photographs or making blueprints of sensitive government premises and installations. It also allowed authorities to search individuals on the basis of suspicion alone and, contrary to the usual criminal procedure, shifted the burden of proof to the accused: 'It was for him to prove that he was there with no illegal intention.'[11]

This more stringent law was passed in an atmosphere of heightened suspicion against foreigners, especially Germans. Kaiser Wilhelm's policy of *Weltpolitik*, adopted in 1897, had launched an Anglo-German naval rivalry, and popular literature stoked fears of rampant German espionage in Britain. William Le Queux's sensationalist *Spies of the Kaiser* (1909) prompted near hysteria with its depiction of a pervasive German fifth column ready to rise up in the event of an Anglo-German confrontation.[12] Churchill played a prominent role in the introduction of security legislation, especially the OSA of 1911, and his approval the previous year led the way to the compilation of an unofficial, secret Register of Aliens, prepared by MI5 with the help of the police. By 1913, the nascent MI5 Registry contained the names of some 28,000 aliens potentially to be arrested, deported or monitored in the event of war.[13]

Possibly the greatest coup of early British counter-espionage was the 'spy round-up' in 1914. HOWs had enabled the interception of suspected German agents' postal correspondence in the run-up to the war, although 'The Detective Branch (G) . . . refrained from arresting known enemy agents whenever this course could be pursued without immediate danger to the safety of the country. The correspondence of agents and spies was intercepted, examined and sent on, as a rule without emandations [*sic*].'[14] In this way, MI5 clandestinely monitored the Kaiser's espionage network and identified its members, building up a clear picture of its organisation 'with the principal object of paralysing the German spy system, in case of war, by one powerful blow'. Indeed, Scotland Yard, with information provided by MI5, was able to arrest twenty-one of twenty-two identified German spies within twenty-four hours of the onset of hostilities.[15]

Once war began, the OSA of 1911 was overridden by the much more draconian Defence of the Realm Act (DORA). Its constituent Defence of the Realm

Regulations (DRR) provided the government with more intrusive measures, including mass censorship – of personal correspondence as often as of the popular press – and the internment of those suspected of communicating with the enemy. The classification and control of information for security and investigative purposes was fundamental to both OSA of 1911 and DORA.

Yet despite the value of interception, the authorities hesitated to extend censorship beyond the HOW system. In part, they argued that mass censorship was simply not practicable. Over time, however, the expediencies of war and the necessity of controlling the availability of information to the enemy prevailed. Mass censorship superseded HOW requirements for interception. Later still, they concluded that MI8 (Cable Censorship) and MI9 (Postal Censorship) 'were possibly of more value as preventative organisations than any other single existing department'.[16] The effort was enormously expensive and labour intensive – MI9's one-person staff in 1914 had grown to 4,871 by 1918. Postal censorship was shown to be of such importance that MI9's postwar review concluded that in a 'future universal war', a censorship department would need to start out with no fewer than 4,000 staff members to complete its task effectively.[17] By way of comparison, MI5's total staff in the early twenty-first century numbers 3,000.[18]

From the German Menace to the Red Menace

Even before Britain's entry into the First World War, the concept of an outside power inciting unrest within the country held considerable currency. The notion continued to carry weight in the interwar period but focused on a different foe. Attention turned from Germany to the threat of Bolshevism, and the intelligence services often focused on socialists and political dissidents who might be doing the Soviet Union's bidding. Domestic dissent, especially when seen as radical or socialist, had been deemed a threat even before the Russian Revolution. Reginald McKenna, Churchill's successor as Home Secretary in 1911, had authorised early on the interception of letters and telegrams of political organisations such as those of the suffragists.[19] Sylvia Pankhurst's MI5 file, for example, dates from 1914.[20] But after 1917, the establishment of a communist state in place of the tsarist empire exacerbated older fears.

After the war, the government continued its surveillance of political dissidents and subversives, issuing HOWs to authorise the monitoring of not only the Communist Party of Great Britain (CPGB), but also influential individuals who were pro-Soviet socialists. The investigations into the activities of

Albert Inkpin (secretary of the British Socialist Party) started in 1916 and continued well after he became the CPGB's first General Secretary upon its founding in 1920.[21] Although there is no complete list of cases, the interception of correspondence via the HOW had an impact over the succeeding years much like that of censorship during the war, underpinning the investigations into the activities of the CPGB's founder-members and many other socialists and communists.[22] Even a cursory glance at MI5's personal files shows how impressively widely MI5 cast its net. The information gained from intercepted correspondence created a web of surveillance and provided initial clues for counter-subversion and counter-espionage operations.

During the war, the government had not been alone in its concern that an outside power was inciting unrest inside Britain. Conservative private groups formed to challenge what they saw as pernicious effects of German influence such as pacifism.[23] They stood for tradition, empire and *Britishness*. But in addition to nationalism, the economics of big business, bolstered by ideas of protectionism and autarky, also played a part in the foundation of groups like the British Empire Union (BEU). Sir George Makgill (11th Baronet of Kemback) was a leading voice of the Anti-German Union, which advocated 'No German labour, no German goods, no German influence, Britain for the British'.[24] At about the same time, he founded the BEU to promote 'the Extirpation – Root and Branch and Seed – of German Control and Influence from the British Empire'.[25] Many in these groups went on to participate in early fascist/patriotic organisations such as Rotha Lintorn-Orman's British Fascisti (BF), which formed in 1923. So, ironically, the roots of British fascism were in part anti-German.

In the 1920s, these groups began to emphasise the threat of organised labour and communism. Decrying the *red menace*, they pointed to the peril created by domestic communism, a new fifth column with a new name. Unlike the German threat, communism attacked the very core of British imperial capitalist beliefs. The members of the BEU and BF saw themselves as the counterweight to socialist militancy and their role as the defence of the established order against the spectre of Bolshevism at home.

Signals Intelligence

In the interwar period, as during the First World War, MI5's counter-espionage operations were crucially assisted by other services' signals intelligence capabilities. Since the late nineteenth century, cable and wireless telegraphy (known as w/t) had also become a vital medium for communication in war and diplomacy, and hence a security concern, as well. The Boer War had made plain to British authorities the necessity of cable censorship.[26] The historian Sir Michael Howard has even suggested that radio introduced 'virtually a fourth dimension of war'.[27]

The decryption of Soviet communications complemented the intelligence produced by HOWs, which might be viewed as the intercepts' physical counterpart.[28] GC&CS – the amalgamation of Room 40 and MI1(b) – had moved to the Foreign Office in 1922 from the Admiralty, where it had first lodged upon its creation in 1919. Although its officially recognised function was to 'to advise as to the security of codes and cyphers used by all Government departments and to assist in their provision', secret instructions also ordered it 'to study the methods of cypher communications used by foreign powers'.[29] It was generally assumed in 1919 that military and naval radio intercepts would consume most of GC&CS's future time and energy, but it actually focused primarily on deciphering diplomatic telegrams sent over international cables, MI1(b)'s area of expertise. A sample of GC&CS's decryption output between November 1919 and January 1920 also shows that the countries covered by MI1(b) during the war accounted for over fifty percent of GC&CS's output, whereas countries covered by Room 40 only accounted for about fifteen percent.[30] One could argue, therefore, that MI1(b)'s analysts were not only greater in number than Room 40's but were also more productive.

Yet from 1919 to 1933, Soviet Russia was held to pose the greatest threat to British security, and the greatest cryptanalytic work against Soviet Russia came from the remnants of Room 40, not MI1(b). Despite the security of tsarist codes, the Bolsheviks discontinued their use and instead relied on inferior systems, badly compromising the security of their communications. Russia had also suffered the loss of a number of tsarist cryptographers after the revolution, including Ernst Fetterlein, who immigrated to the UK and led Britain's cryptographic assault against Soviet Russia with considerable effect.[31] As the historian Christopher Andrew has noted, 'During the ten months of the Anglo-Soviet Trade negotiations which followed [head of the Soviet delegation Leonid] Krasin's arrival in London at the end of May 1920, the single most important source available to the British Government was the Soviet diplomatic traffic decrypted by Fetterlein and his assistants at GC&CS'.[32] Until 1927, the British had almost unfettered access to Soviet communiqués. Then, however, the British Government publicly acknowledged SIGINT success against the Soviet Union, prompting the Soviets to switch to unbreakable one-time cypher pads.[33]

Success reappeared in the 1930s. John Tiltman, who had worked on Soviet Russian intercepts in India, together with Dillwyn 'Dilly' Knox, a Room 40 alumnus, broke the Comintern's radio traffic, supplying the decrypts, code-named *MASK*, from 1930 to 1937.[34] Indeed Tiltman is said to have 'all but invented the modern science of deciphering . . . diplomatic and military intercepts', no doubt accounting for why he was GC&CS's chief codebreaker and deputy to A. G. Denniston. He later served as deputy-head of GCHQ and earned a place in the NSA's Hall of Honour as well.[35] Fetterlein and Knox (like Tiltman) also went on to play distinguished roles at Bletchley Park, the centre of British codebreaking operations during the Second World War. Denniston summarised GC&CS's interwar accomplishments when he wrote that:

> Between 1919 and 1939 GC&CS obtained knowledge of the cryptographic methods used by all powers except those which had been forced, like Russia, to use the One Time Pads or who like Germany had moved to machine encipherment, or those with contiguous European land boundaries who could use landlines to ensure cipher security.[36]

GC&CS's proficiency probably waned over the 1930s, but between 1919 and 1935 British SIGINT was 'possibly the best on earth' – even if GC&CS's ability to warn policymakers of German intentions in Eastern Europe just before the Second World War fell short of the task.[37] Through much of the interwar period, however, it provided senior civil servants and policymakers with direct insight into Soviet diplomacy and operations, such as the funding of the *Daily Herald* and a diamond smuggling syndicate.[38] Intercepts also acted as a counterweight to the sometimes dubious and patchy HUMINT reports coming out of Soviet Russia. Historically the 'INTs' worked best when they worked together.

Counter-espionage and Tradecraft

The methods of investigation varied according to the tradecraft of the target, so it was 'impracticable to attempt a summary of the principles of counter-action', according to MI5's in-house history. It is possible, however, to classify with some precision how the cases were initiated. Wartime regulations gave security services far more leeway, but before the war, leads came from a variety of sources. Externally, they came from informants, military and naval intelligence, government workers, the police and chance events such as a returned letter or an overheard conversation. Internal sources included the Precautionary Index, 'spy contacts established in pursuing and investigation'; and HOWs, which were the most important.[39] During the postwar years, HOWs would again prove to be one of MI5's essential tools. Also, peacetime intelligence acquired from other civilian departments such as SIS and GC&CS was extremely important, as it had during the First World War.[40]

MI5 archival documents detail the three stages of a counter-espionage investigation: discovering the enemy agent, collecting the evidence and either arresting the agent or 'nullifying' the agent's efforts.[41] These operations are subsumed by the 'cardinal principles of preventative legislation', which provides a more comprehensive schematic for the security and counter-espionage process and emphasises the interplay between the three stages. The ten cardinal aspects are information, communication, records, counter-action, examination, identification, classification, control, censorship and protection.[42] Dating from before the war, they remained equally important afterwards, although the HOW replaced censorship and the security services' ability to control individuals diminished significantly once DORA was lifted. But the patient investigation, attention to detail and role of timing that were all implicit in the principles remained as integral to counter-espionage as ever.

These last features had as much to do with the characteristics of the individual officer as with the broader machinery of espionage. The psychology of human relationships – notions of trust, motivation, and persuasion – sat at the centre of agent-handling and agent operations, but it is one of the most difficult aspects to capture. Available documents from the immediate post-First World War era stop short of laying down abstract rules of tradecraft, but they do articulate the character and qualities sought in the officer. Despite the range of circumstances an officer encountered, he (officers were predominantly male) remained the constant in the equation. Failure or success in espionage and tradecraft resulted as much from such intangible qualities of character as imagination, intuition and persuasion as they did from technical skills like shadowing, letter opening and lock picking. As a 1920s description of the ideal SIS officer puts it:

> He should be a gentleman, and a capable one, absolutely honest and with considerable tact and at the same time force of character . . . [and] experience shows that any amount of brilliance or low cunning will not make up for the lack of scrupulous personal honesty. In the long run it is only the honest man who can defeat the ruffian.[43]

MI5's internal history concludes similarly that 'The qualities required of the investigator are mental alertness, elasticity, knowledge of men, intuition, an accurate and powerful memory combined with imagination, judgment to choose the right method of handling a case and the moment to strike'.[44] The officer is responsible for the recruitment and handling of sources, and as such is responsible for recruiting good sources and handling them well. Although officers still required a certain intelligence administration to perform the tasks of spying with optimum proficiency and to provide secret information for policymakers, the intelligence operative was only as good as his tradecraft.

The First World War Legacy and Administrative Reorganisation

The wider intelligence bureaucracy in 1919 has been compared to a giant balloon. During the war it expanded into 'unexpected shapes and inspir[ed] in its rise some hot air but also a burning blast of energy that turned it into a highly mobile and far-reaching instrument'. After the war, however, owing to new priorities and budget cuts, it 'rapidly deflated, and inevitably failed to regain its shape'.[45] The result was that a confused architecture with overlapping responsibilities oversaw intelligence once the war ended.

On the one hand, this misshapen structure had benefits. One report noted that 'the British system represents a reasonable and practical compromise between two undesireable [*sic*] extremes, that of complete disorganisation on the one hand and of bureaucratic absolutism on the other'.[46] It followed very much in the tradition of British improvisation and pragmatism. On the other hand, the same report observed, 'The great disadvantage [of a decentralised system] is the want of co-ordination of the various branches of the public services for preventative purposes and the standardising of administrative instructions and routine'.[47]

Correcting inefficiencies and tightening control was the purpose of the Secret Service Committee (SSC), which convened periodically between 1919 and 1931.[48] Lord Curzon headed the first meeting in early February 1919, which addressed two broad concerns: '(a) What was being done at present by the Secret Service branches of the several Departments; (b) How that work could be best co-ordinated with a view to the necessary action being taken with the utmost promptitude'.[49] A chief issue was how to handle information flow and prioritisation. Walter Long, First Lord of the Admiralty, had prompted the formation of the SSC with a memorandum noting that the armed services' intelligence organisations had efficient channels to notify ministers of cases of pressing importance but that civilian intelligence lacked a comparably effective system.[50] Civilian intelligence had acquired an urgent importance since the war's end as domestic labour unrest and revolutionary activity, as opposed to foreign espionage, created new fears that were both deep and extensive.

To remedy these concerns, the SSC created the Directorate of Intelligence (DI), which 'did little more than regularise the existing situation'.[51] Scotland Yard, the Metropolitan Police Special Branch (MPSB), had been in charge of monitoring anarchists and Fenians since the late nineteenth century.[52] As head of MPSB, Sir Basil Thomson made significant strides in this direction, keeping an eye on pacifists and working with PMS2 (the intelligence branch of the Ministry of Munitions).[53] During the war, it aided MI5's investigations into German espionage, which gradually expanded to include political subversion and labour unrest as well. Yet it was later noted that 'in this direction the work of Mr. Basil Thomson has grown far beyond his ordinary functions'.[54] Nonetheless, it was agreed to place Thomson at the head of the DI.

MI5 suffered the most of any agency. Indeed, the creation of the DI pushed it closer to obsolescence than it had or would ever again come in the first hundred years of its history. Its budget, like that of SIS, was cut to fund the new organisation.[55] SIS, however, saw its charge grow while the scope of MI5's shrank. Within a year, Thomson informally agreed to cede all anti-Bolshevik work overseas to SIS, which was granted permission to maintain a 'skeleton organisation in all foreign countries'.[56] The arrangement was formalised in 1931 after the SSC recommended that SIS maintain exclusive control over foreign intelligence. Although MI5 was given, at that point, responsibility for all security intelligence, its jurisdiction until then was confined to counter-espionage and subversion in the armed services. So when both its and the armed services' budgets shrank after the war, its stature followed suit.

MI5 had little money with which to operate and its staff size was accordingly diminished. One Cabinet estimate shows that MI5's £100,000 budget for 1918–1919 was reduced by almost two-thirds (to £35,000) the following year (or roughly £4.1 million to £1.36 million in today's terms).[57] MI5's wartime funding had reached a peak of £8,000 per month, but by 1922 this was reduced to roughly £1,600 per month, with further reductions the following year.[58] MI5's role, limited as it was to security in the armed services, also shrank dramatically as the armed services adjusted to peacetime operations. That MI5 staffed 133 'officers and civilian officials' at the Armistice but no more than sixteen 'officers and civilian officials' in 1929 brings home the broad sweep of MI5's decline during the 1920s – 'MI5's least influential decade'.[59] Likely as a result, MI5 managed few cohesive agent operations in the immediate postwar period – a sharp contrast to the now legendary adventures of SIS officers in Revolutionary Russia.[60]

Nor did MI5 receive great moral support at the ministerial level. The 1921 SSC contemplated scrapping MI5 altogether.[61] But Thomson plummeted as

1 Major-General Sir Vernon Kell (1873–1942), founding Director-General of The Security Service (MI5). The longest-serving director of the Service, he was unceremoniously sacked in 1940 by the new Prime Minister, Winston Churchill.

fast as he soared, and his rise and fall both seem to have been functions of personality conflicts as much as of the desire for greater bureaucratic efficiency. During his tenure, Thomson had great support from influential figures like former Director of Naval Intelligence (DNI) Sir Reginald Hall (who entered parliament as a right-wing Conservative MP in 1918), current DNI Sir Hugh Sinclair, Chief of the Imperial General Staff (CIGS) Sir Henry Wilson, together with

Cabinet ministers Long, Curzon and Churchill – who were all as passionately and unabashed anti-communist as he. Like Hall, Thomson shared a tendency for flamboyance, whereas Hall believed Kell to be 'short-sighted and timorous'. Though it is doubtful he was referring to Kell's spectacles, his eyeglasses added to his studious look, complemented his linguistic abilities and symbolically underscored his perpetually frail health. Discreet and reserved, Kell did not command attention.[62]

Yet it was not Kell but Thomson who went to the bureaucratic gallows, for the DI was abolished and Thomson forced to resign in October 1921. Thomson met his demise for two intertwined reasons.[63] First, he exaggerated the threat of organised labour and subversion to raise his profile. With budgets dwindling, he wielded intelligence as a political tool, particularly against Kell, whom he disliked. Developments in SIGINT also challenged the authority of the DI's reports. The unquestionable authenticity of GC&CS intercepts helped undermine reports based on forgeries emanating from sources in the Baltics. The fraudulent documents showed how the duplication of efforts undermined proved channels of information and could cause major diplomatic embarrassment – an ironic turn of events given that the desire to avoid redundancy had led to the directorate's creation in the first place. The 'cumulative effect' of the poor intelligence Thomson provided undermined his and his office's credibility overall.[64]

It is doubtful that poor human intelligence work hurt Thomson as much as his proclivity to politicise what information he did gather. Jousting over raw intelligence reflected in part a central weakness of the intelligence architecture – the absence of a unifying analytical agency. No such permanent body existed in the UK until the formation of the Joint Intelligence Committee (JIC) in 1936.[65] As official historian of Second World War British intelligence, Edward Thomas, has written of the JIC, 'On the face of it, the idea of drawing intelligence contributions from departments and inter-departmental agencies and putting them together seems so sensible, if not obvious, that it must cause surprise that it was evolved over so long a period and with such difficulty.'[66] Until the JIC was created, however, ministers, their aides and a variety of administrators were their own analysts. As has since been argued of such situations, 'When a welter of fragmentary evidence offers support to various interpretations, ambiguity is exploited by wishfulness. The greater the ambiguity, the greater the impact of preconceptions.'[67]

Yet the overall intentions of Bolshevik Russia were unambiguous, and there was also real evidence as to the means they employed towards their very clear ends. GC&CS did, for instance, uncover evidence of Soviet funding for subversive propaganda.[68] Other evidence was sometimes fragmentary, however. Soviet involvement in labour unrest was not as uniform or straightforward as some believed, and in these instances, Thomson found what he wanted to find and at times presented correlation as causation. Given that Soviet intentions were indeed so clear, he garnered support from government hardliners when he provided them with information that fit what they believed had to be true. In other words, the intelligence analysis and process was to some extent beholden to ministers' suppositions, and this proved especially problematic with Conservative ministers and labour unrest in the 1920s.

Lines of Authority

It was not until the late 1930s that the intelligence services began to act with a real sense of communal purpose, a transition that first required the emergence of national rather than merely departmental intelligence services.[69] Individual departmental concerns had dominated the collection of information during the war, but the forging of GC&CS from MI1(b) and Room 40 took the first step towards creating services of interdepartmental purpose. Though SIS officially came under Foreign Office purview in 1921 (as did GC&CS in 1922), it served multiple departments. The creation of a DI was also an attempt to bridge departmental interests, but after its collapse, Special Branch returned to the control of Scotland Yard, leaving security intelligence split between its focus on domestic civilian threats and MI5's focus on subversion within the armed services. Though the two agencies were encouraged to 'maintain the closest possible liaison' so as 'to avoid the chances of there being any "no-man's-land" between the civil and military surveillance', technically MI5 could not investigate subversion unless it affected the armed services, and Metropolitan Police Special Branch (MPSB) could not investigate subversion if it did.[70] The 1921 SSC noted the practical difficulties this caused: 'A Communist, working in naval or military circles at Portsmouth or Aldershot, may spend his Sundays making revolutionary speeches in Hyde Park. The former of these occupations is a matter for research by MI5; his week-end relaxations bring him into the preserve of the Special Branch.'[71] MI5's official history later referred to this split responsibility as 'an obvious mistake'.[72]

Neither was the issue of duplication resolved. The SIS maintained agents on the British mainland as well as abroad. Once again, the notion of consolidation arose when the disjointed nature of counter-espionage prompted Hugh 'Quex' Sinclair, who had succeeded Cumming as 'C' upon the latter's death in 1923, to launch an SIS takeover bid for MI5. When the SSC convened in 1923 and 1925, it addressed this idea as a possible solution to the continued inefficiencies in intelligence, but eventually it supported retaining MI5.[73] Dissolving MI5 remained on the table well into the 1920s, however.[74] Despite his failings, Kell – the sole director through this period – should be given least part of the credit for MI5's continued survival.[75]

It was not until 1931 at the last meeting of the SSC, however, that bureaucratic wrangling over intelligence responsibility was put to rest. At that point MI5, renamed the Security Service, became Britain's primary domestic and imperial security intelligence service, accountable to the Home Office.[76] SIS's purview was relegated to human intelligence collection outside of British territories. MPSB remained accountable to the Home Office and would retain executive powers – it was the only service permitted to make arrests.

Bureaucratic tussling clearly hampered the work of the intelligence services between the World Wars, but it alone was not to blame for shortcomings. The DI's short life certainly highlights the limits to which the inherent organisational problems of 'coordination, control, incentives, the sharing of information, and intelligence decision making' across agencies can 'be solved, or even substantially mitigated, by reorganisation.'[77] Yet the problems the intelligence establishment faced after the First World War were partly rooted in the informality of those reorganisations and the failures of individuals to make clear the new lines of the changed intelligence bureaucracy. Even two years after the watershed 1931 reorganisation, Sir Eric Holt-Wilson (Kell's deputy) noted that the Directorate of Military Intelligence, the War Office, was still 'only aware in a vague way' of MI5's new status. Though memoranda had informed police around the country, no single document accurately recording MI5's transition from the War Office to an interdepartmental security intelligence service has ever been found. It appears to have been an oral agreement.[78]

The recruitment and training of officers was similarly loose. Recruitment relied on personal introduction.[79] For SIS, training appears to have been done only on the job.[80] As Petrie noted of MI5 in the interwar period, 'Training took place under the eye of a responsible officer and was acquired in the school of experience. There was nothing in the way of a regular "course", though the War Office used to send some officers to receive instruction.'[81] Little wonder that Sir Dick White, who joined MI5 in 1935 and rose to Director-General (DG) before eventually becoming chief of SIS, later described his training as 'risibly perfunctory.'[82] Indeed informality remained a salient feature of intelligence between the wars, evolving slowly and haphazardly into formality as amateurism developed into professionalism.

The interwar period was a difficult time for MI5. It suffered a severe re-
duction in funds, and the loss of virtually all its staff after 1918 could not help
but have profound consequences for its operational effectiveness and account
in large part for its slow restart after the war. These deficiencies were later
highlighted by its need to recall wartime officers to service during the General Strike of 1926. Retrenchment hurt not only its ability to manage daily operations but also detracted from its institutional memory and skill base, for
'knowledge is costly to transfer, especially knowledge that is based on intuition or [that] . . . involves knowing how to do something rather than knowing
facts or procedures that can be communicated as a set of directions'.[83] In short,
people mattered. There is little evidence that there were manuals on the mechanics of counter-espionage from the early years, no directions for the arts
of tradecraft.[84] MI5 likely lost far more years of experience to staff reductions
than a calendar might suggest for so short a span of years. Yet what continuity in personnel it did have allowed MI5 to retain enough knowledge to sustain
itself during the interwar period. The Registry, too, linked MI5 from one era
to the next. Security instruments and structures inherited from MI5's wartime
experience proved to be the essential tools of its interwar operations. Putting
these characteristics into context is essential to understanding the evolution of
both MI5 and the larger British intelligence community's progression in the interwar period. Methods, structures, and people all mattered. The institutions'
histories mattered, too.

CHAPTER 1

Official Cover

Nikolai Klishko and the Russian Trade Delegation

I N the 1920s, barely after the birth of modern tradecraft during the First World War, both signals intelligence and human intelligence came to affect the conduct of British foreign policy towards the Soviet Union and vice versa. The context in which the art and science of spying evolved began immediately to shape its development as well. External affairs and foreign policy, as well as domestic politics, all played a role in changing the craft of surveillance. So did administrative and bureaucratic wrangling.

After the UK and USSR emerged from the hostilities that accompanied the Soviet withdrawal from the Great War and separate peace with Germany, the context created by the Russian Civil War and the early years of the new revolutionary state created a situation in which the two nations struggled towards an uneasy and incomplete *rapprochement.* As a piece of this awkward diplomatic dance, they worked to seal a bilateral trade agreement.[1] Yet even as they did so, domestic trade disputes buffeted consecutive British Governments, administrations that were also moving from one domestic political crisis to another. It was hard for many to separate in their minds the fear of Soviet Bolshevism and the concern about socialists and communists within the British population. For some, the British labour movement became a kind of domestic parallel to foreign Bolshevism – all of it threatening.

Nikolai Klishko, secretary to the Russian Trade Delegation, became the focus of British security concerns as soon as the delegation arrived.[2] He may not have been a Cheka officer, as recent research has revealed, but he was certainly central to the Cheka's London mission.[3] He stood at the nexus of Bolshevik covert operations and effectively served as a prototype for the 'legal resident' – Soviet intelligence officers operating under official cover. The Klishko case foreshadowed the story of British counter-espionage and surveillance of later KGB residents.[4]

Soviet funding of the British Communist Party also complicated the trade negotiations. Never before had a foreign power subsidised a British political party, and revelations about Soviet funding of domestic communists had a frosty effect on the trade talks. Klishko's involvement in two networks offers insight into how that funding may have occurred. His links to the Moscow-linked, clandestine Kirchenstein courier network suggest that communist operatives communicated with Moscow by means not regularly intercepted by signals intelligence, and his ties to a transnational diamond smuggling syndicate also testify to the complexity of early Soviet agent operations.

In an era of overt hostility to the still new regime, it was crucial for the Bolsheviks that Klishko conduct his intelligence work in secret. Much of Prime Minister David Lloyd George's Coalition Cabinet was loath to deal with the revolutionary Soviet government at all. With typical conviction, Churchill told the Oxford Union in November 1920, 'The policy I will always advocate is the overthrow and destruction of that criminal regime.'[5] Since British conditions for any kind of diplomatic understanding demanded that the Bolsheviks cease subversive propaganda, it was a practical necessity for Soviet operatives to employ seamless tradecraft to conceal their extracurricular activities.

Maintaining covert communications was a fundamental tenet of tradecraft, yet Klishko and his contacts failed to do so, and this had serious diplomatic consequences. Klishko, due in part to his role in diamond smuggling, was a vital conduit for funding subversive activity in India. British knowledge of this covert aspect of Russian diplomatic activity threatened to derail Anglo-Soviet relations, such as they were, and negotiations throughout the early 1920s. This awareness was a direct result of the Soviets' poor tradecraft and lack of communications security, demonstrating that although good tradecraft can produce good intelligence and create political dividends, the converse is also true: poor tradecraft can easily sabotage foreign policy objectives.

Identifying Klishko

Scotland Yard and MI5 had been familiar with Klishko long before the trade negotiations – indeed even before the Russian Revolution. A political refugee from tsarist Russia, he had been employed in Britain as a technical translator by the armaments firm Vickers. Authorities first investigated him in 1910 for suspected arms smuggling to Russian revolutionaries. Though no evidence of this could be found, his involvement with known nihilists and the Herzen Circle, an anti-war and revolutionary organisation, ensured his inclusion on the Scotland Yard watch list.[6]

After the Revolution, fears arose that he might have leaked information on munitions contracts to Maxim Litvinov, V. I. Lenin's representative in Britain from 1917 to 1918, with whom he had shared living quarters during the war.[7] MI5's interest in Lenin himself had first revolved around his relationship with Germany, for it was thought he might be a German agent. As the war ended, however, Britain came to consider Bolshevism a threat in its own right, and so Lenin remained a concern.[8] An 'undeniable source' reported that Klishko was 'very friendly with LENIN and shared his views'.[9] By the middle of 1918, MI5's M. W. Bray had come to see Klishko as the 'most dangerous Bolshevik here', and wrote that he was 'more than ever convinced of the necessity of sending KLISHKO out of the country'.[10] Although the initial deportation process in Britain stalled, events in Russia precipitated Klishko's incarceration and deportation on other grounds.

On the heels of the assassination of Moisei Uritsky, head of the Petrograd Cheka, and of the attempted assassination of Lenin by Dora Kaplan at the end of August 1918, the Cheka arrested Britain's representatives in Russia, including head of mission Robert Bruce Lockhart, for a plot developed with the infamous spy Sidney Reilly to overthrow the Bolshevik regime.[11] MI1(c), as SIS was then called, had operated in Russia throughout the war, serving as liaison to tsarist officials in monitoring German troop movements on the eastern front. It also produced anti-German propaganda under the Anglo-Russian Bureau, of which the novelist Hugh Walpole was one founder. Though the Revolution quickly disrupted this kind of collaboration, for several of Walpole's colleagues – Bruce Lockhart, Paul Dukes and the writer Arthur Ransome – the espionage relationship with Russia would continue.[12]

After the Revolution, SIS's mission in Russia changed from collaborating with the tsarist regime to collecting information about the Soviets.[13] But from the time of the mission's return to Britain until the signing of the Trade Agreement, the United Kingdom had no official representative to report back on political developments inside Russia. To discern Russian intentions towards Britain, officials relied on signals intelligence, SIS stations in Central, Northern and Eastern Europe, and the surveillance of Soviet representatives in Britain.

Daily Herald

In September 1918, Klishko was among those detained in Britain 'with a view to securing the safety of British subjects in Russia'. He and Litvinov were then repatriated in exchange for the safe passage home of the arrested Britons stuck in the Soviet Union.[14] 1919 found Klishko in Stockholm, but he returned to

London in May 1920, officially as secretary to the Russian Trade Delegation and also unofficially as the first resident of Soviet intelligence in Britain. Given changes in British intelligence architecture, primary responsibility for Klishko's case passed from MI5 to the DI to Scotland Yard.[15]

After a year of negotiations, the Anglo-Soviet Trade Agreement was signed in March 1921. Leonid Krasin then returned to Britain in May as the head of the Soviet Trade Delegation, promising as per the agreement (but against most expectations), not to 'interfere in any way in the politics or internal affairs of the country'.[16] For the British coalition government, the Bolsheviks' promise to cease meddling in domestic affairs and stirring revolution in the East had not only been a central condition of the trade accord but remained an ongoing concern. Indeed, secret intelligence had already given the lie to Krasin's promises, and this created an icy air at the reception ceremony for the returning Soviet Trade Representative. SIS agents and diplomatic intercepts ('Blue Jackets', or 'BJs') revealed that only a few months before Krasin's first trade meeting in spring 1920, a Bolshevik agent in Sweden had given the sympathetic *Daily Herald* editor George Lansbury some five hundred tons of paper worth £25,000 (or £850,000 today).[17] Moreover, Klishko had that summer signed off on a telegram reporting that 'we are making use of the "Daily Herald" for purposes of information and agitation'.[18] Tempers ignited again soon after the arrival of Lev Kamenev (head of the Moscow Communist Party and President of the Moscow Soviet) to London in August 1920, when intercepts revealed that he was also intimately involved in additional secret subsidies to the *Daily Herald* and encouraging unions to strike.

Nor did knowledge of the intercepts remain private; on the contrary, the texts were released to the press. *The Times*, among other papers, reprinted eight messages between Maxim Litvinov (now Deputy Commissar for Foreign Affairs) in Copenhagen and Georgi Chicherin (Commissar for Foreign Affairs), including Chicherin's instructions to:

> point out who will give [Lansbury] orders and regulate the numbers of copies. . . . Manuscripts will be sent to him through [Bolshevik representative in Sweden] Strom and Reval [Tallinn]. We now pay 2,000 Swedish crowns for paper. Strom will gradually repay this sum. We, on the other hand, will continue to pay for the paper until the whole of the 500 tons has been paid for. He will pay a small sum as commission.[19]

Litvinov's subsequent message, that the *Daily Herald* merited Soviet subsidisation because it 'acts as if it were our organ', enforced the perception that it was merely a Soviet proxy.[20]

Lloyd George had initially taken a stoic view of the Bolsheviks' covert deal-ings. Deciding against the Delegation's immediate expulsion, he reasoned that there was 'an undoubted advantage in our being able to tap these messages as it gives us real insight into Bolshevist interests and policy. . . . If these delegates were expelled, then that source of information would be cut off.'[21] Following the publication of the intercepts, however, political pressure demanded he take action. Consequently, and with a great show of anger, he summoned Kamenev and ordered his departure for his 'gross breach of faith' (though in fact he was scheduled return to Russia anyway).[22] Krasin and Klishko remained in London to continue negotiating, Litvinov stayed in Copenhagen, and the channels of funding and propaganda remained as open as ever.

The Soviet officials in charge of the negotiations had noted their concern about the security of their communications in the months before Kamenev's deportation. In mid-July 1920, Klishko had requested not only a new cipher to replace the MARTA system then in use, but 1,000 additional keys. This was re-jected on the grounds that that number could not be produced in such a short time. A month before his expulsion from Britain, Kamenev had also urged 'great caution' with communiqués, believing MARTA to be insecure. Chicher-in, too, issued a warning to 'take all possible measures to safeguard the keys of deciphered messages. Specially secret messages must be re-ciphered.' But Lit-vinov, in Copenhagen, was not as worried as the others, stubbornly insisting: 'I propose to continue using MARTA, even if it is obsolete.'[23] This argument continued right up until the publication on 19 August 1920 of the decrypts that triggered Kamenev's September departure.[24]

Although *The Times* had openly stated that the 'wireless messages have been intercepted by the British Government', the Bolsheviks foolishly, and for the British almost miraculously, continued to use the same code. Not all So-viets were sanguine about the problem, however. A telegram sent by Mikhail Frunze (commander-in-chief of the Southern Red Army Group) to Lenin, Trotsky, Chicherin, the military High Command and the Central Committee addressed the issue explicitly:

> The most secret correspondence of the Narkomindel [Commissariat for Foreign Affairs] with its representatives in Tashkent and in Europe is known word for word to the English, who have organized a network of stations designed particularly for listening to our radio. . . . The general conclusion is that all our enemies, in particular England, are *au courant* with all our internal military operations and diplomatic work.[25]

Evidently Chicherin took the warning seriously. The following week (26 December 1920) he sent a telegram to Krasin in London informing him:

> We have ascertained that our actual cypher systems do not present sufficient power of resistance, and that our cypher correspondence is deciphered and become known to the governments of countries hostile to us. Having this in view, no really secret information, the discovery of which could compromise us and cause serious harm to the 'Republic' or the 'Party', should under any circumstances be sent by radio or by the telegraph of a foreign state. Such information should be sent by couriers, and anything particularly secret mentioning names and so on should, even in this event, be sent by cypher.[26]

In this way, Chicherin, the head of Soviet foreign affairs, tacitly acknowledged in correspondence with Krasin, the head of the Trade Delegation, that the Soviets were engaging in secret, subversive activity in Britain – operations that would harm Soviet interests if revealed. Ironically, of course, the telegram also informed the British of the changes.

Kirchenstein

That month, Chicherin instructed Krasin to use a courier for important correspondence, and the first clues surfaced almost immediately in Britain that a Soviet courier network existed. A batch of letters belonging to 'John' or 'Jack Walker' was discovered aboard the SS *Sterling*, which navigated the South Shields (Newcastle) to Bergen (Norway) sea lane. 'Johnny Walker', handwriting analysis later established, was actually Jacob Kirchenstein, an American citizen of Lettish (Latvian) origin.[27] The letters, addressed to 'one of the chief agents' of the Comintern and to the Latvian representative on the Executive Committee of the Comintern (IKKI) in Moscow, indicted Kirchenstein for a litany of abuses, asserting that he:

> was of high standing in the Third International from whose headquarters he was in immediate receipt of orders; that he was a self-confessed enemy agent residing in the United Kingdom as an unregistered alien; and that he was there engaged at the head of an organisation for distributing Bolshevik propaganda and for facilitating the passage of Bolshevik agents to and from Russia as stowaways. He was also cognisant

of, though not hopeful about, the organisation of a Red Army in this country.[28]

Here was definite proof of a subversive conspiracy directed from Moscow. In April and May 1921, intercepted correspondence continued to show that Kirchenstein was instrumental in the despatch of propaganda and propagandists to British colonies, as well.[29] In fact, Soviet activities in the East proved one of the most contentious issues for the British throughout the negotiations.

In September 1921, the same month as Kamenev's departure, Kirchenstein received instructions from Osip Piatnitsky (the head of *Otdel Mezhdunarodnykh Svyazey*, or OMS, the Comintern's International Liaison Department) via Narkomindel and the Trade Delegation in London *not* to liquidate his organisation, suggesting that such a disbanding had been considered. The same month, Lord Curzon, then the foreign secretary, presented to the Soviets documents obtained by SIS in Reval (Tallinn) and Berlin that purportedly showed evidence of Soviet interference in South Asia.[30] Perhaps Curzon's challenge prompted Piatnitsky's directive. Kirchenstein's MI5 file suggests that these particular pieces of evidence were forged, although representative of actual Soviet activities. Regardless of what prompted the directive to Kirchenstein that autumn, he followed the instructions and took 'special precautions to sever any direct connection with the Communist Party headquarters, whom he regarded as politically unreliable.'[31]

At the beginning of 1922, some of the Soviet funding passing through Kirchenstein's shipping channels reached the formerly Fabian and increasingly communist-dominated Labour Research Department (LRD):

> The connection between the Russian Trade Delegation and extremists in the Labour Research Department, such as [Robin] Page ARNOT and C[lemens] PALME DUTT, was significant in light of the definite information that Moscow was inclined to regard this organisation as more fertile ground than the [CPGB], which had not been giving results proportionate to the sums allowed by the Third International for propaganda purposes. There is no doubt that the [LRD] has subsequently become the real driving force of the revolutionary movement in this country. C. PALME DUTT, one of its most influential members, on his own admission receives his instructions direct from ARCOS and the Russian Trade Delegation.[32]

Arnot and Dutt were both leading lights in the CPGB.[33] Dutt later spent time in Moscow and worked in the British Communist Party's Colonial Bureau.

Arnot, like Clemens's brother Rajani, was a founding member of the British Communists; he was also among the twelve senior CPGB figures arrested in 1925 for incitement to sedition.[34] So even if Kirchenstein mistrusted CPGB headquarters, the funds still reached the staunchest of communists and fervent CPGB supporters in the UK.

Kirchenstein received Piatnitsky's instructions to maintain his network via the Russian Trade Delegation. Given Klishko's position as Cheka operative and Delegation Secretary, it is probable that he was also involved in the decision. Kirchenstein was also assisted by Peter Miller, the cypher clerk at the Delegation, with whom Kirchenstein later roomed. Another Latvian, Miller was known the British 'to be at the centre of Bolshevik intrigue in this country, and has been proved in the past to have been associated with the dubious activities of Nicolai Klishko'.[35] Scotland Yard had an additional reason to be interested in Miller because, based on his appearance, it was thought he might be 'Peter the Painter', the Latvian anarchist behind the infamous 1911 gunfight in London's East End known as the Sydney Street Siege.[36] The 1923 HOW on Miller was granted because 'this man has again been reported as intermediary between the Russian Trade Delegation and the Communist party in this country and as an agent of the Third International. In the past he has been definitely proven as an associate of Klishko in his dubious activities.'[37] In other words, suspicion of Kirchenstein was enhanced by his association with Miller, and Miller was a suspect because of Klishko. The reasoning led the British to put Klishko at the apex of the Soviet spy organisation in Britain.

The reality of early Comintern/Soviet networks might not have been as hierarchical as that analysis presupposed. Soviet involvement with the fledgling CPGB and other left-wing movements was then fluid. It is unquestionable, however, that the Comintern lavishly funded left-wing parties and propaganda in the immediate postwar period. In 1919, the Comintern allocated more funds to British communists than to those in any other country.[38] Until Klishko's return to England in May 1920, Theodore Rothstein had been the primary figure disbursing Moscow's funds. With these funds, he was chiefly responsible for bringing together the various left-wing parties to form the British Communist Party in the first place.[39] But the CPGB, while theoretically centralised, was not monolithic. It suffered from factionalism, and tensions existing at higher levels meant that the disbursement of funds was never well rationalised.[40] After he officially joined the Delegation in 1920, Rothstein bitterly complained to Litvinov that 'even my formal appointment does not give me sufficient authority in the eyes of my colleagues who look upon me as a provincial . . . Klishko does not allow me to transmit anything from newspapers or other sources', an accusation which Klishko subsequently denied.[41] So although the Trade Delegation took over the role of funding surveillance and agitation when it arrived in London, Klishko's relationship with Comintern operatives and the CPGB may not have been completely straightforward.

Nonetheless, by his own account, Klishko acted as the CPGB's 'cash box'.[42] By the end of 1921, the Party had received from Moscow some £60,000 (£2.25 million in today's figures).[43] But just as Kirchenstein believed King Street to be politically unreliable, Klishko claimed the Comintern approached funding with 'criminal recklessness', and he therefore asserted nominal independence over subsidies.[44] The nature of Klishko's relationship with Kirchenstein is not explicitly described in Scotland Yard's reports, but given Klishko's role with the Cheka, and if the Trade Delegation controlled Soviet funds, their activities probably overlapped. Scotland Yard suspected they had done so in the past.[45] The extent to which Comintern and GPU courier networks cooperated is unknown, however.[46]

Even if Kirchenstein was not under the direct authority of Klishko, his network was likely representative of other networks operating at that time.[47] Indeed, his agent network appears to have been prototypical. His MI5 file notes that in March 1922, he 'was still receiving both instructions and funds from the Third International by means of Lettish seamen and also through the Soviet diplomatic bag'. These paths undoubtedly continued after 1924, when Kirchenstein began formal employment with the ARCOS Steamship Company, a subsidiary of the Russian Trade Delegation.[48] The use of shipping companies for covert communication was not unique to Kirchenstein's network in the interwar period. The defector Walter Krivitsky later told MI5 that Soviet military intelligence (Fourth Department/GRU) had also organised a courier network based on shipping crews at the time Kirchenstein operated. According to Krivitsky, the GRU courier network, which operated from 1926 to 1937, recruited some two hundred agents from those working on ships sailing between the UK, Holland and Scandinavia with the help of local sympathisers such as the Dutchman Edo Fimmen of the International Transportworkers Federation.[49] These networks were maintained in the event that the Soviet Union became embroiled in a war that would force the closure of its embassies and cut off its lines of communication.[50]

At the time of the trade negotiations, the issue was not so much about maintaining communications as maintaining their secrecy – about, that is, good tradecraft. For the most part, the Trade Delegation failed at this task. Courier services were employed to avoid censorship, but Kirchenstein's network

did not completely escape detection, as the very existence of his MI5 file attests. Nonetheless, the more than fifty letters that were actually intercepted
are not as revealing as might be expected, although they do give an indication
of Kirchenstein's contacts and movement. That they did not disclose more was
in part because he and his and associates were aware of British security methods. In one letter to his wife, Vallie, he writes, 'Don't send me those packets.
All the envelopes were split open and on each one could be read to whom they
were to be given over. The postman hesitated and asked me a lot of questions
before he gave them to me.'[51] He was evidently aware that addresses connected
to him would provide further leads for counter-espionage investigations. To
another associate he urged, 'When you write, write cautiously without touch-
ing upon politics as the censorship of the letters at this end has to be reckoned
with.'[52] Although letters were often examined surreptitiously during the war,
the sloppy tradecraft in this later instance alerted Kirchenstein to his being under surveillance.[53] Forwarding the poorly resealed letters to him did not conceal the security services' activities. Then again, their actions might have been
a deliberate signal to warn him that he was under surveillance. Whatever the
reasons, the effect was to curtail the amount of information communicated in
subsequent letters, therefore cutting also the amount of intelligence collected
and making it hard to monitor Kirchenstein and his agents. Based on MI5 case
files, definitive statements regarding Kirchenstein's or Klishko's activities are
difficult to make: this concealment was exactly the function of their tradecraft.

Russia's Imperial Jewels

MI5 had a source ('E. R.'), who tipped them off as early as May 1920 to the
potentially divergent agendas of those within the Soviet Trade Delegation.
Krasin was said to be 'playing the game, and is only really interested in business', whereas Klishko was reported 'to be far keener on propaganda than business'.[54] Such descriptions mirrored the press's notion of the genteel Krasin as a
'bourgeois Bolshevist' and Klishko as a 'bombproof Bolshevist'.[55] Though some
sources suggest that Krasin's dealings were not completely above board either,
the great many more MI5 and Scotland Yard files on Klishko likely reflect the
greater suspicion of his role in covert activity.

Klishko's involvement in dubious money transfers kept him squarely in the
sights of MI5 and SIS. The CPGB's declared intention, according to Basil Thomson, was 'to fan the already existing flames of discontent, to foment revolution

and finally to bring about revolutionary action.'[56] At the time of the CPGB's emergence, Thomson later recounted, 'A large quantity of unset diamonds to the value of nearly £2,000,000 sterling were [sic] placed on the English market and disposed of in packets valued at £30,000 each with the stipulation made that payment should be made only in French notes which could not be traced.'[57] Thomson, known as something of a sensationalist, likely exaggerated the diamonds' value (£2 million in 1920 would be roughly equal to £68 million today), but diamonds there definitely were, and Klishko's subsequent activities suggest that he was involved.[58] In 1922 he was at the centre of a 'very puzzling deal' in Warsaw. Found to be in communication with 'a man who signs himself "Sam"', the intercepted post probably revealed an extensive diamond smuggling operation. It was learned that 'Sam' (thought by SIS to be Samuel Rabinoff, who was already implicated in 'certain illicit dealings on the part of the Russian Trade Delegation') and the 'G. P. Group' (thought by SIS to be associates of the Armenian Gronik Papazian) were in a position to receive certain 'goods' and 'parcels' at a discounted rate from the Polish government, which in turn received the 'parcels' from Moscow. Extraordinary amounts of money were involved: the G. P. group paid $500,000 for the first parcel and were willing to pay an additional £1.5 million for future parcels.[59] According to the report, 'the recurrent use of the word "parcels" as well as other peculiarities of the deal indicates jewels.' The SIS representative in Warsaw soon discovered that Rabinoff and Papazian had shared a room at the Hotel Bristol Warsaw earlier that month, an amateur tradecraft error that allowed SIS to prove they knew each other and connect their activities. Additionally, an SIS report (i.e. human intelligence) showed that Papazian had been negotiating deals with Krasin in Holland, a known centre for the diamond trade.[60] Basic slips in tradecraft therefore permitted security and intelligence services to connect the dots, drawing a rough picture of diamond smuggling operations across Europe.

Subsequent inquiries showed that the G. P. group had acted in cahoots with the Polish government and with the approval of Moscow. The jewels stood as Soviet security on unpaid reparations to Poland as stipulated by the Treaty of Riga, which formally ended Polish–Russian hostilities with its signing on 18 March 1921. It followed the Polish–Soviet armistice of October 1920 and coincided with a flood of diamonds pouring onto the British market. The documentation is fragmentary, but according to intercepted letters the G. P. Group somehow sought to exploit the beneficial terms of the Anglo-Soviet Trade Agreement to sell the jewels.[61] The documents convey not only British dismay at the 'connivance' of the Soviet and Polish Governments but also strongly imply that using the agreement to govern the transaction breached its terms. That the conspirators in the G.P. Group expressed an urgency to complete the transactions before the expiry of the accord underscored the utility of the agreement to the operation and, in the eyes of MI5, hinted at wrongdoing.[62]

The exploitation of favourable trade terms extended beyond reparations. SIS suspected that Klishko and his partners were themselves embezzling some of the proceeds. 'Klishko has a finger in the pie', one report reads. A letter from Rabinoff insisted it benefited Klishko to 'get things going before the two years are up, which is next March', referring to the end of the agreement in 1923. SIS reasoned that the advertisement for Russian crown jewels in British newspapers at the time of the 1922 report likely emanated from the Russian Trade Delegation 'because it is difficult to see who else would have put them in'. The ensuing publicity would bring attention to the sale of the jewels once in London. Thus it was suggested that 'Klishko and "Sam" are using their advance knowledge of this transaction to get a percentage out of "the G. P. group"'.[63]

Of far graver consequence from the British point of view was evidence that money gained from jewel transactions funded propaganda. Two weeks after the CPGB's founding and in the wake of Lansbury's trip to Scandinavia, Francis Meynell, one of the *Daily Herald*'s directors, submitted his resignation when it became public that he had accepted gold from Russia amounting to £75,000 (£2.55 million today) to be held 'in trust for the Third International and to be offered to the *Daily Herald* as the need arose'. The news undermined Lansbury's insistence that the *Daily Herald* operated independently of the Soviets.[64] Krasin claimed complete ignorance of the transaction when meeting with Lloyd George, as did Chicherin in an official communiqué to Curzon.[65] Meynell's later testimony, however, tells a different story. He admitted having taken many 'jewel-trips' to Scandinavia, smuggling precious metals from Denmark, Sweden and Finland in a marvellous variety of concealments. Butter jars and chocolate creams were but two examples. However, the smuggled diamonds had a distinctive Russian cut, tipping off Scotland Yard to the jewels' provenance.[66] Even more revealing, Meynell insisted that Krasin and Kamenev were also responsible for bringing a large quantity of diamonds and platinum to London when they arrived for a round of negotiations in July 1920.[67] It took Moscow several years to publicly acknowledge interest in selling Russian imperial jewels (let alone owning up to having subsidised the *Daily Herald*). It could hardly have been mere coincidence that the eventual decision to publicise the jewel sales in early 1923 fell just before the expiration of the Trade Agreement.[68] Given his later collusion, it is also hard to imagine that Klishko, the 'bombproof Bolshevist', was not already participating in jewel smuggling operations at the time of the delegation's arrival.

Curzon Ultimatum

A major proviso of the Anglo-Soviet Trade Agreement called for the end of hostile Soviet activities against British colonies in the East. Problematic for the communists, however, was that the measure directly conflicted with the purpose of the Comintern, whose express mission was to coordinate and inspire global proletarian revolution.[69] Officially, Bolshevik Russia reiterated the fiction that the Comintern operated separately from Moscow. Thus it offered lip service to British grievances while actively supporting subversion in British colonies. In September 1920, the Comintern organised the First Congress of the Peoples of the East in Baku. Although the gathering accomplished little in terms of organising revolution – the First Congress was also the last – it captured London's attention and put pressure on politicians to reach an understanding with Moscow. Almost two thousand delegates heard Comintern chairman Grigori Zinoviev implore: 'Comrades! Brothers! We call you to a holy war above all against English imperialism!'[70] Moscow's feigned impotence regarding the workings of Comintern was difficult to maintain once Zinoviev rose to the Politburo in 1921. The Bolsheviks, however, thrived in the face of diplomatic adversity. The same year, they established a Communist University of Toilers in the East, with centres in Moscow and Tashkent, to train revolutionaries in propaganda and subversion for missions throughout Asia and India in particular.

The issue of Bolshevik propaganda in the East was especially close to the heart of Lord Curzon, former Viceroy to India (1899–1904, 1904–1905) and current foreign secretary (1919–1924). He had been prominent among those urging Lloyd George to scupper trade negotiations following the revelation of the Litvinov-Chicherin intercepts in August 1920. Three years later, he led another drive to expose Soviet duplicity. In May 1923, Soviet representatives received a note from the Foreign Office threatening to break all relations if Soviet subversion in Central and South Asia did not halt immediately. Rather than presenting vague charges, as they had in the past and which the Soviets consistently met with blanket denials, Curzon submitted irrefutable proof of Soviet complicity: '[His Majesty's Government] are content to rely exclusively upon communications which have passed in the last few months between the Russian Government and its agents, and which are in their possession, and upon the recorded acts of the Soviet Government itself.'[71] With the intercepts as proof, the note recounted past objections and enumerated Soviet transgressions in Afghanistan, Persia and India. Curzon highlighted, for instance, the November 1922 arrest of seven Communist Indians trained at Communist

University of Toilers in the East who attempted to travel into India for propaganda purposes under the auspices of Russian civil and military officials. Indian officials had also systematically intercepted correspondence from Comintern operative M. N. Roy (alias Norendra Nath Bhattarcharji) to his Tashkent-trained agents in India.[72]

The note presented damning evidence that the Soviet delegation in London had given logistical support for communist operations in India. Klishko was singled out for having had financial responsibility for at least one of them. This was hardly surprising since he had been implicated in passing currency to agents in other operations, such as Kirchenstein's courier network.[73] Investigations traced a number of £1 bank notes cashed by suspected revolutionaries in India to London. The bank notes in India corresponded to the same notes issued to one 'Nicolai Klishko' through Lloyds Bank and the Russian Commercial and Industrial Bank.[74] It was indisputable, therefore, that currency handled by Klishko and the delegation had been transferred to subversives in India.[75] Klishko's official position made his connection to subversive activity particularly problematic. It was exactly this accountability and traceability that good tradecraft sought to prevent. For whatever reason, Klishko suffered from a serious lack of foresight. Undoubtedly Scotland Yard was correct in suspecting that his disappearance from London soon after the note's publication confirmed the truth of the charges against him.[76]

Curzon's determination to route the Soviets revealed to them British codebreaking abilities. This had important costs. It is true that, in the short term, the ultimatum resulted in diminished Soviet activity in South Asia. The Narkomindel cabled numerous representatives in the East with orders to scale back operations.[77] In forcing Klishko's departure, the démarche also dispatched one of Britain's most reviled guests. Yet in the long term, Curzon's manner of indignant confrontation probably hurt more than it helped Britain. SIS later learned that, only a year after his disappearance, Klishko had joined the Russian Trade Delegation in Constantinople.

Klishko's move could not have soothed Curzon's anxiety about British isolation at the meetings of the Peace Conference of Lausanne, the last of the First World War's treaty negotiations, which had been convened to reach a settlement with Turkey.[78] Clearly seen as linked to the possibility of a Soviet-Turkish alignment,

> Klishko's arrival bears a close relation to the request recently made to Ismet Pasha [Kemal Atatürk] by the Soviet Government that Turkey should authorise the opening of a number of Russian Consulates on

Turkish territory near the Iraq and Syrian frontiers. These Consulates are apparently to be centres for espionage and propaganda.[79]

Thus Curzon had exposed Klishko as an accomplice to subversive activity in Asia only to see him reappear in Asia Minor and continue to threaten British imperial interests.[80]

As long as Klishko had been in London, the security services could monitor his activities; once he went abroad, their task became much more difficult – which highlighted the great disadvantage to the British that derived from the Curzon Ultimatum. Before 1924, signals intelligence gave the British direct access to Soviet instructions sent to their London Trade Delegation. It also provided vital clues leading to postal interception, which in turn allowed for more thorough surveillance of Soviet agent networks. After the note, the Soviets changed their codes, and the British lost, if only temporarily, the 'real insight into Bolshevist interests and policy' afforded by their secret knowledge, as Lloyd George had warned would happen. It was perhaps the lack of signals intelligence that prevented an earlier discovery of the agent network that Klishko left behind. In the meanwhile, investigations into the extent of Soviet influence on labour unrest intensified.

CHAPTER 2

Counter-subversion

Labour Unrest and the General Strike of 1926

T HE Anglo-Soviet Trade Agreement of 1921 did not put an end to Bolshevik activities in Britain. It did not dampen Soviet propaganda, attempts
to meddle in British domestic affairs, or the British fear of their doing so. Indeed, concerns that the Soviets were attempting to influence British unions
and workers led to a political crisis and influenced Parliament's decision not to
ratify a second trade pact, which the two nations had negotiated in 1924. It also
led Parliament to vote no confidence in the still new Labour government barely
after it had gained power for the first time.

Earlier that year, Prime Minister Ramsay Macdonald had formally recognised the Soviet Union, the first in a series of events that led to his party's
ouster in October. In the autumn, when the government dropped its prosecution of the communist John Ross Campbell, who had been accused of encouraging revolutionary action, Parliament's passed a resolution of no confidence
in Macdonald. The third general election in less than two years was called for
the end of October.

It was then that SIS supposedly intercepted a letter ostensibly written to
the CPBG by Grigori Zinoviev, the head of the Comintern. The missive urged
the mobilisation of labour and indicated that the Russian trade delegation, in
the midst of renegotiating the terms of the trade agreement, would provide the
necessary funding. The letter, almost certainly a forgery, was published on the
eve of the general election. To some, it provided yet more evidence that the
Labour Government was ill equipped to confront communist subversion, and
Baldwin campaigned on the dangers of socialism. Nonetheless, Labour gained
million votes in the October 1924 election but was unable to surmount the To-
ries' landslide victory, gained mainly on the back of the Liberal vote's collapse.[1]

Unrest characterised British intelligence as well as politics, and inter-ser-
vice tensions again found a forum in the reconstituted SSC. As organised labour came together and appeared increasingly potent, the government sought
tighter coordination and more efficiency in British intelligence.[2] Prompted by

the Zinoviev letter, 'Quex' Sinclair used the 1925 SSC to try to put himself at the head of an amalgamated intelligence branch – a suggestion that stirred considerable dissent from the heads of other services.

Then, in late April 1926, a call for a general strike by the leaders of the Trades Union Congress (TUC) led Conservative Prime Minister Stanley Baldwin to aver that such a work stoppage would come 'nearer to proclaiming civil war than we had been for centuries past.'[3] Indeed, he saw the strike less as an industrial conflict than as a threat to the most basic tenets of law and order: 'It is not wages that are imperilled, it is the freedom of our very constitution.'[4] By some counts, the strike was indeed remarkable. Never before had Britain seen industrial action on a scale like it, nor would it again. More working days were lost to industrial disputes in 1926 than in 1912, 1921 and 1979 combined.[5]

Yet despite the huge number of productive hours lost, the strike was really not so remarkable after all. In fact, the background to the General Strike was more important than the strike itself, which only lasted nine days and ended with relatively little violence. The General Strike's unspectacular resolution was also surprising. In the end, for both the CPGB and the Comintern, the work action was an unmitigated failure and a massive anti-climax. The revolution it was believed to presage never occurred, prompting serious questioning by rank and file members of militant unionism who had been encouraged by communist propaganda. It is also uncertain to what extent the CPGB even posed a threat to the British establishment writ large: it never gained more than three percent of the vote in its entire history, prompting some historians to conclude that 'revolution, perhaps, is not to the British taste.'[6]

With the benefit of hindsight, it has often been thought that the intelligence services' perception of the threat posed by the CPGB – and even organised labour as a whole – was a paranoid overreaction.[7] Many in the government, the security establishment and the public had believed that industrial unrest was directed from Moscow and funded by 'Red Gold', which those privy to MI5's intelligence knew not always to be the case. Nonetheless, whether due to their true fears or as a political ploy, some ministers voiced greater alarm than did the secret services. Home Secretary William Joynson-Hicks ('Jix'), for example, was dissatisfied with these findings and continued to push for causal connections. Although the defence of parliamentary authority necessarily presumed a central role for the security and intelligence services, there existed a fundamental weakness in the intelligence apparatus at the time – the absence of a joint method of assessment, such as the JIC, which was not founded until

1936. Yet despite the absence of an objective analytical intelligence function, and accepting that Churchill was a doomsayer and Jix 'saw a communist under every bed', it is nonetheless true that the CPGB's failure to influence dramatically the General Strike and instigate a general uprising was not for lack of trying.[8]

Secret Service Committee

At the June 1925 meeting of the Secret Service Committee, Permanent Under-Secretary (PUS) of the Foreign Office Sir William Tyrrell pointed to a gap in the security establishment's ability to deal appropriately with Soviet agents and their British comrades. Noting that the investigation of domestic communist activities was closely tied to the nation's foreign policy towards the Soviet Union, he argued that:

> There were two possible courses to follow as regards the Soviets, either to attack them on every departure from the rules of international courtesy, thus giving them the advertisement for which they craved, or, so far as possible, to treat them with neglect. If the latter policy continued in favour, as at present, it was essential that a close and complete watch should be kept on the activities, individual and collective, of soviet [*sic*] agents in the United Kingdom.[9]

He told the committee that although Sinclair, then 'C', had provided 'a mass of information' on Soviet activities overseas, the nation needed a similar system for collecting intelligence on the Communists' 'equally dangerous activities in civil life'. Although Tyrell's points reiterated concerns the SSC had voiced six years earlier and which had led to the creation of the Directorate of Intelligence, the government had remained limited in what it could actually investigate. The British Communist Party's activities occupied a grey area in the law: although some of its members were conspiring with a foreign power to illegally subvert the government by extra-parliamentary means, the party itself remained a legal organisation.

Moreover, as Tyrell noted, even though Britain was 'in substance . . . at war with Russia', it could do nothing to counter enemy actions outside of espionage.[10] Over half a century later, John Bruce Lockhart, a former Deputy Chief of SIS, described the political aspects of the later era's analogous problem in a way that gave detail to Tyrell's plaint:

The Communist Party ... [is] actively trying to destroy parliamentary government. Surely this is treason? Yet it cannot be treason since the Communist Party is a perfectly legal party. ... Moreover much of their work is perfectly open. ... The right answer is not easy to find, but until an effective answer can be found, democracies are asking the security services to fight the battle with one hand tied behind their backs.[11]

The problem was organisational as well as legal, however. Even permissible investigations were hampered in that Britain had no domestic equivalent to SIS. In 1925, MI5 was not yet the service it would become in the 1930s. Its jurisdiction was confined to security issues involving the armed forces. As Kell explained to the Committee, MI5 was 'responsible for what might be described as home security'. But he also said:

The term 'counter-espionage' as a description of its work was no longer entirely applicable: counter-espionage proper at present formed only a small part of it. He was responsible for ... the safety of the armed forces of the Crown in this country, both in respect of foreign espionage and communist interference.[12]

MI5 dealt with all issues related to the military, and Scotland Yard attended to those involving civilians. In Kell's opinion, the division was 'quite distinct'.[13] He conceded that the Soviets might be using the same operatives to propagandise on both the military and civilian fronts, but he also insisted that their most common practice was to establish cells within the armed forces, as well as in arsenals and dockyards. And those cells, he argued, came under his purview.[14] MI5 did not in fact assume responsibility for all counter-intelligence in Britain for another six years, and until then SIS also ran agents on the British mainland.[15]

Tyrrell was not alone in expressing scepticism about the efficiency of British intelligence. Nor was this meeting the first time in 1925 that the Committee had gathered to address the question. Sinclair proved the most vocal within the services about the need for consolidation: 'All the different branches ought to be placed under one head and in one building in the neighbourhood of Whitehall, and to be made responsible to one Department of State, which ought to be the Foreign Office.'[16] Since the Foreign Office was responsible for SIS, a consolidated intelligence service would have come under Sinclair's control.

In a thinly veiled reference to Kell and Holt-Wilson, Sinclair acknowledged that any attempt to modify MI5 would meet resistance 'due to the length of time during which certain officers had served the department'.[17] Nonetheless, he pushed his case, maintaining that MI5's activities directly overlapped with both SIS and Scotland Yard and argued that consolidation would be the inevitable outcome of any attempt to 'draw the line between espionage and contre-espionage, for both were concerned solely with foreign activities'. Sinclair explained that 'M.I.5. looked to him to obtain information from abroad relating to spies working in the United Kingdom and then to follow up on that intelligence at home.' But, he pointed out, MI5 'had no agents and had to rely on informers and the interception of mail for whatever information they were able to gather domestically'.[18] Consequently, Sinclair insisted, SIS necessarily employed agents inside the UK 'in order to cross-check information received from abroad'.[19]

Although their targets were often the same, SIS and MI5's collection systems at this time were somewhat different. When Kell met the SSC, he echoed Sinclair in saying that 'he had no "agents" in the accepted sense of the word, but only informants'. He also stated, however, that he might use agents on an ad hoc basis if needed and would consult Scotland Yard if he had doubts about whom to use and 'might even borrow a man from Scotland Yard'. These differences in approach can be traced back to the services' establishment in 1909 when, for the first six months they worked closely, occupying the same building. But according to Kell:

> They then found that their methods of work were so entirely different –
> C's essentially secret and his own largely in the open – that their cohabitation had to be determined. This difference continued today: C worked entirely through secret agents, he himself [Kell] mainly through chief constables, commanding officers and other avowable channels.[20]

Kell maintained 'close communication with chief constables who wrote him direct and were able to discriminate between his function and those of Scotland Yard'.[21] Holt-Wilson also described an MI5 intelligence collection system by which,

> all enquiries by foreign naval, military and air attachés were recorded, with answers given, and any information deliberately withheld in giving those answers. These records were passed to M.I.5., who tabulated them, and thus knew exactly against what to be on their guard, and could give appropriate warning to those in possession of secrets which were in demand amongst foreign powers.[22]

MI5 compiled the intelligence obtained from 'C, Scotland Yard, chief constables, commanding officesrs, the General Post Office, and other official and private informants' and catalogued it in the Registry.[23] So though there were changes in how MI5 perceived its role from its founding through the 1920s, the underlying system essentially remained the same.[24]

As Kell noted, MI5 depended on a close working relationship with the Metropolitan Police Special Branch (MPSB) and chief constables to identify and track suspicious individuals and to recruit and handle informants. With scant resources – in 1925 MI5 employed a mere ten officers and twenty-five staff – it had little choice.[25] Assistant Commissioner for MPSB, J. F. C. Carter, explained to the SSC that when MPSB was created in 1884 'at the time of the Fenian outrages' its task was primarily 'investigatory' in nature, but 'it seldom had occasion to resort to arrest'. The definition of MPSB's duties was 'somewhat nebulous', he said, but 'roughly speaking, they might be described as the operations side of intelligence'.[26]

Scotland Yard employed some 1,200 plainclothes policemen, 136 of whom were Special Branch.[27] S.S.1. acted 'generally as the liaison office on foreign revolutionary matters between Special Branch and the Home office, on the one hand, and the Special Intelligence Section of the Foreign Office on the other, thus acting virtually as the Home Section of S.I.S.' S.S.2 processed the intelligence received from across the intelligence services. Special Branch dealt with 'all matters of a political-revolutionary matter'.[28] S.S.1. and S.S.2 only employed a handful of officers. The group at S.S.1. included Captain Guy Liddell, who later became head of MI5's B Division (counter-espionage) during the Second World War.

By the mid-1920s communism had come to pose a new challenge to counter-intelligence. During the First World War, intelligence had waged a war against a foreign nation, but that shifted in the interwar period to an intelligence battle against a political and ideological movement. Although the Soviets' goals were not difficult to grasp in their broadest outlines, it was not as obvious how to proceed in light of Bolshevik intentions. To uncover revolutionary and subversive agents, MI5 chiefly relied on methods of intelligence collection already in place from the First World War.

Threat Assessment

The perceived threat from leftist labour was multifaceted. The 'Triple Alliance' of miners, railwaymen and transport workers' unions, an association that had been reconstituted in 1919, headed the list. It was augmented by the founding in 1924 of the General Council of the TUC, whose responsibilities included promoting 'common action by the trade union movement'. Then, too, the British Government saw itself as confronting a related threat in the perceived alliance among organised labour, the Labour Party and the Soviet Union.[29] Despite the fact that Labour roundly rejected affiliation with the CPGB soon after the latter's creation, and even though the first Labour Prime Minister Ramsay MacDonald had warned that 'we shall never be free from danger' as long as the Comintern existed, the Zinoviev scandal in 1924 appeared to confirm the existence of a tripartite alliance involving unions, the Labour left and the Soviets.[30] On the heels of MacDonald's downfall in November 1924, the TUC's General Council sent a delegation of prominent labour leaders to Moscow for the first of the year's series of highly publicised meetings between British communist and labour leaders and their Soviet counterparts.[31] This increase in Anglo-Soviet trade union fraternisation reaffirmed the fear that Moscow was in cahoots with the unions, that both foreign governmental and domestic organisations aimed to subvert the British government's authority and promulgate a people's revolution. Despite the Curzon Ultimatum, one Foreign Office review of communist activity determined that throughout 1925 'anti-British activities have continued unabated, increasing in scope and boldness'.[32]

No doubt the Anglo-Russian Trade Union Conference of April 1925, held at the offices of the TUC's General Council in London, fit that conclusion. Mikhail Tomski, member of the Presidium of the Central Executive Committee of the Soviet Union and President of the All-Russian Central Council of Trade Unions, presided over the discussions about whether the TUC should join an international labour union, likely the Moscow-dominated Red International of Labor Unions (RILU). The TUC subsequently submitted a resolution recording its:

> appreciation of the General Council's efforts to promote international unity, and urges the incoming General Council to do everything in their power towards securing world-wide unity of the trade union movement through an all-inclusive international federation of trades unions [sic].[33]

The conference's initiatives were then buttressed at the Scarborough Trades Union Conference the following September, where, as one sympathetic historian puts it, 'Perhaps the most consistently militant TUC ever held to date [1969], welcomed and ratified all that had been done by the British Delegation to Russia, by the General Council, and by the [Anglo-Russian] Joint [Advisory] Council.'[34] It appeared that the Soviets were usurping the British trade union movement. Only months before, at the Scarborough Conference, IKKI had agreed on the principle of reorganising the British, French and German Communist Parties along military lines, including:

> (a) The introduction of the principle of strict centralisation. (b) The abolition of all factions. (c) Direct contact with the strike movement of Trade Unions through revolutionary Strike Committees attached to Central Committees of Communist Parties. (d) Internal and external control by the creation of special Control Commissions in each Party. (e) The armament of Parties under the control of the Military Bureaux of the Central Committees.[35]

To those already convinced that King Street (CPGB Headquarters) did Moscow's bidding, that Lenin's 'Twenty-One Points' of Comintern membership had subordinated the British Communist Party under the Soviet principle of 'democratic centralism', it now seemed that Moscow was now doing the same with British labour unions.[36]

British authorities viewed the TUC's heightened militancy and increasingly close ties with the Soviets with acute apprehension. The consolidation of the trade unions under Soviet control was viewed as being at the very least an unacceptable encroachment into domestic affairs. At worst, it constituted a preliminary step towards inciting revolution. In 1921, the Comintern had formally adopted Lenin's 'Twenty-One Points', explicitly calling for 'all national communist parties [to reorganise] on an industrial basis and to work upwards from the rank and file to the capture of official trade union positions'.[37] By late 1925, one Foreign Office review of the communist movement in Europe asserted that Moscow planned:

> to make the Trade Union General Council the directing organ of the whole Trade Union movement; to capture that Council, and to use it as a medium for bringing about a General Strike, supported by Continental Action; and to evolve therefrom a general upheaval, culminating in mass violence.[38]

Yet the CPGB did not give its full support to the General Council of the TUC until after the Party had founded the National Minority Movement (NMM) in 1924. The NMM, an offshoot of the Party, was described in the same Foreign Office Review as the 'principal medium, or Advanced Guard' of Soviet policy.[39] Its first head, Tom Mann, worked closely with Soviet help from the RILU (also known as the 'Profintern'), Mikhail Tomski and others to radicalise labour and harness the trade unions for Soviet ends. The NMM's intentions were unambiguous. The 'aims and objects' were:

> To organise the working masses of Great Britain for the overthrow
>   of capitalism, the emancipation of the workers from
>   oppressors and exploiters, and the establishment of a Socialist
>   Commonwealth.
> To carry on a wide agitation and propaganda for the principles of
>   the revolutionary class struggle, and work within existing
>   organisations for the National Minority Movement programme
>   and against the present tendency towards social peace and class
>   collaboration and the delusion of the peaceful transition from
>   capitalism to socialism.
> To unite the workers in their everyday struggles against the exploiters.
>   To maintain the closest relations with the Red International of
>   Labour Unions.[40]

The CPGB's 'All Power to the General Council' campaign, which suggested that it – and Moscow by proxy – thought that it could actually gain control of the TUC through the NMM, led Scotland Yard to conclude that:

> Several trade union leaders of national reputation [who] identified themselves with the programme and policy of the National Minority Movement are, in effect, the junction at which communist infiltration from below, i.e. through the rank and file, meets the communist permeation from above, i.e. Russian influence working on leaders of the British trade union movement.[41]

The remarkable growth of the NMM in its first years convinced Zinoviev that Britain could become 'the centre of gravity for the further development of world revolution.'[42] According to the Minority Movement's records, the number of organisations represented at its annual conference nearly doubled from 271 in January 1925 to 443 in August 1925, and the numbers of members represented by the delegates to the conferences supposedly grew from 200,000 in

1924 to some 957,000 in March 1926.[43] Although these figures are likely exaggerated, the NMM's rapid expansion formed an alarming backdrop to the regularly intercepted telegrams and postal correspondence passing between Moscow and King Street, such as this one from July 1925:

> The economic crisis which is maturing all over England is, in our opinion favourable for conducting the most energetic campaign for a general strike provided the economic demands and political slogans are dexterously combined . ... It is imperative that the **party influence which is gaining strength in the unemployed should be consolidated and extended** by all means available. It is particularly desirable to make use of the unemployed in the campaign against fascism and militarism. In this respect the unions of ex-servicemen and the organisations **could produce large cadres of hardened and energetic fighting men**. ... We advise you, while applying all efforts to the **organisation of a general strike of coal miners, transport, metal and textile workers**, not to stop work in **recruiting new elements from amongst the soldiers and sailors**. Only an alliance of the proletariat with the soldiery can overthrow the bourgeoisie and its government.[44]

That same month, the miners' union threatened a work stoppage, and the railway and transport unions appeared likely to support them. On the cusp of so broad a strike, the government agreed to a six-month extension of fast-expiring subsidies to the mining industry. 'Red Friday', as the 31 July 1925 compromise became known, confirmed – on all sides – the power of the triple alliances.

Some have concluded that the Minority Movement was largely unsuccessful at commandeering the union bureaucracies, instead finding its strongest support at the local level.[45] To the security services at the time, however, local support merged with the high-profile fraternisation between prominent labour leaders and Soviet representatives to suggest that communist domination of the labour movement was a distinct possibility. This was, moreover, the Comintern's boldly expressed strategy.[46]

Alexei Losovski, the Secretary-General of the Red International of Labour Unions, arrived in Berlin a few weeks after Red Friday to outline a 'program of action' to the German Communist Party in anticipation of industrial unrest in Britain in early 1926. According to an SSC report:

> This programme provided for a simultaneous strike in Germany, France and England and possibly in Belgium which would affect the miners, the

metal workers, the transport, post and telegraph workers. It was anticipated that the strike would be of six months' duration and primarily of
an economic nature; but as it progressed, political demands would be
advanced, and care would have to be taken to avoid provoking extreme
measure on the part of the authorities.[47]

A. J. Cook, the Secretary General of the Miners' Federation of Great Britain
and the former head of the Miners' Minority Movement (MMM), a sub-sec-
tion of the NMM, attended the meeting and emphasised the importance of the
last point – that the workers should not provoke the authorities.[48]

But in October 1925, Baldwin's Government, and Jix in particular, were
already sufficiently provoked to move against the CPGB leadership without
having to worry about the publicity that would be guaranteed by a later era's
demands that the government protect civil liberties. With a general strike
seemingly imminent, the government struck at the heart of the communist
movement in Britain. Intercepts and informants had for some months been
indicating that the CPGB, on Soviet orders, was planning to launch a new propaganda campaign aimed at inciting sedition in the armed services and urging
men to 'turn their guns on the masters as the workers had done'.[49] The police
raided CPGB headquarters and the offices of the NMM, the Young Communist
League (YCL) and the *Workers' Weekly* newspaper and arrested twelve prominent communist leaders, eight of whom belonged to the ten-member Political
Bureau of the Party.[50] Convicted under the Incitement to Mutiny Act of 1797,
their sentences ranged from six months to one year.

The imprisonment of most of the CBGB leadership weakened the party's
operations but did not end them. While British communists remained in custody, the Comintern filled the void. As one historian concludes, 'The party, with
the help of the [Comintern], coped. It did not collapse. It would be ready, up to
point, to meet some of the challenges that would arise during 1926.'[51] Although
the strictly top-down command relationship between Moscow and King Street
was merely the perception of British authorities (and equally the wish of some
senior CPGB members), the domestic communists were not so autonomous
that Moscow could not help. Moreover, Moscow wanted to be involved; it aimed
to use the agency of the CPGB and the unions to pursue its revolutionary interests. That was exactly what British security services investigations sought to
prevent. As one post-Second World War document on MI5's responsibilities explains: 'The Security Service is not a secret political police and is not concerned,
for instance, with British Communists or Fascists on account of their political

views but as the potential instruments of Foreign Powers and thus having a bearing on high policy as factors in a military situation.'[52]

Operations

Before the General Strike of 1926, the government had already twice declared a State of Emergency due to industrial action.[53] As a result of the strikes of July 1921 and April 1924 and work stoppages that were narrowly averted, the government developed elaborate contingency plans to secure the provision of essential goods. It also instituted security measures to ensure the maintenance of law and order and began tasking the intelligence services to stay abreast of communist machinations. Emergency regulations laid the legal framework for law enforcement agencies, MI5 and the military to impose martial law in the event of a civil emergency. The latter two of these were to be brought in as a new 'defence force' that would serve as an auxiliary to assist the domestic law-enforcement agencies that normally operated under civil law. Limited resources obliged MI5 to search for alternative means of fulfilling its duties. The temporary recruitment of ex-MI5 officers, for example, was a response to MI5's having few permanent staff. [54] Thus both the *modus operandi* and much of the staff during the General Strike came from the First World War.

Military intelligence, an important component of the Defence Force, was to carry out, as intelligence B services, actions of a 'defensive, preventive, negative and precautionary' nature (as distinct from intelligence A services, which were to be 'concerned with the acquisition of the positive information required for the conduct of active military operations against opposing force').[55] B services included 'special instructions for military authorities on the prevention of sabotage and damage', 'precautions against enlisting in the Defence Force communists and disloyalists who might act treacherously or levant with their arms', and 'arrangements for close intelligence liaison with the civil police intelligence services, and with well-informed loyal citizens'. All cases of suspected espionage were to be referred to MI5.[56]

By 1926 MI(B) consisted entirely of MI5 officers under MI5 Deputy Director-General (DDG) Holt-Wilson. The organisation coordinated with other government agencies but was also charged with a considerable amount of intelligence collection.[57] Information categorised under two headings: 'As acquired by troops' and 'As acquired from civil sources', and the entire process was intended to address nine concerns:

(i) POLICY, PLANS, and INTENTIONS of opponents: forecasts
relating to possible centres of disturbance.

(ii) ACTIVITY of opponents, such as sabotage and other acts of
violence or intimidation.

(iii) PROPAGANDA of opponents and its effects.

(iv) RESOURCES of opponents, including armament and traffic in
arms; of inter-communication; transport, supply, financial and
economic questions.

(v) MORAL [*sic*] of opponents: the attitude of their various groups
towards each other and their relations with Communist, Sinn
Fein and similar organisations.

(vi) MORAL [*sic*] OF GOVERNMENT FORCES.

(vii) UNDESIRABLES present in the Government Forces.

(viii) LOYALTY of the local authorities and population generally,
including the Press.

(ix) GOVERNMENT CIVIL AND MILITARY POLICY AND
MEASURES their general effect; proposals and modifications.[58]

Placing agents and informants inside unions, communist cells and government forces was critical to fulfilling collection tasks. Human intelligence assumed a primacy in security operations because it allowed the services to keep a finger on the pulse of public sentiment, troop morale and communist activity.

With the expiry of the 'Red Friday' subsidies due on 1 May 1926, Jix feared that the regular police force would be insufficient to quell the expected mass protests and that even the Defence Force might be inadequate to the task of providing essential goods to the public. Although special constables were 'quietly recruiting' volunteers, Jix wrote to Baldwin that 'the time has come to really have the button not only there but with the names of individuals attached to each button'.[59] So in September 1925 the government formed the Organisation for the Maintenance of Supplies (OMS), whose purpose was 'to register and classify those citizens of all classes and of either sex who are prepared to render voluntary assistance in maintaining the supply of food, water, and fuel and the efficiency of public services indispensable to the normal life of the community' in the event of a general strike. The official communiqué asserted that the OMS:

> has no aggressive or provocative aims. It is not formed with any idea
> of opposing the legitimate efforts of trade unions to better the status
> and conditions of their members, and it is in complete sympathy with

any constitutional action to bring about a more equitable adjustment of social and economic conditions. If however, in order to secure a particular end, an attempt is made to inflict severe privation on the great mass of the people who have no direct part in the actual dispute, this Organisation of Citizens, serving the interests of the general community, will place its entire resources at the disposal of the constitutional authorities.[60]

At least some of these volunteers came from extreme right-wing organisations, the remnants of the British Empire Union, and the Economic League set up by George Makgill during the First World War.[61] For those like Makgill, Bolshevism inspired the same resistance that Germany had animated. The closeness with which these groups cooperated with the government is indicated by the fact that Makgill served on the Supply and Transport Organisation (STO), a subcommittee in part responsible for the development of the OMS and other contingency measures.[62]

The Supply and Transport Committee (STC), of which the STO was a sub-committee, also affirmed the emergency framework devised in 1921 (when the STC was known as the Industrial Unrest Committee) authorising the evocation of martial law.[63] It also issued the cautionary message that although sensitive and necessary sectors of the economy such as coal and food might be protected, intelligence officers needed to distinguish between legitimate strikers and agitators:

> Trade Unions have a definite, legal, valuable and responsible position in the country. The army must not make the mistake of approaching the officials of a Union or Federation of Unions as though their existence was illegal or even antagonistic to the national welfare. When they are directly or indirectly involved in the apparent cause of violence and disorder, it will nearly always be found that their own authority has been usurped by irresponsible communists, anarchists or local hot-heads out for personal advantage or plunder only . . . Intelligence officers must beware of prying into bona-fide Trade Union organisation work and membership, as though they were exploring a conspiracy.[64]

It also urged the army to wage a 'battle for hearts and minds', noting that 'the military security branch in each Command must make itself popular with all classes, official and private. Avoid all arbitrary and jack-boot methods and statements and sabre-rattling.'[65]

So by 1925, the government had solid emergency structures in place, the culmination of some six years' planning since the first meeting of the STC and the STO. The government's two-pronged approach of decapitating the CPGB leadership structure and solidifying contingency plans for civil unrest meant the government faced the prospect of a general strike in 1926 with confidence. Or as Jix put it a couple of months before the General Strike, 'There is now very little remaining to be done before the actual occurrence of any emergency.'[66]

As anticipated, the miners called for a work stoppage to begin on 1 May 1926. In solidarity, the TUC threatened a general strike to begin at midnight on 3 May unless the government entered into negotiations. The Prime Minister, however, declared a state of emergency 'in consequence of the cessation of work in the coalfields', triggering MI5's emergency measures.[67] Contingency plans focused on four critical areas: labour, transport, food and order. The government called for committees to recruit labour and ordered the navy and army to prepare to break stoppages and take over Hyde Park to establish a 'transport and milk depot'. It also issued advertisements for special constables in the event that the police also went on strike.[68] Negotiations between the Cabinet and the TUC collapsed, with Baldwin refusing to continue negotiations if the TUC did not call off the impending strike. The TUC stood firm, and the General Strike began at midnight on 3 May 1926.[69]

MI5 tracked suspect individuals and pockets of unrest during the Strike, writing up situation reports – the 'P. reports' of MI(B). Although the reports did not follow a set format, they typically detailed the activities and movements of some of those involved in revolutionary groups, providing descriptions of individuals, addresses, background information and a list of their associates. The reports also listed labour and political groups to which they belonged. Although, as one former SIS officer has said, the 'bigger picture is seldom clear' when submerged in the 'microcosm of case-work', thorough case files and good record keeping created continuity and forged connections where none was necessarily apparent.[70] MI5 was able to build a clear picture of trouble spots and link networks of agitators and subversives by indexing the information for cross-referencing, as had been done during the First World War.

Aldershot[71]

On the night of 4 May, after the first full day of the Strike, five agents arrived in Aldershot, southwest of London, 'for the purpose of gaining general information and Intelligence'. The five agents, identified in the reports as *A*, *B*, *C*,

D and *E*, each adopted a fictitious history of a cover identity. *A* travelled as a South African visiting a friend and *B* as his chauffeur. *C* posed as someone en route from London to Winchester looking for employment. *D* and *E* operated as a team, with the story that they were partners in a small motor business. The ability to move in a crowd without attracting attention has been termed *going grey*.[72] Using obvious, but nonetheless important tradecraft, the three groups spent the night in different hotels under their assumed identities, hotels that likely reflected the social status of their respective covers, a potentially obvious but nonetheless important demonstration of consistency with their cover identities. Later British intelligence instruction teaches us that cover identity is not a costume but an entire persona.[73]

Agents *A*, *B*, *C*, *D* and *E* maintained a low profile, gleaning information from casual encounters. A grocer's wife told *A* and *B* 'there was a great deal of "anti-King" feeling among the Railwaymen'. A soldier's wife told them 'her husband's regiment could absolutely be relied on', but they also reported that one officer indicated the morale of his troops was 'rather bad'. Aldershot had experienced an 'intensive campaign' of Communist propaganda during the previous months, in which agitators threw leaflets over the walls of the barracks, distributed literature to troops 'under the trees in the evening', and chalked subversive messages on the pavement. It may have had some effect on local feelings.

Agents *C*, *D* and *E* 'operated in the lower parts of town', mingling at 'various bars and eating houses frequented by soldiers'. Rare for British agents during this period, they adopted the stance of *provocateurs*, baiting soldiers with subversive political conversation. They found nobody, however, 'with any disloyal feelings. In most cases, when political arguments were started the soldiers finished their beer and left at once'. This does not appear to be unique, for MI5 received other reports that when communists had 'systematically lured' Royal Marines posted at the Deptford Cattle Market (London) into a local public house and plied them 'with drink and Red propaganda', they had little success. Rather, the report stated, their attempts merely resulted in 'the consumption of an inordinate quantity of beer'.[74] In Aldershot, the agents reported that not only the armed forces, but also 'the ordinary working men and labourers seemed to be perfectly loyal', and although there was 'a distinct tendency to sympathise with the Miners', there was little sympathy for the General Strike. That night the agents attempted to observe communist propagandists in action, but 'as it was a pouring wet night, it was decided that no Communist propaganda would be spread for obvious reasons and therefore observations were discontinued at

11.45'. Information provided by the agents makes it possible to piece together a picture of the town as being quite resistant to communist propaganda, and although the communists sometimes affected the mood of the soldiers, over-all morale was good. Agents *A* and *B* were, moreover, able to discover enough of the subversives' propaganda methods to enable the authorities to develop means of countering them.

Stratford-upon-Avon[75]

Not all surveillance bore fruit, of course, except perhaps in honing skills and developing tradecraft. Agents in Stratford-upon-Avon submitted a report that serves today to give us more information about what the agents did than it helped MI5 at the time. The summary notes the activities of the local socialist R. H. Webb in great detail:[76]

> 11.15 Entered station, occupied by Station Master, 2 Clerks, and refreshment woman. Remained in booking-office with the 3 men [he met previously], talking in undertones. Sounds as of a quarrel. Our agent got the impression that WEBB had a shadow escort. 12.15 Left Station, walking along pavement under the Bridge. Next picked up on Shottery field path, where he ran and disappeared. Picked up again by chance on Shottery Rd going towards Shottery. Opposite a farm on right he turned left into a field, disappeared among some allotment huts, finally entering first brown hut on left. Was at once joined by two men. Joined by several more. Agent did not know how they arrived at entrance of hut on the far side. Silence for 5 minutes.

Although the report does not indicate Webb's importance, it is a good example of the raw intelligence MI5 received throughout the strike. Surveillance enabled the security services to establish a target's routine movements, a baseline from which to gauge irregularities. It also allowed observers to catalogue and investigate the target's destinations and acquaintances. Deviations from patterns of activity alerted observers to suspicious activity, such as covert meetings.

It seems clear from the report that Webb knew he was being followed. Perhaps his 'shadow escort' noticed the agents and tipped him off. Webb's running gave away to the agents that he knew of their presence. Had he shown more awareness, he might have allowed them to follow as he led them away from his intended rendezvous. Instead, he continued with his arrangements and led the agents to his meeting place. Their working as a team undoubtedly made trailing him easier. One Cold War intelligence veteran notes that it takes four people to trail one target on foot (and five cars to shadow one target car).[77] Teamwork allowed the agents to give the target more space – once dropped by one agent on foot; the suspect can be picked up by another. If done correctly, the more people used, the more likely invisibility is assured. In this case, at least two men trailed Webb. These agents were not well skilled, however, and Webb spotted their presence.

'Lying by the roadside 75 yards from the hut', the two agents continued their surveillance. Two women came past their hiding place and entered the hut, after which the agents counted five individuals who exited and looked around – 'they were obviously very ill at ease'. The two women left, 'probably to take up posts of observation'. Meanwhile, 'One agent tried to crawl across the field, but was half way across when someone from the hut shouted "Show yourself".' The agents' positions had been compromised. Someone with binoculars looked on from the hut while several individuals approached the agent still lying by the roadside. Two others tried to cut off the other agent, who had retreated to the main road. He 'took to his heels and he did not wish to be closely seen'. Someone yelled at him, 'What the Hell are you doing here?' to which he replied 'What's it to do with you?'. The agent then continued back to Stratford, and the other observed six men 'cross the allotment towards Evesham road, hurriedly. Time 1.10p.m.'

Taken independently the details mean relatively little (even if the verbal exchange does provide comic relief), but building case files often required meticulous attention to seemingly arbitrary details. Many times insignificant details encountered at the beginning of a case might prove to be central in retrospect. Cataloguing these insignificant pieces of information might have provided links and leads later in the case that had not been perceived in the earlier phases of the investigation. Copious paperwork thus became an integral aspect of agent operations. No other information on Webb exists in MI5's General Strike file, but dead-ends are a reality of espionage and counter-espionage.

A Resourceful Agent[78]

Two days after the Strike's conclusion, MI(B) received a report from a determined and resourceful agent about the offices of the *Daily Herald*, which as of 1922 was jointly controlled by the TUC and the Labour Party.[79] 'There was a constant hum of action emanating from the offices of the Herald and the neighbouring house occupied by Williams', the agent wrote. 'Men going up the staircase of the offices, women coming down, people going into and others emerging from Williams' house. This decided me to attempt to force an entry.' According to the agent, he pushed his way to the offices, which were 'well defended by a gang of say 100 men.' He knocked on the door, from which hung a sign reading 'Committee meeting', and two 'stalwarts' permitted him entry without hassle. The agent observed '18 men sitting on chairs lined round the wall. One darkish fellow, clean shaven, fairly well dressed, black hair, age about 22, height 5ft 6" . . . taking down resolutions and writing out minutes. He had been holding forth before I had gained admission.' The agent appears to have kept calm. Instead of beating a hasty retreat, he carried on as if pursuing a normal course of action. 'I walked up to his table, asking whether his name was BLACKADDER. He said "No, Blackadder, has gone up to the Central Committee".'

His knowledge of at least one of the committee member's names spared the agent from a potentially ugly scene. As he turned to go, the man 'then caught the eye of one of his stalwarts and turned round short on me, rising from his seat. "Who are you?" I said "Alright comrade, I am P. B. correspondent of the I. I.". He said "You will find Williams next door; go to see him. He may give you some news".' It is uncertain what a 'P. B. correspondent' was, let alone if the 'I. I.' news corporation in fact existed. The importance of the incident lies in the agent's creation of a cover to justify his activity in the *Daily Herald* offices.

Aside from overhearing that the committee was in the process of writing a manifesto, the agent gleaned important information from Williams's wife on leaving the office. 'Have you any news?' he asked. 'Well the men are solid to a man,' she said, adding that 'They will not go back unless they are taken back in their old places', referring to the question of the re-employment of workers following the strike. The agent further learned that news of lower wages had angered the strikers. 'What are the men going to do about it?' 'Yes, there is going to be a riot', she told him. The agent reported to his officer straight away. There is no record of a riot having erupted, but the presence of a resourceful agent meant that the security services were alerted to the volatility of the situation.

Strike's End and Aftermath

The TUC leadership unconditionally called off the General Strike on 12 May 1926. The OMS and emergency services had worked: 'The efficiency with which commercial road transport functioned during the crisis appeared afterwards to be the most vital if not most spectacular success of emergency administration.'[80] The TUC's inability to cause serious shortages weakened its bargaining position. The availability of both oil and electricity allowed OMS volunteers to meet the demand for most necessities. The strike did not occasion widespread violence. There was no connection between a communist presence and violent protest. In London, the 'communists exercised little influence', in part because most CPGB-affiliated organisations were raided early in the strike, their printing presses confiscated or dismantled, and their meeting places 'kept under constant observation' (again a function of human intelligence). Although a few areas reported communist activities, most stated it was 'negligible' or 'nil'.[81]

The CPGB's failure to influence dramatically the course of the General Strike was due in part to its own mismanagement, its misreading of its relationship with the TUC and its fundamental misunderstanding of British public sentiment. The same could be said of Moscow. MI5 and Scotland Yard's successful contingency planning made the CPGB's failure all the more emphatic. In the end, 'Jix was far better prepared for the General Strike than the Communists in either Britain or the Soviet Union.'[82] The CPGB's post-mortem of the strike concluded that it had 'not sufficiently mobilized the very scanty resources at our disposal', but the same cannot be said of the security services, which also operated with insufficient resources.[83] Perhaps Kell was referring to the retired First World War officers called back to work during the strike when he wrote to the MI5 staff, 'I desire to thank all Officers and their Staffs, also the Ladies of the Office, for their splendid work and co-operation during the General Strike. The manner in which all hands have put their shoulders to the wheel shows that the ancient war-traditions of M.I.5 remained unimpaired.'[84]

The lack of public support for the strike also strengthened the Government's ability to maintain order. Baldwin's overall leadership has been described as using constitutionalism as its 'strongest weapon', and that was certainly true of how the government approached the General Strike. [85] Its framing of the conflict as a constitutional confrontation was forcefully propagated by the *British Gazette*, a broadsheet edited by Churchill during the strike, with one front page featuring an article on Baldwin's insistence that 'the General Strike is a challenge to Parliament and is the road to anarchy and ruin'.[86] Baldwin himself encouraged the public to support the Government over the radio waves of the newly formed British Broadcasting Company (BBC).[87] Not only did the strike fail to halt necessary services, the shift of focus from treating it as an issue of industrial conflict to one of subversion alienated much of the public from the workers' cause.[88]

Ultimately the CPGB concluded at its Eighth Congress that the Party had failed 'to prepare for the coming struggle'.[89] Scotland Yard concurred: 'The strike, when it actually occurred, was too big a thing for the Communist Party to handle.' Yet it also concluded that its 'failure was not due to lack of effort'.[90] An MI5 informant reported a conversation between J. T. Murphy (an executive and founding member of the CPGB) and William Brain (a Midland Organiser for the CPGB), in which Murphy (it can be assumed) admitted the CPGB's failure to concentrate on the armed forces – to inspire mutiny and sedition – despite Moscow's insistence that 'this work was one of the most important tasks'. But Murphy thought that 'the effort made was not itself worrying', rather, 'the manner of the effort was all wrong'. He apparently believed that Moscow's instructions accounted for the lack of success, telling Brain that the faulty methodology was 'clearly realised by the Communist Party leaders here who know more about the psychology of the British soldiers than Moscow does'. He concluded that the most recent propaganda efforts in the military had been 'practically nil', but also insisted, 'The minute this trouble is over it will be necessary to sit down and sift the whole question with a view to organising propaganda in the Services on a proper systematic basis and on the right lines.'[91] Thus the failures of the CPGB did not in any way indicate surrender.

Few in the intelligence and security services equated the end of the General Strike to the end of the 'red menace' either. One Scotland Yard report ventured:

> It is not possible to predict whether the general strike will or will not recur. ... The fact remains however that, had that been no communist propaganda, there would have been no general strike. On the one hand there was a strong and determined Government reinforced by a loyal Army, Navy and Police force and backed by the overwhelming mass of a law abiding people adverse to coercion and gifted with considerable powers of adaptability and improvisation: on the other hand were a handful of amateur revolutionaries and a few million organised workers. In the face of formidable odds, the latter contrived seriously to interfere with the life of the whole nation and effectively suspend nearly all constructive work and ordinary trade. Admittedly a failure and a blunder, the General Strike, whether regarded as a single incident or a rehearsal was and unless revolutionary propaganda is checked or counteracted, must remain, a menace.[92]

In the eyes of communists, the General Strike was one battle in a larger war. CPGB expenses were underwritten by the USSR, and according to Scotland

Yard, the Comintern had allocated the CPGB £16,000 in 1925 (almost £775,000 today).[93] But one MI5 informant with intimate knowledge of Soviet operations stated it was £20,000.[94] Other sources suggested that the sum was nearly £99,000.[95] The Soviet defector Krivitsky later wrote, with some exaggeration perhaps, 'At no time has any single Communist Party in the world managed to cover more than a very small percentage of its expenses. Moscow's own estimate is that it must bear on an average from ninety to ninety-five percent of the expenditures of foreign Communist Parties.'[96] From its funds, the CPGB also supported other organisations such as the NMM, which also depended almost entirely on Moscow, 'for its income from individual subscriptions and affiliation fees was negligible.'[97]

Jix's determination to prove the links between the trade unions and the CPGB and the Soviets continued after the Strike ended. On 11 May 1926, A. S. Hinshelwood wrote to Liddell's colleague at Scotland Yard, H. M. Miller (noted for his 'tendency to excess of zeal', according to the 1925 SSC), with information that he had been contacted by a source at the *Daily Mail* who had, in turn, a source in the Bankers Clearing House. Miller's source reported that ARCOS paid £300,000 (£14.5 million today) to the Cooperative Wholesale Society, which later that day disbursed the same amount to 'strike funds'.[98] For Jix, the correlation showed that the Soviets were 'without doubt providing money on the first day of the General Strike for the financing of the strike'. This was wishful thinking. Only a few days later, he admitted that there was 'no reason to connect the two transactions'.[99] In the absence of any analytical oversight that could bring together existing evidence, ministers became their own analysts. At times, this led to alarmist conclusions (although the politicians of later generations have proven that they are still perfectly capable of ignoring proper intelligence analysis that contradicts their policy objectives).

As with the Zinoviev affair, the evidence offered to exemplify Soviet misconduct did not support British claims. However, the allegations were substantiated by other documents, some of which Jix released to demonstrate the existence of the financial dealings. The Soviets had indeed sent money to help the strikers. An impressive £100,000 (or nearly £5 million in today's terms) was wired to the TUC General Council, which rejected the offer so as to avoid accusations that it was beholden to Moscow.[100] One MI(B) report documents an officer's interview with Ivan Maiski (an ARCOS executive member and later Soviet Ambassador to the UK), who 'took exception' to certain implications in the British media that the Soviets were funding the strikers. The officer duly responded that any transfer of funds from the USSR required government approval, and so any funds received tacitly implied the Soviet government's consent. Maiski coyly replied, 'We cannot prevent the workers of Russia to come to the assistance of other workers', a disingenuous claim by any account.[101] Again, the Soviet intention was to intervene, even if events unfolded against their wishes.

The fact that the TUC refused Soviet aid, like the comments of J. T. Murphy above, points to larger fissures in the perceived TUC-CPGB-Moscow alliance. That relationship was particularly fraught with difficulties. Though some members of the TUC, such as the NMM, strove for revolution, key union leaders saw the strike differently. Following Red Friday in July 1925, Walter Citrine, General Secretary of the TUC, viewed with uncertainty the wisdom of a prospective general strike, correctly believing it would lead to the government intervention he sought to avoid.[102] Nor did his conception of the trade union movement reflect the revolutionary ethos espoused by the NMM, CPGB, and most of all, Moscow. According to Citrine:

> The British trade union movement has its roots very deeply in economic soil, and, unlike some of the Continental movements, it is not so susceptible to revolutionary change that at the wave of a wand it can become suddenly transformed. It has been built up to redress immediate economic injustices, not to change violently and fundamentally the social system in accordance with an abstract theory.[103]

Hence, understanding the British trade union movement as being simply an extension of Moscow was based on flawed reasoning. On the other hand, some communists thought it was exactly this compromising, reform-minded unionism that had undermined the General Strike. For Rajani Palme Dutt, the strike's failure underscored the need to move definitively away from 'old sectional trade union action' towards a universal, militant unionism directed by a highly centralised Communist party.[104] Dutt's influence on the party meant that this sentiment led to increasing rigidity in CPGB doctrine generally.

In Moscow, some located the failure of revolutionary spirit to take hold in Europe in the mid-1920s in the changing nature of the Comintern – and indeed the Soviet Union as a whole. Stalin's consolidation of power in the mid-1920s saw the triumph of 'socialism in one country'. An emphasis on stability transformed the role of the Comintern from harbinger of international revolution to defender of Soviet national interests.[105] For Trotsky, the notion of Soviet 'national' interests amounted to apostasy – or more accurately, the revolution's betrayal. He later lambasted the development of a 'conservative bureaucracy', which he believed was responsible for the 'treachery' behind the failure of popular movements such as the General Strike.[106] Although the USSR wavered between engagement and isolation, Soviet participation in international politics during the 1920s ultimately roped it into the status quo in important ways.

Under Stalin, Soviet intelligence collection began to change correspondingly – both in targeting and methods. Diplomatic normalisation with Western European countries brought increased sensitivity to Soviet relations with national communist parties. The General Strike in particular graphically demonstrated to the Soviets both that they could not defeat Britain through the labouring class and that working too closely with native communists caused immense diplomatic headaches. From the British perspective, the General Strike justified and brought renewed attention to organised labour and the CPGB. Events in the late 1920s further persuaded the Soviets of the need to change their strategy while the same events convinced the British to maintain theirs.

CHAPTER 3

Recruitment and Handling

Macartney, Ewer and the Cambridge Five

I N 1927, the Anglo-Soviet relationship ruptured, and agent operations lay behind the break. One set of treasonous activities, those of the Macartney case, occurred within the context of several international incidents of considerable importance: the coup in Poland led by Marshal Jozef Piłsudski, the quickly following assassination of Soviet diplomat Pyotr Voikov in Warsaw, the Chinese civil war (including the Peking raid by British authorities), and more directly, the ARCOS raid of May 1927 and subsequent war scare. Viewed altogether, it is easy to understand why Wilfred F. R. Macartney's attempt to give classified British military information to the Soviets struck British security and intelligence officers as being not only grave, but urgent, and why, too, they sought to arrest Macartney and his handler, German-born Soviet operative Georg Hansen, when the opportunity arose. Recent literature has highlighted risk-taking as a 'quality essential' to today's intelligence operatives, but as the Macartney case shows, there is a fine line between risk-taking and bad judgement.[1] The Macartney case also serves to highlight an early iteration of the 'recruitment cycle': spotting, assessing, developing, pitching, formalising, producing (handling) and terminating.[2] Macartney's history illuminates why he came to the attention of Soviet recruiters, what motivated him to spy, the particular characteristics that made him attractive to a Soviet recruiter, how he was spotted, and how he might have been assessed.[3]

A second case, that of William Norman Ewer, concluded shortly after Macartney's trial. The fact that Ewer, a Trinity College, Cambridge graduate who spied for the Soviets in the 1920s, was detected more rapidly than Kim Philby in the 1930s was due chiefly to his more primitive tradecraft. Under the cover of the Federated Press of America (FPA) and his job as foreign correspondent for the *Daily Herald*, Ewer ran a network of agents and informants that provided him – and the Soviets – with information from a number of government offices, some of which came from turned detectives in Scotland Yard. The Soviets and the CPGB, thus forewarned, were able to take appropriate action to protect their interests from counter-espionage operations. Revelations

2 Wilfred Macartney (L) and Second World War double agent Edward Arnold Chapman ('Agent Zigzag') (R), who were charged with violation of the Official Secrets Act. (31 March 1946)

that Scotland Yard detectives had been compromised in the end worked in MI5's favour. After years of deliberating on the appropriate division of labour among the intelligence services, in 1931 the SSC handed MI5 control of all British counter-subversion and counter-espionage – civilian and military. Nonetheless, the methodical undermining of British security from the inside represented a coup for early Soviet intelligence – though one later dwarfed by the success of the Cambridge Five (Anthony Blunt, Guy Burgess, John Cairncross, Donald Maclean and Kim Philby).[4]

Macartney's Background and Motivations

Wilfred Macartney first came to the attention of British intelligence because of his own foolish self-promotion. In a display of pitiable indiscretion and equally poor judgment, he publicised his interest in and previous connection to intelligence in the autumn of 1926, following the General Strike. An article he wrote for the *Sunday Worker* caught the attention of Sir Stewart Menzies, later the chief of SIS from 1939 to 1952. Macartney, 'The Monocle Man', claimed to have worked for the Foreign Office in Greece and to have received war decorations from both Greece and Serbia. What drew attention to him, however, was his assertion that he had also worked for the 'Secret Service' in Turkey, coupled with his lambasting of the Trades Union leadership for their betrayal of striking workers.[5] Menzies notified MI5's Joseph Ball, who had served MI5 during the First World War and who correctly suspected that Macartney was the 'Sub. Lieut. M' who had once governed an island and had squandered a £67,000 fortune – what would amount to well over £3 million today.[6] Menzies also alerted Guy Liddell of Scotland Yard.[7] Soon after, Liddell wrote to Ball that his investigations into Macartney revealed that in addition to having joined the CPGB, Macartney had agreed to write more articles for the *Sunday Worker* to provide warning of future attacks on 'Reds' based on information gathered from 'past acquaintances in the Service', and more generally to find out 'how much is known of the Communist Party at the Home Office and Whitehall'.[8]

Scrutiny of Macartney increased, and Liddell passed along further information, gleaned from an informant, that Macartney had 'been taken in by a man named Messer in Glasgow, who is a member of the Red Secret Service'.[9] Messer was not an unknown; MI5's file on him dated back to 1916, when he had attracted attention for his political agitation in 'Red Clydeside', Glasgow's historically radical industrial centre, where he protested against British involvement in the First World War.[10] Formerly of the Shop Stewards Movement, Messer was affiliated in the mid-1920s with Kirchenstein's clandestine courier network, so Macartney's association with Messer fuelled the security services' interest.[11]

The CPGB had expelled Macartney shortly after his enrolment, however, under the misconceived suspicion that he was spying on them.[12] In fact, soon after Macartney's expulsion from the party, Scotland Yard's own watchers observed Messer shadowing Macartney. Yet despite CPGB and its Soviet advisors' mistrust of Macartney, his acquaintance with Messer and brief membership in the CPGB earned him British suspicion as well. Thus he was under observation by both sides, and an MPSB informant provided Liddell with the necessary information to impose a HOW on Macartney's communications and correspondence.[13] The HOW then provided the foundation for the collection of the evidence leading to Macartney's arrest and conviction not long after the surveillance began.

Macartney was an early example of an upper-middle class youth turning to the communist myth-image. By all accounts, he had a privileged upbringing and a promising career as a civil servant as well as a substantial private income. His father made him a director of his Malta-based company, one of the largest tram contractors in the world, when Macartney was only twelve. By the time Macartney was fourteen he was earning £200 per year – a respectable sum given his age – and had a banking account in the United States.[14] After his father died, Macartney left for the United States to attend university while his brother assumed operations of the business and dealt with lawsuits over his father's will.

At the age of sixteen, Macartney enlisted for the Great War. One of his postings was under Compton Mackenzie in the Eastern Mediterranean, where he worked in military intelligence, managing incoming reports from SIS agents in Asia Minor.[15] 'Working with Compton Mackenzie and Hope-Johnstone was exciting for me,' Macartney later wrote. 'Ciphers, agents' reports, inter-departmental jealousies, international intrigues added to my not inconsiderable experience, making me regard life and the war less credulously than was usual among boys of my age.'[16] After Greece, he was sent to France (for a second time), where he sustained a (second) wound, and was captured. He later escaped by jumping off of a train and then made his way back to the UK, where he was decorated.[17]

Although Macartney came from an affluent family, stood to inherit a fortune and returned to Britain as a decorated war hero, he was deeply disillusioned with the status quo. In London he found 'the slim soldier on leave from the fighting line, hard as nails, vital, and physically attractive, could compete successfully with the fat-gutted war profiteers, but the ex-soldier in mufti had no chance against the stout and prosperous postwar entrepreneur. Heroes slumped and the day of the sugar-daddy arrived.'[18] Like many of his generation, Macartney felt betrayed by the society and government that had sent him to war. He gradually turned to communism. 'I have said we do not become Socialists all at once, and I am honest to say that once upon a time I was far from being a Socialist,' he explained.[19] Indeed, he wrote, 'My story would be an easier to write . . . if I could say that I had actually thought like Siegfried Sassoon and others like him during the beastliness of those dreadful years, but I just didn't. I stayed with the twentieth century. When it thought war I thought war, and when it decided the war was over I decided the same thing.'[20] Before he grew intoxicated by communism, however, Macartney had been intoxicated by liquor. In London, he lived the life of a *flâneur*, squandering what remained of his inheritance after years of litigation aimed at supporting his extravagant lifestyle. Macartney seems to have been part of the first wave of champagne socialists – and one wonders whether it was champagne or socialism that commanded his loyalty more.

The acronym M. I. C. E. summarises the four typical motivations for spying: money, ideology, compromise and ego.[21] Macartney's motivations, as far as can be discerned, accounted for three of the four (money, ideology and ego). His own explanations for his behaviour varied. At times he waxed ideological – 'the only chance for the huge majority of mankind . . . is a Communistic revolution leading to the replacement of a system of universal exploitation, degradation and horror by a Communistic economy in which human beings shall enjoy the full fruits of an [sic] universal abundance'.[22] At other times, he was frank about the financial incentives – 'it cannot be denied that for money [I] took on the job of obtaining information for a foreign Power'.[23] To historian Gill Bennett, the political passion of anti-materialism was a cover for its opposite, 'By 1925 [Macartney] was almost bankrupt and claimed to be a convert to Communism, although he seems to have regarded it as a business opportunity rather than a spiritual home'.[24]

To the Soviets, Macartney must have appeared to be easily recruitable but not very trustworthy. If the qualities of a potential agent often included exploitable weaknesses and vices (though noble attributes might also be exploited) – what might be called *entry points* – Macartney fit the model. Alcohol, debt, sexual involvements, insecurity and other factors all served as exploitable behaviours. In the mid-1920s, Macartney was drunk, destitute, idle and idealistic, showing great weakness. A description of Soviet practice suggested that there must have appeared about him plenty to leverage.[25] At that point, again following Soviet practice, he would most likely have been enlisted 'either by means of a direct or a veiled offer. The direct offer can be made only when the person in question is in difficult material circumstances or is known for his previous espionage activities'.[26]

Macartney also had connections to the military and high society and boasted a background in intelligence. In short, he was an ideal target for recruitment – but that is not the same as being an ideal agent.

Monkland

Although Macartney's newspaper articles aroused concern, Liddell's investigations and background check led Ball and Menzies to conclude that Macartney was 'no longer worth powder and shot from our point of view'.[27] Nor did Desmond Morton of SIS give much credence to Macartney's claims, later testifying that he believed Macartney to be 'an inveterate liar and crook'. He similarly dismissed Macartney's professed ties to British intelligence:

I further knew he had given himself out on occasions as a member of the British Secret Service, the true fact in this respect being that at one period in the war he was Military Control Officer on an island in the Aegean, the work he did there entitling him to call himself a member of the Secret Service about as much as the work of a Solicitor's Office boy would entitle the latter to call himself a lawyer.[28]

Soviet intelligence apparently disagreed, but Macartney's poor judgement and poor tradecraft ultimately proved the British assessment of his overall value a better one.

It is unclear exactly when Macartney met Hansen ('Johnson'), his Soviet contact, but Macartney notes that he met George Monkland, whom he tried to recruit, through a mutual friend at the Ritz in London in 1924.[29] Two years later Macartney asked Monkland for information on arms shipments from the UK to the Baltics. Macartney attempted what the Soviets called a 'camouflaged enrolment': Monkland was at first an unwitting accomplice.[30] When Macartney gave Monkland a detailed questionnaire on various questions of military importance, however, it confirmed Monkland's growing suspicions. Macartney's wartime superior, Compton Mackenzie, later wondered, 'Why Macartney should have foolishly supposed that Mr. Monkland would lend himself to such a transaction.'[31] Indeed, Macartney's failure in the assessment and development phases of the recruitment cycle precluded his success in getting Monkland on board. Quite the opposite occurred: Monkland contacted Admiral Sir Reginald 'Blinker' Hall (Director of Naval Intelligence during the First World War), who then set up a lunch with former Deputy Chief of SIS Freddie Browning to discuss the case. Hall and Browning passed the case to Morton rather than to MI5 directly. Following Browning's instructions, Morton contacted Monkland to set up a meeting the next day, using the code word 'emerald' and introducing himself as 'Peter Hamilton'.[32]

Morton then began to run Macartney's agent against him. On 2 May 1927, Morton contacted Jasper Harker of MI5 to inform him:

We have received a report originating from the G.P.U. [Soviet foreign intelligence] in Paris as follows:--'W. F. R. Macartney . . . is now acting as an agent for the Soviet in connection with British Aircraft matters and the British Air Force. He arrived in Paris on the morning of April 29th, having crossed from England by the previous night's boat. Here he is going under the name W. F. Hudson. . . . He is in touch with a certain George Monkland . . . [and] expects to receive reports on British Air Force matters from England . . . He intends to post these reports when received back to England to George Monkland, who has been instructed to pass them on to the head of the USSR espionage.'[33]

Morton asked to be kept informed of the results of investigations into two addresses Macartney was using and over the next month some eleven more addresses were added to the warrant the Home Office had issued. The additions included addresses in Berlin and Paris, with the justification: 'Strongly suspected of being the secret service agent of a foreign Power.'[34] The case was considered important enough that Kell and Sinclair personally reviewed its details.[35] MI5 files show that the Macartney case, like many others, was conducted as a joint operation between MI5 and SIS. While Kell and Sinclair kept themselves abreast of the developments, Morton and Harker ran the case, with Morton handling Monkland.

True to MI5 tradition, they decided to leave the suspect in place and methodically build up evidence as Macartney exposed his contacts. First, however, it was necessary to evaluate their new informant: was Monkland legitimate? As was standard, the initial step was to check the Registry for a trace to see whether Monkland had come to MI5's attention in the past. The result was noted as *N/T*, for *no trace.* Kell then obtained a HOW to tap Monkland's telephone, although Kathleen Sissmore (later Jane Archer) concluded the telephone check was 'not illuminating'. As far as the case was concerned, it may not have been; but for the historian interested in understanding British counter-espionage operations, Sissmore's notes provide fascinating insight into MI5 surveillance methods and target analysis at the time. The report's telephone checks detail Monkland's acquaintances' addresses, nicknames, the time and frequency of the calls, the subjects of the calls and the callers' relationship to the target (i.e. Monkland). Regarding his habits, for example, Sissmore noted that Monkland did not seem to work and slept late after big nights. It was also gathered that he 'had had bad luck lately backing horses', thus indicating an awareness of his vices, potential entry and leverage points. Tracking Monkland's movements was straightforward, with notes on where he went, with whom, and why.[36] Thus the case handlers could construct a baseline for Monkland from which to establish inconsistent behaviour, unusual contacts and abnormal activities. They would then be able to cross-check his given statements with their own observations to determine the validity of his claims.

By 9 May 1927 Monkland gave 'Hamilton' (Morton) Macartney's questionnaire. Three pages in length, it concerned itself with air force mobilisation capabilities, personnel, armament, technical specification of airplanes and requests for drawings and documents, among other things.[37] Morton recognised the document as the 'work of an expert' and concluded that it 'could only have had origin in the Government Offices of a foreign power', most likely 'compiled by the united efforts of several experts'.[38] He was correct. Questionnaires were a common tool used by Soviet intelligence at the time. They were devised by specialists in the Soviet Union and distributed to residents abroad. After translation into the appropriate languages, residents then passed them to agents. The Soviets had employed the questionnaire method for several years, but with limited success. With nearly sixty percent of the questions left unanswered in some countries, the questionnaires potentially revealed more about the Soviet Union than the country to be spied on. Concealing the extent to which one nation knew sensitive information about a target nation could be as important as acquiring the target nation's secrets. The questionnaire, at times accompanied by 'book length lists of foreign military technology' coveted by Moscow, expressed what the USSR knew, thought it knew, and thought it needed to know. Taken together, these presumptions could hint at larger strategic intentions. As in the Macartney case, the questionnaire was also acutely vulnerable to disinformation when an agent was compromised.[39]

ARCOS

Three days after Morton forwarded the questionnaire to Harker, Monkland's tapped telephone recorded a call from 'Mr. McCarthy' (who Harker believed was 'undoubtedly that of our friend McCartney [*sic*]'), frantically advising Monkland to hide 'those papers' because 'they raided the Russian Headquarters to-day'.[40] Scotland Yard had moved in on the ARCOS headquarters because it had received information from 'X', a 'British subject of undoubted loyalty', who had received information from 'Y', a disgruntled former ARCOS employee, that among other illicit documents, a British Signals Training pamphlet had appeared at ARCOS. SIS passed the information to Kell, who after satisfying himself with the authenticity of the information, proceeded to organise the 12 May 1927 raid on ARCOS with Scotland Yard. The foray itself was shambolic and ultimately failed to recover the sought-after document.[41]

Nonetheless on 26 May, Arkadi Rosengolts (the Soviet Chargé d'Affaires) received an official Note informing him of the British Cabinet's decision to sever relations with the Soviet Union. The note complained that despite the Soviets' previous assurances to the contrary, they continued to engage in subversive activities in 'abuse of diplomatic privilege'.[42] Even if a face-saving reaction to the raid's failure, the decision was the culmination of six years of diplomatic spats. Foreign Secretary Austen Chamberlain later wrote that the Government broke relations 'not only because of the constant hostility of Soviet agents to the British Empire and other parts of the world, but because their agents had interfered in our domestic concerns' despite repeated warnings that Soviet interference in British domestic politics would be grounds for breaking relations as stipulated at the establishment of Anglo-Soviet trade relations in 1921.[43]

Outwardly the Soviets took the British announcement in stride, but their confidence belied a deep-seated unease about the implications of British actions. As the historian Zara Steiner explains, 'Neither Stalin nor Chicherin had anticipated the London decision. Failing to appreciate the extent of British anger over the activities of the Comintern or the strength of public feeling mobilised by the Conservative diehards, the Soviet leadership overreacted to the diplomatic rupture and indulged in worst-case scenarios.'[44] In the mind of Moscow, the severing of relations morphed into a prelude to invasion, and Litvinov declared that 'The rupture of diplomatic relations cannot be regarded otherwise than as an acceleration of war preparations, for it can have no other object and would be absurd from the point of view of England's own interests.'[45] Cutting ties gave evidence to the Soviet conviction that Britain had always been on the brink of war with the USSR, and that the ARCOS raid was merely incidental: 'The decision of the British Government to sever diplomatic and economic relations with the USSR is no casual or unexpected event connected with the raid on Arcos and the alleged disloyalty of the Soviet trade organizations.'[46] Even still, the break came as an unwelcome surprise. One British diplomat in Helsingfors (Helsinki) reported that 'the Anglo-Soviet rupture is having the effect of shaking the Bolshevik Government to its very foundations.'[47]

Amid Moscow's mounting panic, a White Russian émigré assassinated the Soviet envoy in Warsaw, Pyotr Voikov, on 7 June 1927. The ever-paranoid Stalin pinned responsibility on British intelligence, again construing the incident as a precursor to a general British invasion. The Soviets had been keenly sensitive to the threat of an attack ever since the British occupation of northern Russia in 1919 and support for the White Russians during the Russian Civil War. The Soviet press went so far as to liken Voikov's assassination to that of Archduke Ferdinand's in 1914. The subsequent propaganda blitz and calls to prepare for a British invasion in the summer of 1927 – now known as the 'War Scare' – gave the entire Macartney case, especially his attempts to steal information on British aviation capabilities, renewed gravity.[48]

During the summer of 1927, Macartney was, by his own account, 'buzzing about between London, Paris, and Berlin, writing idiotic letters to Mr.

Monkland, all of which the Intelligence Department had photographed by the Post Office in transit.[49] Macartney had worked on censorship during the war and was well aware of military intelligence's significant suspect indices. Curiously, however, he failed to establish secure communications with his own agent, breaching a fundamental precept of tradecraft and agent handling.[50]

Monkland told Morton that Macartney planned to travel to Paris at the beginning of June 1927 under the name of 'W. F. Hudson' to 'interview the big men there who are now presumably going to run direct [*sic*]' Soviet intelligence in Britain. Macartney hoped to learn 'whether the whole business was going to be reorganised as from Paris or whether it was all going to close down' as a consequence, it would seem, of the Anglo-Soviet rupture. Monkland also told Morton that a Scotland Yard informant, 'Barton', had forewarned Macartney of the ARCOS Raid.[51] Later investigations would show this claim to be highly improbable. It is likely, though not certain, that the raid was a last-minute decision.[52] Moreover, had Macartney known about the raid in advance, it is inexplicable that he did not alert his handler or ARCOS officials.

Other questions arose as well, particularly with regard to Monkland's reliability. Morton raised the point in a letter to Harker:

> Monkland's letter of the 30th May . . . does not add to what he had already told me on the telephone. In fact, typical of the man I should judge, he omits several small pieces of the detail he told me previously. As you say, honest or dishonest, he is not a trained observer. As regards his suggestion that he should to go to Paris sometime with Macartney, financed by us, the answer is for the moment 'I don't think'. Don't you agree? Knowing Monkland's private life, I do not see why we should pay for a spree for him in Paris. Therefore . . . I have left the matter open, while putting on a restraining hand in my reply.[53]

It should come as no surprise that those consorting with Macartney would themselves exhibit dubious integrity. But as suggested in the passage above, it is unclear whether Monkland was deliberately deceptive or simply absent-minded. In any case, it became apparent that handling Monkland required special attention to detail.

Although Monkland did not express a *need* to go to Paris, using British intelligence was a way to secure a lifestyle that he could not otherwise afford. Morton tapped into that desire and used it to ensure Monkland's cooperation. Monkland had convinced Macartney that he had an agent who could supply valuable information. When Monkland requested that Morton provide him with the appropriate 'chickenfeed' to entice Macartney and encourage further correspondence, Morton rewarded Monkland in terms he would appreciate: money (in this case £50).[54] Morton thereby maintained his access to Macartney, and Monkland achieved his goal.

Macartney's counterfeit passport information was important to Morton and Harker.[55] Without knowledge of it, security officials could not have tracked Macartney's movements. Its details allowed them to monitor Macartney as he passed through Britain's security fences and to coordinate successfully his surveillance with Continental counterparts. By mid-July Macartney was in Paris, and Morton received a steady stream of reports, including intercepted letters from SIS representative 'Franck', Wilfred 'Biffy' Dunderdale, about his activities there.[56] In one letter intercepted by 'Franck', Macartney advised an acquaintance that he was preparing to depart for Berlin, a hub of European espionage, to 'see somebody of great importance'. The individual's 'paramount influence' owed to his position as a 'People's Commissaire' and his place on the committee of the Katorga Club, an elite group of revolutionaries (that included the head of Soviet foreign intelligence, M. A. Trilisser) who had each spent a minimum of ten years in Siberia at the Katorga labour camps under the Tsar.[57] Macartney, an informal recruit rather than a trained spy, was again exhibiting poor tradecraft, for he was clearly unaware that the security and intelligence services methodically intercepted his mail.[58]

Macartney, ever the opportunist, also offered his services for hire. A fantasist, he went about it with incredible bravado. Dunderdale forwarded another intercepted letter in which Macartney – apparently quite out of the blue – offered to work for Prince Carol of Romania, who unsurprisingly declined the proposition.[59] That Macartney believed Prince Carol would accept such an overture from a complete stranger speaks to Macartney's warped sense of reality. After the rejection, the French police notified Morton of Macartney's departure on 12 August 1927.[60] On his way to Berlin he passed through London, where MI5's watchers coordinated to see that his arrival and departure were covered.[61] His importance to the security services is evident from the door-to-door surveillance he received as he moved to and from the Continent.

'Mr. Johnson'

Monkland met Morton, in the latter's guise as 'Hamilton' at 4.30 p.m. on August 1927 at 23 Hertford Street, near Hyde Park Corner across from Curzon Gate (alas, poor Curzon, communist intrigue even harassed his monuments). Morton learned at the meeting, and from a subsequent letter, that Monkland had received £38 for information he sent to Macartney. Some of the money was for 'Mr. Johnson', who was due to arrive from Berlin (on a Belgian passport so he could open a bank account). 'Mr. Johnson' was actually the second 'Mr. Johnson', the first having proved incompetent and been replaced. Maintaining the cover name on the one hand concealed the number of agents working in Britain; on the other hand, if the name were to be discovered, intercepted correspondence might be decoded more easily.

Macartney told Monkland that the new 'Mr. Johnson' was 'frightfully interested in the man who can produce and ship arms' (Monkland). With Anglo-Soviet antagonism increasing daily, Macartney insisted, 'All the "Mr. Johnsons" in existence knew that war between Russia and England was inescapable, had been so instructed from Moscow and were to act accordingly.' While this 'inevitability' meant that Macartney ran additional sub-agents to gather more military secrets than Monkland alone could provide, it did not mean that the overall execution of the operation improved. Despite his 'frightful interest' in meeting Monkland, the second Mr Johnson (Hansen) proved as inept as his predecessor. Monkland explained, 'The 2nd JOHNSON lost my address and made a muddle of everything and was sent elsewhere as a consequence', thus delaying their meeting.[62] In later years, the Soviets were typically successful in intelligence collection and operations but poor in intelligence analysis. In the case of Macartney, Soviet intelligence was deficient all around. MI5 exploited mistakes in tradecraft as they occurred.

In consultation with Scotland Yard, MI5 decided not to arrest Macartney for possession of a false passport when he returned from a trip to Berlin in early November.[63] Instead Monkland was left in place to make further observations. Macartney told Monkland that he had finally managed to schedule an appointment with representatives in Berlin after earlier frustrated attempts given that 'all his old friends had been replaced'.[64] Their 'replacement' in November 1927 coincided with the arrest and expulsion of the leaders of the 'Left' opposition in Moscow: Leon Trotsky (Commissar for War), Grigori Zinoviev (head of Leningrad Party and Comintern), Lev Kamenev (head of Moscow Party), Karl Radek (Rector of the Chinese Workers' University of Moscow and editorial board member of the newspaper *Izvestia*) and Khristian Rakovsky (first deputy Chairman of the Council of People's Commissars). Stalin's purge extended beyond elite political figures to include elements of Soviet intelligence.[65] It is possible, therefore that Macartney's Berlin contacts were not merely replaced, but recalled to Moscow for liquidation – a prologue to the Purges of the 1930s that would strike down such other intelligence operatives as Teodor Maly, an instrumental figure in the handling of the Cambridge Five, among others.

For the British intelligence services, more important than the fate of the Soviet operatives in Berlin was the news that the new Johnson (Hansen) had contacted Monkland (via Macartney) to arrange a meeting. The British decision to continue running the operation bore fruit, but not without some complications owing to Johnson's poor tradecraft. It is self-evident that spies want to see the defeat or limitation of counter-espionage operations directed against them. They do not, however, want to confuse an asset when arranging a personal meeting. Inadequate attention to detail could be fatal to even as simple an operation as a meeting. As Monkland explained to Morton, 'I have at last heard from Johnson and am to meet him at 7.o.c. to-morrow evening. You will remember where, no doubt, M. [Macartney] is going to wait at my flat in case Johnson comes there as he does not say in his letter where I am to meet him, and it is so long since our meeting place was arranged that he may mean to call on me at home.'[66]

The meeting place, in the end the same as the first one, favoured Johnson. Sissmore wrote to Valentine Vivian at SIS, 'You will remember that the rendezvous previously arranged between Johnson and Monkland was at the Marble Arch Cinema. As you know 23 Hertford Street is a most difficult place to keep under observation, but we are doing our utmost to make arrangements to cover this interview with a view to establishing the identity of Johnson.'[67] MI5's watcher John Ottaway was assigned to observe the meeting. Nearing 7.00 p.m. on 17 November, he saw a man enter the Marble Arch Cinema Tea Room:

> Age – 25 to 27. Height – 5'8" or 5'9". Complexion – pale. Hair – brown. Clean shaven, somewhat high cheekbones, thin face, medium build, broad shoulders, slovenly gait, turns toes inwards appearance of a Belgian or Russian. Dress – Grey jacket suit and overcoat, grey soft felt hat, dark brown shoes with crepe heels.

The man removed his overcoat and sat at a table. Monkland entered the tearoom a few minutes later, a red book in hand as Macartney had instructed.[68] The man, spotting the red book, greeted him. Johnson and Monkland spoke for about forty minutes according to Ottaway's report. They then parted, but Ottaway continued trailing Johnson.[69]

A Soviet tradecraft manual published several years after the Macartney case declares it 'absolutely incumbent upon the intelligence officer and the informant to establish whether they are being shadowed and to make sure that they have come to their rendezvous completely "clean" and that neither of them has brought to the meeting a "tail" behind himself'.[70] Although Johnson took evasive action, such as using various forms of transport on his way to the meeting, and though he did pause at several junctures to check, he failed not only to note his tail but also to shake it. Whether by foot or by vehicle, typically surveillance is done in teams.[71] However, there is nothing in Ottaway's report to suggest that his operation included other officers. As such, the incident suggests that Ottaway's surveillance skills were as good as Johnson's counter-surveillance technique was weak.

MI5's shadowing staff makes almost no appearance in the existing literature on British intelligence.[72] It was, however, one of the oldest departments. The *watchers* predated MI5 itself, tracing their origins to 1903, and some of MI5's early tradecraft, such as surveillance, had been imported from Scotland Yard and consisted of basic Edwardian investigation techniques.[73] Indeed, 1903 also marked the beginning of William Melville's tenure at the then-primitive MI5.[74] Melville, the original 'M', had formerly worked for MPSB and became MI5's first head detective when the organisation was formed in 1909. Watcher John Ottaway was also a former Detective Superintendent of Scotland Yard.[75] He had probably 'retired', as Melville had done, before secretly joining MI5.[76] The shadowing staff's history recounts the difficulties in 'obtaining, training, and keeping suitable staff for this very difficult and usually very dull work'.[77] Ottaway, like Melville before him, inevitably drew upon skills learned earlier at MPSB.

The tedium of surveillance sometimes comes through in Ottaway's reports. Arriving at 12 Redcliffe Gardens, Ottaway noted that Johnson 'evidently had no key as he halted on the doorstep before going in.' It is unclear whether Johnson was supposed to have had access to the house, but it would have been in keeping with the rest of the operation if he had and had once again blundered. Nonetheless, 'a smart saloon four seater motor car No. XY 4895' arrived ten minutes later, the driver of which showed him through the door. At 9.50 p.m., the same man left the flat accompanied by a young woman. Ottaway kept his surveillance going until after midnight, but Johnson did not reappear.[78]

Although a HOW was filed for the address the next day to establish Johnson's identity, it proved superfluous.[79] Early on the morning of 17 November, Sissmore received a call at home from F. B. Booth at the GPO.[80] He informed her of a telegram addressed to 'Hamilton' from Monkland: Macartney intended to meet Johnson at 3.00 p.m. that afternoon at the Hampstead Tube station. She must have rushed to the office, as she noted, 'I immediately saw Ottaway.' He reported that the previous night's surveillance had gone as planned. She wrote, 'I immediately went down to C.S.I. [Kell] and informed him of the developments in this case.' Kell, in turn, telephoned Vivian and Morton at SIS, requesting they come see him 'at once'. They expressed no objections to the proposed arrest of

Johnson and Macartney that afternoon. In fact, both Vivian and Morton 'considered this entirely an M.I.5. case', an unexpected position considering that SIS and MI5 collaborated extensively on the operation and that Morton had handled Monkland throughout. Shortly after the meeting, just after noon, Kell finalised the operation with Scotland Yard, and 'Macartney and Johnson were, accordingly, arrested at 3 o.c. on the afternoon of the 17th November as arranged'.[81]

Despite the successful prosecution of Macartney and Hansen, his former wartime boss, the novelist Compton Mackenzie later observed that 'the apparent ineptitude they [the intelligence authorities] displayed over several months was equalled only by the obvious ineptitude of Macartney himself'.[82] In his view, the intelligence services acted prematurely and succeeded in closing a promising case with only Macartney and Hansen to show for it. Had they continued to run the operation, they might have discovered a more extensive web and apprehended more important spies. The decision not to arrest Macartney earlier on simple passport fraud allowed MI5 to arrest Hansen, as well. Had MI5 waited longer, who else might have been exposed? In 1940, MI5 undertook an extensive debrief of Soviet defector Walter Krivitsky, and some of the findings have startling implications about the Macartney case.[83] Krivitsky told interrogators that 'one man who was earmarked to act as head agent' in London was Krivitsky's own assistant Max Maximov-Unschlicht, who had served as head of the Fourth Department in Nazi Germany and was the nephew of Jósef Unschlicht, Cheka founder Felix Dzerzhinsky's one-time deputy.[84] According to Krivitsky, Hansen's 'association with MACARTNEY . . . was only incidental to his visit. His main purpose was to ascertain the best means of establishing UNSCHLICHT in the United Kingdom, and if possible, to prepare for his residence here'. Instead, 'the proposal to use him in this capacity was cancelled in November 1927 after the arrest and imprisonment' of Hansen, who he confirmed had been employed by the Fourth Department.[85] Apprehending Unschlicht would have more than compensated MI5's patience. Of course, MI5 had no way of knowing what the future might hold – but that was exactly Mackenzie's point. Then again, the early apprehension of Hansen might have averted later security disasters. Deciding when to conclude an operation has always been a challenge for security and intelligence services. Acting too early, they risk the fruits of not having allowed the case to develop and accusations of having exaggerated the immediate threat. Acting too late, they can be blamed for failing to have protected vital security interests or worse, failing to have saved innocent lives.

Mackenzie believed the timing of the decision to act against Macartney was one of political expediency: 'The claim on behalf of the public interest will be noted, for if a cynic should ask himself whether the public interest does not seem to coincide almost too perfectly with the interest of the Conservative Party.'[86] It certainly suited Austen Chamberlain and Jix – not to mention Stanley Baldwin – to publicise evidence of Soviet espionage after little proof had emerged to justify the blunders of the ARCOS raid and the subsequent Anglo-Soviet rupture. The possibility of political machinations from within the security and intelligence services also remains open to question, but there is nothing in Macartney or Hansen's MI5 files to suggest political manipulation by the Conservative leadership or otherwise.

Mackenzie's suppositions aside, the Macartney case was accounted an MI5 success in the 1920s, overall 'MI5's least influential decade.'[87] Indeed, the 1920s saw repeated attacks on MI5's very existence. Nonetheless, at a time when MI5 was at its weakest and most understaffed, cooperation between MI5 and SIS, however tense it sometimes grew, was necessary to compensate for MI5's limited resources. The Macartney case demonstrates how closely the two agencies could cooperate and the solid results possible when they did, as was also evident in the concurrent investigations of W. N. Ewer and the FPA.

W. N. Ewer and the FPA

William Norman Ewer had first aroused the interest of MI5 in 1915, when he gave a passionate pacifist speech at a rally, fitting Basil Thomson's profile of the post-First World War pacifists who were 'busy tearing off their disguise and re-appearing under their proper garb as revolutionaries.'[88] Though the retrenched MI5 failed to keep track of Ewer immediately after the war, it renewed its interest in him in 1924, when the 21 November edition of the *Daily Herald* contained this notice:

> Secret Service—Labour Group carrying out investigation would be glad to receive information and details from anyone who has ever had any association with any Secret Service Department or operation—Write in first instance Box 537, Daily Herald.[89]

MI5 had at least two reasons to be intrigued. First, the Secret Service was supposed to be a secret, so any group interested in its operations was naturally suspect. Second, and more worrisome, was the *Daily Herald*'s links to the CPGB and Bolshevik Russia. Just a month before, the Zinoviev Letter scandal had broken, and MI5 assumed that the appearance of the letter just a month after the election was a Soviet/Comintern attempt to infiltrate the security system.

'Jasper' Harker, head of MI5's B Branch, sent one of his agents, 'Dan Rein-mann' ('D' in the reports), to respond to the notice in the hope that he would be able to penetrate the 'Labour Group' and find out more. When he answered the notice, a second, this one signed 'Q. X.' (later determined to be Ewer), appeared in the paper. The men arranged to meet, but 'Q. X.' did not appear. Harker, with some sophistication, anticipated that Reinmann might be observed by a third party, so he sent Ottaway to watch both 'D' and to keep an eye out for other surveillance. The importance of the case is reflected in the resources put into surveillance, which, in the 1920s, relied on HOWs and on following targets on foot. Even without other means available to it, MI5's deployment of watchers represented a substantial investment in the case given its limited staff.

Ottaway noted in his subsequent report that while Reinmann waited, he was kept under observation 'by an individual posted inside the extreme west entrance of the gate of the entrance to Hyde Park'.[90] One modern manual on surveillance notes, 'The ideal operator could be described as being the "Grey Man", or Mr. "Nobody" but a Mr. "Everybody" who looks like Mr. "Average".[91] Ottaway did not know that the man ('A' in his report), Walter Dale, had had professional experience in surveillance operation as a police officer some years before. Nonetheless, Dale failed where it counted most – he was recognised as staking out the site. It must have been Dale's technique rather than his appear-ance that gave him away, for according to Ottaway's description, he did not appear distinctive:

Age about 38; Height about 5'9"; Complexion—similar to the yellow brown tan after service in India; Hair—dark brown—clean shaven; Nose—straight, flat, with slight upward turn at the tip; Build—average; Clothes—light grey trilby hat, white collar, grey tie, overcoat dark brown frieze. Black shoes. Umbrella with plain crook handle.[92]

Ottaway's systematic approach to Dale's description was likely adopted from detective methods.[93] MI5's files are replete with such descriptions, which formed an important part of surveillance work. Ottaway's recognising Dale ('A') at a meeting several days later had a decisive impact.

Q. X. contacted Reinmann the following day, 'tendering his sincere apolo-gies' and suggesting that they meet again. In a scenario foreshadowing the tra-decraft of Cold War espionage, Q. X. recommended that 'in order that there should be no mistake in recognising you, will you please be seated at a table near the entrance coming up from the Strand and carry with you or be reading a copy of the "Daily Herald".[94] The questions submitted to Reinmann at their meeting were along the lines of how the 'Secret Service' worked and if agents were employed in the Labour movement and who they were. He also told Reinmann that the Labour movement had decided to create its own secret service to combat the government's. The information was sufficient to justify a HOW on Box 573 of the *Daily Herald* given the potential breach of the Official Secrets Act.[95]

Continued surveillance of Reinmann's meetings bore fruit. On 4 February 1925 Ottaway observed a meeting between Reinmann and 'B' (most likely Ewer again) inside the 'Bodega Wine Bar'. On following the two out, Ottaway recognised individual 'A' (Dale), the same man whom he had seen in the park, 'watching from the corner' of a nearby street. After Reinmann, MI5's agent 'D' had departed, Ottaway noted that 'A then followed B to check if he was being followed, then himself took a circuitous route to see whether he, too, was being followed'. Convinced, incorrectly, that he was not, Dale continued on to the ARCOS offices, where he waited outside for forty minutes before a woman, 'about 28, height 5 ft. 5 or 6 inches, brown hair (believed to be bobbed), face powdered, medium build, smartly dressed in a brown skirt', later identified as Rose Edwardes, joined him. They lunched at Lyons Restaurant, High Holborn, and then Dale followed Edwardes to the Law Courts, where, Ottaway speculated, she might have been employed as a secretary at the Admiralty and Probate Division. Ottaway then tailed Dale to Outer Temple, 222–225 Strand, W. C., which was discovered to house, among other business, the Federated Press of America.[96]

Two days later Ottaway and fellow watcher Henry Hunter ('HH') easily recognised the pair again having lunch at the Lyons Restaurant. This time the officers followed them to the Soviet Embassy at Chesham House. Edwardes was in the building for roughly ten minutes while Dale kept watch outside. Next they went to the post office where, subsequent MI5 enquiries revealed, Edwardes paid a telephone bill for the FPA in the name of William Norman Ewer. The connection between the FPA and the Soviet Embassy was now a strong one. The HOW put on the FPA telephone line produced 'immediate results', showing calls to prominent communists, ARCOS, John H. Hayes of the Vigilance Detective Agency (and former policeman and an organiser of the 1919 police strike), and Boris Said, another suspected Cheka operative who had been connected with Klishko in an arms deal in Murmansk in 1922.[97]

The HOW on postal correspondence turned up evidence that was even more astonishing. Regular packets addressed to 'Kenneth Milton', a cover name for Ewer, contained 'copies of despatches and telegrams from French ministers in various foreign capitals to the Quai D'Orsay [and] reports on the French political and financial situation', often including 'typed and unsigned covering slips in English guarded or code language'. A further discovery was that the packets occasionally included messages from 'Anne' in Paris to 'C. P. D'. Upon consultation with the Indian Political Police, MI5 concluded the messages were from Evelyn Roy, wife of M. N. Roy (recently expelled from France and now living in Moscow) to Clemens Palme Dutt (the noted communist and brother of the dogmatic, radically uncompromising CPGB Executive Committee member Rajani Palme Dutt).[98] MI5 soon discovered the provenance of the packets when one of the reports sent to 'Milton' appeared almost verbatim in a *Daily Herald* article on 8 May 1925 'from your correspondent George Slocombe', the paper's Paris correspondent and manager of FPA office's there, which resulted in a HOW on all correspondence to and from his home and work addresses.[99] In a period of a couple of months, Ewer had gone from being a communist journalist to being considered a central figure in an international spy ring, all because of the decision to place a notice in the *Daily Herald* asking for information on the British secret service.

MI5 then operated in conjunction with SIS in Paris to monitor Slocombe's correspondence. At the beginning of March 1925, Booth (MI5's GPO liaison officer) informed Harker, 'It is only possible to post letters for Paris on the mail trains which include a P. O. [Post Office] sorting van and that a responsible man belonging to the latter looks out for all addresses which are on check; there is, therefore, no gap in the system in this way'.[100] MI5 covered the domestic side of the communications, while SIS covered the Paris side. Considering that Ewer knew his correspondence was monitored, at least according to information later given by his assistant Albert Allen, Slocombe's exposure was a first-class blunder on Ewer's part.[101] Among the central tenets of tradecraft, the protection of a source would come only after securing the ability to secretly obtain the information sought in the first place. Slocombe's exposure jeopardised future information and put Ewer at risk, which also compromised the secrecy of the operational methods, aims, and weaknesses of his intelligence network.

Although the precise nature of Ewer and Slocombe's relationship is uncertain, it can be said that Ewer was Slocombe's conduit for funds and information and so bore significant responsibility for Slocombe's handling and protection. If money is any indication, which it surely is, Ewer compromised a valuable agent. Intercepts revealed that Ewer was paying Slocombe an average of 18,000 francs in 1925, an extraordinary sum if it is true that, as reported by the informant Allen, the annual Soviet allotment to the CPGB totalled $20,000 – or some $327,000 today (though that amount may have been as many as four times greater).[102] Most of Slocombe's funds went towards operating costs. He doled out 8,000 francs to obtain information locally, and the rest – surely less a slice for personal expenses – was used to bribe French officials for Foreign Ministry despatches from Rome, Sofia, Bucharest and Belgrade.[103]

Slocombe's correspondence also revealed that he was in contact with Soviet intelligence. Harker learned from Morton that several letters to M. Borgeand, 17 Rue d'Astorg, Paris had been posted by one Winstone of Durrants Hotel, Manchester Square. That address, the French Police had ascertained in the course of their ongoing investigation into Russian espionage against the French government, was 'where the Chief of the Comintern Secret Service attached to the Russian Embassy meets his agent', and in telling Morton this, the French also commented that 'it seems possible that correspondence from the Outer Temple might possibly be going to this address, or, at any rate, it might be regarded as a spy address'.[104] Together with information already available – the history of the *Daily Herald* and the Soviet Trade Delegation, Ewer's connection with the *Daily Herald* and the FPA, Chesham House's funding of the FPA (including contacts with the CPGB and ARCOS), and the diplomatic intercepts from Paris to the FPA – this last connection with the suspected Bolshevik secret agent in Paris 'confirmed', according to SIS, 'what we already knew, that the Federated Press of America is secret Intelligence Bureau of the Komintern [*sic*]'.[105] Yet they should have been prepared to go one step further, for according to MI5 interviews in 1928 with Allen, former assistant to Ewer at the FPA, both he and Ewer had worked for the Cheka.[106]

'Allen'

On 21 May 1928, Sissmore noted that although the FPA organisation had apparently ceased functioning before Allen's HOW was cancelled, the surveillance 'had shown us that Allen was in great financial straits'. She proposed that 'by means of a second H.O.W. we might now be able to ascertain what Allen's present circumstances are and whether he is still on friendly terms with Ewer, Rose Edwards [*sic*], Dale and his other old associates. If this is not the case, possibly he might be led to tell us something of his former work'.[107] Now spotted and assessed, once Allen was recruited as an informant, Sissmore discovered that Ewer, acting under Soviet intelligence officers, regularly received information from two moles inside MPSB.

It was only due to Sissmore's initiative that Harker suggested to Kell that Allen 'may have quarrelled with his former employers, a fact which might be disclosed from his correspondence, and should this be discovered, it is obvious that we might be able, by careful approach, to get valuable information from him'.[108] Two days later a HOW was duly applied on Allen's address.[109] Yet once again, it took Sissmore's prodding before anyone took action on what they were learning. On 12 June 1928 she once again wrote to Harker:

> You will see that the H.O.W. on Albert Allen is producing nothing but demands for the payment of various debts . . . So far, no letters have been seen from any of his old friends at 50 Outer Temple, and I think there can be little doubt that he is not now receiving assistance from them. Do you think that now would be a good time for Mr. Ottaway perhaps to make Allen's acquaintance? Judging by the rate at which Allen is getting into debt, it seems that, if we delay much longer, Allen will be in such low water it will be a very much more expensive matter to make any attempt to extricate him from his difficulties for a quid pro quo.[110]

Clearly Sissmore sought to exploit Allen's insolvency to gain intelligence. Yet she was also judicious, aiming to maximise collection and minimise expenditure.

Two days later, following discussion with Ottaway and Kell, it was decided that Ottaway would approach Allen with the cover that he belonged to an 'anti communist or anti socialist organisation'.[111] Ottaway accordingly introduced himself to Allen as 'G. Stewart of the Anti-Communist Union' and claimed that he had been sent to ask about Allen's involvement with the FPA. Ottaway's offer to pay for useful information overcame Allen's initial surprise and suspicion. Despite Allen's later boast that he had been employed by the Cheka, it was clear by the time MI5 approached him in 1928 that any belief he might once have held in a Soviet tomorrow had long since dissolved. He admitted to being in financial straits and agreed to provide 'Stewart' with information on the FPA, ARCOS and other Russian 'intrigues' but only under the condition of anonymity and a fee of £1,500 (roughly £76,000 today).[112]

The motivations of agents and informants were not always straightforward, and Ottaway quickly sensed another dimension to Allen's motivation: 'His late masters evidently have let him down, and he seems embittered in consequence.'[113] Although Britain was experiencing the rise of bitter ideological confrontation, one cannot claim Allen's reversal to be even a little politically motivated. Collaborating with MI5 did not necessarily constitute a rejection of ideals, and in any case because 'Ideology very rarely, if ever, motivates treason.'[114] Allen did not constitute that rare case. He betrayed and consequently destroyed the secret organisation that he helped run for eight years for revenge and money, and MI5 eagerly accommodated him.

Ever aware of MI5's purse-strings, Ottaway nevertheless told Allen that he was 'positively certain that [his] people would not pay such a large sum' as the former communist operative was demanding. Allen replied, 'Well I suggest that as they are most likely in touch with one or other of the Government Depts. [*sic*], they should go there, and for preference I would recommend Colonel Kell's department.'[115] He then further enticed 'Stewart' by revealing his knowledge of the Photostat Department at the Post Office, where intercepted mail was opened and copied, and his awareness of leaks emanating from the Foreign Office and MPSB. That succeeded in getting Ottaway's attention, and soon after the case was handed back to Harker, Ottaway's superior.

In late July 1928, Harker duly introduced himself to Allen as someone who 'came from Colonel Kell'. Aware of Allen's position, Harker 'did not think it wise to attempt to take notes' during the meeting, presumably because it would have made Allen uncomfortable. His overall sensitivity to Allen's state of mind clearly put the former Soviet agent relatively at ease:

> I very quickly found . . . that we were on quite good terms, and, by treating him rather as my opposite number, found that he was quite ready to talk up to a point. He is, I think, a man who is extraordinarily pleased with himself, and considers work which he did for some eight years for the Underground Organisation known as the FPA was admirably carried out, and has not received quite that recognition from its paymasters that Allen considers it deserves.[116]

By all indications, he tried to make Allen feel as comfortable as possible, responding to Allen in a way conducive to conversation. According to Harker's example, tradecraft requires insight into motivations as much as an expertise in procedure. He had to size up people and situations, often quickly, and use that knowledge carefully.

The documents suggest that Harker trod softly, but with determination. He urged Allen to disclose the names of colleagues, but Allen was reluctant: 'I do not want to give away my late boss, because, personally, I was very fond of him.' Why he was fond of the person he also felt had slighted him need not detain us: emotions are often convoluted. Harker proceeded:

> I thought that this was suitable opportunity to stimulate Allen's imagination so I said to him—'Perhaps I could tell you the name of your late boss, in which case you would not be placed in such a position.' I then wrote the initials 'W.N.E.' [William Norman Ewer] on a piece of paper, and showed them to Allen saying, 'That was your late boss wasn't he?'[117]

That the technique worked makes Allen appear an amateur, but perhaps Harker sensed that Allen's loyalty to his former superior was not unshakeable.

Harker simply needed to provide Allen with a scenario in which he could convince himself he had never technically betrayed his boss. Allen replied to Harker's question, 'Yes, "Trilby", "Trilby" is a good fellow and damned smart.'[118] 'Trilby', as Harker knew, was what Ewer's friends called him.[119] Ewer was in fact 'known to a generation of journalists' by the sobriquet, having acquired it in his youth on account of his habit of going barefoot, 'like the heroine of George Du Maurier' (author of the popular late-Victorian novel *Trilby*).[120] Eventually Harker talked Allen down to £75 per meeting, subject to change based on the quality of information at the discretion of Harker's superiors, Kell and Holt-Wilson, and the information began to flow.[121]

Ewer had first enlisted Allen in 'about 1921' on the recommendation of John (Jack) Hayes, a former police officer who headed a private investigation company and knew Allen through other work they both did with the Federation of Prison and Police Officers, which Hayes also ran.[122] Ewer had been looking for a 'good man' to investigate a publication by White Russians in London, a newspaper calling itself '*Pravda*', which was a counterfeit of the official Bolshevik newspaper in Russia. This tallies with Ewer's later comment that the secret organisation was 'purely counter'. 'Someone', Allen vaguely said, suspected that Basil Thomson was involved with the newspaper. It is unclear what exactly transpired, but eventually the issue was raised in the House of Commons. Ewer was pleased with Allen's work and asked him if he would be willing to do other jobs, to which Allen agreed, 'and in a very short time he discovered that Ewer was running a secret service organisation in this country on behalf of the Russians.'[123]

Allen only discovered that he was working on behalf of the Russians after the fact.[124] Soon after he was told the truth and did not object, he was put in touch with none other than Nikolai Klishko, an integral figure in Cheka's London operations. Klishko directed Allen to set up an office in his apartment for future work with Ewer and provided the requisite funds.[125] That arrangement was later compromised by bad tradecraft, however, when the 'indiscretions of a Russian agent' who repeatedly called on Allen at midnight brought undue attention to the office and forced it to relocate.[126] It was later in 1923, when Ewer was on 'holiday' in Moscow, that 'the decision was taken to run the organisation under the cover of a branch of a news agency, the Federated Press of America.'[127] According to Allen, from that point until the ARCOS raid, money for the FPA, the CPGB and other socialist organisations came from America in dollars via the Soviet Embassy, proving that Soviet meddling in British internal affairs had anything but ceased with Kamenev's expulsion.[128]

So if Ewer worked for Soviet intelligence, why did he draw attention to himself by advertising his interest in the British secret service operations only one month after the Zinoviev Letter implicated the Bolsheviks in a conspiracy against the British Government – and in a Bolshevik-linked newspaper, no less? It would have been counter-productive to have attempted to collect information on a secret intelligence service by announcing the intention to do so in a subversive newspaper. Ewer's decision appears clumsy and imprudent. It could, however, have been an attempt to build wheels within wheels:

> Prima facie, the advertisement inserted in the 'Daily Herald' was to enable Ewer to obtain agents who would be useful to him. Equally obviously, it was likely that the Security Service would attempt to put someone in touch with the persons behind the advertisement; and he may, therefore, have hoped that this would give him the opportunities to penetrate our organisation and obtain information about it either by method of observation or double-cross, or both.[129]

Indeed, Ewer admitted to as much after the war.[130] His testimony attests to a fairly high degree of sophistication on either his own part or that of his handlers. Just as MI5 had anticipated that their agent 'D' would be watched, Ewer anticipated that MI5 would surveil the meeting. Allen's own explanation did not mention any intention to penetrate MI5, but he did state that the notice was placed 'with the object of catching out' the agent who would respond (and whom they thought would most likely be Dan Reinmann). Reinmann had previously tried to penetrate leftist groups and was already suspected, correctly in the end, of being an MI5 informant. Surveillance of Reinmann led Ewer's watchers to MI5 offices, and all FPA association with him thereafter ceased.[131] Although bringing himself to the attention of MI5 seems a costly trade-off for exposing an informant, it is worth remembering that the Cheka's foreign intelligence department (INO) concentrated most of its early efforts on 'counter-revolutionary' activity.[132] The overriding concern was to silence counter-revolutionary organs like the fraudulent '*Pravda*', expose traitors and 'catch out' informants like Reinmann, even at the expense of 'blowing' the Cheka's own agents.[133] Maybe Ewer was expendable, but because the hidden hand of Soviet intrigue was revealed as well, the enterprise proved a pyrrhic victory for the communists. The strength of espionage is in its secrecy, and the handling of this secret agent did not adequately protect that secrecy. The publication of the notice eventually compromised much more than just the informant that the Soviets were willing to sacrifice: it also led to the exposure of Soviet intelligence and its agents and, ultimately, the end of a valuable network.

Ewer could not have known that Allen would later relate the operations of the FPA in detail to MI5, but he nonetheless invited scrutiny of the organisation and its personnel by attracting MI5's attention. The scale of Ewer's folly became even more apparent with Allen's disclosure that Ewer had had two sources inside Scotland Yard. The sources gave Ewer the names both of individuals under surveillance and of those to be stopped by the Alien Officers at the ports (a security fence), both lists of great importance for Bolshevik counter-surveillance.[134] With such information, Allen explained, 'Any move that S. Y. was about to make against the Communist Party or any of its personnel was nearly always known well in advance to Ewer who actually warned the persons concerned of proposed activities of the Police.'[135] Allen insisted that the only surprise was the ARCOS raid, and that was because the officers conducting it were initially told they were going to Government Dockyards, which had indeed been the case.[136]

Harker asked Allen why, if he had inside information, he was not aware that MI5 had taken out a HOW on him and Ewer, to which Allen replied that MI5 had obviously not informed Scotland Yard.[137] Allen was correct on this account.[138] Had Scotland Yard been informed of MI5 and SIS activities, Ewer and Allen surely would have known. When Allen first began his work for the FPA, under his real name Arthur Lakey, he had provided a potential female recruit with an address where she could stay. Soon after, Ewer told Lakey that he was under surveillance and that Scotland Yard had taken out a HOW on the address he gave to the recruit, suggesting that the woman was an MI5 plant. Lakey subsequently dropped all contact with her and changed his name to Albert Allen.[139] MI5 withheld information from Scotland Yard not only about the intercepted mail from Paris, but also about its domestic operations against the FPA. This is possibly the one case where the infighting and animosity between British intelligence services seems to have improved internal security.

Allen's other serious allegation entailed major leaks coming from the Foreign Office and the Colonial Office. According to Allen, 'The information which was supplied from the India Office was considered by the Russians to be extraordinarily good, as also that from the Colonial Office.'[140] It came from an agent named Karandikar, also known as 'The Sheik'.[141] He was paid £10 per week for the information he obtained from secretaries in those respective offices.[142] Although Lord Curzon had died in 1925, an attentive ear could surely have heard a faint moan floating from his grave. Before his death Curzon had bellowed endlessly about the mortal threat posed by the Bolsheviks in India.[143] He was not known for understatement, but leaks from the Foreign Office and the Colonial Office did have grave implications, especially considering the objectives of the Comintern and the function of Communist University of Toilers in the East. The wife of M. N. Roy (who had himself trained twenty-two students for revolutionary work in India) was in Paris and in contact with Ewer.[144] Information acquired by Russians from these offices would have been a great boon in devising future agent operations in India and other British colonies.

Featherstone

Allen's revelations required immediate investigation. Although surveillance showed that the FPA had shut down following the ARCOS raid, its participants might still have been active in other capacities. Investigators tracked Rose Edwardes down to her Leigh-on-Sea address in Essex, where they found she commuted regularly to the Featherstone Typewriting Bureau at the Featherstone Buildings in Holborn (London). Seven months of additional observation determined that Dales, Holmes and Ewer met there twice a week, always providing Edwardes with ample material to type up.[145] Allen's information and other enquiries led Harker to conclude 'we have now established the face that the organisation, which EWER was formerly running as the F.P.A., is still operating', and the investigation was revamped with the aid of 'observation, telephone checks and HOWs'.[146] The entire surveillance apparatus was mobilised once again.

Retracing steps led to Walter Dale, the watcher first observed at the Reinmann meeting, who then unwittingly led investigators to two of his acquaintances, soon identified as Hubert Ginhoven and Charles Jane of Scotland Yard. MI5 had found Ewer's inside informants, the moles.[147] Patience and meticulously careful work had exploited Dale's lapse in tradecraft. As one MI5 officer concluded, 'Dale's extraordinary lack of caution in choosing the same rendezvous for each meeting, can only be put down to carelessness occasioned by long standing practice'.[148] Complacency is ever, of course, a hallmark of poor agent operations. The British, however, remained careful and decided not to prosecute Ginhoven or Jane after their arrest on 11 April 1929. One likely reason was to avoid any public enquiry or discussion into the methods of the secret services. MI5 was also probably keen to protect the identities of Allen and the officers involved from public scrutiny.

After Dale's arrest, the recovery of his diary further laid out how Ewer's network operated. It confirmed that Dale had been the intermediary between Ewer's group and the MPSB officers for some time, proving that Allen had held out on the specifics of the Scotland Yard leak, probably, as historian Victor Madeira suggests, in the hope of reaping larger payments from MI5.[149] The diary also described his duties in detail, including the observation of British intelligence officers, surveillance of expatriate Russians, provision of lists of politically and socially prominent individuals who might interest the Russians, and counter-surveillance of Russian agents, including Ewer and FPA employees. For five years, he and other detectives maintained 'unremitting surveillance' on the sites and employees of British secret intelligence agencies, including SIS and GC&CS, which included noting officers' licence plate numbers and trailing them to their homes. In sum, Allen's information and the diary led one officer to write, 'It became abundantly clear that for the past ten years, any information regarding subversive organisation and individuals supplied to Scotland Yard by SIS or MI5, which had become the subject of Special Branch enquiry, would have to be regarded as having been betrayed to Ewer's group', an astounding admission by any account, and a major victory for Soviet intelligence.[150] Moreover, although this was not voiced at the time, Soviet intelligence may well have continued to exploit access to MPSB information had Ewer and his agents not employed such slipshod tradecraft.

Evolving Recruitment Strategy: 'Illegals' and the Cambridge Five

The events surrounding the trials and convictions of Macartney and Hansen again served both to confirm and invigorate preconceived, and not necessarily unjustified, notions about British and Soviet intentions towards each other. When the worlds of secret intelligence and diplomacy met, the result was frequently one of posturing and double-speak. In this case, these were mixed with a large dose of paranoia. So even if the war scare was chiefly a function of the Soviet Union's internal politics, as studies have suggested, it nonetheless had significant international repercussions, not least in the field of Soviet foreign intelligence operations.[151]

Indeed, the continual controversy surrounding the implication of CPGB members in espionage scandals prompted Moscow to discourage the use of local communists as agents in the belief that their exposure handed Western nations an easy propaganda victory.[152] The fallout from incidents like the ARCOS raid and the Macartney case provided an impetus for the USSR to separate itself officially from subversive and covert activity in Europe. Instead, the Soviets pushed for the expansion of operations using *illegals*, building on its tentative forays of this type in the United States in the early 1920s.[153] SIS liaison with the French security service (Deuxième Bureau) furnished MI5 with an agent's report that explained the new strategy in detail:

In 1927 the authorities in Moscow decided to change their methods which they judged to be no longer sufficiently secret and which constantly threatened to bring about diplomatic complication. The sections of the G.P.U. were shorn of a part of their power which was handed over to illegal organisations[,] the chief or 'resident' of which was of superior rank to any of the other G. P. U. agents left in the Embassy. For the purposes of cover the illegal agents usually pose as business men or proceed to set up commercial companies, the business activities of which usually remain nebulous. Contact is kept up between the Embassy section and the secret section by means of one or more skilful agents. . . . The secret agents or 'residents' of the G.P.U. are almost invariably recruited amongst the citizens of foreign countries so that the Soviet authorities may, should any awkward incidents occur, disclaim all responsibility. Should Russian citizens be employed in these capacities they are always provided with false passports of other nationalities. In addition to the aboved [*sic*] described organisms there is also a mobile section of well tried agents mostly consisting of Germans, Hungarians, Letts [Latvians] and Austrians.[154]

The shift in strategy was significant: *legal* residents now operated from within an embassy and under official cover; *illegal* residents operated outside of the embassy and without any ostensible link to it. One highly skilled agent was the only connection between the two. Under these circumstances, tradecraft assumed an entirely new importance as Soviet operatives attempted to afford Soviet officialdom with plausible deniability.[155] Ideology bound the Bolsheviks to revolution, but circumstance forced them to accommodation with international diplomatic norms.[156] In attempting to forge this dual policy, ensuring the invisibility of clandestine operations was paramount. As such, clandestine statecraft assumed a level of importance equal to and sometimes greater than overt statecraft, and the employment of tradecraft was at its core.

With regard to the French report, Vivian noted that there was 'nothing particularly new in all this' (the legal/illegal arrangement). The report must therefore have been representative rather than unique; in other words, MI5 and SIS were *au courant* with the developing Soviet collection system. But understanding the principle of illegals was a far cry from identifying them. Thus liaison, as with the French, was of tremendous importance. Throughout the interwar period there are numerous instances when the Deuxième Bureau and SIS successfully collaborated and coordinated in the field (*vide* Slocombe) regardless of tensions that may have existed at a higher political level. During the course of Dunderdale's fourteen years in Paris, for example, he became close friends with Gustave Bertrand, the Deuxième Bureau's chief signals officer.[157] This kind of working relationship paved the way for later Anglo-French liaison such as the development of the Double-Cross System and collaboration between the Free French and Jedburgh teams of the Second World War.[158] Indeed, liaison became a cornerstone of intelligence work that continues to this day.[159]

Yet British preconceptions hindered counter-espionage efforts. As illustrated here, MI5 reasoned that the CPGB and the working class likely represented the largest source of recruits for Soviet intelligence. While MI5 and SIS were slow to recruit from Britain's hallowed halls, the 'Great Illegals' presciently saw that the burgeoning idealism of university campuses offered ripe picking grounds for future agents. By the early 1930s, Soviet illegals had developed a recruitment strategy targeting idealistic young students with prominent backgrounds who were studying at top universities in the belief that they would rise quickly to the corridors of power. Arnold Deutsch wrote to the 'Centre' (Soviet intelligence headquarters) explaining,

> Given that the Communist movement in these universities is on a mass scale and that there is a constant turnover of students, it follows that individual Communists whom we pluck out of the Party will pass unnoticed, both by the Party itself and by the outside world. People will forget about them. And if at some time they do remember that they were once Communists, this will be put down to a passing fancy of youth, especially as those concerned are scions of the bourgeoisie. It is up to us to give the individual [recruit] a new [non-Communist] political personality.[160]

Although MI5 and SIS may have been aware of the new operating strategy using legals and illegals, neither was aware of the new Soviet targeting and recruitment plans.

MI5 and SIS, both of which had been cut back in the 1920s and expanded only slowly in the 1930s, lagged behind Soviet intelligence in recruiting from Oxbridge in the interwar years.[161] SIS's culture, like MI5's, was predominantly colonial-military in character. Many senior officers rejected what they considered the effete intellectualism of university types. The irascible Claude Dansey, later SIS chief Sir Stewart Menzies's deputy, was fond of saying, 'I would never willingly employ a university man.'[162] He would later write, 'I have less fear of Bolshies and Fascists than I have of some pedantic but vocal University Professor.'[163]

British intelligence, especially SIS, retained a strong strain of social elitism, as personified by Menzies, an Old Etonian who had worked as deputy to

Sinclair in the 1930s and succeeded him as 'C' in 1939. Although Philby thought of Menzies 'with enduring affection', he wrote that 'his intellectual equipment was unimpressive, and his knowledge of the world and his views about it, were just what one would expect from a fairly cloistered son of the upper levels of the British Establishment'.[164] The secretive nature of SIS meant that new recruits were often drawn from among the acquaintances and insular social clubs enjoyed by men like Menzies. These fissures worked in favour of Philby. Coming from a prominent family, the old-boy network facilitated his entry into the intelligence and diplomatic communities.

CHAPTER 4

Penetration Agents (I)

Maxwell Knight, the CPGB and the Woolwich Arsenal

K NOWING an opponent's intentions is among the most useful pieces of information to bring to any confrontation.[1] But as history has shown with some painful regularity, getting it right can be brutally difficult. In deciphering the layer upon layer of signalling that occurs in international relations, penetration agents, those trained by to infiltrate a hostile organisation, provide one of the best means of distinguishing between the real and the counterfeit, the overt and the secret, and the secret and the mysterious.

The difference between secrets and mysteries is often critical: 'Secrets are things that are potentially knowable', whereas in mysteries, 'there are no clear-cut answers, often because the other leaders themselves do not know what they are going to do or have not worked out their problems'.[2] The difficulty of assessing intentions, a complicated endeavour in the best of circumstances, is exacerbated when the adversary operates in a covert or clandestine manner, in secretive cells, and perhaps using legal political processes to shield illegal activity. MI5 experienced this problem when trying to counter the subversive activities of communists in the 1930s, as they had in the 1920s. British security and intelligence services knew full well that the broad goal of the USSR, through the CPGB, was to stoke the flames of rebellion in Britain, but the communists' operations intended to effect sedition were not nearly as apparent. Security intelligence knew the *what* of communist ideology but not necessarily the *how*, *when* or *who* of Soviet operations.

Maxwell Knight, who gave his name to MI5's 'M. Section' (M.S.), helped to fill part of the knowledge gap through the use of penetration agents.[3] In an apparently rare discussion that directly addresses tradecraft, Knight made no secret of just how important he considered such agents. 'The proper function of M.S.', he wrote, 'lies in the recruitment and operation of agents who are trained for the purposes of penetrating subversive political bodies, and for the investigation of suspicious individuals or groups of individuals'.[4] These ideas about recruitment and agent-handling, seldom laid out with such candour, illuminate MI5's agent operations against the CPGB at that time.

Following the 1931 reorganisation of the security and intelligence services, MI5 (which had become officially known as the 'Security Service') was less constrained in its investigation of covert communist activity. The arrest of the two communist moles in MPSB in April 1929 and the links to communism among some of the Invergordon Mutineers (who were mostly lower-deck sailors protesting a Navy pay cut) in September 1931 lent urgency to MI5's expanded responsibilities.[5] As Knight put it later, 'It was decided that it was vitally essential [*sic*] to increase our knowledge regarding the Communist Underground Movement.' To do this, however, 'It was clearly necessary for someone to be worked in from the bottom.'[6] Knight had clear ideas about how to do this, but he stressed, it was not possible 'to lay down any golden rules' on the recruitment of agents.[7]

Knight had very particular ideas regarding recruitment – especially about the use of women as agents, the character of agents and the best ways to work agents into hostile organisations. Some of these ideas are exemplified in his handling of Olga Gray – Miss 'X' as she was known in his reports and later court proceedings. She provides, too, an early example of and testament to the idea that 'the most valuable modern Humint [*sic*] asset is the long-serving agent in place.'[8]

The psychological aspect of Knight's tradecraft played a significant role in the operation's success. Gray spent seven arduous years leading a double-life that ultimately led to the 1938 arrest of Percy Glading and his accomplices at the Woolwich Arsenal for having breached the Official Secrets Act. Yet Gray did not discover Glading's involvement in espionage until she had been working for the CPGB as a double agent for several years, and given how long she stayed inside the party and the mental strain it caused her, Knight's ability to keep her going was crucial.

Glading, who ran the Woolwich Arsenal spy ring, was the subject of frequent surveillance by the British security and intelligence services due to his prominence in the CPGB. At the forefront of organised labour for much of the 1920s, he was an active member of the Amalgamated Engineering Union (AEU) and the Red International of Labour Unions (RILU). Glading also travelled incognito to India in 1925 on behalf of the CPGB to meet M. N. Roy 'in order to study Indian Labour conditions and to encourage the growth of the Communist Movement in India.'[9] On his return he attended the Colonial Communist Conference in Amsterdam and presented a report on his findings. Back in the UK, Glading became involved with the National Minority Movement (the most pro-Soviet of trade unions) after the General Strike in 1927. Both he and his wife had also been linked to the clandestine, Soviet-linked Kirchenstein courier network and to communist agitator James Messer, which suggested to British officials that Glading was a conduit for the Comintern in the early part of his career.[10]

In the late 1920s and 1930s, communist activism in security-sensitive industries such as armaments became an increasing concern for MPSB and MI5. Glading's own activity made headlines in 1928, when he and other colleagues were dismissed from their positions at the Woolwich Arsenal after refusing to renounce their communist beliefs. The incident fitted into a larger trend of forced redundancies for ideological reasons in the defence industry.[11] Authorities did not want active communists in the labour force in the sensitive defence sector because of security concerns. Reports received from Indian Political Intelligence (IPI) – such as one noting that 'GLADING had prepared a report of all shipyards, munitions works, dockyards and arsenals where Strike Committees or "Red Cells" existed: efforts were to be made in these and all industrial centres to cause trouble'[12] – raised the distinct possibility of subversion at the heart of Britain's defence capabilities. The mutiny at Invergordon and sabotage at the Portsmouth Dockyard a few years later substantiated fears in MI5's eyes

3 Percy Glading, labour activist turned Soviet agent, led the Woolwich Arsenal spy ring before being unmasked by an MI5 operation.

that communist activists were engaged not only in simple propaganda but in a strategic effort to undermine British security.[13] By the mid-1930s, MI5 reports suggested that Glading's interests were expanding from domestic subversion to international espionage. In light of this, it must have been with more than idle curiosity that MI5 received news of his decision to leave the CPGB in 1936–1937.[14] Glading's intentions only became clear once he approached Gray in 1937, which marked the beginning of the operation that would eventually lead to his arrest and the unravelling of the Woolwich Arsenal spy ring.

Although Glading was successfully prosecuted, some have pointed out that MI5 failed to apprehend his Soviet handlers, one of whom, Teodor Maly, might have led them to uncover the Cambridge Five spy ring. One historian has suggested this was because MI5 suffered from a 'lack of imagination'.[15] During this period, it was generally held that the biggest internal communist threat came from the working class and the CPGB, and the Woolwich Arsenal case certainly seems to fit that mould. Yet the Soviet Union's greatest agents were being cultivated in Britain's elite universities and would soon be entering Whitehall. This complaint against MI5 is not entirely fair, however, for even though we usually think of Soviet intelligence as being the first espionage service to recruit agents from Oxbridge, Knight did attempt to penetrate the intellectual communist left by recruiting Oxford-educated and future Labour MP Tom Driberg.[16] MI5 was not as bereft of insight as some have claimed.

The Two Recruitments of Olga Gray

Little is known about Olga Gray other than that she was born in 1906 and was initially approached by MI5 when she was twenty-two. The sole account of her background and personality before and after her dealings with MI5 comes from Knight's biographer, Anthony Masters, who managed to track her down in Canada many years later, when she was in her seventies.[17] She was, he wrote, 'temperamentally well suited' for work with MI5:

> She needed excitement as well as a sense of belonging, even if that belonging was wholly based on deceit. She possessed a photographic memory and a strong, dominant personality that was entirely convincing with its consistent show of commitment and loyalty. She was also headstrong and highly insecure.[18]

A much earlier internal summary of the case described her similarly, stating that Knight had been 'impressed by her intelligence and patriotism and

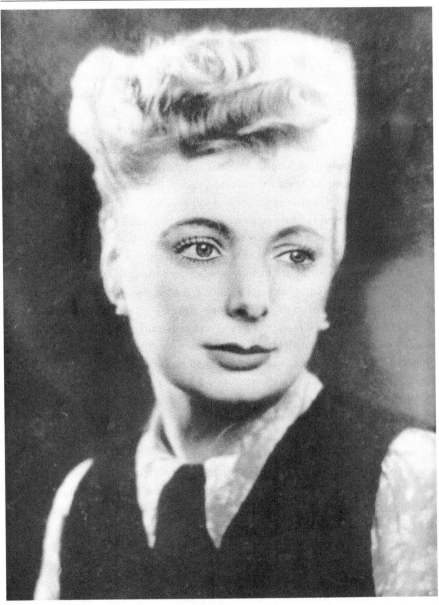

4 Olga Gray, MI5's agent who became secretary to the leader of the Communist Party of Great Britain – Harry Pollitt – and penetrated the Woolwich Arsenal spy ring. (1938)

realised that she was uninterested in her job and would like an opportunity to do something more worth while [*sic*]'.[19] Gray's combination of ambition and restlessness probably gave Knight useful leverage.

Those who handle agents, like great salespeople, would be psychologically attuned since their ability to persuade requires exploiting an individual's extant tendencies, desires or weaknesses. Doing so with sensitivity requires an immense amount of dedication. As Knight noted, 'The running of agents is most definitely a full-time job.' Like the doting lover, 'the officer-in-charge must, to all intents and purposes, be at the beck-and-call of the agent.'[20] Or as one former SIS officer described it, recruiting and running an agent is akin to the act of seduction.[21] Gray and Knight must have had a close relationship, though not as close as he had with another of his agents (and MI5 staff member), Joan Miller, with whom he lived for several years.[22] Generally, Knight believed a close relationship with his agents was good practice. 'He [the officer] must at all costs make a friend of his agent: the agent must trust the officer as much – if not more than – the officer trusts the agent; and that basis of firm confidence must be built up,' he wrote. To this end, 'The officer running an agent should set himself the task of getting to know his agent most thoroughly,' extending to 'the agent's home surroundings, family, hobbies, personal likes and dislikes,' all of which could be brought to bear in running the agent during operations.[23] Knight needed to know how best to use an agent, and once in an operation, he needed to know the agent's limits and capabilities. The best kind of person for an officer's task, he wrote, was that 'he shall be, or shall learn to be a man of wide understanding of human nature; one who can get on with and understand all types and classes.'[24] Officers required empathy, awareness and psychological insight: in other words, the human touch.

Women played a prominent role in Knight's operations. Some of his views on women clearly challenged the status quo of his era. He noted, 'It is frequently alleged that women are less discreet than men: that they are ruled by their emotions, and not by their brains: that they rely on intuition rather than on reason; and that Sex will play an unsettling and dangerous role in their work. My own experience has been very much to the contrary.' Knight did not hold that women were not different than men, but believed rather that feminine traits in a 'properly balanced' woman could be of utility. He wrote, for example, 'That a woman's intuition is sometimes amazingly helpful and amazingly correct has been well established.' Knight ascribed female intuition to emotional complexity, but remained adamant that women were not 'exclusively ruled by their emotions' as was often contended. Even so, he thought female intuition could be listless and required an officer's 'guiding hand.'[25]

Perhaps Knight was merely identifying what we would now call 'emotional' or 'social' intelligence.[26] Ironically, the same aptitude was essential for the agent's handler – almost always in that era a man – and one that Knight himself

5 Charles Henry 'Maxwell' Knight (1900-1968), considered one of best case officers in MI5's history, was behind many of MI5's interwar triumphs, such as the penetration of the Woolwich Arsenal Spy Ring and the Right Club. He later became a celebrated naturalist at the BBC.

clearly possessed. Quite simply, the *human* element of *human* intelligence cannot be overlooked. As such, less quantifiable aptitudes, like the ability to build rapport, gain confidence and inspire trust, can acquire greater importance than analytic intelligence in an agent operation. Indeed, in Knight's experience, the 'academic mind', the paragon of analytic intelligence, had not proved suited either to being or running an agent.[27]

Knight also believed that women were more discreet than men. Men, he later recorded, were responsible 'by far greater proportion' than women for 'loose talk' during the Second World War. A woman's ability to keep secrets was, he believed, a function of her vanity, which expressed itself in innocuous, typically superficial ways such as appearance and dress.[28] A man, on the other hand, suffered from conceit, the result of which was an attempt to 'build himself up', leading to boasting and one-upmanship.

Though the Second World War popularised the notion of the seductive spy with posters such as 'Keep Mum, She's Not So Dumb', sex and espionage share a long relationship. Knight was certainly not the first to address the question of female agents and sex. On that subject 'a great deal of nonsense has been talked and written', he remarked. In Knight's experience with Olga Gray and others, he concluded the most important consideration was that the agent be well rounded, or in his words, 'a normal, balanced person'. In relation to sex, this meant that agents 'should not be markedly over-sexed, or under-sexed: if over-sexed, it is clear that this will play an over-riding part in their mental processes; and if under-sexed they will not be so mentally alert, and their other faculties will suffer accordingly'. On balance, though, he considered an under-sexed female agent was preferable to an over-sexed one, writing that 'It is difficult to imagine anything more terrifying than for an officer to become landed with a woman-agent who suffers from an overdose of Sex.'[29] Not all would agree with Knight's conclusions, but in any case, we should presume that he perceived the blonde Olga Gray much like a latter-day Goldilocks: the degree of her sexuality was *just* right.

Knight still recognised the value of a physical attraction as useful in acquiring information, for he understood that 'A clever woman who can use her personal attractions wisely has in her armoury a very formidable weapon.' Equally though, he was quick to emphasise that he was 'no believer' in 'Mata-Hari methods'.[30] Far better, he observed, for a female agent to establish a relationship with a target based on companionship and sympathy:

> I am convinced that more information has been obtained by women-agents, by keeping out of the arms of the man, than ever was obtained by sinking too willingly into them; for it is unfortunately the case that if a man is physically but casually interested in a woman, he will very speedily lose his interest in her once his immediate object is attained;

whereas if he can come to rely upon the woman for her qualities of companionship and sympathy, than merely those of physical satisfaction, the enterprise will last the longer.[31]

So however much physical temptation might achieve short-term gains, Knight was far more interested in extracting maximum value from his agents and maximum information on his targets. The benefit of a long-term source was that 'it did not go out of date'.[32] But a source who requires physical persuasion to share information (whether by pleasure or pain) will likely be of only temporary value. This suggests that a long-term penetration strategy should attempt to appeal to morals and ideology rather than fear, lust or greed (although there are prominent examples to the contrary).[33]

Personal qualities mattered little if the agent did not have access to information, of course, and so a potential recruit's entrée was fundamental. Knight held that 'one good agent, carefully trained and well placed, is worth half-a-dozen indifferent agents'.[34] The 'quality' of an agent, then, would have been a measure of the level of access that agent had to information and how discreetly that information was obtained. Knight would have agreed with the head of the Second World War's Double-Cross System, John Masterman, who later pointed out that quality intelligence did not necessarily come from a traitorous 'high-grade' source, such as a minister, but rather concluded that the 'highest-grade agent is often a low-grade man'.[35] One reason Knight recruited women was that 'any woman possessed of some secretarial ability offers unique opportunities for exploitation' for:

No official or other single individual ever has the same opportunity for obtaining information covering a wide area as does a clerk or secretary. A woman so placed will have a much wider grasp of the day-to-day doings in a movement, than any of the officials of the movement will ever dream of.[36]

We only have to imagine a secretary's filing cabinet to grasp the immense power the position holds – appointments, contacts, memoranda, briefs. The secretary is at the hub of an organisation's information system, so Gray's own background considerably influenced Knight's decision to use her as an agent.[37] Her experience as a trained secretary did more than give her a legitimate cover; it also provided her with a seemingly innocuous position from which to observe an incredibly wide range of the CPGB's operations.

Gray was an early example in a long tradition of secretary spies. As practitioner-turned-academic Michael Herman has written, 'The most dangerous spies throughout the Cold War were West German secretaries supplying the East German intelligence service with secret documents; the most dangerous of an agent's weapons is uncontrolled access to a Xerox copier.'[38] Closer to home, even as Gray penetrated the CPGB, another young secretary began spying for the Soviets. Melita Norwood, the 'Spy Who Came In From the Co-op', joined the British Non-Ferrous Metals Research Association as a secretary in 1932 and was recruited by the NKVD (as the OGPU had been by then relabelled) in 1937.[39] Unfortunately for the British, MI5 and Scotland Yard did not put together the clues to her identity contained in Glading's notebook after his arrest in 1938, and Norwood retained her post through the Second World War. She was able, therefore, to provide the Soviets with top-secret information on the 'Tube Alloys' project, Britain's nuclear weapons research programme.[40]

The best way for an agent to penetrate an organisation was to be invited in, Knight held, asserting that the approach to an organisation 'should if humanly possible always be made by the body to the agent, not the agent to the body'.[41] In other words, having recruited the penetration agent, the organisation running the operation and the mole-in-waiting had to arrange for the new spy to be recruited by the hostile organisation targeted for penetration. Knight based this reasoning on his understanding that an agent who aggressively pursued entrance into a secretive organisation might provoke suspicion and that having received an invitation from an established member of that organisation would provide *bona fides* in the event of later suspicion and even investigation.

This fitted well with Knight's conclusions about the best kind of training for an agent, which he saw as work in the field, 'be it in ever so humble a capacity'.[42] The agent should begin to attend the organisation's public meetings, for example, to become a familiar face. Even before that though, Knight encouraged agents to acquaint themselves with the target organisation's literature that they might demonstrate a sincere interest in the cause. The probable outcome, he believed, would be 'some casual personal contact with some adherent or official of the organisation in question'.[43] Accompanying this jump into fieldwork would be necessary training in technical tradecraft, 'such as when, where and how to take notes, memory-training and accurate description of individuals, etc., etc.'[44]

Knight envisioned penetration as a gradual process of assimilation. As he emphasised to Olga Gray, he did not expect immediate gains but fully anticipated waiting several years for meaningful results.[45] Reducing pressure to provide 'tactical' intelligence minimised Gray's exposure to risk and allowed her to concentrate on building relationships and gaining access to sensitive material for a more comprehensive view of the organisation and its operations.

On Knight's instructions, Gray came to London in 1931 and began to attend meetings of The Friends of the Soviet Union (FSU), part of an international Congress that advocated policy on behalf of the Soviet government – in reality a front organisation funded and run by the Comintern.[46] As an 'interested and sympathetic enquirer', she made several acquaintances, among whom was the FSU Assistant Secretary. Her cover as a typist for an author who kept odd hours meant she was able to oblige when subsequently asked if she would volunteer for the League Against Imperialism (LAI) and then, soon after, to work as secretary for the Anti-War Movement. Both of these organisations were also Comintern fronts.[47] It was in this capacity that in late 1932 she came to know Harry Pollitt, General Secretary of the CPGB (1929–1939, 1941–1956), and Percy Glading, who had joined the LAI a year before Gray and become one of its paid officers.[48] 'As a matter of course', Gray later testified, she was then 'required' to join the CPGB.[49] But as Knight was keen to emphasise, 'Miss "X" had not applied to become a Party member and had not even announced that she was a completely convinced Communist … she had been invited to join the Party; and she had therefore taken the first major step, without laying herself open to any accusation of "pushing".[50] Knight's telling Gray to take a softly-softly approach, letting it appear that she was hired on their initiative rather than her own, and his not pressuring her for immediate results provided a model of how to bait CPGB members effectively.

Luck – being in the right place at the right time – undoubtedly played some role in Gray's successful penetration. Yet Knight had also created his own luck: the way he handled Gray invited the circumstances leading to her recruitment by the CPGB. Patience and training enabled Gray to become close to two of the CPGB's most influential members, Pollitt and Glading. Getting close to Pollitt, the former secretary of the National Minority Movement, was a great coup. Once called the 'English Lenin', Pollitt had been under surveillance since 1921.[51] In 1931, the year before Gray met Pollitt, MI5 had tapped his telephone, intercepted his post, arranged with SIS and foreign intelligence (the Belgian Sûreté, for example) to have him followed when outside of the UK, and received regular MPSB reports with excerpts from his speeches, meaning that informants had attended his speaking events.[52] Gray added to this array of surveillance from her benign position as secretary with an invisibility that increased her access to information. 'She had attained that very enviable position', Knight wrote, 'where an agent becomes a piece of furniture, so to speak: that is, when persons visiting an office do not consciously notice whether the agent is there or not.'[53]

The LAI, like the FSU and the Anti-War Movement, was a product of the efforts of German-born Willi Münzenberg, one of the Comintern's best operatives and propagandists.[54] In the early 1930s, when Glading was a prominent member, the LAI was involved with Comintern operations in India and China and launched a prominent campaign in support of the Meerut conspirators – the thirty-one Indian Communist and Labour leaders arrested in 1929 on charges tantamount to sedition.[55] Glading himself wrote a nineteen-page pamphlet on the case (*The Meerut Conspiracy Case*), published by the CPGB in 1933 just after the accused were sentenced.[56] Soviet defector Krivitsky later described how Britain's colonies occupied a central position in Soviet strategy. India was especially important, undoubtedly because Stalin was 'convinced that the Achilles heel of the British [was] in India and the Near East'.[57] Olga Gray's access to Glading put her in a position to secure international as well as domestic intelligence, therefore, information with important strategic implications.

It was not long before Knight's patience and Gray's fortitude bore fruit. Glading, like many Comintern operatives, had been given rudimentary training in tradecraft at the Lenin School when he was in Moscow in 1929 and 1930.[58] He soon put it to use, though it was actually Pollitt who first approached Gray, asking her in 1934 whether she would undertake a 'special mission'. According to Gray, Pollitt explained she would be 'carrying messages from here [Britain] to other countries'.[59] Glading followed up the inquiry, probing if she would like to 'take a trip a trip abroad for the Party'. In this situation, like others, Gray played a passive role and, by being coy in responding to the first request, forced Pollitt and Glading to take more than the initiative of just the initial approach. Knight approvingly recalled, 'With very becoming self-restraint, Miss "X" did not appear too keen'. But Glading continued to sound Gray out, and it finally emerged that Gray's destination was to be India.[60] With the Meerut Conspiracy case freshly concluded, her mission as a courier had the potential to provide valuable insight into CPGB connections to Comintern operations on the Subcontinent.

Only a broad description of Gray's trip to India remains, though the journey fitted a pattern typical of Comintern activity. The Comintern's *Otdel Mezhdunarodnykh Svyazey* (OMS), the International Liaison Department, was the organ through which communist parties received funding and directives. Pollitt gave Gray a large sum of cash, in pounds (which she apparently smuggled out in sanitary pads) to be exchanged for dollars in Paris, where she met Glading in June 1934.[61] There, Glading gave her additional instructions and a questionnaire for Communist leaders in India.[62] She then embarked for Bombay.

Knight later reflected on why Pollitt and Glading chose Gray to act as courier. He concluded, probably correctly, that her anonymity played a large part in the decision. 'In my opinion', Knight wrote, 'the two principal reasons were: - a) The fact that Miss "X" had never obtruded herself into public Communist activity, and had therefore – in the eyes of the Communists – probably never come to the notice of the Police: b) – The fact that she possessed a "clean" British passport.'[63] In later terminology, she was a 'green skin'; she had a clean record. Before the Second World War, known communists were at times refused visas to some parts of the Empire, and an attempt by a known individual to obtain one might have alerted the authorities to CPGB activities. Glading might also have known that port security was an important part of Britain's surveillance apparatus. As a recognised communist himself, he stood a good chance of being detained and the mission of failing. It would seem the value of Gray's anonymity outweighed the potential risk of sending someone so inexperienced.

Despite this caution, the communists did not make adequate travel preparations for her, and it is possible that she might have been detained at the port had Knight's department not lent a helping hand:

> They were proposing to send her to India during the monsoon period – a time of the year when normal people do not choose to travel to India; they proposed that she should stay there for a matter of only a few weeks, another unusual circumstance; and the Party shewed [*sic*] themselves so out-of-touch with general social matters, that they did not realise that an unaccompanied young English woman travelling to India without some very good reason stood a risk of being turned back when she arrived to India as a suspected prostitute. Our department was faced with a peculiar situation whereby Miss 'X' had to be assisted to devise a cover-story which would meet the requirements necessary, without making it appear to the Party that she had received any expert advice. This was no easy task but eventually a rather thin story of a sea-trip under doctor's orders, combined with an invitation from a relative in India met the case.[64]

Knight put the communists' poor tradecraft down to the fact that Gray's mission was largely organised by the CPGB and not Soviet intelligence – as Glading's own trip had been in 1925. Yet often the divide between national communist parties and the Comintern was blurred. Glading himself had been trained by the Soviets and the CPGB frequently acted under orders from Moscow. His mission amounted to an out-sourced Soviet operation, but because he and his peers had only limited training, Comintern clandestine activity often retained an amateurish flavour in the early 1930s. In the end, only with MI5's input into the communists' tradecraft, was Gray's mission successful.

Gray's six-week journey succeeded without incident, thanks in part to the scheming of M. Section. MI5 files contain little follow up on the consequences of the trip, but if Gray made contact with one of Knight's agents, as she suggested, then it can be presumed that her activities and contacts in India were observed by local officials, and possibly Comintern lines of funding and communication were discovered.[65] Sadly for Gray, her health deteriorated after her return. Knight sympathised: 'As may be readily understood, she was tired, suffering from some nervous strain; and rather disposed to feel that she had done enough. Her health suffered something of a break-down, and she retired from the scene.'[66] In fact, she suffered a full nervous breakdown and was admitted to National Hospital for Nervous Diseases. Knight apparently visited her every day – which, while a commendable gesture, is inexplicably bad tradecraft.[67] Her covert position could have easily been spoiled had either been under surveillance.

After some time recuperating, Gray took a new job not connected to spying. But normal life did not last long. Glading soon approached her again, asking her to work as Pollitt's personal secretary at CPGB headquarters, clearly testifying to her competence and credibility in the eyes of CPGB officials – and to the quality of Knight's handling. Knight was pleased by the prospect, and, despite her health problems, urged her to return to the field.[68] But only a short time elapsed before Gray again fell ill. She explained, 'The work was very hard and after three or four months I informed the officer of the Intelligence Department for whom I worked [Knight], that I found the work too great a strain and would prefer to drop my connection with the Communist Party and return to ordinary life.'[69] Knight was again sympathetic to her situation – 'some years of literally leading a double life, cut off from most her friends, and under conditions of considerable strain' – and accepted her decision to resign her position at the CPGB, but he did ask her to keep in touch with Glading and other officials.[70]

Percy Glading and the Woolwich Arsenal

With his long and active history in communist politics, Glading's decision to leave the Party in 1936–1937 and sever all connections with it must have surprised MI5. It must also have been viewed with suspicion. Intelligence collected by Knight's agents suggested that his interest in military secrets had only just begun.[71] His departure from the CPGB also coincided with increasing instability on the international scene. In 1936 the League of Nations was fast crumbling:

Hitler reoccupied the demilitarised Rhineland in the spring, and soon after, Mussolini hailed a new Roman empire when Ethiopia's Emperor Haile Selassie fled to Britain. Summer brought the beginning of the Spanish Civil War, and civil war in China continued unabated until the end of 1936, when the Communists and the Nationalists agreed to a temporary truce in order to counter the advancing Japanese Army. In the terse words of historian A. J. P. Taylor, "'International Anarchy' had come again."[72] The ideologically charged atmosphere – as evidenced at the Olympics in Berlin that summer and embodied by the Soviet and Nazi pavilions at the World's Fair in Paris a year later – made it an unlikely time for Glading to withdraw from politics. Come winter 1937, any questions regarding his actual intentions were answered. Glading requested Gray's services once again.

As instructed, Gray continued to see Glading in a friendly capacity. He broached the subject of a new arrangement over lunch in February 1937. It sounded fairly innocuous. He asked her to lease a flat and make it available for occasional private meetings for him and his associates. Gray assumed this meant colleagues from the LAI. The lease would be in her name, as would contracts such as telephone and electricity, but she would not have to pay for anything; the Party would cover it all. She would not even have to work for Glading in a traditional sense, so she could retain her current position. Yet she was still apprehensive about becoming involved with Glading again.[73] Ultimately, Knight's powers of persuasion won out, and she agreed to another operation.

Knight noted that Glading's recruitment technique had become more sophisticated. The apparent facility and generosity of his offer belied a degree of entrapment. Clandestine operations inherently require invisibility, and Gray's clean record provided a suitable front to shield Glading's activities, which he clearly wished to keep below MI5's radar. It was the same reason she had been chosen to go to India, but putting her name on the lease and utilities contracts also bound her to Glading, because she would be relying on his paying the bills. Knight observed, 'Glading therefore had what one might term a "hold" on her.'[74] He had created a relationship of dependence.

Knight, too appears to have had a hold on her, though a psychological rather than financial one. She may have agreed to enter into the operation of her own free will (indeed it was she who informed Knight of Glading's offer), but considering her fragile psychology and articulated reluctance, it seems fair to assume that Knight did some manipulating of his own, seeing the operation's potential as outweighing the risks it posed to Gray's mental health. It is not impossible, in other words, that he viewed Gray as an indispensable agent but expendable person. Nonetheless, he must have understood that any agent's continued success depended upon her well-being. Indeed, this alone could account for Knight's earlier visits to the hospital. Convincing agents to act in ways potentially against their own best interests appear to be as much a part of handling them as are other elements of tradecraft.

Glading charged Gray with finding the flat but gave two specifications: 'Firstly: It must not be in a block because there must be no porter. Secondly: It must not be in the Notting Hill Gate District.'[75] Both were issues of tradecraft, and the reasons behind them were sound enough. Glading wanted to conduct his activities away from prying eyes. The existence of a porter introduced a possible leak in what he likely intended to be an otherwise airtight operation. He also wanted to distance himself spatially from underground Communist activity. Notting Hill Gate is around the corner from what was then the Soviet Embassy at Kensington Palace Gardens, where many operations were orchestrated.

With Knight's help, Gray found a suitable flat, at 82 Holland Road, though strangely it was only a few blocks away from Notting Hill Gate. She signed the lease at £100 per year, the cash for which Glading gave to her monthly in addition to giving her funds for furnishings.[76] He further instructed her to have three sets of keys made, two of which he would keep for future rendezvous.[77] Glading led Gray to believe that his activities were under the auspices of the CPGB, but as Knight astutely commented, 'It seemed in the highest degree unlikely that the C.P.G.B. would go to all this expense and trouble merely to provide a room where Party members could occasionally meet, for there must have been dozens of completely safe places in London, where such matters could be conducted.'[78] Glading's cover might have convinced Gray, but little did he realise he needed to convince MI5 as well. With the use of a penetration agent, Knight lifted the lid on Glading's covert arrangements in ways even Gray need not have understood.

More questions were soon answered in the form of one 'Mr. Peters'. Unknown to Knight at the time, and revealed by Walter Krivitsky three years later, Peters was in fact Teodor Maly (also known as Paul Hardt), one of the 'Great Illegals' and a handler of the Cambridge Five. On 4 April 1937, Glading brought him to the flat, apparently to evaluate Gray's suitability for the operation. She must have passed, because after that visit, Glading began to speak 'fairly openly' about his work. At this point it became clear that he – and now she – was in some capacity working for Soviet intelligence.[79] Later Glading brought more people to the flat: a 'bumptious' Austrian – the *illegal* Arnold Deutsch – and 'the Stevenses' (or 'Stephenses'), who, it would transpire, were married Soviet operatives Willy and Mary Brandes.[80]

Neither Glading nor Deutsch maintained covers. Willy Brandes and Teodor Maly, on the other hand, conducted their work using covers involving commerce, just as previous agent reports had indicated illegals would do. Brandes ostensibly represented two American firms (Phantom Red Cosmetics and the Charak Furniture Company), and Maly worked for Gada (a shell company based in Holland and an OGPU front for agent operations in France, Belgium, the Netherlands, Luxembourg, and primarily Britain).[81] It was under his Gada cover that Maly ran J. H. King, a Foreign Office cypher clerk.[82] Through the apartment, the one strategically placed penetration agent Olga Gray linked Knight with some of the Soviets' most effective operatives and sensitive operations.

Glading revealed to Gray that 'the real purpose of the flat was to provide a place where certain photographing of documents could be safely undertaken.'[83] The documents, he explained, were 'borrowed' and 'very secret'. This would occur about once a week, and the typical procedure would involve their being picked up in the evening, photographed overnight, then returned in the morning – he did not say to whom any of this would be done. Glading proposed that Gray find a new job, one that would be part-time, so that she could do more work for him. She would also be trained in the use of a miniature camera.[84]

As Knight later noted, Glading drew Gray into this new round of illegal work slowly. At first he simply asked her to rent the flat for the Party. Once she was bound by contracts, he then revealed he was working directly for the Soviets, thereby making her an accomplice.[85] Finally, his earlier promise that she could keep her job dissolved as he pressed her to take a part-time position that would allow her to work directly for him and photographing secret documents. In this latter phase, he was still not entirely forthright, telling her the documents were borrowed. By engaging her in small tasks of an increasingly illegal nature, he increasingly implicated her in the operations.[86] Presumably these steps were taken for his safety, for if she were made complicit in the crime, she would be less likely to denounce him. Yet by involving her more, he also further incriminated himself.

The first photographic session took place in mid-October 1937. Glading had asked Gray to purchase a 'really heavy, steady table … something in the nature of a refectory table' for the photographic work. Knight was eager for Glading to accompany Gray on the errand so surveillance might secure positive visual identification should it be needed later as evidence. Gray, 'with considerable skill', coaxed Glading into joining her.[87] With the refectory table installed several days later, 'Mr. Stevens' and his wife Mary (the Brandeses), arrived at the flat to test the photographic equipment. Gray subsequently reported the Stevenses were 'clearly foreigners', and that Mary spoke to her husband in French.[88] Gray also told Knight that the group practised using a Leica camera (which Krivitsky later noted was the Soviets' favourite) to photograph London tube maps.[89] She also observed that 'Mrs. BRANDES was by no means an expert photographer and she was decidedly nervous about her ability to use the apparatus effectively with only a small amount of practice'. This is hardly the image of a slick undercover operative. Nor was Glading impressed: '[He] told Miss "X" that he was annoyed with Mrs. BRANDES' incompetence and again said he thought it would be a good thing for Miss "X" herself to take a course in photography.'[90]

There is no record of Gray taking photos, and Mary Brandes returned three days later as planned to take the first set of clandestine photographs. She arrived with the documents concealed in 'a bundle of rolled newspapers', telling Gray the job would require about forty-two exposures. Edgy, she also asked Gray to take her tea and go into the bedroom while she completed her work. When she left the flat after ten that night, she left the negatives, giving Gray the opportunity to note the names and numbers of the documents. Meanwhile, Mary Brandes was followed from 82 Holland Road to Hyde Park Corner, where she met her husband and the later-identified George Whomack, a gun examiner from the Inspector of Naval Ordnance Department at the Woolwich Arsenal.[91] Gray's notes from the photography session enabled MI5 to identify one set of plans as being one of the only five extant copies of the blueprints of a naval gun mounting. Three of the copies had been issued only two weeks early to the defence firm Vickers, the Admiralty and the Ordnance Factory of the Woolwich Arsenal.[92] This indicated that some of Britain's most up-to-date defence technology was being given to the Soviets almost as soon as it was developed.

Two weeks later, Glading informed Gray that 'the Stevenses' had been recalled to Moscow owing to their daughter's ill health. Much to Glading's annoyance, Willy Brandes asked him to handle his sources until, Glading inferred, they could be taken over by Brandes's replacement. Glading complained that most of Brandes's contacts were 'purely mercenary' and fumed that handling them would be time-consuming because 'there were so many'. He also recognised that the responsibility would expose him to more risk.

While he did not expect 'Mrs. Stevens' to return, he believed that 'Mr. Stevens' would return for a week sometime after Christmas, at which time the photography sessions would resume. In the meanwhile, Glading took the stand and camera equipment to his own flat for additional work. He explained that he could not find a stand for his own camera and that one of his projects had been a 'rush job' of poor quality made difficult because he had to use a pile of books.[93] Here, we get an inside look at what was more often than not the rather mundane reality of espionage. Although blueprints for top-secret armaments falling into Soviet hands was of great significance, the image of a spy balancing his camera on a tottering stack of books exemplifies the extent to which espionage during this period was often a labour-intensive and shoe-string affair that sometimes bordered on the farcical.

On 20 January 1938, Glading telephoned Gray to invite her for lunch the next day and to request the use of her flat for 'something important' that evening.[94] It might have been related to a several-hundred page book she knew he had planned to copy during the previous weekend (16–17 January).[95] Gray notified Knight of the developments and then met Glading as he had asked. After their lunch at the Windsor Castle Bar, he told her to meet him at the flat at 6.00 p.m. Gray, who thought they would begin taking the photos when she arrived, found that a perturbed Glading had already set up the equipment but still needed to collect the 'object to be photographed' at 8.15 p.m., copy it, and then return it that same night.[96] Glading was also 'very worried' that neither Brandes (who was scheduled to return) nor his other contact would show up. Behind Glading's anxiety lay the fact that he was running out of money and still had 'stuff parked all over London'. He feared that 'Russian dilatoriness' would force him to borrow money to pay those keeping all of Brandes's things. Not only did he not like the Russians personally, but he believed that the fact that they were 'nearly always illegally resident' brought unnecessary risks to operations.[97]

Gray told Knight all this as soon as Glading left the flat that evening, but he was likely already being monitored anyway. It is not clear why the hammer fell that particular evening, but Knight later wrote:

> In January 1938, it was understood that GLADING was contemplating an important piece of copying, which was to be done at the flat; and by this time it was practically certain that the documents in question were emanating from Woolwich Arsenal … The Authorities therefore had to face the fact that this sort of thing could not go on for ever [*sic*], and eventually a decision was taken to formulate a plan by which GLADING and the other parties concerned might be arrested and searches carried out at the exact time when it was planned to photograph the next document.[98]

In the end, he was not arrested in the act of photographing the documents but of passing them. It is possible that Knight planned for the apprehension to occur at the flat, but Glading arrived and left early and so delayed his arrest.

Although Glading's departure that night was not anticipated, Knight was flexible and moved quickly to shut his venture down.

The post-mortem of the case notes that "'Miss "X" rang up and stated that GLADING had just left her flat and was proceeding to Charing Cross station where at 8.15 p.m. he was to meet a man from whom he would receive the material to be photographed.' At the expected time, one of the MPSB officers waiting at Charing Cross spotted Glading, who five minutes later greeted Albert Williams, an examiner at the Department of Chief Inspector of Armaments at Woolwich, where Whomack worked.[99] After he handed Glading a 'brown paper parcel', both were apprehended. The officers escorted Glading and Williams to Scotland Yard, where the parcel was opened and found to contain four blueprints of a pressure bar apparatus, a mechanical engineering device frequently used in the development of military hardware. The men were searched, and Glading's diary confiscated as evidence. Scotland Yard also 'ransacked' his house:

> Two cameras and other photographic material were discovered there, in addition to an anti-tank pistol-mine and other material relating to his espionage activities. Spools of film found in GLADING's house were printed by the photographic department at New Scotland Yard, and were found to constitute a copy of a textbook on explosives used in the Services, 1925 issue. Photographic plates found at the same time were revealed as negatives of five prints relating to fuzes [*sic*] designed for use by aeroplanes against submarines.[100]

One of the negatives showed a portion of wallpaper later found to match a room in Williams's flat that had been converted into a photography studio. This further affirmed Glading and Williams's collusion.[101] Then, just over one week later, Whomack and a certain Charles Munday were also arrested.[102] Glading subsequently received a six-year sentence, and Williams and Whomack were given four and three years, respectively. Munday was acquitted.[103]

For reasons of security, Gray did not appear *in camera*, but she nonetheless received the judge's plaudits for her role in the case. Justice Hawke remarked that she 'must be possessed of extraordinary courage', and noted that 'she has done great service to her country.'[104] The kudos did not ease the disappointment she felt after the case's conclusion, however. Despite all of the attention Knight had bestowed upon her during the course of the operation their relationship ended abruptly with its conclusion. According to her, after the trial she was treated to lunch at the Ritz by an anonymous colonel, thanked, and given a £500 cheque for her services. There her relationship with MI5 ceased, and soon after, she left for Canada.[105] No account exists of Knight meeting her after the trial. In older age she bitterly recollected, 'I was a 50 shillings a week spy ... Then I was dumped. In those days the adrenaline really flowed but since then the excitement has never been rekindled. That's why I feel so restless – and my abilities remain so unfulfilled.'[106] If her account is to be believed, it raises questions about the sincerity of Knight's relationship with her. It would seem she believed her capabilities were bypassed rather than made use of in future operations, but perhaps in her seventies she glossed over the impact the case had had on her nerves at the time. Moreover, contrary to her feelings of unfulfilled potential, there may have been a simple, practical reason why Gray could not continue as an agent: her cover had been blown.

As for Knight's thoughts about Gray after the case, there is no record. It is not possible to say if his concern for Gray extended beyond the operational. He did apparently ask her older brother, a high-ranking police officer, to act as her bodyguard, which shows some degree of concern for her, but it is unclear whether this was of a professional or personal nature.[107] Nor can we illuminate more broadly the extent to which Knight created a personal bond with his agents during the course of an operation. If we take Gray at her word, his approach would appear to have been objectively attentive but subjectively dispassionate, with Knight displaying the kind of concern one might towards a chess game. The pieces may take on great importance, but they must at times be sacrificed to defeat the opponent. With victory in hand, Gray appears to have become irrelevant.

Many would agree that the Woolwich case 'reinforced MI5's false assumption that the chief danger to British security was provided by the CPGB'.[108] Nonetheless, this conclusion begs for nuance. The CPGB *was* the recruiting ground for Glading, Whomack and Williams – and other suspected and convicted subversives, as well. The damage these spies wrought did not, however, compare with the damage that would be wrought by the Cambridge Five. With MI5's attention fixated on threats emanating from the CPGB (to say nothing of the fascist threat), Soviet illegals Deutsch and Maly were more easily able to target Britain's elite universities and their upper-class students. This has led some, like historian Richard Thurlow, to conclude that MI5 'often lacked imagination in counter-intelligence because it was unable to perceive the sophistication of Soviet propaganda, recruitment and organisation'.[109]

Yet we have since learned that MI5 did, in fact, investigate Britain's elite educational institutions. In 1923, for example, MI5 and MPSB began examining two professors at Trinity College, Cambridge: Professor Pyotr Kapitza, the future Nobel laureate in physics who worked under Ernest Rutherford at Cavendish Laboratory, and Maurice Dobb, the outspoken Marxist economics tutor.[110] Nor does Thurlow's argument take into account Knight's attempts to penetrate the radical left at Oxford. The recruitment of Tom Driberg (the future Labour MP and Baron Bradwell) as agent 'M8' gave him access to the 'Café Communist' set at Oxford – although the CPGB later expelled Driberg in 1941 after Anthony Blunt exposed him.[111] Knight also recruited Bill Younger at Oxford to supply him with information on the communist activities of his peers.[112] MI5 was clearly not oblivious to the ideological fomentation occurring at Oxbridge.

At least three accounts recognise that Glading, while once a prominent Party member, conducted his work on the whole without Party leaders' connivance. As Knight wrote, 'It is necessary to make clear the fact that although GLADING was a member of the Communist Party of Great Britain, the last episode of this case was conducted and operated by the Soviet Intelligence Authorities, without the general knowledge of the Communist Party leaders.'[113] Another summary report states:

> The British subjects employed in GLADING's espionage organisation appear to have been exclusively members of the Communist Party of Great Britain. GLADING himself was, of course, one of the most prominent members. These persons all have appeared to have dropped open Communist Party Work, and in some cases to have resigned from the Party as soon as they were recruited for espionage work.[114]

John Curry, in the official postwar history, also wrote: 'Percy Glading and his assistants were all British subjects and were all members of the C.P.G.B. who dropped Party work as soon as they were recruited. The Party had no official knowledge of their activities, although certain Party officials were fully informed.'[115] While it is true that this does not invalidate Thurlow's conclusion, each account nonetheless justifies MI5's focus on the Party: Glading *had been* a prominent CPGB member, and the Cambridge Five *were* involved in communist activity. Dobb inspired Philby to work for the Comintern in Austria, and Burgess and Blunt were enough enthused by Communism to travel to Moscow – only soon after to disassociate themselves with communism and their communist friends, as Philby did. Still, MI5's interest in Cambridge's older academics, like Dobb and Kapitza, exceeded its interest in the students. If Deutsch's or Maly's tracks had been followed from the Glading meetings, they might have led MI5 to the student communists in Cambridge, and investigations into the CPGB and communist-affiliated organisations might not appear as unimaginative as they seem in retrospect.

Still, at least two factors hindered, if they did not preclude, the expansion of operations against Soviet espionage and communist subversion. Although the accusation of unimaginativeness is debatable, MI5's lack of resources is beyond question. In October 1937, around the time when Glading re-recruited Gray, MI5 staffed a mere sixteen officers in B Branch, of which a scant four held responsibility for counter Soviet and communist espionage.[116] With the threat of war looming in 1937, MI5 was reorganised in preparation. The already limited funding that had dogged it throughout the interwar period did not increase, however, and the lack of money brought it to a breaking point.[117] MI5 simply did not have the wherewithal to investigate all it might have wanted.

The second prohibitive factor was the war itself. Even if MI5 began to identify the Soviets' agents and understand their tradecraft – first from Glading, then from J. H. King in 1939, and finally from the debriefing of Krivitsky in 1940 – the war cut those efforts short. In the late 1930s, MI5 began to suffer from a problem that security and intelligence services would continue to face later: 'the tyranny of the tactical'.[118] Small clues potentially pointing to a much larger pattern, strategy or event were regularly overwhelmed by more imminent threats. Given finite resources after September 1939 and, especially, after May 1940, MI5 suffered an overload of suspected reports of potential fifth-column activities and the need to vet them. Efforts focused almost exclusively on countering the threat from the Axis powers, and the Foreign Office ordered MI5's counter-Soviet operations to cease once the USSR entered the war as an ally in 1941.[119]

The fact nonetheless remains that the apprehension of Glading did not yield all it could have done. In the end, MI5 successfully prosecuted Glading and two low-level armaments employees. Although not insignificant, these results paled in comparison with what might have been discovered had Deutsch, Maly or even the Brandeses been apprehended. All four escaped without being properly identified, let alone interrogated. MI5 also missed the Melita Norwood lead. Glading's notebook contained information that could have led to her, but, oddly, it seems never to have been pursued.[120] As noted earlier, Norwood went on to work for the Tube Alloys project, providing secrets on British nuclear developments to the Soviets throughout the war.

Still, Knight's work in M. Section cannot be considered unimaginative. It shows, too, that the Soviets were not unique in their ability to run long-term penetration agents. Knight recognised as much: 'The interest of this case lies in the example it provides of the operation of an agent on a long-term basis.' It was almost solely due to Gray, who 'over a long period of time, was able to work herself into the complete confidence of the key-man concerned', that MI5 had the success it did against the Woolwich Arsenal spy ring.[121] Knight believed this long-term approach was especially effective against the Soviets because it exploited their own methods:

In dealing with Communism in particular, it should be borne in mind that the Russians are past-masters at the art of long term policy, and that it is not unusual for a Soviet agent to be 'plaa4nted' in some position in order to carry out work which will probably not fructify in a matter of years. To combat this, therefore, it is obviously imperative to employ counter-espionage agents who are worked on the same policy, and with the same degree of patience.[122]

In other words, he advocated a symmetrical response to the Soviet attack. His skill in implementing that response is why MI5 still honours him today.[123]

One former practitioner wrote later that the first of the 'Ten Commandments of Counterintelligence' is to 'be offensive'. Knight, in handling Gray's penetration of the CPGB, understood early what future intelligence officers continued to propound. He showed early in the twentieth century that 'the key to [counter-intelligence] success is penetration'.[124] With the Soviets as 'past masters' of long-term penetration, Knight used their strategy in counter-espionage, thereby turning a seemingly reactive and defensive concept into a proactive, offensive strategy. He would use the same strategy to investigate Britain's fascist groups.

CHAPTER 5

Penetration Agents (II)

Maxwell Knight, Fascist Organisations and the Right Club

THROUGH the 1930s, as Hitler's Germany and Mussolini's Italy grew more menacing, MI5 expanded its focus beyond what had been its almost singular efforts to counter Soviet and communist activity. Turning to the domestic fascist threat it had begun investigating in the early 1930s, Knight's M. Section spearheaded MI5's investigation into Britain's fascist organisations. Generally regarded as the best agent-runner in MI5's interwar history, if not the history of the agency as a whole, Knight earned his reputation not only from his successful penetration of the Woolwich Arsenal spy ring, but also as a result of his infiltration of fascist groups. He was no doubt aided in great part by his experiences in the political right before he joined the government to take on communist subversion and Soviet espionage.[1] Although the fascism of the 1930s was a different beast than the fascism of the 1920s, Knight's own previous affiliations and personal connections with some on the right made him particularly well suited to charting their activity.[2] As the one-time Director of Intelligence for the British Fascisti (BF), he understood not only the fascist mind-set but also the mechanics of the organisations and the people involved. He first honed his skills while taking part in the right-wing movement of the 1920s. It was during that time that fascist groups had become increasingly sophisticated, as demonstrated by the development of paramilitary wings and, in some cases, intelligence branches. The British Empire Union (BEU), which had been founded during the First World War by George Makgill, provides one such example. It was linked in turn to the Industrial Intelligence Bureau (IIB) – the group in which Knight had begun his intelligence career by spying on left-wing groups before was recruited to the government.[3]

Knight's departure from the fascist movement and his entry into MI5 had coincided with the extreme right's distinct movement towards anti-Semitism and eventually pro-German and pro-Italian sentiment. Yet when he left fascism to work actively against the connections of his own past, those links nonetheless provided him with a valuable pool of recruits for the agent operations he conducted after joining MI5 in 1931.[4] Knight's work with the three agents who penetrated the viciously anti-Semitic Right Club during the suspenseful period of the Phoney War exemplified the skill in agent recruitment and handling with which he became identified.

Though this particular fringe group posed little direct challenge to the political status quo in terms of electoral power, as other groups such as the British Union of Fascists (BUF) were feared to do, its links to the diplomatic community gave the Right Club the opportunity to exert a potentially disproportionate influence on British politics. Not only did Knight and his agents effectively penetrate the Right Club (a feat in its own right), the intelligence they collected led to the detection of a spy in the US government. These fascists' secret dealings with Tyler Kent, a cipher clerk in the American Embassy, almost caused irreparable damage to the British war effort after belligerencies began in September 1939. Knight's brilliant tradecraft may well have affected the course of the war.

Emergence of the Fascist Threat

British fascism in the 1920s differed substantially from the fascism of the 1930s in its constitutional character, as the earlier domestic fascists had no plans to usurp the functions of the properly constituted authorities.[5] Indeed, even Winston Churchill extolled the anti-communist stance of Mussolini, who had inspired the creation of the BF. As late as 1933, he praised 'the Roman genius' of Mussolini, 'the greatest lawgiver among modern men' – though he stopped well short of advocating fascism for Britain.[6] Thus it is not as surprising as it may at first seem that in the mid-late 1920s, Knight and his private network of agents began to work directly under Morton at SIS, where they were known as the *Casuals*. Morton sought to exploit their contacts 'to uncover channels of funding and instructions emanating from Moscow, and thereby to check and confirm SIS reports received from overseas'.[7] Amateurs like Knight were skilful enough at collecting intelligence on communists that SIS saw their value.

In 1933, two years after Knight and the Casuals were transferred to MI5, M. Section was given the additional responsibility of investigating fascism and the BUF, whose creation in 1932 had given a jolt to the flagging fascist movement.[8] Following a lull in extreme right-wing activism in the late 1920s, the BUF marked (and sparked) the resurgence of the British far right. Knight understood its potential for growth:

Although in a very disorganised and loose state at the moment, given a leavening of reliable subordinate officers and live constructive political programmes, it will be more than possible to weld [the BUF] into a very formidable organisation, and there can be no doubt that the interest in Fascism in the moment is greater than at any other time since the initial Italian experiment.[9]

With Hitler's assumption of the German chancellery as the backdrop, uniformed marches and huge rallies raised the BUF's profile, as did the concerted publicity campaign launched by Lord Rothermere's *Daily Mail*. At its zenith in the summer of 1934, the BUF counted some 40,000–50,000 members.[10] It was never more than marginally successful at the polls, but its sheer visibility, as in its paramilitary processions, exaggerated the threat it posed to the status quo.

With the first rumbles of the Nazi war machine in Germany, Knight's M. Section attempted both to plant agents in and recruit agents from the BUF. HOWs played a central role. However, unlike its approach to the CPGB, the Home Office consistently denied MI5's requests for HOWs for Mosley and his principal deputies, perhaps as a result of domestic political pressure for the appeasement of fascism or maybe as a function of an inherent Whitehall bias against the working class and socialism.[11] Nevertheless, MI5 was one of the first departments of government to recognise the potentially threatening nature of British fascism even as it found that political expediency often restricted it from aggressively pursuing its investigations.[12]

The growing menace of the fascist movement was personified by William Joyce, who became the BUF's 'Director of Research' (i.e. propaganda) in 1934. Joyce boasted a history of street fighting and a collateral razor scar across his face. His zeal and skilful oratory led to the rapid ascendancy of his passionate promotions of bigotry and violence. Given his place 'at Mosley's right hand', his character was of considerable importance to Knight, who observed:

> He has always been of a very precocious intellectual development, with tremendous personality and energy. His greatest failing is that his mental balance is not equal to his intellectual capacity. As an Irishman his is naturally a person of very definite opinions and these opinions always tend towards extremes. He is, for instance, a rabid anti-Catholic, and a fanatical anti-Semite.[13]

Joyce's tendency to extremism did not, however, lessen his ability to wield influence among fascists or, Knight feared, beyond them. 'If Fascism were to progress in this country and become more powerful, then Joyce would be a man who would undoubtedly play a very prominent part in affairs,' Knight

6 William Joyce (1906–1946), 'Lord Haw-Haw', was an American-born Irish fascist who fled to Germany and broadcasted pro-Nazi propaganda during the Second World War. After being captured at the war's end, he became the last person in Britain to be hanged for treason.

concluded.[14] Once again, Knight displayed his astonishing skills of judging character, his insight into people and his critical faculties for running agents – all aspects of his tradecraft.

The BUF's resounding defeat in the 1935 general election pushed it further from mainstream politics.[15] Financial straits also exacerbated rifts within the group, culminating in the departure of several prominent officials, including Joyce, John Beckett and John Angus MacNab, all of whom went on to found the pro-Nazi British National Socialist League.[16] Knight had prophesised right before the split that if the BUF were to collapse, it would 'not mean the last of JOYCE … JOYCE knows what he wants in life, and is out to get it. I feel somehow, despite the fact that I dislike the man intensely, that in him there is someone who might one day make history.'[17]

The Right Club

Joyce's anti-Semitism was mirrored throughout the far right of British and European politics at the time. Though anti-Semitism may have been latent in modern British far right politics (and even British society generally), the 1930s heard these delusions vocalised as never before. Hitler's Germany contributed to this trend, and the likes of Joyce, Ramsay and others increasingly looked to it for inspiration. The British Government, in turn, increasingly became the target of the far right's bilious diatribes. One of Ramsay's political motivations was to cause such controversy over 'the Jewish question' that the Conservative Party would 'cleanse itself from Jewish control'.[18] He and others interpreted resistance to this campaign as yet more evidence of the manipulative Jewish hand he wanted to expunge. By 1939, the rhetoric reached such a pitch that the fascist movement could no longer be viewed as a potential bulwark against communist subversion; the Establishment now found itself threatened by extremists on both sides of the political spectrum. Looking to Hitler's anti-Semitic policies for guidance, Fascists had become the negative complement of the militant left.[19] And only down the road from 82 Onslow Street, Chelsea, where Joyce once taught language students (except Jews), resided Maule 'Jock' Ramsay MP. [20] He had been intimately involved with violently anti-Semitic groups like The Link and The Nordic League (on whose Council he was a leader) before founding his own extremist group, the Right Club, in May 1939.[21]

While the Right Club was meant to be a secretive organisation, Ramsay, the Conservative MP for Peebles and South Midlothian (south of Edinburgh), did not conceal his anti-Semitism. He wrote bluntly that, 'In the autumn of 1938 I was made acquainted with the fact that the power behind World Revolution was not just a vague body of Internationalists, but organised World Jewry.'[22] He held that Jews had instigated widespread social upheaval since the Middle

Ages and that the Russian Revolution and the Spanish Civil War provided but the most recent examples. These social eruptions were 'part and parcel of one and the same Plan, secretly operated and controlled by World Jewry, exactly on the lines laid down in the Protocols of the Elders of Zion'.[23] The *Protocols*, a fake text 'discovered' in the late nineteenth century, had actually been contrived by an Okhrana official. It purported to expose the Jewish plan for world domination and served for Ramsay and his ilk not only to validate their prejudices but to establish 'proof" of a Judeo-Communist conspiracy.[24] The third of the protocols, for example, states, 'We support Communism', and the tenth proclaims, 'Our Goal – World Power'.[25] Although level-headed authorities denounced the forgery shortly after it began circulating, this conspiracy theory persevered despite the abundance of evidence pointing to the text's illegitimacy.[26] Even today it continues to beguile. It is cited in Hamas's 1988 Covenant and regularly appears on Islamist websites as confirmation of the Zionist plot to control the world.[27]

Had one wanted to find others engaged in anti-Semitic ranting in 1939, the Russian Tea Rooms off of Queen's Gate Mews in fashionable South Kensington would have been a good spot to haunt. It was owned and run by Admiral Nicolai Wolkoff, the tsar's Naval Attaché in London before the Revolution. His daughter, thirty-six-year-old Anna, a naturalised Briton, frequently met acquaintances at the restaurant to discuss politics. She and Maule Ramsay, who lived nearby, became the most prominent members of a community forged in a common desire to purge the government of Jewish influence and a common admiration for Nazi Germany. It was not his anti-Semitism *per se* that brought Ramsay and the Right Club to the attention of MI5, however, but his anti-Semitism *qua* pro-Nazism. Knight noted that Ramsay 'addressed meetings of the Nordic League at which he made statements regarding his policy of anti-Semitism which were frankly pro-German in tone, and almost amounted to incitement to riot. These early reports showed that it was clearly necessary to have an agent inside the Right Club'.[28]

Knight does not appear to have approached espionage theoretically, and it is hard even to determine to what extent he planned the coordinated penetration of multiple agents into the Right Club. He later wrote that he did not believe it was possible to 'lay down any golden rules' about the recruitment of agents, insisting that 'nothing more than a few generalisations and examples can be of any practical help'.[29] One of these generalisations, seemingly informed by his work on the Right Club case, was his preference for the centralised coordination of agents. He thought it better to employ a structure in which 'all agents operating in the particular field of activity are "run" by one particular section of the office' to one in which 'agents would be run by individual section officers in the Divisions concerned, these officers being the persons who are also dealing with the research into the matter under investigation'.[30] Knight considered six agents to be the maximum an officer could handle with effectiveness, in part because the amount of time and dedication required to run an agent necessitated an officer's highly focused attention.[31]

Understanding the agents' strengths and weaknesses was key to how Knight operated. Centralised agent running afforded a synchronicity precluded by the compartmentalised approach of a decentralised system. 'While it is seldom that one agent knows personally, or knows of the identity of another agent,' Knight wrote, 'it is quite possible for the operating officer or officers to work his group of individuals as an efficient team dove-tailing their activities into the general strategic plan, and organising their tactics accordingly.'[32] Running agents on a centralised basis increased efficiency by allowing agents to be tasked with more specific targets. Their coordinated efforts generated synergy. The centralised approach suggested by Knight provided the opportunity to implement a targeting and collection strategy within and across cases, rather than confining tradecraft and agent operations to a narrow assembly of tactics.[33]

'M/Y'

Knight sent three agents into the Right Club, and all three played a role in unravelling the Kent-Wolkoff conspiracy. Yet the very important work of Marjorie Mackie, the first he used, and Helene de Munck, the second, has been unduly overshadowed by that of Joan Miller, in part because of her 1986 memoir, *One Girl's War*.[34] Although Miller's role was hardly negligible, the intelligence collected by Mackie and de Munck was pivotal to procuring the case's conclusive evidence.

Mackie, whom Miller described as 'a cosy middle-aged woman who will always remind me of Miss Marple', first became acquainted with the Ramsays in 1931 through the Christian Protest Movement, an organisation which campaigned against the persecution of Christians in the USSR.[35] Knight himself had probably met Mackie in this anti-communist context. When he contacted her in the summer of 1939 to request her services, it was not the first time he had done so: 'Miss A. had previously worked for M.I.5. in connections with other matters, and had therefore received some training' in tradecraft.[36] At the very least, she knew how to collect and pass information to Knight without compromising her clandestine position.

Under Knight's instructions Mackie contacted Ismay Ramsay, Maule's wife, and was invited to tea a few days later. The meeting consisted of an anti-Semitic, anti-Masonic tirade by Ismay Ramsay, who exaggerated her own role in describing the Right Club 'as an organisation of persons concerned to propagate her views'. All other accounts, however, point to Maule Ramsay and Wolkoff, also great egotists, as leading the organisation. Before departing that afternoon, Ismay Ramsay gave Mackie a copy of the *Protocols of the Elders of Zion* to study, and Mackie soon after joined the Right Club (August 1939).[37]

As their relationship developed over the following months, Ismay Ramsay expressed the Right Club's interest in penetrating government offices, especially the Foreign Office and Postal Censorship.[38] With this information in hand, Knight arranged for Mackie to apply to for a position in Postal Censorship. She thus became an agent working for MI5 working for the Right Club working for Postal Censorship.[39] She was, that is, a penetration agent working as a penetration agent, a double agent working as a double agent. If Postal Censorship was unaware of her special status in M. Section, she was necessarily sustaining two covers – one for the Right Club and another for Censorship, a feat demanding extraordinary psychological discipline and self-awareness. It was Knight's job to assuage her anxieties, task her next moves, and manage the intelligence she collected.

Ismay Ramsay's probing reflected her great interest in Mackie's new position at Censorship, but Knight had coached Mackie on how to answer questions she might be asked. When 'Ramsay pressed her for details as to how she had managed to get the job', a 'suitable story was given'. Knight apparently tried to stick to the truth whenever possible to minimise the chance of complications if Ramsay were to question Mackie again at a later date. The truth is easier to remember than a fabrication and so provides tighter security. It also meant that Mackie's story could be corroborated if the Right Club inquired further. On learning of Mackie's involvement with the registry, Ramsay asked if she handled the personal files. When she said she did, the matter was dropped. Just the question, though, revealed that Ismay Ramsay – and others too – were concerned that MI5 might be operating against the Right Club.[40] Indeed, it became clear over time, at first through inference and later explicitly, that Right Club members were aware that their organisation might attract the interest of the security services. This may have been a result of the group's inflated sense of importance – in the beginning it seems fair to characterise the Right Club as no more than 'Maule Ramsay, Kent, five women with eccentric views and three MI5 agents'.[41] Nonetheless, the desire of these members to have informants in government departments would justify MI5's attention.

At a subsequent meeting, Ismay Ramsay returned to the details of Mackie's work. She inquired into the specifics of Mackie's workplace: the layout of the offices, the facilities available and the precise nature of her responsibilities. She was keen to learn whether Mackie might make acquaintances in other departments, which Mackie answered should be possible via the communal canteen. The Right Club leaders were anxious to scout out new recruits, so Ramsay greeted Mackie's response positively, saying, 'Yes, I think when it comes to a show down you will have work to do.'[42]

On being introduced to Maule Ramsay several months later, Mackie faced another grilling. She reported that Maule subjected her to 'practically three hours of third degree' over her political views and her role at Censorship. Like his wife, he expressed great interest in her possible connections to other Departments, asking her quite pointedly, 'Do you know any people in M.I.5.?' She replied in the same way she had to Ismay: 'Probably by sight through seeing them in the canteen, but that is purely guess work.'[43] She did not press her position onto the Ramsays. She baited them with suggestions and allowed them to believe they were taking the initiative, while leaving herself plenty of room to manoeuvre, just as Olga Gray had done with Glading. Her suggestions were vague but sparked their interest. In this way, under Knight's control, Mackie successfully laid the set piece for the introduction of further agents.

By the time of Mackie's introduction to Maule Ramsay, she had become an integral feature of the organisation and was already close to Anna Wolkoff, to whom Ismay Ramsay had introduced her in December 1939. Wolkoff described herself to Mackie as 'Ramsay's chief agent' and considered the two of them as Ramsay's 'two aides-de-camp', insisting that they were 'the only two people who do any work for him'. In a twisted sign of affection, Wolkoff dubbed Mackie 'the little Storm Trooper'. Wolkoff even proposed that Mackie should ride in the same car as Nazi *SS* chief Heinrich Himmler 'when it came to a triumphal procession.'[44]

Wolkoff's enthusiasm for Nazi Germany was not in itself against the law, but Mackie's observations clearly put her within the camp of suspected fifth columnists, the idea of which was igniting popular and political imaginations in Britain. Defence Regulation 18B already permitted the detention of those deemed prejudicial to the safety of the realm. Knight hoped that by leaving Wolkoff in place and allowing Mackie to collect intelligence, he would gain a more comprehensive picture of the Right Club's associates and their activities.

Mackie's insider account revealed that the Right Club comprised several different 'rings', the innermost of which involved itself with more than simple

7 Anna Wolkoff, daughter of the last imperial Russian Naval attache in London, was a key member of the Right Club. The organization was part of a right-wing movement that supported Germany and opposed Britain's entry into the Second World War. She was implicated in US diplomat Tyler Kent's efforts to leak sensitive Anglo-American communications to the Axis powers.

propaganda. As Knight's other agents would soon discover, the Right Club's propaganda campaign masked a worrying interest in higher politics, 'which suggested that espionage might not be so far removed from its activities as might at first have been supposed'. Wolkoff, 'the most diligent worker in this inner circle', thus became Mackie's primary target.[45]

On 25 February 1940 Wolkoff came into the Russian Tea Rooms 'agog with information'.[46] It was at that point that Mackie learned that the Right Club maintained active correspondence with contacts in Germany through a third party in the Belgian Embassy. Jean Nieuwmanhuys (or Neumanhaus), the legation's second secretary, was receiving German-bound communiqués through either Mary Stanford, a Right Club member and regular fixture of the British far right during the period, or Wolkoff herself.[47] He then shipped the letters using the Belgian diplomatic bag to the Comte de Laubespin, an official at the Belgian Ministry for Foreign Affairs, whose wife, the Comtesse, collected them and passed them on to William Joyce.[48] Joyce had immigrated to Germany in 1939 and begun broadcasting English-language Nazi propaganda into Britain (for which he was executed after the war). Knight was still not sure what the letters contained, nor of the finer points of how the system of passing information worked, but the intelligence Mackie provided led him to suspect with greater certainty that 'Wolkoff may be working for the enemy'. Stanford's correspondence with Margaret Bothamley, who had immigrated to Germany like Joyce, enhanced those suspicions.[49] Several days later, the first of numerous HOWs was imposed on Wolkoff and her family.[50] Thenceforth the noose slipped ever tighter around Wolkoff and the Right Club.

'M/I'

By the end of February 1940, Mackie was but one of several sources building the case against Wolkoff and the Right Club's members. On the first of the month, Knight had deployed another agent who in time collected substantial intelligence on the purpose and contents of the communications sent through the Belgian legation. It undoubtedly helped that his new plant, Helene de Munck, was herself Belgian. It further helped that this twenty-six-year-old spinster was also a professed anti-Semite who had known the Wolkoffs for several years.[51] So although she did not exhibit the most estimable qualities, her views did not limit her abilities as an agent. Part of Knight's skill was his ability to engage the right person for a given job. Indeed in this case, de Munck's bigoted views probably helped rather than hindered her penetration of the Right Club, as the operation capitalised on her character, however distasteful. Of overriding importance was the success of the operation. Hence, the suitability of the agent, not the likeability of the agent, proved the most important factor in recruitment.

De Munck's motivation for working with Knight is harder to ascertain. Like Mackie, she seemed at one point – or on some level – to have agreed with the targets she was tasked to undermine. Mackie had belonged to an extreme right-wing group, and de Munck's anti-Semitism fit the Right Club ethos. Both were also independently familiar with the Club's leading members. What then motivated them to turn on these acquaintances? Surely Knight's powers of persuasion had a great deal to with their decisions, but their rationales, how they articulated their reasoning to themselves, remain unknown.

During April and May of 1940, de Munck saw Wolkoff 'constantly'. She reported that 'sometimes a day would pass without our meeting, but then I would see her several times a day'. Meetings with the Right Club were often held at the Tea Rooms. Yet, likely under Knight's instruction, she 'never joined the Group [the Right Club members] at their table ... except when they asked me to'.[52] This tactic reflected Knight's practice of coaxing the target towards the agent, rather than vice-versa.[53]

De Munck employed it to great effect on the evening of 9 April 1940 (coincidentally as Germany invaded Denmark and Norway).[54] Over dinner at the Tea Rooms with Admiral Wolkoff, de Munck offhandedly remarked that she had an acquaintance in the Romanian delegation (which was untrue). Wolkoff immediately brought Anna to the table, where she asked whether the contact was in a position to get mail to Germany. Demurely, de Munck said she believed so, because in the past he had delivered letters to 'an uncle' who lived in Romania. Anna reportedly became 'extremely excited'. 'Why didn't you tell me this before?' she exclaimed. De Munck explained that her contact was leaving for Romania within forty-eight hours, so it would be necessary to have the letters immediately if Anna wanted them sent. Wolkoff 'then produced from her bag an envelope addressed to Herr W. B. Joyce, Radfunkhaus, Berlin'. By the evening's end, Knight had in his possession this crucial piece of evidence linking Wolkoff to Joyce.[55]

Letter opening formed an important component of counter-espionage tradecraft for MI5 in the first half of the twentieth century. Copious examples of copied letters can be found in MI5's personal files. Renegade MI5 officer Peter Wright has since given a detailed description of his first visit to the Post Office Special Investigations Unit some years after the period at hand.[56] There is little to suggest that the operations he observed had fundamentally changed in the interim. In all probability, Knight sent the letter to such a letter-opening facility. After having it opened, copied and resealed, he arranged for Wolkoff's letter to be sent on to Romania. Complications arose when Wolkoff indicated she had forgotten to include something in the letter. De Munck hastily retrieved the letter from Knight and returned it to Wolkoff. On 11 April, Wolkoff arrived at de Munck's flat requesting the use of her typewriter. She typed a note in German and sketched an emblem of an eagle and a snake, which Wolkoff explained 'was the sign for all the agents of her Group'.[57] The note asked Joyce to broadcast that a certain Lord Ampthill had been present at a Freemasons' meeting in 1931, and, more generally, noted that it was important to hear more about Jews and Freemasons.[58] This was to be more fodder for her anti-Masonic, anti-Semitic campaign. She closed the letter with the Right Club standard 'P. J', or 'Perish Judah.'

Wolkoff did not know the exact contents of the other, encoded letter, but she told de Munck 'it contained facts relating to Jewish activities in England, intended for the use of William JOYCE ("Lord Haw-Haw") in his propaganda broadcasts from Germany'. Later deciphering also revealed the letter to include 'commentary on JOYCE's broadcast, together with suggested improvements, and items of political news'.[59] To de Munck, though, Wolkoff claimed that when Joyce made use of the information, 'It would be like a bombshell'.[60] Wolkoff resealed the letter and gave it to de Munck, who again passed it on to Knight. It was important that the letter arrive at its destination in order to ingratiate de Munck with Wolkoff and thereby embed her further in the group. Knight also sought to ascertain '(a) if the letter reached JOYCE, what acknowledgements would be made; and (b) to explore further the activities of these treacherous individuals'.[61] Watching and waiting would reveal more about their operational methods, future plans, and accomplices.

Following the successful delivery of the letter to Lord Haw-Haw, de Munck rose in Wolkoff's appreciation. Knight then instructed de Munck to casually introduce her family in Belgium into conversations with Wolkoff, who took the bait and began to ask more about de Munck's Belgian connections.[62] In particular, she wanted de Munck to make contact with Guy Miermans, the Right Club's 'principal agent' in Belgium, the next time she visited her family. Miermans was in possession of a Russian document Wolkoff wanted translated. She also had information and literature to pass to other contacts there. De Munck duly went to Belgium at the end of April 1940 and carried out the assignments given to her. Wolkoff was particularly keen to see de Munck do so because of creeping doubts she had regarding Nieuwmanhuys. De Munck's conversations with the Right Club contact in the Belgian Foreign Office, de Laubespin, put those fears to rest.[63]

While de Munck was in Belgium, Knight busily investigated other leads relating to the Right Club. Tyler Kent also piqued M. Section's curiosity. He had first come to MI5's attention in 1938 when he was observed dining with Ludwig

8 Tyler Kent, a disgruntled cypher clerk in the American embassy in London, was arrested and stripped of diplomatic immunity for passing secret Roosevelt-Churchill correspondence to Germany and Italy at the beginning of the Second World War.

Mathias, a naturalised Swede and suspected Gestapo agent, but the signifi-cance of this trace did not become apparent until later.[64] M. Section agents first reported Kent's entry onto the scene at the end of February 1940. By the end of

March, he had been positively identified, linked to the US Embassy in London, and observed to be close enough to Anna Wolkoff that she regularly borrowed his car.[65] Kent frequented the Russian Tea Rooms, and Wolkoff told Mackie that he was 'a most interesting man' of 'our way of thinking'. A month later he was introduced to Maule Ramsay and, according to what Ismay Ramsay told Mackie, he sometime afterwards joined the Right Club.[66]

As M. Section pursued this new avenue of inquiry, an extraordinary, and strange, incident occurred.[67] On 18 March 1940, Vernon Kell received the second of two letters from Wolkoff, who had met Kell on a previous occasion – her father, the Admiral, had numerous government contacts. Whereas the first letter had been filled with banalities, the second included text with potential security implications. It served to follow up on a warning imparted by her brother, who had supposedly learned from an acquaintance in the Ministry of Information that if Wolkoff continued her 'anti-government' activities, she would find herself 'inside' (i.e. imprisoned). If this were true, she wished to protest the charge adamantly.[68] Interested to find out who alerted her brother to possible government action against her, Kell fulfilled her request for council.

The following day, 19 March 1940, he and 'Captain King', Knight's usual alias, welcomed her into the War Office. She began with an exaggerated display of gratitude for being granting the interview, but Knight quickly sought to deflate her sizeable sense of self-importance: 'As I did not want her to think that we had been over-eager to reply to her letter I said that while Sir Vernon was perfectly willing to hear what she had to say our main interest was to discover the identity of an individual who was wrongly representing that he had sources of official information.' He reckoned this 'rather took the wind out of her sails', but he also noted that she maintained her composure and 'did not for a moment lose her grip on the situation'. Ironically, most of the interview actually consisted of Wolkoff's repeated attempts to elicit information from Knight rather than vice versa. She tried to get out of him a definitive answer as to government's stance towards her and her group's activities. Knight apparently parried her advances with success.[69]

Referring to the Right Club's campaign to use the blackouts to sneak around and paste pro-German and anti-Semitic posters where passersby would see them in daylight, Wolkoff brazenly admitted that she was 'an ardent "stickyback" performer'. Knight 'pretended to treat this as a great joke' and made the point that stickybacks were not in themselves an offence, but posting them in prohibited areas was. Rather pointedly Wolkoff asked 'if it was an offence to hold anti-Jewish views'. His riposte was that 'this was rubbish and she knew it was'. 'She could think what she liked about Mssrs. Lyons and Montagu Burton,'

Knight explained, 'but if she threw a brick through their windows she was punished for wilful damage, not for her views about Lyons and Burton.' Her demeanour then changed, and she adopted an attitude of complete understanding. Knight held, however, that he was 'quite convinced that the object of her letter and the object in her mind during the interview was to put a smoke screen up regarding the activities of herself and her associates, to endeavour to obtain information as to the intention of the authorities regarding these'.[70] With his agents in place, Knight stood a good chance of determining her true intentions.

Overall, Knight contended 'it was a real pleasure to cross swords with someone of Mrs. Wolkoff's character', noting that she was 'an extremely clever woman with a considerable amount of superficial charm'. It seems he entertained a certain respect for her. He conceded,

> If I had not been so well supplied with information about this woman's activities, she could easily have made a complete fool of me. She was plausible and cunning to a degree and exceptionally good at twisting the circumstances surrounding her real activities into something which appeared quite harmless though a trifle eccentric.[71]

But he was not deluded: 'She is also a first-class liar,' he wrote. Knight's comments reinforce the notion that a mastery of details is key to case handling. Thus the fundamental importance of MI5's Registry again comes to the fore. The basic system of indexing developed at the time of the Service's foundation formed the backbone of his agent operations.[72]

Miller

In mid-April Knight infiltrated yet a third agent into the Right Club. Mackie's intelligence especially underscored the Ramsays' desire to recruit sources within government offices. Knight decided to provide one, Joan Miller. [73] Miller is, incidentally, in large part responsible for the widely held belief that Knight was homosexual. Despite their living together for some time, she claimed their relationship was unconsummated – as, she also claimed, had been Knight's marriage to his first wife, Gladwys (née Poole), who committed suicide in 1935.

Though Miller may have harboured contempt for Knight later in her life, she nonetheless admitted to his 'charm of rare and formidable order'. She wrote that his voice was 'hypnotic' and that on meeting him she was 'captivated'. It also took her little time to observe his 'ability to instil confidence and enthusiasm in his subordinates'.[74] None of this should come as much of a surprise, though, considering his success in recruiting agents. Recruitment has been compared to a game of seduction, and Knight displayed charm in spades. So while Knight may have been heterosexual, homosexual, impotent or asexual, in the annals of intelligence history he will remain a recruitment Casanova.

Knight believed that understanding the history of agent operations was important. Miller's training included a 'step by step' review of Olga Grey's penetration of the Woolwich Arsenal spy ring so she could 'learn how a really dedicated agent worked'. Only then did she start her assignment against the Right Club. It was here that Knight executed his 'dovetail' strategy.[75] Mackie had laid the groundwork, and de Munck provided the corroboration. As trusted Right Club members, these two agents would act as independent verification of Wolkoff's thoughts on Miller, much like SIGINT corroborated progress with German agents run in the Double-Cross System.[76] Miller began frequenting the Russian Tea Rooms at various times of the day, 'sometimes bringing along an innocent friend to lend colour to the deception I was engaged in'.[77] This tactic was again part of Knight's strategy of having the body approach the agent, not the agent the body. One day Mackie noticed her. Up to this point, Mackie was apparently unaware that Miller was working for Knight. Mackie later submitted that 'on the 9th April 1940 I was in the Russian Tea Rooms ... when a girl came in for dinner, *whom I now know to be* Miss Joan MILLER'.[78] She recognised her from the canteen and joined her at her table. Later Wolkoff came to the table and Mackie introduced her. When Miller left, Mackie told Wolkoff that they worked in the same building. Several nights later, Wolkoff asked Mackie to bring Miller for dinner 'as she thought that Miss MILLER might be useful to her, if she could convert her to her way of thinking'.[79] Miller passed what she referred to as the 'vetting' and began the process of solidifying a friendship with Wolkoff. Later Miller wrote that 'it was difficult to get close to her as she was filled with mistrust, but once she'd accepted you, Anna was capable of impulsive and generous acts'.[80] The 'generous acts' undoubtedly refers to a dress Wolkoff gave her. Miller apparently never realised that the gift was a ploy, but Mackie recounted a meeting she had with Wolkoff on 23 April 1940:

> ... late that evening Anna came to see me in very high spirits. She said that the dinner had gone off very well, that 'the child' was quite unsuspecting, and that she was going to make her a present of a dress which she had shown her and which Miss MILLER had admired. She said that she had a very good reason for doing so. One of her objects in making this present, she said, was to get a letter of thanks out of Miss MILLER.[81]

Early in the investigation Knight learned that 'like many Russians' Wolkoff was highly superstitious, being interested in 'spiritualism, clairvoyance, astrology and in fact anything to do with the Occult'.[82] De Munck shared this interest, and Knight encouraged her to play up her skills in those areas as a means of getting close to Wolkoff. One afternoon de Munck invited Wolkoff to tea to teach her how to see into the future, and so part of their meeting was spent 'staring into pieces of silver in a glass of water'.[83] De Munck also claimed to possess the ability to discern character from handwriting, hence Wolkoff's desire to elicit a sample from Miller. De Munck had already gained Wolkoff's approval to some degree by producing a flattering reading of Wolkoff's own character from writing. She had first produced her own, 'extremely accurate' character sketch, but M. Section then 'suitably edited and embellished' it before it was successfully shown to Wolkoff. As Knight noted, 'Whether or not those who read this account share a belief in this ability is beside the point.' The importance of the matter lay in the ability to exploit Wolkoff's superstitions and produce actionable intelligence.[84]

Suspicious of Miller, Wolkoff had already asked de Munck to 'keep an eye' on the young woman. Now she called on de Munck again, requesting her to do a character reading based on a thank you letter she had acquired. Knight consequently informed de Munck that Miller was working for him so that she would produce an amendable reading. De Munck recorded:

> When Anna received a letter of thanks from Miss MILLER she gave it to me, and asked me to make an analysis of the character of the writer … . I reported to Anna, who thinks that I have a gift akin to second sight, that the writer of the letter should be made use of without her knowing it.[85]

Thus de Munck both ingratiated herself to Wolkoff and secured Miller's place in the group. As Knight later reflected, this set of interactions demonstrated the importance of understanding a target's character, an ability that relies not only on intuition but also on meticulous attention to detail and thorough record keeping 'on the personal characteristics, strengths and frailties of the subject'.[86] In this way, a comprehensive understanding of the target was a central part of Knight's tradecraft. It revealed the best method of exploitation and hence the most effective way to run agents.

For all these efforts, however, it remains unclear what Miller ultimately contributed to the overall operation. Judging from MI5 records, Mackie and de Munck – not Miller – were responsible for the bulk of actionable intelligence against Kent and Wolkoff. Only the knowledge of hindsight, however, would suggest that the efforts to use Miller were not of great value. At the time, it was unknown what intelligence she might be able to collect. It is also possible that Knight's purpose was to use Miller simply to strengthen the positions of Mackie and de Munck. Mackie would prove her worth to the Right Club by providing a source in MI5, and de Munck would endear herself to Wolkoff by providing another character reading. Multiple points of reference bounded Knight's uncertainties about the Right Club's intentions. In this case, and probably others, it therefore seems safe to say that as far as penetration agents go, the more the merrier (and the better informed).

Churchill–Roosevelt Correspondence

In April 1940, MI5 was beginning to view the Kent-Wolkoff relationship with increasing alarm. On the 23rd, Mackie first reported that Kent was passing Wolkoff secret information. Wolkoff told her that she had seen 'the signature of one Liddell of the Military Intelligence to a letter concerning American radio detectors and Hoovers'. What she had actually seen was correspondence not about vacuum cleaners, however, but letters between Guy Liddell, then deputy-head of MI5's B Branch and J. Edgar Hoover, Director of the FBI, discussing the purchase of Radio Direction-Finding equipment. Significantly, Wolkoff had dined with Kent the night before.[87] The coincidence implied that Kent had taken the documents and showed them to Wolkoff. Yet another report, dated a week earlier (also likely informed by Mackie, despite when it was she said she first knew that Kent and Wolkoff were in league), suggested Wolkoff was gleaning much more than simple signatures from him:

> It is confirmed by our special source that this woman [Wolkoff] is obtaining a lot of information through Tyler KENT of the American Embassy. She dined with this man at the Russian tea Rooms on Friday, April 12th. Anna WOLKOFF reports information which she says comes from him to her various associates but there is every reason to believe that whatever information he gives her is subsequently distorted in order to increase its propaganda effect. For instance, she told her cronies later in the evening of the 12th that KENT had informed her that the North Sea battles then in progress had been grossly exaggerated, that only minor skirmishes had taken place and that the propaganda from the British about this action was merely to cover the heavy naval losses we had sustained at Scapa Flow. She also disseminated a story purporting to be based on an interview which Mr. [Joseph] Kennedy, U.S. Ambassador, had recently had with Lord Halifax, in which Lord Halifax is alleged to have told Mr. Kennedy that the reason why the British navy had been

unable to stop the Germans landing in Norway was on account of dense fog. Mr. Kennedy is then alleged to have asked Lord Halifax why the fog did not impede the Germans also. On returning to the American Embassy Tyler KENT alleges (according to Anna WOLKOFF) that Mr. Kennedy said: 'How can England hope to win the war with a daft fool like that as Foreign Secretary.' Anna WOLKOFF herself obviously attaches tremendous importance to this contact.[88]

Intelligence that Kent, a bitter isolationist, was both divulging military secrets and actively trying to undermine British diplomacy with the United States made the Right Club's stickyback campaign look innocuous by comparison. While Wolkoff relished this sort of political intrigue, British security and intelligence officials did not. Following the Nazi-Soviet Pact of 23 August 1939, Britain saw itself as facing a united German-Soviet behemoth on its own. Securing good relations with the United States was of the greatest importance.

On 11 May, the day after Churchill assumed the premiership and Hitler's Panzer divisions tore through the Ardennes, Mackie reported that Wolkoff visited her in a triumphant mood and explained how she had managed to steal and copy a key and then pilfer and copy some documents. She also mentioned she had been at Kent's flat the previous evening, which suggests that Kent and Wolkoff's relationship was not completely transparent and that Wolkoff had an agenda of her own.[89] Two days later Mackie reported that Wolkoff, Enid Riddell (another Right Club member), and Kent dined with an Italian, but Mackie had not been told his name. The only clue was a passing remark: 'It is something to have a name like a tin of fruit,' Wolkoff had said.[90] At the time, this information must not have painted a clear picture. Yet considering the link to Joyce, a new mysterious Italian acquaintance, and the possibility of documents possibly stolen from the cipher clerk Kent, it must definitely have seemed like something was rotten in South Kensington.

Further inquiries filled in the blanks. The documents Wolkoff obtained were in fact messages between Churchill (then First Lord of the Admiralty) and Roosevelt regarding a trade agreement 'which was to the very great benefit of the U.S. at the expense of other neutrals'.[91] The 'tin of fruit' Italian, or 'Mr. Macaroni' as Kent knew him, was one Duca del Monte, the assistant military attaché to the Italian Embassy, and was understood to have connections with Italian intelligence.[92] Mackie learned that Wolkoff had arranged for copies of these communiqués to be given to del Monte. Wolkoff's motivation, as she explained to Mackie, was that 'one does not like to see one's country making such fantastic blunders', and added, 'Italy was charmed to receive the copies of the letters.'[93] She must have assumed the Italians would make use of the information to torpedo any kind of Anglo-American agreement, leaving Britain on its own and giving Germany the advantage.

In the interwar period, the suspicion Washington held for London – and vice versa –often revolved around economics. Roosevelt had refused to support the faltering British pound in 1933, while his administration's adoption of 'open door' policies that sought to break up autarkic trading blocs being formed by Germany and Japan also targeted Britain's protectionist imperial trade system.[94] Even after Germany's invasion of Poland laid plain the possibility of an all-out European war, factions in the US government who supported the UK during the Phoney War nonetheless maintained concern that Britain might use the circumstances to strengthen its hand in international trade. Indeed, some continued to hold this view throughout the war. Needless to say, Britain viewed American policies as an attempt to undermine its economic position and similarly suspected the United States of using neutrality as a mere economic tool at a time when Britain braced itself for yet another Continental conflict.[95]

The role of shipping, central as it is to international trade, meant that Churchill's position in the Admiralty gave him a prominent role in the debate. Churchill was, and remained, a staunch advocate of Anglo-American cooperation even as others in the Cabinet approached the relationship with caution. Consequently, during his time as First Lord he was eager to foster an understanding with Roosevelt, who in turn also saw the value of an ally in the Admiralty. Their amicable intentions were evident in their exchanges.[96]

The correspondence seen by Kent revealed that the US administration was not quite as neutral as it hoped that many, especially some in the US electorate, preferred to believe. Kent believed Roosevelt was misleading the public and felt duty-bound to expose the transgression. In fact, from September 1939 to May 1940 (from the first message until Churchill became Prime Minister) the notes only numbered thirteen in total (nine by Churchill and four by Roosevelt).[97] Although the communication was not extensive, it was potentially explosive.

At least two critical issues were under discussion, information about both of which would have been available to Kent, and therefore Wolkoff, the Italians and the Germans. The most urgent was the trade agreement that Wolkoff had referred to in conversation with Mackie. She most likely meant discussions surrounding the British navicert policy, a regulation developed during the First World War and resurrected in December 1939 to offer the equivalent of a commercial passport for neutral vessels delivering cargo through the British blockade.[98] The Roosevelt Administration and many American businessmen believed that the navicert policy unfairly targeted American ships. The matter came to a head in early January 1940, when the Royal Navy seized an American ship, the *Mooremascun,* and refused to release it or its cargo without proper documentation. The incident was eventually resolved after Churchill's intervention, and he informed Roosevelt that he had given 'orders last night that no American ship should in any circumstances be diverted into the combat zone around the British Isles declared by you. I trust this will be satisfactory.' The following day Churchill sent another message requesting the President's discretion regarding their agreement to avoid other neutrals' quite legitimate charges of discrimination.[99] Roosevelt responded a few days later with sympathy and an explanation of political realities in the United States:

> I think our conversation in regard to search and detention of American ships is working out satisfactorily – but I would not be frank unless I told you that there has been much public criticism here. The general feeling is that the net benefit to your people and to France is hardly worth the definite annoyance caused to us. That is always found to be so in a nation which is 3,000 miles away from the fact of war. I wish so much that I could talk things over with you in person – but I am grateful to you for keeping me in touch as you do.[100]

On the one hand, Roosevelt's pointing out that some Americans found British policy annoying must have grated; Britain believed it was executing a perfectly legal exercise as part of its war strategy. On the other hand, Roosevelt clearly acknowledged Britain's frustration with America's disconnect from European reality, ensconced as it was across the Atlantic. For Kent, the correspondence's candour and understanding implied a sort of unholy collusion that, he believed, presaged America's eventual involvement in a European war. By exposing this relationship, Kent hoped to mobilise isolationist Americans against Roosevelt and sabotage the president's chance for re-election in November 1940, thus preventing a future Anglo-American wartime alliance.

As far back as October 1939, Kent would have also seen correspondence relating to a second issue, the American Neutrality Zone. It was in fact this correspondence that first alerted Kent to the Churchill–Roosevelt connection.[101] In concert with other American nations not members of the British Commonwealth, the United States delineated a 300-mile radius around the continent and issued a declaration barring entry to belligerent vessels.[102] It claimed responsibility for patrolling these waters. Privately to the British, Roosevelt argued that the United States, by assuming responsibility for the security of the Americas, would free British ships for operations elsewhere. In exchange, however, he requested base rights in the British territories of Trinidad, Saint Lucia and Bermuda.[103] Although Washington implied it would provide the British with intelligence on German ship movements, British shipping had already begun to suffer attacks by German warships, and Churchill was understandably anxious about the vigilance with which the US authorities would conduct its policing. 'We do not mind how far south the prohibited zone goes,' one of his cables announced, 'provided that it is effectively maintained. We shall have great difficulty in accepting a zone which was only policed by some weak neutral. But of course if the American Navy takes care of it, that is all right.'[104] Yet he also insisted that should America fail in its duty to monitor German ships, Britain would be forced to enter the zone in order to do so.

Churchill even offered to provide naval technology to aid the American effort: 'We should be quite ready to tell you about our ASDIC [Anti-Submarine Detection Investigation Committee] methods whenever you feel they would be of use to the United States Navy and are sure the secret will go no further.'[105] ASDIC, whose name was given to the British underwater detection system it developed, was at that time more sophisticated than the Americans' Sound Navigation and Ranging (SONAR). Although the Royal Navy was not convinced of the American ability to keep the technology secret, the mere idea that Churchill raised the suggestion spoke to the extent to which the British and Americans were cooperating. But had word of the offer reached the public, the US claim to neutrality might have been jeopardised, hampering Roosevelt's attempts to aid the British. Its exposure might also, therefore, have precluded later agreements, such as the important Destroyers-for-Bases deal in September 1940, which stemmed from the Neutrality Zone discussions.

The fear was that the American public's becoming aware of the extent of Roosevelt's cooperation might have damaged the president's re-election bid in the autumn of 1940. Moreover, by creating a breach in the burgeoning Anglo-American relationship, it could also have seriously cobbled the British war effort. The information contained in the correspondence, Knight later summarised, would have been 'of the greatest value to the enemy' and 'might do incalculable harm to the Allies, were it conveyed to Germany.'[106]

Yet there was every reason to think that it might already have been revealed to both Germany and Italy.[107] In April, Wolkoff had boasted to friends that 'information which she obtained from KENT had been successfully communicated by her to the Italian Government' – communicated, that is, with the help of MI5. That MI5 had managed to intercept this communication did not defeat Wolkoff's purpose. The letter given to Mackie had been ready for sending, indicating that it would have been sent by other means had the opportunity arisen.

And it clearly had gone through, since Joyce had confirmed in April the receipt of her message over the airwaves by inserting the word 'Carlyle' into one of his broadcasts.[108] British SIGINT also intercepted messages from Rome to Berlin containing 'practically everything from Ambassador Kennedy's despatches to President Roosevelt, including reports of his interviews with British statesmen and officials.'[109] Knight wrote that 'it became obvious that in Tyler KENT, Anna had a source of information which she was using to the detriment of this country', and that in light of her correspondence with Joyce, 'there was ... abundant evidence that Anna WOLKOFF was indeed to be classed as an enemy agent.'[110] Once again, Knight's tradecraft had permitted an intelligence coup in this discovery of a major security breach.

Denouement – Kent's Arrest

Despite his diplomatic status, Kent soon learned his position was no less tenuous than that of Wolkoff and other suspected fifth columnists. As arranged by Liddell, on Saturday 18 May 1940, Knight called on Herschel Johnson, a veteran diplomat at the US Embassy, to lay out the case against Kent. After the briefing, Knight observed that Johnson was 'profoundly shocked'. The information gleaned from Wolkoff, said to have originated with Kent, had 'more than a substantial basis of truth', Johnson informed him. He urged Knight to take action against Wolkoff, but Knight hoped to coordinate any action against her with that which would be taken against Kent. Johnson 'promised the fullest co-operation', and told Knight he would get back to him shortly.[111] After the meeting, Knight submitted the paperwork for Wolkoff's detention under Regulation 18B of the Emergency Powers (Defence) Act, which was signed the following day by the Home Secretary, Sir John Anderson.[112] Knight then telephoned Johnson to brief him on plans to apprehend Wolkoff the next day. Johnson said that the Americans 'would take as strong action as possible regarding Tyler KENT', and that the suspension of his diplomatic immunity was under serious consideration.[113]

On the morning of Monday 20 May 1940, Ambassador Kennedy received notification of an extraordinary decision from Washington: 'Upon receipt of your telegram Tyler Kent is dismissed from government service as of this date. Please so inform him. You are therefore authorized to waive immunity for Kent.'[114] That morning, Knight, accompanied by US Embassy official Franklin Gowan and three officers from Scotland Yard, surprised Kent at his flat. They also surprised the woman in his bedroom, Irene Danischewsky, the Russian émigré wife of a shipping magnate who had been the subject of MI5 investigations for suspected ties to Soviet intelligence.[115] Kent was instructed to dress and go with the officials to the US Embassy.

Inside his flat, the officers found 'an amazing collection of documents'. In a summary report submitted to Sir Robert Vansittart (former Permanent Under-Secretary and then chief diplomatic adviser to the government), Knight described 'copies of secret and confidential code telegrams between various United States Embassies and Washington, together with memoranda obviously made by Kent himself, which even on casual examination were clearly of the very highest importance, not only to the United States Government but to the Allies'.[116] Although the Churchill–Roosevelt correspondence he had gathered was indicative of the type of information Kent had access to, it was not the extent of his thefts. Even before a full inventory of the documents could be compiled, Knight wrote that 'It is quite clear that some of the information relating to the military position of the Allies was so vital that in the event of its being passed on to Germany, the most disastrous consequences would ensue.'[117] In all, 1,500–2,000 pages of documents were recovered, including evidence that documents had been photographed.[118] They also found correspondence with officials in Berlin in which Kent requested a transfer to the German Embassy and a mysterious red leather-bound book later revealed to be the Right Club's membership list of roughly 235 men and women, including Peers, MPs and business leaders.[119]

At the US Embassy, Knight met Kent in person for the first time and found him arrogant and pretentious. The son of a diplomat, Kent had a skill for languages but had never made the cut as a foreign service officer, instead taking a position as clerk. This inferior position likely inflamed his considerable self-esteem.[120] Even casual observers picked up on his haughtiness. The legendary journalist (and wartime SIS officer) Malcolm Muggeridge caustically depicted Kent as 'one of those intensely gentlemanly Americans who wear well-cut tailor-made suits, with waistcoat and watch-chain, drink wine instead of highballs, and easily become furiously indignant. They always strike me as being somehow a little mad.'[121]

Knight interrogated Kent in the presence of Kennedy.[122] He tried to overwhelm him with the amount of information he already knew about his activities – what later interrogators came to call the 'all-seeing eye' approach.[123] Knight told Kent that he could prove he had been associating with Wolkoff, who, he could also prove, was in communication with Germany, entertained 'hostile associations', and was involved in pro-German propaganda. Kent himself had just been found in possession of classified documents in breach of the US security code. Knight intoned: 'You would be a very silly man if you did not realise that certain conclusions might be drawn from that situation, and it is for you to offer the explanation, not us.' Yet Kent gave no quarter.

Knight continued, pressing Kent to reveal the contents of the locked, red ledger found in Kent's room (the membership list). Kent pleaded ignorance, maintaining he was simply holding it for Ramsay. 'Don't you think it strange that a member of Parliament should come to you, a minor official in an Embassy and give you a locked book to take care of for him?' prodded Knight. Kent again replied blandly, 'I don't know', to which Knight retorted, 'You are adopting a sort of naïve attitude which doesn't deceive me for a moment. You are either hiding something or … ', Knight began to say, but Kent interrupted, 'Well, the fact remains that I don't know what is in that thing and I havn't [sic] seen it open. He simply requested that I keep it for him.'

Kent continued to obfuscate throughout the questioning, barely even conceding knowledge of the Right Club or his acquaintance with Wolkoff and Ramsay or admitting his association with suspected Gestapo agent Ludwig Matthias. After some rounds of questioning, Knight said, 'I am going to speak now extremely bluntly. I am afraid I must take the view that you are either a fool or a rogue because you cannot possibly be in a position except that of a man who has either been made use of who knows all of these people.' But the appeal to reason and circumstantial evidence failed to elicit information. Kent's smugness was impenetrable.

Knight's mounting frustration with Kent's flippancy is palpable even in the typed words of the transcript. 'It is not for me to discuss the question of your position with regard to these documents belonging to your Government, because that is not my affair at all. But your explanation about this appears to me to be extremely unconvincing; and your explanations of every point raised are unconvincing,' Knight said. Kent continued to prevaricate: 'Well give them to me again and I will try to be a little bit more clear. You mean the fact that I had the documents at all?' Kent had asserted that the documents in his possession were for his personal interest only. He even had the audacity to profess his ignorance regarding the illegality of possessing the confidential documents. Of his collection of official papers, he said, 'I think in the future it would have been very interesting.' With practically audible exasperation Knight replied, 'You know you are in an extremely ------ If you were English you would be in a very difficult position. You don't impress me by your cocky manner.' Indeed, Kent seemed to be taking things light-heartedly. He later claimed he was unaware of the severity of his situation.[124]

His position might have begun to dawn on him when Kennedy asked Knight, 'If you prove that she [Wolkoff] is in contact with them [the Germans, presumably] she is more or less a spy. If the United States Government decides to waive any rights they may have, do I understand that that might very well make Kent part and parcel of that.' Knight replied, 'Subject to the production of evidence under the law, yes.' Knight's impatience likely stemmed in part from the certainty of his case, but realising that Kent would not budge, he decided to end the interrogation: 'I think honestly that at this state nothing very useful is to be got by carrying on this conversation.'[125]

Knight questioned Kent again a week later. Part of an interrogation's purpose is to compare a subject's statements with other known facts, or to return to the suspect at a later date to check for discrepancies in his testimony over time. In this case Kent's initial statement was proved false by other subsequent investigations. He had said that the photo negatives found in his room came from one Hyman Goldschmit, a former employee at the embassy from whom Kent claimed to borrow a camera to take pictures. Actually, Wolkoff had hired a certain Nikolai Smirnoff to take the pictures, though the latter was apparently oblivious to the conspiracy he had joined. During this second round of interrogation, Knight initially encountered the same obstinacy from Kent:

> His general attitude throughout the interview was one of apprehension, defiance and muddled thinking, but during the two hours questioning, in which time the utmost patience was exercised on our part, he refused to give us the name of the individual concerned. I pointed out to him several times that whatever it was finally decided to do with him, his position was extremely serious.[126]

Kent, too, had begun to understand this. Knight reminded him that if deported back to the United States he would have to face the FBI, which, he suggested, 'would in all probability not display the same patience' as MI5. 'He did not like this,' Knight wrote. Knight must have known that with diplomatic immunity waived, Kent was likely to be tried in the UK and not deported. No matter though, his ruse was successful. Kent informed him he would like some time 'to think it over.'[127]

In their next session Knight noted that Kent's 'manner was much more respectful.' Apparently the idea of an FBI investigation had frightened him and elicited some cooperation. In his report on the interrogation, Knight wrote that Kent 'informed me that he had been thinking matters over and he wished to re-consider his position and explain exactly how he came to be mixed up in what he described as "all this"'. Knight said he was more than willing to listen. It was in this way that Knight later extracted a formal statement from Kent, who quickly and fully implicated Wolkoff. He claimed to have lent her the documents but was ignorant of her intentions to photograph them. He also described his dinner meeting with Wolkoff, Enid Riddell, and the man he knew as 'Mr. Macaroni'. It was clear that any loyalty Kent might have had for Wolkoff had evaporated.[128] Kent had revealed that even a cowardly opportunist could be in a position to do great harm to Britain and the United States.

The American response to the Kent-Wolkoff affair was unequivocal. 'Nothing like this has ever happened in American history', Assistant Secretary of State Breckinridge Long claimed.[129] That is, nothing he knew about or admitted to. Throughout the interwar period itself, the Soviets spied in the United States, though not as comprehensively as they did in Britain.[130] On reading the sixty-seven-page list of compromised documents, Long recorded in his diary:

> They are a complete history of our diplomatic correspondence since 1938. It is appalling. Hundreds of copies – true readings – of dispatches, cables, messages. Some months every single message going into and out from the London Embassy were copied and the copies found in this room. It means not only that our codes are cracked … but that our every diplomatic manoeuvre was exposed to Germany and Russia … It is a terrible blow – almost a major catastrophe.[131]

If Long's words emphatically expressed the strategic consequences of Kent's activities, Kent's erstwhile boss in Moscow, Ambassador William Bullitt, expressed his dismay in more personal terms. He condemned Kent, claiming that he was a 'rotter and always had been'. He told one official, 'The sooner you shoot him the better'. He believed that the 'effect in America would be excellent' and that it would serve as a lesson for other contemplating similar action, repeatedly telling the official, 'I hope you will shoot him, and shoot him soon: I mean it.'[132]

Kent was not shot. Nor was he made a public example, as he was tried *in camera* amid substantial secrecy. Of the few accounts of the trial to appear in the press in October, one headline read, 'Even Police Barred at Old Bailey'.[133] The US State Department permitted some of the correspondence to be submitted as evidence, but rejected its release long after the trial due to the politically sensitive nature of its contents. As Long said, they might 'implicate the Chief [FDR]', and that was unacceptable while so many in the United States remained opposed to helping Britain or doing anything that might lead the nation closer to war.[134] Thus the Kent case sat in relative obscurity while Kent himself served time in Britain during the war. His doings gained some notoriety towards the end of the war, however, and after he was deported back to the US in 1945, where the political climate had changed enormously.[135]

The Kent-Wolkoff affair also prompted the expansion of existing domestic security regulations in the UK. For those in the Cabinet seeking more rigorous application of the Defence Regulations, the Kent-Wolkoff case provided the justification. Here was proof that the German fifth column was a clear, present and powerful threat to British security. The Kent-Wolkoff case acted as the catalyst for the implementation of Defence Regulation 18B(1A), which sanctioned the internment of those with connections to subversive organisations and came into force only two days after Kent and Wolkoff were taken into custody.[136] Guy Liddell wrote in his diary that 'It seems that the P.M. takes a strong view about the internment of all 5th columnists at this moment and that he has left the Home Secretary in no doubt about his views. What seems to have moved him more than anything was the Tyler KENT case.'[137] Thus began the mass internment of suspected subversives in Britain, one of the most controversial and drastic security measures in modern British history. Among the first to be interned were Maule Ramsay and Oswald Mosley, followed in quick succession by the leadership of most of Britain's fascist and anti-Semitic groups.[138]

Had the information obtained by Kent been exposed to the American public, and had information on Anglo-American cooperation been exploited by the Axis powers, the course of the Second World War might possibly have been different. We cannot know, but that is exactly the point: when intelligence is successful, it is preventive. MI5 recognised a potential threat to security and sought to neutralise it before it occurred. Yet the full seriousness of the threat posed by the Kent-Wolkoff conspiracy was only revealed by the successful penetration of the Right Club by M. Section agents.

Infiltrating the Right Club was difficult and complicated. Maxwell Knight had needed to recruit suitable agents, handle them throughout the operation, and coordinate their activities based on the intelligence they collected. Through a dovetail strategy, he used them to verify information and embed still others into the group. He exploited their particular abilities brilliantly, using Helene de Munck's penchant for the occult, for example, against Anna Wolkoff's superstitions. De Munck was also able to employ her claimed skill of character reading to convince Wolkoff to use Joan Miller. Similarly, Knight deployed Miller as a way to prove Mackie's usefulness to the Right Club when it was learned that they were anxious to recruit sources in the government. Like a puppet-master, Knight deftly manoeuvred his agents to the unsuspecting and misplaced delight of his target audience.

He also understood the value of good officers, that an agent-runner 'shall be, or shall learn to be a man of wide understanding of human nature; one who can get on with and understand all types and classes.'[139] Agent handling is bound to have a certain immutability because it is rooted in human relationships. Knight manipulated those brilliantly. Good tradecraft was also integral to the dexterous handling of the Soviet defector Walter Krivitsky, to whose case we now turn.

CHAPTER 6

Defection and Debriefing (I)

Walter Krivitsky

A FTER Soviet intelligence officer Walter Krivitsky defected to the West in 1937, he offered his receivers tremendous amounts of information and great insight into one of modern Europe's most closed societies, one whose clandestine activities often left rivals ignorant and weak in the face of its subversive onslaught. Krivitsky's debriefing in London, conducted over the course of four weeks in January and February 1940, occupies a singular place in the annals of MI5. The debriefing was the first of its kind, the earliest attempt at what would later become a standard practice in handling defecting or active enemy agents. It was MI5's first experience interrogating a former Soviet intelligence officer, its first opportunity to directly question a former illegal about the machinery and tradecraft of Soviet intelligence. The novelty of Krivitsky's debriefing does not alone, however, account for its prominence in MI5's history. The seamless nature of the debriefing's planning and execution, the expertise and diligence of the officers who conducted it, and the quality and quantity of the information it produced have led some MI5 insiders to regard this case as the moment when MI5 came of age.[1]

A comparison of Krivitsky's experiences in Britain and the United States, to which he had emigrated in 1938, contrasts the differences in security intelligence between the two nations, dramatically highlighting MI5's relative sophistication at the time.[2] Even given that his arrival in America occurred under very different circumstances than his arrival in Britain, disorganisation and a degree of incompetence or inexperience, at least as regards this case, are likely explanations for Krivitsky's encountering a hostile US immigration service, parochial government officials and small-minded bureaucrats. His potential value as a high-ranking former intelligence operative was lost on the FBI until after his death. Krivitsky's experience in America also revealed a nascent conflict between law-enforcement and intelligence gathering in the United States.[3]

Although Britain's intelligence services are by no means strangers to power struggles, MI5 and SIS both grasped the importance of Krivitsky's defection and worked closely to ensure he was brought to London for the extensive and landmark debriefing, an event recognised as ground-breaking even at the time. Unlike the American FBI, both MI5 and SIS benefited from the presence of counter-intelligence officials who were knowledgeable about the Soviet Union and its intelligence services. Officers such as MI5's Jane Archer understood the Soviet threat as an international rather than simply local phenomenon and were thus able to exploit Krivitsky's knowledge in terms of strategic intelligence rather than just domestic criminal activity or something to be treated merely as an accessory to institutional prestige.

Krivitsky's case argues for an understanding of debriefing as a process involving much more than discrete question and answer sessions, just as agent-handling extends beyond the technical transmission of information (which is, however, still of vital importance) to a more developed understanding of officer-agent psychology.[4] MI5's handling of Krivitsky showed that the skills required in a debriefing shared much with the tradecraft of running agents. In their handling of this defector, British intelligence officers anticipated the conclusion of a later CIA study, which found, 'The defector, to be sure, is not truly a clandestine source. . . . Nevertheless it is usually desirable to employ clandestine tradecraft in the reception, exploitation, and protection of a defector.'[5] Another CIA veteran later wrote, 'Interrogation is quintessentially a manipulative enterprise, as is agent handling.'[6]

There are also important differences between debriefing and agent running, not least of which is the operating environment.[7] On the one hand, debriefing a defector does not entail the hazards accompanying a rendezvous with an agent. On the other, there is another class of hazards inherent in the mind of the source. Just as great cleverness is required to overcome physical barriers to operations, so tremendous wit must be summoned and trained upon psychological barriers in order to elicit useful information – actionable intelligence – in the debriefing.

The defector entering a debriefing, like the agent meeting his handler, has on some level agreed to the principle of sharing information, but what the defector knows does not pass to the debriefer by osmosis. There is plenty of scope for unintentional confusion, unintentionally withheld information, resistance and ambiguity. The defector might know something of importance but not recognise the knowledge or consider it important (i.e. the 'unknown knowns' of Rumsfeldian epistemology).[8] Astute psychological insight is required to overcome resistance and allow for competing ideas of importance to play out. The debriefer had to assess the reliability of the defector and the veracity of all proffered information.[9] Like other forms of human intelligence, a debriefing deals in the realm of human interaction, and necessarily involves the judgement of character, the apprehension of motivations and expectations, and the ability to navigate prevarications.

While evidence of this psychological insight is lacking in US documents on Krivitsky, much of it is in evidence in MI5's records. The whole notion of defection was a relatively new phenomenon, and the newly budding field of British psychology provided little direction in general and no analyses at all of the psychology of defectors.[10] But as Krivitsky's arrival in Britain was expected (unlike his appearance in the US), MI5 and SIS were able to coordinate sufficiently to ensure his visit went as smoothly as possible. In anticipation of the questioning, they wrote preliminary, informal character assessments of a kind that has evolved and become standard operating procedure not only for defectors, but for agents and foreign leaders as well.[11] Working in 1940, MI5 and SIS sailed into uncharted territory, providing the compass by which later debriefings would be steered.

British intelligence officers aimed to impress Krivitsky with their knowledge, competence and discretion. Their motivation was not simply pride; they understood that Krivitsky was a professional, and they hoped to gain his respect and cooperation by showing their own professionalism. They went to considerable lengths to take care of Krivitsky's needs, from living and customs arrangements for his family in Canada while US immigration issues were being resolved to providing entertainment while he was in London – all in the hope he would reciprocate with cooperation and openness.[12] Overseeing Krivitsky's travel and accommodations even in the midst of a desperate wartime struggle for survival also enabled intelligence officials to control his environment, yet again anticipating a Cold War truism that 'the better the control the better the outlook for success' in counter-intelligence interrogations.[13] The elimination of outside interference permitted officers to concentrate on their relationship with Krivitsky, establishing rapport and decreasing his resistance to unlocking his encyclopaedic knowledge about Soviet intelligence operations in Britain and elsewhere.

The spectrum of information provided by Krivitsky was comprehensive and somewhat daunting, including details about passport forgeries, secret inks, training at the Lenin School, penetration and decomposition in the army, White Russian activity and subversion in the British Empire. At the end of the four weeks, the debriefing had yielded the identities (and often aliases) of over seventy Soviet covert officers or agents operating abroad, most of whom were previously unknown to MI5.[14]

In retrospect, the most important and controversial information he provided were the identities of Soviet illegals Arnold Deutsch and Teodor Maly.

Neither Deutsch nor Maly was operating abroad at the time of Krivitsky's defection (Deutsch had been recalled to Moscow and Maly had been liquidated), but Krivitsky nonetheless provided some of the earliest and most valuable clues about the existence of the Cambridge Five spy ring and methods of Soviet intelligence.[15]

Krivitsky in America

Krivitsky and his family arrived in New York aboard the transatlantic liner *Normandie* on 10 November 1938.[16] At Ellis Island, the US immigration clearing point, he presented papers giving his real name, Samuel Ginsburg, and the visitor's visa he had been issued in France showing that he was in America to do private research on the history of the Soviet Union. Officials neither expected nor welcomed his arrival. Krivitsky avoided any mention of his experience in intelligence but did concede to immigration officials that he was a former high-ranking officer in the Red Army. When asked whether he was a deserter from the Red Army, he replied, 'I consider myself a deserter because I broke up with the government and the party.'[17] It was not this, however, that caught officials' attention. Rather it was the inadequacy of his funds relative to his proposal to travel to Stanford University to conduct research. The immigration officials duly rejected the Ginsburg family's entry. It could be argued that immigration had fulfilled its preventative security function, but it was preventative security wholly lacking an intelligence dimension, one the British had cultivated since the First World War.[18] Krivitsky appealed to authorities to check with the French government, in order to validate his identity, but to no avail. Eventually he was released on bail secured through his erstwhile secret agent and future writing collaborator Paul Wohl (who had recently established himself in the United States), and with that, one of the Soviet Union's most experienced and high-placed spies took up residence in New York.

Once the US government became aware of his former position in Soviet intelligence, largely through articles Krivitsky published in a weekly newspaper, the security agencies were still unable to coordinate effectively to exploit his information regarding US security. Ironically, it was Krivitsky himself, likely hoping to extend his expiring visa, who contacted the State Department to offer information on Soviet intelligence. Loy Henderson, an old Russia hand and head of State's Russia desk (and an acquaintance of Tyler Kent), noted in a memorandum that he and Krivitsky 'discussed at length certain aspects of Soviet developments with which he was particularly familiar'. If the FBI case files are any indication, a discussion at length did not mean a discussion in depth, even if intentions were good, as were Henderson's. Krivitsky returned to Henderson two months later to express concerns for his safety, after being confronted by a former OGPU colleague. On that occasion, the most Henderson reported was that 'he asked [Krivitsky] several questions' about the organisation of Soviet military intelligence in the US, which revealed to him that it operated along two lines, legal and illegal residencies. The fact that the Soviets operated illegally in other nations ought not to have come as a surprise. MI5 had tracked the Soviets' use of legal entities as fronts for operations and the use of illegal agents for well over a decade.[19]

Krivitsky's information shed considerable light on the darkness that then represented the US understanding of Soviet intelligence, and understanding the structure of Soviet intelligence was surely of vital import to US officials. Yet little was done to learn from his knowledge. Only three short documents in the FBI's over 500-page file on Krivitsky involve Henderson's conversations with him. The only other record of the discussion is a memorandum from the State Department on Krivitsky's knowledge about passport fraud.[20]

The OGPU's pursuit of Krivitsky likely intensified after he began to publish biographical articles in the popular press. Though Krivitsky told Henderson on his first visit that he intended to live quietly in the United States, only a few months later he began to gain notoriety for his condemnation of Stalin in articles such as 'Why Stalin Shot His Generals'. In that piece, he revealed a secret pact between Stalin and Hitler, which Krivitsky claimed Stalin negotiated just as he purged the Red Army of its high command.[21] His articles caused controversy and provoked the ire of the American left, which met the notion of a Nazi-Soviet pact with derision. MI5, meanwhile, patiently collected these articles, forwarded by Canadian counterparts.[22]

It is likely that the dearth of US government documents on Krivitsky collected during his lifetime reflects the degree of importance (or lack thereof) the government placed on his defection when he showed up on American shores more than it reflects on the Americans' less organised intelligence bureaucracy.[23] All matters with an international dimension had been the responsibility of the State Department. In 1936, however, Secretary of State Cordell Hull ceded responsibility for surveillance of communists and fascists to Hoover, bluntly urging him to 'go ahead and investigate the hell out of those cocksuckers'.[24]

Contrary to the FBI's official mandate, these investigations were not aimed at arrests and prosecutions, as no crimes had yet been committed, but were reconnaissance intended to inform foreign policy. True to fashion, Hoover continued to expand his jurisdiction until he was granted central authority over counter-espionage and subversion, a purview he finally cemented by a presidential order on 1 September 1939, the same day Germany invaded Poland. He had not, however, shifted his ways of thinking from those of law enforcement to those of security intelligence. Instead, in the interim between 1936 and 1939, Hoover tended to use his new found powers to blackmail and stymie political opponents at least as much as to investigate unions and domestic socialists, fascists and others he considered subversives.[25] On the eve of what many in the United States saw as the 'European Civil War', Krivitsky found himself in the midst of a US civil servants' war.

The failure to probe Krivitsky was the result of Washington's notorious turf battles, with the subsidiary reason that the FBI was imbued with an ethos geared to criminal investigation rather than intelligence-gathering.[26] The FBI's uncomfortable (and many would say incompatible) roles as both national police force and intelligence agency lay at the heart of the problem. The FBI garnered prestige with high-profile arrests and headline-grabbing cases. As Krivitsky had committed no crime, there was little motivation to investigate him.[27] But one purpose of intelligence is to prevent headline-grabbing events from occurring in the first place. The event itself is approached from opposite ends: intelligence operatives chase leads that *may* result in an event; law enforcement tracks evidence to an event that already occurred. These responsibilities lead to fundamentally different mentalities: one deals in an uncertain future, the other in a certain past.[28] Thus when the FBI arrested the Soviet resident Gayk Ovakimyan in 1941, it appears they treated it no differently than they would have an isolated criminal case.[29] Unlike MI5's officers in dealing with Krivitsky, they did not appear to understand the case in terms of larger Soviet intelligence strategy.

When Hoover read Krivitsky's articles on Soviet intelligence activity in the United States, he likely saw it not as an opportunity to gather information, but as a public indictment of FBI failures and, more important, as potential fodder for his political opponents. Only several months before, a tip-off from MI5 had led to one of the largest spy round-ups of the American interwar period. However, fourteen of the eighteen spies arrested in Guenther Gustave Rumerich's German 'Crown' network escaped without prosecution during the ensuing interagency bickering over the case. The presiding judge invoked Hoover's wrath by blaming the FBI.[30] Thus Krivitsky's assertion that the OGPU operated with impunity on US territory further undermined Hoover's push to consolidate control of US security intelligence and law enforcement in his hands.

Yet the FBI left the Krivitsky case primarily in the State Department's hands, as indicated by the fact that the FBI investigators appear to have interviewed

Krivitsky only twice before his death. When they did, it was only about the specific case of Moishe Stern (alias Emil Kléber), whom Krivitsky believed to have been liquidated.[31] The FBI Special Agent questioning him disagreed, noting that Krivitsky's statements contradicted 'facts previously developed in this investigation'. From this one meeting, it was also concluded that Krivitsky 'accepts his own conclusions as facts and so relates them and that in reply to a question he would state his opinion as fact, rather than admit a lack of definite knowledge'.[32] The Special Agent was clearly unprepared for this debriefing. There is no indication that any attempt was made to mine other fields of information. Nor, if the documents accurately reflect the atmosphere of the interrogation, were great strides made to generate rapport, a prerequisite of successful elicitation.[33]

Later, in a letter to the US Attorney General during inquiries into the circumstances of Krivitsky's death in 1941, Hoover wrote, 'Krivitsky has never furnished any information of value to this bureau'.[34] This might not have been the case if the State Department and FBI had coordinated more effectively and made a concerted, methodical effort to debrief Krivitsky. Isaac Don Levine, who ghost-wrote Krivitsky's publications, had, for example, been contacted in summer 1939 by Whittaker Chambers, a Soviet courier for an American spy ring, who (partially inspired by Krivitsky's book) was anxious to escape from Soviet intrigue. He had long conversations with Krivitsky, the two of them piecing together Krivitsky's knowledge of the handlers he knew, and Chambers the operatives he dealt with in the United States. The information would have been invaluable to US counter-intelligence – had there existed any substantive notion of counter-intelligence in America. Levine attempted to connect Chambers with the President, but instead Chambers met Adolf Berle at the State Department. At Berle's home on 2 September 1939, Chambers named over twenty US government officials working for the Soviets, including State Department officials Alger and Donald Hiss. Inexplicably, Berle failed to notify the proper security authorities, either at the FBI or State itself, and FDR appears to have disregarded Berle's subsequent memorandum on the subject altogether.[35] Consequently nothing immediately came of Chambers's revelations, just as nothing came of Krivitsky's. No action was taken against any of the information Chambers provided until well after Second World War ended, and thus for the entirety of the war the Roosevelt administration played host to a bevy of Soviet spies.[36]

The public announcement of the Nazi-Soviet Pact on 23 August 1939 dispelled many of the suspicions held about Krivitsky and confirmed him overnight as a nationally recognised expert on Soviet affairs. A symbol of his vindication was his invitation to speak at a forum on instability in Europe, held at the elegant Waldorf Astoria Hotel in New York and opened by none other than President Roosevelt and the First Lady. There, Krivitsky appeared alongside such influential figures as philosopher Sidney Hook, British ambassador Lord Lothian and Hoover.[37] It also brought more official recognition in the form of a subpoena to appear before the House Committee on Un-American Activities, known also by its acronym, HUAC and also as the Dies Committee, after its chair, the Democratic congressman Martin Dies of Texas.

The transcripts of the Dies Committee hearing are remarkable for two reasons: the Committee's elementary line of questioning and its unbelievable naïveté. One of the Committee's counsellors, Rhea Whitley, asked Krivitsky a volley of questions such as 'Are [the Soviet secret police's] operations outside of the territory of the Soviet Union very extensive? Does it operate in many countries?'[38] Whitley's questions may have been simple for the sake of putting the facts on record, but the transcripts' consistent confusion of 'Chekov' for 'Cheka' does not argue strongly for the Committee members' expertise.[39] The same might be said of others in the government. After his testimony, one congressman railed against Krivitsky for 'posing as a patriot', and a senator who rejected Krivitsky as 'nothing but a phoney' called for his immediate deportation.[40] Though appearing before the Committee might have bolstered Krivitsky's authority, Dies's authority was simultaneously being eroded. Hoover believed Dies to be angling for his position as director of the FBI and so directed a smear campaign against him, spreading 'derogatory information' to the President down to contacts in newspapers.[41] In any event, Krivitsky came away from the hearing dismayed. He later told acquaintances that Dies was a 'shithead' and that the committee members were 'just ignorant cowboys'.[42] Alienating those from whom one wants to elicit information is probably not the wisest tactic. It seems reasonable to assume the ineffective questioning resulted from competing political agendas and poor communication and coordination within the government.

The British Reaction

Krivitsky published his memoir to wide readership several weeks after his appearance before the Dies Committee. One book review stated that Krivitsky was 'certainly the most discussed writer in New York, and possibly in America'.[43] His work was closely read in other quarters as well. While the US media pilloried him and figures in the US government and even some in the British

Foreign Office discredited him, MI5 busily assessed the veracity of Krivitsky's claims.[44] After the initial publication of his articles in the *Saturday Evening Post*, MI5 compiled them for cross-referencing – and the first record in MI5's Krivitsky file predates even those notations.[45] MI5 found that the information contained in his *Saturday Evening Post* articles was 'wholly corroborated by [earlier] M.I.5. records' and 'contained a great deal of information of additional interest'.[46]

MI5's B Division became highly engaged, however, after British officials in Washington met with the Russian-born journalist Isaac Don Levine. Levine revealed to Victor Mallet, the Chargé d'Affaires at the British Embassy, that Krivitsky had told him in confidence of the existence of two Soviet agents in sensitive positions in the British government.[47] 'One is KING in the Foreign Office Communications Department', Mallet's subsequent despatch reads, 'the other is in cypher (sic) [*sic* in original] department of Cabinet Offices but name unknown.' 'KING selling everything to Moscow', he also reported. The latter of the two agents, according to Krivitsky, was a 'Scotsman of very good family, a well-known painter and perhaps a sculptor'. Mallet further added that Krivitsky refused to identify the man because 'he likes him' and believed from having worked with him during the Spanish Civil War that the man was 'not acting for mercenary motives but through idealism and sympathy for the "loyalists"' (i.e. the anti-Franco Republicans, whom the Soviets supported)[48] MI5 subsequently concluded that 'the Scottish artist, communist and idealist' was 'a totally different person' than the man in Spain (whose identity they 'knew').[49] Nonetheless, Levine's information led Mallet to the conclusion that Krivitsky was 'clearly not bogus as many people, particularly the American communists who were furious at his revelation in the *Saturday Evening Post*', tried to make out. He did, however, suggest that 'Krivitsky, being a Russian refugee, would probably expect to be paid if you want to put someone on to pumping him for information'.[50]

MI5 quickly located 'King' and established that he had indeed spied for the Soviets, passing Foreign Office documents from the Communications Department to a Dutchman, the illegal Hans Christian Pieck, from 1935 to 1937.[51] The plain-text communiqués from King at the Foreign Office could be compared to their encoded counterparts and so gave the Soviets a great advantage in attempts to break British cyphers. Unbeknownst to Krivitsky, the investigation led to King's arrest in a matter of weeks and a ten-year prison sentence for breach of the Official Secrets Act.[52] Krivitsky thus appeared knowledgeable not only about Soviet strategic intentions given his prediction of the Nazi-Soviet Pact but also about specific Soviet intelligence operations. His *bona*

9 Jane Archer, MI5's first female officer, was described by Soviet double agent Kim Philby as one of MI5's best officers. A Soviet expert, she played a key role in debriefing defector Walter Krivitsky. Archer was dismissed for insubordination at the beginning of the war and joined SIS (MI6). As seen here, she was also a trained barrister.

fides established, Jane Archer, one of MI5's sharpest pre-war counter-espionage officers, wrote to Valentine Vivian, the head of SIS's counter-espionage section, 'Personally, I am convinced from [Krivitsky's] articles, and the scraps of information that LEVINE has obtained from KRIVITSKY and given to our Ambassador in Washington, that if we wish to get to the bottom of Soviet military espionage activities in this country, we must contact KRIVITSKY.'[53]

British government officials began to arrange for an interview with Krivitsky. In preparation, MI5 also began to assess his character. Krivitsky's own writings provided the foundation for discerning his motivations and expectations. His explicit motives and self-portrayal told only a part of the story. Although ideology played a decisive role in Krivitsky's defection, fear and revenge also spurred him on.

In his published memoir, Krivitsky pinpoints the exact moment he broke with the Soviet government. At the height of the Purge in Moscow, Paris-based fellow illegal and close childhood friend Ignace Reiss (alias Ignace Poretsky, alias Ludwig) expressed his 'crushing disillusionment' with the Soviet Union following the arrest of the Red Army's Marshal Mikhail Tukhachevsky, a hero of the Revolution. Reiss wrote to the Central Committee of the Communist Party, 'Up to now I have followed you. From now on, not a step further. Our ways part! He who keeps silent at this hour becomes an accomplice of Stalin, and a traitor to the cause of the working class and of Socialism.'[54] Denouncing Stalin was a treasonable offence even at the best of times, but denouncing him during the Purge guaranteed the swiftest retribution. The deputy head of the Foreign Department of the Cheka, Mikhail Shpiegelglass, then in Western Europe with 'plenipotentiary powers to purge the foreign services', confronted Krivitsky in Paris with Reiss's intercepted letter. As Krivitsky later wrote,

> To his insistent suggestion that I take a hand in organizing the 'solution' of the Reiss case, so as to establish my own loyalty in the eyes of [OGPU head Nikolai] Yezhov and Stalin, I finally replied that I would have nothing to do with any such undertaking. *At that moment I realized that my lifelong service to the Soviet government was ended.* I would be unable to meet the demands of Stalin's new era. . . . I had taken an oath to serve the Soviet Union; I had lived by that oath; but to take an active hand in these wholesale murders was beyond my powers.[55]

Krivitsky's turn from Stalin, however, was not a turn from either socialism or the spirit of the Revolution. Indeed even his position on liquidation remained ambiguous to the extent that his refusal to take an active part was accompanied by his silence about his own passive contribution to other wet operations that must have taken place. Only just before Reiss sent his denunciatory letter to Moscow, Krivitsky tried to reason with him: 'The Soviet Union is still the sole hope of the workers of the world. Stalin may be wrong. Stalins will come and go, but the Soviet Union will remain. It is our duty to stick to our post.'[56] Krivitsky's disillusionment was confined to Stalin; he still believed in the Soviet project.

It is difficult to overstate the profundity of what defection must have meant for a professional intelligence officer and committed communist like Krivitsky. He had joined the Comintern when he was roughly twenty years old, operating

10 Walter Krivitsky, the Soviet military intelligence officer who fled to the United States to escape assassination by colleagues, was secretly debriefed by MI5 in London. Krivitsky gave MI5 clues to the identities of the most damaging double agents in twentieth-century British history: the Cambridge Five. He was later found dead in a Washington, DC hotel room under mysterious circumstances.

secretly behind Polish lines during the Russo-Polish War in anticipation of a march on Warsaw by Tukhachevsky.[57] As the introduction to MI5's summary report on Krivitsky reads, 'GINSBERG adopted whole-heartedly the cause of the Bolshevik revolution, and became a staff officer of the Red Army early in his career. He joined the Fourth Department of the Military Intelligence about 1919, and from that time became known as KRIVITSKY.'[58] The liquidation of the Red Army high command, including Tukhachevsky, under whom Krivitsky had served, came very much as a personal blow. It represented a betrayal of what he risked his life fighting for. Working for Soviet intelligence meant his identity, both in name and substance, was intricately tied to the state.[59]

Levine later recalled that in his interview at the British Embassy in Washington, he had tried to impress upon Mallet 'that Krivitsky's service in Soviet military intelligence had been motivated by ideological, and not mercenary, considerations, that his ambition was to serve the Allies in the fight against Hitler and in this manner redeem himself for his services to Stalin, now Hitler's ally'. Just as his commitment to Bolshevik Russia was ideologically motivated, so was his defection. Krivitsky did not consider himself, but the regime, to be the traitor to the Revolution.[60] Levine noted, 'Ideological espionage was still a fairly new phenomenon in those days, and Mr. Mallet was obviously surprised at my description of Krivitsky and his motives.'[61] Mallet must have been surprised; he had only just insisted to the Foreign Office that Krivitsky, 'being a Russian refugee', would seek money in exchange for cooperation. In his writing and to his associates, Krivitsky portrayed himself as persecuted despite his deep loyalty to the Soviet Union, his ideological integrity, and his dedication to higher principles. Taking advantage of these grievances, MI5 showed that one nation's traitor can be another nation's ally.

Understanding well the psychology of the now public figure Krivitsky, the British Embassy warned MI5 that he might prove difficult to deal with and that inducing him to travel to Britain might not be easy: 'Krivitsky is rather vain as result of his success as an author'. Perhaps, the cautionary text continued, 'prestige of rank in French Intelligence Service might be best bait'. The Embassy was at the same time urging officials at home to bring Krivitsky to London because he had more information that he had become reluctant to share with Levine following an argument.[62] O. A. 'Jasper' Harker, the head of B Division, quickly rejected the notion of including the French and thought it 'imperative that KRIVITSKY should be seen as early as possible'.[63] He requested that Lord Lothian begin inquiries with the US government to ensure that an attempt to bring Krivitsky to Britain would not meet any official obstacles. It became increasingly clear, however, that Krivitsky himself might prove the biggest obstacle. Britain at this point lacked experience with the 'difficult' defector psychology. In 1940 there was no precedent by which to judge Krivitsky, no case to which to compare his debriefing's progress. Krivitsky created the precedent. An SIS source suggested that dealing with Krivitsky was not straightforward – he was a career spy after all. In December 1939, Vivian forwarded Archer a scathing report on Krivitsky written by 'a very reliable source who provides the Lovestone correspondence' (presumably a source with access to the outspoken anti-Soviet American communist Jay Lovestone).[64] Vivian prefaced the note by writing,

> Our Representative in sending this says that personally he thinks that the source is being rather hard on KRIVITSKI [*sic*], but at the same time he states that KRIVITSKI does not talk English and is very difficult person to be with. He has a great opinion of his own importance and, if 'buttered up', he may only require his expenses to be paid. Our Representative is trying to persuade him to leave the question of further possible remuneration until he sees you.

The SIS source's report emphasised Krivitsky's ideology and questioned the extent to which he had really turned from Stalin:

> KRIVITSKI [*sic*] may have been thrown out of Russia by Stalin but he is still a Communist. . . . KRIVITSKI has not severed his connections with the Revolutionary movement in any sense of the word. . . . LOVESTONE told me that after KRIVITSKI had testified before the Dies Committee in Washington against Stalin, an FBI executive came to KRIVITSKI and wanted to get some inside information and it was refused because KRIVISTKI 'didn't see why he should help the capitalists in any country, not even America'. . . . KRIVITSKI is a marked man in America. His great aim always was, until the last few days, not to have to go back to any European country under any pretext at all. He does not speak English. I consider this man a traitor, a liar, and a dyed-in-the-wool Communist. My belief is that while he might not be unwilling to stab one of Stalin's men in the back, if it came to a showdown where he had to choose between loyalty to our country or to the workers in his own land, he would revert to type and stab us in the back.[65]

MI5 had to take such a report seriously, despite its vitriol, but it never had been going to take Krivitsky strictly at his printed word. Everyone involved assumed as a matter of course that they would have to pay Krivitsky despite his anti-capitalist stance. Archer had actually asked Krivitsky whether MI5 reports were correct in saying that he had 'appropriated certain funds' from his Department at the time of his defection. He replied, obviously embarrassed, that it was an 'accusation . . . made in order to discredit him', and insisted on discussing the matter later.[66] Archer might have considered him to be protesting too much. Although Krivitsky initially refused payment, except to cover expenses, he did in the end accept a large sum of money from MI5 as recompense for a 'lost contract' with an American newspaper because he had spent time in London.[67]

MI5 also reached conclusions that historians have echoed, including the cynical but perfectly plausible notion that 'though Krivitsky later claimed that it was a sudden upsurge of moral repugnance which had prompted him to defect, there is in fact little doubt that the motive was rather a sudden upsurge in panic', a conclusion supported by the fact that Krivitsky only went to the United States after surviving two assassination attempts.[68] Even Levine, who spoke to Krivitsky's ideological motivations, later conceded, 'The assassination of Reiss determined the conduct of Krivitsky, who realized that his lifelong friendship with his comrade portended his own execution. . . . Krivitsky's break . . . was motivated by dread of Stalin's long arm.'[69] Although Krivitsky's desire for self-preservation constituted an additional layer to his personality and to his motives, as well, it did not necessarily diminish his belief in socialism. Krivitsky's decision to publicise his discontent with Stalin also made it plain that he was 'bent on revenge', as one biographer has noted.[70] MI5's own summary report reached a similar conclusion in its observation that a 'passionate hatred of Stalin, based on the murder of personal friends, relations and colleagues' motivated his acquiescence to MI5's request for a London debriefing.[71] His public lambasting of Stalin and Soviet policy and his revelations to MI5 were ways to strike back at the Soviet leader, whom Krivitsky believed to be hunting him. From MI5's angle, Krivitsky's fear and desire for revenge were possible 'entry points' – points of leverage – in the debriefing. They implied space for compromise and cooperation. Balancing these competing motivations and self-justifications lay at the heart of assessing the defector, just as leveraging them sat at the core of handling him.

The Debriefing in London

MI5 and SIS seem to have been the first historically to engage in the comprehensive and systematic planning of a defector's debriefing. The approach they outlined, albeit in rudimentary form in the files, set a precedent for what became common practice for British intelligence during the Cold War. MI5's methods of pre-empting resistance from Krivitsky can be broken down into at least four areas. First, the officers planning Krivitsky's visit (Archer, Harker, Liddell and Vivian) tried to capitalise on the notion of reciprocity. Through his whole time in the United States, Krivitsky wrangled with the immigration services. By contrast, MI5 and SIS ensured his family easy passage into Canada and helped them with accommodations during his trip to Britain. They also co-ordinated Krivitsky's passage from Canada to his hotel in London. At all points they presented the image of skilled and practised officers (which they were) to appeal to Krivitsky's own sense of professionalism. Second, they hoped their professionalism would help establish their establish authority. Third, in their handling and questioning, MI5 sought to create rapport.[72] Fourth, as a backdrop to this psychological environment, MI5 also asserted control over the physical environment, to whatever extent possible, to help coax information out of Krivitksy. Censorship therefore also played an important part in minimising distractions and focusing Krivitsky's attention while simultaneously ensuring his protection.

MI5 imposed a HOW on Krivitsky, thereby intercepting his post, as part of the effort to 'contain' his visit. It seems logical to assume that when a source volunteers information – as in a debriefing rather than an interrogation – the handler's control over the physical environment diminishes to some extent. The use of unpleasant psychological tactics might quickly increase resistance. MI5 tried to compensate for this variable through censorship and surveillance. Shortly before Krivitsky's arrival, Archer contacted Colonel Allen at the GPO with specific instructions:

> I would be very grateful if the following arrangements could be made in regard to letters addressed to Samuel GINSBERG or General KRIVITSKY at the Langham Hotel, Portland Place, W.1:-
>
> 1) That all foreign letters from countries subject to censorship should be examined by you and sent on with censorship labels attached.
>
> 2) That no letters not ordinarily subject to censorship should be opened for the reasons I explained to you.
>
> 3) That a list of letters not opened should be submitted daily. I am particularly anxious to see whether he receives any letters from Rugby. As we are not opening any letters except those ordinarily subject to censorship, must I have a warrant?[73]

The 'reasons' mentioned in the second point are not made clear and grew out of an earlier telephone conversation, nor do the records make it clear why

Archer was anxious about letters from Rugby, but Allen's response to Archer's question in point 3 shows that MI5 was not adverse to interpreting the spirit rather than the letter of the law when it came to maintaining the secrecy of their operations. Allen wrote,

> Re point (3) This raises a nice point of law. Technically, as we are not a section of the Censor's Dept. I suppose we ought to have a warrant, but in practice, this seems superfluous as the letters would normally be opened by the Censor's [*sic*]. I think therefore we can dispense with a H.O.W. and if necessary, invoke the good offices of the 'Wide Warrant' to cover our misdeeds.[74]

In other words, wartime regulations meant that the Censor would intercept the mail anyway, so it seemed irrelevant which security authority intercepted it. The passage highlights nicely the flexibility afforded to MI5 during times of emergency.[75]

Archer wrote to Vivian a month before Krivitsky's scheduled arrival, 'This is going so splendidly, I feel there must be a snag somewhere'.[76] There was not. After assuring Krivitsky that he would not be prosecuted for previous espionage activities, Vivian finally received word from New York that Krivitsky was 'ready to visit the United Kingdom direct' and was not asking for remuneration. He was scheduled to arrive in Liverpool from Halifax in mid-January. Though Krivitsky made his way to Montreal to deposit his family at his own expense, MI5 and SIS arranged his sea passage, and Sir James Paget, the SIS chief representative in New York, provided him with the substantial advance of $100 (roughly $1,640 in today's terms) for expenses beyond the fare.[77] Krivitsky's only request was to travel cabin class, 'but otherwise wishes his visit to be quite unobtrusive'. There was some debate as to where he should be lodged and what kind of entertainment to provide once he was in Britain. Paget informed Broadway (SIS headquarters) that Krivitsky's 'standard of living is that of a refined journalist' and suggested that 'he should stay at a middle class hotel such as the Cumberland and that his entertainment should be on that scale'. He also stressed that the 'the main consideration is that he should remain unnoticed'.[78]

With these arrangements in place, MI5 received word of Krivitsky's departure from Halifax on 10 January 1940 and only then learned of Krivitsky's intention to stay at the Langham Hotel, leaving Archer only six days to secure new arrangements.[79] The irony was that the Langham Hotel was one of the most expensive and exclusive hotels in London and one of the first 'grand hotels' of Europe, frequented by celebrities, diplomats and royalty. For someone wanting to remain unnoticed, and whose ideology supposedly eschewed such luxury, it was a surprising choice. It seems at least in terms of taste, Krivitsky was not a man of the masses. On the other hand, staying at the Langham would presumably have afforded him a discreet staff and security, important considerations for someone with his level of fear. Whatever the reasons, MI5 obliged.[80]

MI5 aimed to not only to impress Krivitsky on his arrival, but also put him at ease. Memoranda flurried between Archer, Harker, Liddell and Vivian discussing how this could best be accomplished. The first impression would be critical, so it was agreed that an MI5 representative who spoke Russian should greet Krivitsky at the port. Major Stephen Alley, borrowed from T. A. R. Robertson in Section B.3, would meet Krivitsky and escort him to London personally.[81] An indication of the level of secrecy surrounding MI5 and SIS at the time is that it was even considered whether or not to reveal to Krivitsky exactly which Departments were conducting the debriefing. Ultimately, it was deduced that Krivitsky would have little doubt as to whom the interested parties were and that concealing their respective departments might only antagonise the somewhat conceited Krivitsky. Anticipating his haughtiness, Archer suggested, 'As Krivitsky is notoriously a vain man we ought to produce somebody pretty big in the first place. ?Sir Alexander Cadogan [Permanent Under-Secretary of the FO] or Sir Robert Vansittart [former PUS].? D.M.I. ?Major-General Sir Vernon Kell [sic].'[82] No record exists of any of these figures attending the debriefings (and Liddell certainly would have noted it in his diary). Instead, Harker and Vivian, heads of MI5 and SIS's respective counter-espionage divisions, attended as ranking officers, and they assumed responsibility for Krivitsky's requisite 'flattery and tactful handling,' which an SIS officer in Canada had indicated would be necessary.[83]

British security intelligence operated under the strictest secrecy regarding Krivitsky's transatlantic venture. The *New York Times* noted his departure, but his final destination remained unknown to all but a select few.[84] Unlike the wide publicity Krivitsky received in the United States (instigated by his own articles), Harker wrote to Vivian, 'I think it is definitely essential that the Press should have no knowledge that KRIVITSKY is here at all, both in our interests and in his.'[85] The decision to keep Krivitsky out of the news formed a central part of sealing Krivitsky from the 'outside world.'[86] Security was a key concern. Archer had noted, 'He is obviously definitely frightened, and it is in both our interests that as few people as possible should know of his arrival.'[87] Her observations were confirmed by an entry in Liddell's diary. On Krivitsky's arrival, Alley took him to tea, and having no sugar – it was after all wartime London – offered him a saccharine tablet. 'He sheered right off this,' Liddell recorded, 'obviously thinking it was dope or poison.'[88]

One security instrument available to MI5 was the 'D-Notice System', the agreement between the government and the press whereby the press refrains from publishing articles deemed to compromise matters of national security.[89] But as Archer also cautioned, issuing a D-Notice would 'do the very thing we wish to avoid, letting the entire press know that he is here, and we could not exclude the Left Wing press'.[90] Instead it was decided to handle Krivitsky using clandestine tradecraft to ensure his visit remained secret. So Krivitsky, down to his luggage tags, became 'Mr. Thomas' during his journey.[91]

With the 'outside world' safely at bay, Archer, Harker and Vivian could concentrate on the 'internal world' of the actual question-answer sessions. Presenting Krivitsky with a united front was important; the officers had to reach a consensus on methodology. Archer pointed out, 'As the Lovestone source is convinced that KRIVITSKY, though infuriated with the present Soviet regime, is still an ardent communist, we shall have to think out very closely our line of approach.'[92] Harker agreed: 'KREVITSKY [*sic*] still being an ardent Communist and definitely anti the present regime, I take it that an anti-Stalin line is probably the wisest.' However, Harker also insisted Krivitsky be treated with a certain degree of openness. He argued, 'I do not see that there is any good in pretending that we have got KRIVITSKY over here for any other reason than to pump him, and I imagine a certain amount of frankness would probably pay.'[93] If Krivitsky, someone who had spent his career running agents, perceived the officers as being contrived, overly manipulative or especially cagey, it might have increased rather than decreased his resistance during questioning.

While a certain frankness might have encouraged the elicitation of information, too much openness on the part of the debriefers might have displayed vulnerability. Power and knowledge appear to be at the core of a debriefing or interrogation. Playing with what is known and unknown to discover what the source knows and does not know, or knows and refuses to reveal, could be one of the interrogator's greatest tools. Along these lines, prior to Krivitsky's arrival, Archer wrote to Harker, 'We must make up our minds whether we are going to mention KING's arrest and sentence to KRIVITSKY. I presume that that he does not know that LEVINE came to us with KING's name. . . .We must not put him in a rage to start with by letting him know that his thunder has been stolen by LEVINE.'[94] Harker more than agreed, replying that 'it would be fatal' to let Krivitsky know King's fate at the outset of the debriefing process.[95] Not only would this have added to Krivitsky's anxiety regarding police involvement, it might have revealed too much about the extent of MI5's knowledge. Instead they waited to spring King on Krivitsky once he was in London.

Knowing what *not* to reveal thus became as important as what *to* reveal. Both were issues of form and timing. Even if the environment appeared good, there was still the principal matter of figuring out what questions to ask and how to ask them. Archer, Harker and Vivian addressed these concerns as they planned the debriefing. Archer asked Harker, 'How is it proposed to deal with Krivitsky?'[96] Harker asked Vivian, 'How are we to deal with Krivitsky in so far as the long-drawn-out conversations and cross-examinations have to be carried out?'[97] Moreover, they reasoned, asking the right questions required having the right person able to ask them. Archer told Harker that 'Colonel Vivian no doubt will be keenly interested to question him on past history, and both he and ourselves will have a great many questions on Soviet methods and the organisation of Soviet Military espionage organisation here and abroad.' Archer suggested that 'the person to do the major interrogation is Colonel Vivian who has all the Soviet background in his head.' Even so, it was Archer who provided the strategy, based on information from King's agent Pieck, that would in the end open Krivitsky: 'We must I think display to KRIVITSKY a good deal of information we have in order to convince him that we know what we are talking about, but it would perhaps be better if Colonel Vivian could do this as he knows how far he can go without disclosing that we had an agent in Holland.'[98] In this way, the debriefers would appear informed and authoritative. Krivitsky, believing British intelligence already knew what he knew, and possibly more, would see little point in holding back other information. Perhaps this technique, called the 'all-seeing eye', was used with greatest effect soon after Krivitsky's debriefing, when MI5 officers, armed with ISOS (decrypted German radio messages), successfully turned captive German spies into British double agents at Camp 020 as part of the now-famous Double-Cross System.[99]

Despite Archer's inclinations, the documents remain unclear as to whether MI5 or SIS held ultimate responsibility for the debriefing. Harker wrote to Vivian, 'While I think we are both agreed that it is a matter of joint interest to M.I.5. and S.I.S., there is still a little doubt as to who is really going to hold the baby. . . . Both Mrs. Archer and I feel very strongly that you personally, if possible, should take as large a part in this investigation as you can manage.'[100] Ultimately, however, Vivian's schedule prevented him from attending all but the initial sessions, and if the notes submitted on the interviews with Krivitsky are any indication, much of the questioning fell to Archer – and perhaps with good reason: not only was she well-versed in Soviet espionage, she was also a trained barrister.[101]

Like a court procedure, the debriefing or interrogation was a process, though a much less formal one, pivoting on the source's resistance levels rather than protocol. Although debriefing incorporates specific methods, current literature suggests that 'educing information is most productively envisioned as a process, rather than as an applied set of techniques. Moreover, the context of that process should be viewed broadly, not solely (or even primarily) as an across-the-table interaction between an educer and a source.'[102] Understanding Krivitsky's debriefing in these terms illuminates MI5's summary report, which states 'the work represents an attempt to sort out and put into a coherent form a mass of information gleaned from KRIVITSKY at odd moments in the course of lengthy and diffuse conversations extending over three or four weeks.'[103] Honing in on the 'odd' moments when information was 'gleaned' from Krivitsky is very much at the core of this study, for they represent the culmination of MI5's preparation and analysis. Further, they reflect the value of the nuanced psychology of the debriefing process. The 'odd' moments represent the debriefers' successful penetration of Krivitsky's protective barriers. They are the moments of victory.

In the initial stages of the debriefing, Krivitsky showed extreme reluctance to share information, much to the frustration of the officers involved, who noted 'It seemed at first that little was to be gained from the visit.' Rather implausibly, Krivitsky also 'repudiated any suggestion that he had knowledge of, or was in any way responsible for Soviet secret activities in this country, and appeared quite unable to remember the names of the any of his assistants who had operated in or against the United Kingdom.' It transpired that his recalcitrance stemmed from an abiding loyalty to his former colleagues and fear of self-incrimination. It appears that being separated from Soviet intelligence for two years had done nothing to uproot the enormous fear firmly embedded in the mind of an officer who had been close to the purges.[104]

The Soviet security apparatus also viewed interrogations as a process, but one quite different from the British understanding.[105] Its approach to security interrogations sought to generate incriminations. The objective of the criminal interrogation versus the intelligence interrogation differs substantially and will yield correspondingly different information. Whereas the function of the former is to produce evidence leading to conviction, the latter, as practised by MI5 and SIS, is additionally concerned with understanding wider structural and operational details. Thus in the intelligence interrogation, 'Admissions of complicity are not . . . ends in themselves but merely preludes to the acquisition of more information.'[106]

Rather than interrogation based on fear, the British used a softer approach with Krivitsky. There are several indications that from their first meeting, the British intelligence officers tried to lull Krivitsky into disclosing information.

Harker's report on the first interview noted that it took place in Krivitsky's (likely plush) hotel room, not, as one might expect, in a spartan basement room at MI5 headquarters. The session began innocuously with 'a good deal of beating about the bush'. After a while, Krivitsky did 'get down to the facts', telling officers present that he was 'aware' of a Soviet intelligence network operating in Britain, but 'was very anxious to point out that he himself was not responsible for the direction of activities against the U.K', only against Germany. Even then he expressed his desire 'to know what action we would take on his information, as he was convinced that anything we did in the way of arrests, etc., would at once be attributed by the Soviet Government to his activities'. Krivitsky was 'further very anxious to know to what lengths we would go as regards using him personally'.[107] Over the course of subsequent interviews, Harker and Vivian met these worries with reassurances. It took some time to convince Krivitsky that the information he gave would not result in the immediate arrest of those he implicated.[108] Harker and Vivian assured Krivitsky that he would not be used as a material witness and insisted that, 'anything he told [them] would be treated as regards its source with absolute confidence'.[109]

With these guarantees given, Krivitsky finally dropped his bombshell – but it was a dud. His revelation of an agent in the Foreign Office came as no surprise to those at the debriefing. Krivitsky was informed that British intelligence was 'perfectly aware' of the agent, that his name was King, and that he had already begun a ten-year prison sentence. As Harker observed, 'This rather took the wind out of his sails.' The officers then produced a picture of Pieck, King's handler, whom Krivitsky identified. Thereafter Krivitsky 'spoke very freely' about King and Pieck.[110]

Considering his new status as an 'expert', and his high opinion of himself, Krivitsky felt no doubt considerable internal pressure to produce something significant after the anticlimactic reception to his unrevealing revelation. He began to offer information of his own accord as opposed to its being elicited. Harker's report states that he, in consultation with Vivian, decided to tell Krivitsky about King 'with a view to reassuring him', but as Archer had suggested, it also gave Krivitsky the impression that MI5 'knew what they were talking about', and went some way in humbling the prickly Krivitsky, likely raising his esteem for the debriefers and lowering his resistance to them.

In addition to the picture of Pieck, Krivitsky also identified 'Hart' as well as 'Brandes'. Hart likely referred to Alexander Tudor-Hart, the Cambridge-trained doctor who led a medical delegation to Spain during the Civil War, and who was married to Edith Tudor-Hart, née Suschitsky, a Soviet courier in the Woolwich Arsenal spy ring and close friend of Kim Philby's ex-wife, Litzi Friedman.

'Brandes' was Willy Brandes, the operative involved in Percy Glading's espionage activities. Krivitsky claimed to have met him in Moscow.[111] The debriefers could not ask Krivitsky directly about the Cabinet Office source since they were not supposed to know about it, so, Harker wrote, 'We then tried to lead him up to giving us information regarding other leakages.' Leading a source in this way has proven a useful tactic. As one study on persuasion notes, people generally strive to remain consistent in their principles.[112] If a source produces information on his own, he must take responsibility for his decision. In theory, if Krivitsky divulged information on his own, why should he not divulge more?

According to the debriefing reports, Krivitsky informed the officers that 'there had been for some time a leakage of valuable information which emanated from what he described as the Council of State – but which we think must be the C.I.D. [Committee of Imperial Defence] Offices.'[113] Marginal notes however stressed the importance of noting Krivitsky's own words. Krivitsky's understanding of the British government may have been comprehensive, but it was still imperfect. It was important, therefore, to understand what he meant, what he intended to say, rather than to assume he was expressing himself the way they would have. The marginal note, however, disappears in subsequent reports. Perhaps the officers interpreted Krivitsky's information correctly, but even today it is vague as to whom Krivitsky tried to identify (more on this below).

Krivitsky and the officers spoke for an additional two and a half hours that first day. As Harker reported, 'It was difficult to confine the conversation to a particular topic, and he wandered about over various fields of Soviet work and told us a good deal about Pieck, practically all of which we knew.' They planned a meeting for the following day, at which time Krivitsky 'would go into matters in far greater detail, after he had come to terms with us as to what he wanted us to do for him.'[114] It is unclear as to what these terms were, but only three days later, Archer wrote to Vivian saying, 'I had three hours sitting with our friend Walter yesterday. He was much easier and friendly and seemed to remember things better.'[115] So although 'at every point' Krivitsky was quick to assert that he had been concerned solely with Germany during his time as a Soviet intelligence officer, first in the Fourth Department, then (albeit briefly) in the OGPU, he began to make concessions, explaining that 'the general principles on which the third section [of the Fourth Department, in charge of acquiring military information outside the USSR] operates are the same in all western countries.' He expressed confidence that 'from his personal knowledge and from his general experience that, allowing for variants which occur in all intelligence services, the activities of the Fourth Department in the United Kingdom are organised on the lines which he describes'.[116] As Gordon Brooke-Shepherd has rightly noted, 'When Walter Krivitsky sat down in England to begin his extensive interrogation, he was dealing, for the first time since his flight to America, with experts who knew not only what questions to ask but also how to evaluate his answers'.[117] Unlike his experience in America, Krivitsky was gradually put at ease by competent and professional intelligence services.

CHAPTER 7

Defection and Debriefing (II)

Walter Krivitsky

A LTHOUGH MI5 and SIS would not know it for another ten years (except, of course, that the moles Kim Philby and Anthony Blunt did), Krivitsky was providing details on two of the Soviet Union's greatest operatives, the recruiters and early handlers of the Cambridge Five spy ring.[1] It is unclear how many times Krivitsky met with the officers. But by the end of Krivitsky's month-long stay in London, MI5 and SIS had obtained a wealth of information on the structure and operations of Soviet intelligence. At the heart of these revelations was the identification of Soviet operatives. Of those Krivitsky named, perhaps Arnold Deutsch and Teodor Maly attracted MI5's attention the most, as these men ran the high-ranking CID source – the identification of whom was one of the primary goals in having brought Krivitsky to London. Krivitsky insisted that Deutsch, and then Maly, ran a high-ranking source in the CID – now widely accepted as having been one of the Cambridge Five. The question remains, however, as to whether the information Krivitsky provided in 1940 was sufficiently conclusive to have pointed could have prevented one of the worst disasters in British intelligence history.

Krivitsky informed British officials that an Austrian illegal named 'Alfred' Deutsch, holder of a doctorate in chemistry, arrived in the United Kingdom sometime in 1933–1934. The 'bumptious' Deutsch, as Maly described him to Krivitsky, initially arrived with his chief, the illegal resident 'Reiff' (Ignati Reif), but soon brought over his wife and child from Vienna. Strangely enough, Deutsch, who worked under the codename 'Stefan', also brought his mother-in-law not long after. His wife, a trained radio operator, worked on the OGPU staff. Deutsch apparently travelled on his own credentials, making it possible for MI5 to check police files on his entry into the UK.[2] With details from the background check, Archer was able to confirm with Krivitsky that 'Alfred' was in fact Arnold Deutsch. Testifying to the efficiency of MI5's Registry, Archer also ran a check on the name 'Stefan' and found the record of a telephone conversation between a previously unidentified Stefan and Arnold Schuster, the Second Secretary of the Soviet Embassy (and legal resident). Krivitsky identified Schuster as 'the Ogpu man' in the Soviet Embassy in the mid-1930s. Krivitsky claimed he had not mentioned Schuster earlier because he thought he would not have used his real name.[3] This direct contact between the legal and illegal residents was a slip in Soviet tradecraft. If one had been apprehended, it might have led to the exposure of the other and his secret network. The potential implication of embassy officials might have caused further diplomatic complications. Indeed, communications between the legal and illegal residents was typically carried out through a third person, almost always a female courier, Krivitsky said.[4]

Schuster was the nephew of a certain Dawidowicz, an illegal in Holland who ran a textile export firm called GADA, which acted as a front for OGPU operations and provided cover identities for illegals. The same Dawidowicz was a brother of Bernard Dawidowicz, whom Krivitsky claimed to be a resident OGPU officer in London.[5] GADA also served as business cover for Maly while he ran King. In fact, bank notes belonging to King were traced to Dawidowicz, who accompanied Maly to London in 1936.[6] By that point Maly (alias Paul Hardt, Theo, Mann, Peters, Petersen) had replaced Reif, who had been recalled to Moscow in 1935 and made chief of the British section of the INO. There, Reif exclusively handled information passed from Deutsch through Maly.[7]

Two weeks into the debriefing, Krivitsky continued to open up. Archer wrote, 'Mr. Thomas [Krivitsky], then said what he had not told me before', that it was in his capacity as roving officer that he also became involved with Maly in Holland handling the material of Percy Glading.[8] As Krivitsky described it, after 1935 the Fourth Department had no illegal resident in Britain. Rather, 'agents' (by which he certainly meant officers) worked from surrounding countries, such as Holland, France and Sweden.[9] Krivitsky first began to work with Maly in 1935 as part of his assignment to inspect all of the Western European illegal residencies, both OGPU and Fourth Department – thus the American press's description of Krivitsky as the head of Soviet intelligence in Europe. Krivitsky claimed that Maly had been a priest and army chaplain to an Austrian regiment during the Great War, was later taken prisoner by the Russians, and eventually took an active part in the Russian Revolution. Some five years after his work with Maly, Krivitsky insisted Maly was still alive, claiming to have received a letter from him in 1937, although he knew that all of Maly's assistants had been arrested (and likely liquidated) in the purges.[10] Krivitsky was convinced that if Maly were alive, he would 'undoubtedly' use Pieck again, 'as Pieck was one of his best men for recruiting agents'.[11] But Pieck never worked for Maly again. It is possible that Krivitsky received a letter from Maly in 1937, but Maly was in fact executed later that same year. Clearly though, Krivitsky hedged in his earlier claims that he knew nothing specific about Soviet operations in Britain.

Like Henderson at the State Department, MI5 and SIS were interested to learn directly from a former Soviet operative about the existence and procedural relationship between legal and illegal residents, though MI5's records go into considerably more detail than those recorded by Henderson. In the Fourth Department, Krivitsky explained, the legal resident acted as the public face of his illegal counterpart. He was a recognised diplomat, whereas the illegal operated without diplomatic cover. His activities extended to targeting and cultivating potential sources who could be identified to and taken up by the illegal resident.

The legal resident also acted as a post box for the illegal resident and ciphered and deciphered urgent messages for him, though female secretaries usually played this role. According to Krivitsky, an illegal's mail was usually sent and received twice a month. The women serving as secretaries also provided a communications link between the legal and illegal residents. As direct contact could jeopardise the secrecy of an illegal's operations, both the legal and illegal residents employed women as intermediaries when passing information. The reason the messengers were usually women, and the illegal's runner invariably so, is not explained, but it may well be that, given women's role in British society in the interwar period, the Soviets believed them less likely to fall under suspicion. Women secretaries, typists, cashiers, and clerks, Krivitsky warned, 'should be carefully watched'.[12]

The third section of the Fourth Department employed three classes of regular agents abroad: head agents, resident agents and speculant agents.[13] Head agents were Fourth Department staff officers such as Krivitsky himself. Resident agents held permanent posts and fulfilled a support function to the head officer or resident. Speculant agents were mainly Central-Eastern Europeans and usually 'outlaws from their own countries on account of their communist activities'. Krivitsky noted that the early speculant agents, often urbane and sophisticated, were also frequently refugees from pre-Revolutionary Russia, such as Theodore Rothstein.[14] While recognising their necessity, he placed no great faith in speculants, as he considered them particularly susceptible to bribery.[15] Insight into these agents' vulnerability introduced further opportunities to encourage defection.

'Sub-agents' (as Krivitsky called them, although they were actually just agents enlisted by officers like himself) were necessarily recruited locally. They were the footprints of the Fourth Department's invisible steps in any given country. The Communist Party was the primary field from which sub-agents were drawn. The next largest group was made up of fellow travellers, and then, in Britain, the Irish, simply because of their 'anti-British bias which makes their recruitment comparatively easy'.[16] In Britain, recruiting from the CPGB was risky, especially after the ARCOS raid. As Krivitsky pointed out, the legal resident 'can and does call for assistance upon the Communist Party of the country to which he is accredited, but as the Embassy must on no account be compromised, the communist connections are most carefully concealed'.[17] The Macartney case, which helped lead to the temporary severing of Anglo-Soviet relations, also showed how the Soviet Embassy's links to known communists had negative repercussions. It was at least in part a result of the Macartney and Ewer cases that the Soviets introduced illegal residents in Britain the first place.

Usually, an illegal resident began work only after six months *in situ*, during which time he trained one or more assistants. With their help, the agent met 'on a friendly basis various people in different walks of life and [gained] their confidence'. Krivitsky illustrated the process as follows:

> If a man is found to be working in a map making establishment, he would be cultivated, given money and presents, and eventually recruited as a 'sub-agent'. Gradually the 'sub-agent' might get the chance to get a cell formed of three or four men at an armament factory. New recruits are checked up by the Communist Party. Later plans are brought out of the works and photos of these have to be prepared.

Original documents were 'never allowed to be stolen', so photography equipment was necessary to copy the documents before the agent replaced the originals.[18] According to Krivitsky, 'The Fourth Department agent is himself always an expert photographer,' so if material could not be secreted away to another town or country house, pictures could be taken on the spot. Although Soviet officers maintained a full photographic laboratory in London, trained assistants were sent to the sub-agent in possession of the material 'with a small suitcase which contained everything he could want for photographing documents'. They checked into a hotel, set up the makeshift laboratory, and copied the documents in the hotel room – 'always a Leica camera was used'.[19] The material processes of agent operations marked a distinct vulnerability. The discovery of a miniature camera by the authorities could have been compromising; hence the great importance to tradecraft of concealment and other security measures.[20]

Krivitsky was one of the first to provide MI5 with clues of a major leakage of information from the British Embassy in Rome in the 1920s and 1930s. Undoubtedly it operated along the lines illustrated above. In discussing the King case, Krivitsky told MI5 he had himself read a large number of his telegrams and, *en passant*, mentioned that they were not nearly as important as the material the OGPU obtained from the British Embassy in Rome'.[21] To his recollection, Krivitsky connected the name 'Duncan' with the source of information from the British Embassy in Rome.[22] Sixty years later, *The Mitrokhin Archive* identified the Rome 'source' as two sources, the brothers Francesco ('Duncan') and Segundo ('Dudley) Constantini, employees at the British Embassy.[23]

A year after Krivitsky arrived in New York, another defector appeared in America and added more information about the leaks in Rome. The recent declassification of Leon Helfand's MI5 file for the first time allows first-hand insight into the Rome operation.[24] On compiling a summary of the case for the Foreign Office, Sir Frederick Hoyer Millar, a British diplomat in Washington (and later Ambassador to West Germany and PUS of the Foreign Office), lamented, 'I'm afraid this report is rather in the nature of locking the stable door after the horse has gone, but it certainly gives a pretty frightful picture of our Embassy in Rome!'[25]

Three key observations emerge from Helfand's debriefing, and all emphasise the fragility of British protective security in the 1930s.[26] First is the sheer quantity and comprehensiveness of the information to which the Soviets had access. Helfand said that 'in Rome he had read not only our telegrams in and out, but also all reports, print, and internal communications such as minutes between the Commercial Counsellor and the Ambassador'.[27] The possession of British messages *en clair* would have greatly facilitated breaking Britain's coded communiqués.[28] Second is the incredible speed with which the Constantini brothers delivered the material. Helfand said the source 'would bring them documents which had been received, or sent, on only the previous day, and sometimes on the same day'.[29] Finally, the Soviets paid an extraordinary sum for the material. According to Helfand, the Rome source received $10,000 per month, though this was later reduced to $5,000. Clearly, the Soviets regarded the intelligence to be of great value. Indeed, the documents obtained in Rome by the Constantinis included meetings between Foreign Secretary Sir John Simon and Hitler in Berlin; Eden and Litvinov in Moscow; Eden and Polish Foreign Minister Joseph Beck in Warsaw; Eden and Czech President Edvard Beneš in Prague; and Eden and Mussolini in Rome.

Yet even though many of these documents went straight to Stalin, it is not clear that the Soviets used the information as well as they might have, if at all. Given the range of information they collected, for example, it is hard to believe that the Soviets did not also receive the Foreign Office documents regarding Eden's visit to Stalin in Moscow in 1935 (which were also sent to Rome). Yet the Centre, according to *The Mitrokhin Archive*, did not record it as notable.[30] Perhaps, then, the information was received, but tactfully discarded or altered before reaching Stalin. Slutsky and other officials in the INO were reluctant to inform Stalin that Eden believed him to be 'a man of strong oriental traits of character with unshakeable assurance and control whose courtesy in no way hid us from an implacable ruthlessness' or, indeed, Eden's opinion that he was 'perhaps more appreciative of the German point of view than Litvinov's'. In the mid-1930s, higher-ups knew that placation was essential to maintaining their careers and extending their longevity.[31] So even if the Soviets excelled at collecting intelligence, their failure in analysis meant they were frequently *less* rather than *more* informed about their opponent's actual intentions.

The 'Imperial Source' and the Cambridge Five

Krivitsky's information on the CID source, or 'Imperial Source', came to suggest that the footprint of Soviet activity would not be one that British intelligence would readily recognise. The agent he described did not fit the preconceived notion of *communist* that many in British intelligence held. Krivitsky said he thought the 'C.I.D. information came from a person of titled family', but Alley made a point to note that it was 'only Mr. THOMAS's idea'.[32] Archer bluntly told Krivitsky, 'It was very important for me to be able to find out the identity of this man'. Krivitsky said he was 'certain' that 'the source was a young man, probably under thirty', that he was an agent Maly recruited 'purely on ideological grounds', and that 'he took no money for the information that was obtained'. He had been recruited 'on the basis of anti-Hitler work', and, according to Krivitsky, Maly 'or an agent of Maly', convinced him that Stalin was the only man capable of countering the fascist threat and preserving 'the cause of democracy generally'. Krivitsky said the man was 'almost certainly educated at Eton and Oxford' and believed him to be the 'son or secretary of one of the chiefs of the Foreign Office', from whom the 'boy obtained the papers' and 'may probably have taken them home'. He also 'could not get it out of his head' that the source was a 'young aristocrat'. With some prodding, however, Krivitsky agreed that he may have reached this latter conclusion only 'because he thought it was only young men of the nobility who were educated at Eton'.[33]

Krivitsky told Archer that the Imperial Source's information was of such 'vital importance' that even if Maly left the country and King were dropped 'he [did] not think the Soviets would have abandoned this young man'.[34] Moscow began receiving his information in 1936, and Krivitsky himself saw the material when he was last in Moscow in 1937. It took Archer several days of questioning, but finally she wrote to Vivian, 'I think I have now got quite clear all the information [Krivitsky] has about the information from the "Imperial "Council" [*sic*]'. As she explained it:

> This information was always bound up special in the form of a book, typewritten on pale green paper. Only five copies of this book were made up, one for VOROSHILOPP [War Commissar Marshal Klimint Voroshilov], one for ORLOFF [Deputy Commissar for Defence and Commander of Soviet Naval Forces Vladimir Orlov], one for YEZHOV [OGPU chief Nikolai Yezhov], one for SLOUTSKI [INO chief Abram Slutsky], and one for STALIN. The book contained information of high Naval, Military, Air Force and political importance. . . . Walter told me that between 1936 and 1937 he saw two or three books of the same kind containing the same sort of reports. He said that the book did not contain all the reports which were received, which he said went into a very large number of pages. The book was made up, not as we previously understood of a precis of all this information, but extracts literally translated into Russian: where the translator was not sure of the Russian translation, the English word was put in brackets after it.[35]

Archer's last point may seem trivial, but it is significant. It means the information conveyed to Moscow was not summarised or handwritten and then passed on, but that documents were actually being secreted out of government offices, copied and passed on to Moscow while the originals were returned. This indicated the existence a worryingly sophisticated network of spies with some level of technological proficiency along the lines Krivitsky had described.

Krivitsky said he would be able to identify the document he saw in Moscow if it were shown to him again, so Archer duly produced two copies of documents that fit the description Krivitsky had offered. The first was the cover of a CID Imperial Conference document (No. 98), which Krivitsky quickly recognised: 'Yes, I have seen this cover several times in Moscow, in white on black form, in the office of the man who receives the material. This man had a photographic studio adjoining his room and when the copies were made and dried, they were piled on his desk.' But it was the second copy that Archer showed him, part of a 'very secret S.I.S. document' (dated 25.2.37), that Krivitsky had been referring to as what he had seen in Moscow. 'This is the document', Krivitsky definitively stated. Archer noted:

Then followed some general conversation, in the course of which he mentioned again how much more important the agent who obtained the Imperial Conference material was than KING. I said, 'naturally, because if that agent could obtain reports such as I showed you he would have also access to the most important of KING's stuff'. In fact as they had this agent they need not worry, as that was the only agent they would need. On this Thomas suddenly said 'Ah, I now remember this man must be in the Foreign Office'. He then told me a story which will be the subject of a separate note of how a third man was approached by a Dutchman from Holland, and offered to supply material from the Foreign Office. He says he now remembers that he refused to allow this man to be taken on because they already had two good sources in the Foreign Office and he thought to take on a doubtful third would imperil those two. The two agents in the Foreign Office were KING and the Imperial Conference man, of that he seems now quite certain.[36]

An investigation showing that the SIS document never went through the CID validated Krivitsky's certainty, but his certainty was met by increasing uncertainty by MI5 about other details he had already provided about the CID source.

Over a week after he first began to describe the CID source, Archer wrote that Krivitsky still 'harped on' a young aristocrat, who he 'thought' was under thirty, and who he again suggested went to Eton and Oxford. This time he admitted though that 'it was not quite clear' if that description was true or merely fit his image of the English aristocracy. In fact, so firmly embedded is the Soviet notion of the aristocratic credentials of the Cambridge Five that Yevgeni Primakov, former head of the KGB's post-Cold War successor, the SVR, and one of Soviet intelligence's sharpest-ever leaders, still refers to Donald Maclean as a 'Scottish lord' (his father's title was not hereditary), and insists that Maclean's fortune was large enough to have underwritten all Soviet foreign intelligence costs, an exaggeration well into the realm of the absurd.[37]

Krivitsky was now, however, 'perfectly certain' that the source was 'a University man', but he stepped back from his suggestion that he was the son of a 'big man' in the Foreign Office and instead suggested he could equally have been a private secretary. He began also to 'harp on the suggestion that [the source's] name began with P', which he had not done before. Seeing the files years later, the reader's mind jumps to Kim Philby, who might have fitted Krivitsky's description. Educated at the elite institutions of Westminster and Trinity College, Cambridge, he was also son of the renowned Arabist St John Philby, who had wide contacts in diplomatic circles. Philby himself later wrote that

Krivitsky caused him consternation when he learned Archer had 'elicited a tantalising scrap of information about a young English journalist whom the Soviet intelligence had sent to Spain during the Civil War'.[38] In short post-debriefing reports, Krivitsky first said that the Foreign Office source was counted 'amongst the friends' of another 'English *aristocrat* who was to go to Spain to murder Franco'.[39] Only on page eighty-two of Archer's eighty-six page case summary does the reference to a journalist appear. In other words, there is no record of its original recording in the post-debriefing write-ups, so it is unclear when and in what context Krivitsky first told Archer that the young man in Spain was a journalist.

Although the information is buried at the end of Archer's report, it is not an insignificant entry. In the nine-page index to 'Soviet Secret Agents' named by Krivitsky, Maly's entry is about one page in length – much longer than any other. But the way the information is presented is perhaps important. In Archer's final report, the link between the CID source and the English journalist is lost. This passage describes how:

> Arnold DEUTSCH was another of [Maly's] agents in London and it was HARDT [Maly] who obtained highly important information covering the deliberations of the Committee of Imperial Defence. BRANDES was one of his subordinates. . . . HARDT was not a subordinate of KRIVITSKY, but the two men were personal friends. Moreover under the commission given to him in 1935 KRIVITSKY had the right to enquire into HARDT's organisation and in certain cases to give him orders. HARDT's 'service' name was MANN and it was in this name that his instructions and money were sent to him at the Soviet Embassy in London. KRIVITSKY corresponded with him and sent him money through the Soviet Embassy in the name of MANN. Early in 1937 the Ogpu received orders from Stalin to arrange the assassination of General Franco. HARDT was instructed by the Ogpu chief, YEZHOV, to recruit an Englishman for the purpose. He did in fact contact and sent [*sic*] to Spain a young Englishman, a journalist of good family, an idealist and fanatical anti-Nazi.[40]

So even though the link between the CID source and the Englishman in Spain was strong in the initial briefings, it was almost coincidental in the final report. It linked the CID source and the Englishman in Spain only through Maly, who had been dead for three years by the time Krivitsky arrived.

A former FBI special agent who worked during this period has written:

In 1939 [*sic*], if the British Intelligence service had been more on their toes, at least two of the three men [i.e. Burgess, Maclean, Philby] might have been uncovered as Soviet spies. . . . Krivitsky . . . told the British that there were two other Soviet agents in the F[oreign] O[ffice]; one of them, he said, was a Scotsman of good family who had been educated at Oxford and Eton. He mentioned, as well, a third important Soviet agent who was journalist, a man who had been with the Franco forces during the recent Civil War. Now, Krivitsky's details were slightly wrong – Maclean had gone to Cambridge, not to Oxford – but most of his information was correct enough to have identified both Maclean and Philby. However, neither Maclean or Philby came under suspicion, despite Krivitsky's warnings.[41]

There is no indication that the journalist was 'with the Franco forces' – Krivitsky simply said he was sent to assassinate Franco. Moreover, since Krivitsky did not imply that the journalist posed a threat to British security, identifying him would not have been a priority. Third, to fault MI5 for not cross-referencing earlier material directly linking the CID source and the journalist would require, by the same logic, the need to factor in Krivitsky's earlier insistence that the CID source's name began with a 'P'. Yet it was impossible for Philby to be the source because, as a journalist during the Spanish Civil War, he did not have access to the material Krivitsky saw in Moscow in 1937. So although the information may have been 'correct enough', it was fragmentary and buried in a mountain of other vague scraps of information.

Without Krivitsky's insistence that the source's name began with a 'P', Donald Maclean nearly fits the profile. Krivitsky's biographer insists, with references to a 'Scotsman' from 'a very good family', that 'today it is clear that it should have led to Donald Maclean'.[42] Lord Gladwyn (Gladwyn Jebb) also stated many years later that, with the benefit of hindsight, he believed the spy Krivitsky attempted to identify might have been Maclean. He came from an upper-class family; his father, Sir Donald, had been a prominent Liberal MP who had briefly served as President of the Board of Education in MacDonald's second National Government; he had attended Gresham's School and Trinity Hall, Cambridge; he had joined the Foreign Office in 1935; and, not least, he was a 'Scotsman'. These parallels, although striking, become muddied when Krivitsky's debriefing is reviewed in detail. As Lord Gladwyn conceded, Krivitsky's evidence was inconclusive at the time; the Foreign Office did not lack diplomats 'of good family'.[43]

Closer analysis shows that if Krivitsky is taken at his word, the evidence pointing to Maclean is not as obvious as some of the subsequent secondary literature would have us believe. Archer's final report states:

[Krivitsky] is certain that the source was a young man, probably under thirty . . . that he was recruited as a Soviet agent purely on ideological grounds, and that he took no money for the information obtained. He was almost certainly educated at Eton and Oxford. KRIVITSKY cannot get it out of his head that the source is a 'young aristocrat', but agrees that he may have arrived at this conclusion because he thought it was only young men of the nobility who were educated at Eton. He believes the source to have been the secretary or son of one of the chiefs of the Foreign Office.[44]

But Archer crucially prefaced her remarks with the caveat, 'As regards the source of the "Imperial Council" information KRIVITSKY has *little definite information*.'[45] The mention of a father in the Foreign Office is intriguing in light of Maclean's father's prominence, but Sir Donald was not in the Foreign Office; he was an MP. And again, if we expect MI5 to have reviewed the evidence beyond Archer's final report, we also have to entertain Krivitsky's earlier idea that 'the boy obtained the papers from his father who may probably have taken them home'.[46] Sir Donald died in 1932, four years before Krivitsky saw the CID material in Moscow. A postwar note in Krivitsky's MI5 file reads, 'It was clear that in 1940 S.I.S. had identified a document which KRIVITSKY had seen in Moscow. Its title was "Soviet Foreign Policy during 1936". . . . It had been circulated by S.I.S. to the Foreign Office Northern Department, Foreign Office Mr. Leigh, [. . . etc.].'[47] So although Maclean was rising fast in the Foreign Office, it might not have been immediately clear that from his position in the League of Nations and Western Department that he would have had access to the kind of material Krivitsky saw anyway (nor incidentally would have his father, even if he had not already died).[48] None was an artist. The only one of the Five associated with art was Blunt, but Krivitsky did not describe the source as 'a Scot and a communist with artistic tastes', as later reported.[49] In response to Levine's information as given to Mallet, Harker wrote to Jebb with the wish to clarify the information about the 'Scottish artist communist and idealist', but Krivitsky, according to Levine, had actually said that the source was a sculptor.[50] In any case, this information only appears in the Foreign Office correspondence and does not reappear during the MI5 debriefing. Moreover, Blunt was in London (not Spain) during the Spanish Civil War. In 1937 he took up his post at the Warburg Institute, so he could not have passed the documents that Krivitsky saw in Moscow. He did not have access to government files until he joined MI5 in 1940.

The only possible clue Krivitsky gave about Burgess, which applied equally to Blunt, was the oblique suggestion to 'look up names of communist leaders in UK. Name begins with "B". This was HARDT's best recruiting agent.'[51] But Burgess was not a communist leader; he, like the rest of the Five, repudiated links with communism after being recruited by Deutsch (and then handled by Maly). Additionally, Burgess would not have had access to material Krivitsky saw – in 1937 he was a producer for the BBC.

Recently one writer has even suggested that the CID source was John Cairncross.[52] It is unclear how he reached this conclusion. Cairncross did have access to the kind of material Krivitsky saw in Moscow, but not until 1940, when he was appointed secretary to Lord Hankey (who, despite losing his position in Chamberlain's War Cabinet after Churchill became Prime Minister, retained his ministerial rank and continued to receive Cabinet documents).[53] In 1937 Cairncross was moving between departments in the Foreign Office, finally transferring to the Treasury at the behest of Maly in October 1938.[54] Moreover, if MI5 had been looking for a Scottish 'aristocrat' who attended 'Eton', they would not have found this person in Cairncross. Although he was indeed Scottish and a Cambridge graduate, Cairncross came from a working-class background.

No one fits the description of Krivitsky's Imperial Source, but several did share his characteristics. Today we can see that MI5 should have looked for a young, upper-class journalist, educated at elite institutions, who worked in Spain during the Civil War, and whose name began with 'P'. Through this person MI5 could have located his friend, a Scotsman, also educated at elite institutions who worked in the Foreign Office and whose father was or had been prominent in government. At the time, however, Krivitsky's information might equally have led MI5 to look for an Eton- and Oxford-educated Scottish lord whose name started with 'P', whose father was a private secretary at the Foreign Office, and who may (or may not) have counted amongst his friends an aristocratic English journalist in Spain during the mid-1930s. The former is a very different search from the latter. If it had been as obvious then as it is now, Philby and Maclean would have been caught much earlier.

MI5's investigations were hampered, too, by circumstance. Resources previously dedicated to countering the Soviet Union had been diverted to confront the more urgent German threat Britain faced once the war began in earnest. Dick White later told his biographer, 'Our enemy was Germany, not Russia. Our major interest was whether Russia might help the Germans. Krivitsky provided no information about that,' a view which Liddell apparently shared. The same account notes that Krivitsky's 'information was filed and soon forgotten.'[55] Krivitsky's MI5 file records little investigation between his departure from London and his death. MI5's investigations into Soviet espionage all but halted after 22 June 1941, when the Soviet Union entered the war as a British ally. The Foreign Office thenceforth prohibited MI5 from actively investigating Soviet activity in the UK.[56] During the war, Archer, the central figure in the Krivitsky case, left MI5 and began work at SIS – under Philby, who did his best to 'keep her busy'. Blunt was then Liddell's secretary.[57] From these positions Philby and Blunt could monitor and influence counter-Soviet agent operations and reveal vital tradecraft to the Soviets.

It might be said that the vicissitudes and vagaries of Krivitsky's information demonstrate the weaknesses of human intelligence, the full potential of which can only be realised when it is fully incorporated into the rest of the intelligence cycle – when it complements other forms of intelligence collection and analysis. Ultimately, Krivitsky's 'Eton and Oxford' clues bolstered the case against Maclean – but only after the joint US-UK VENONA project had deciphered documents that revealed the existence of a spy in Washington.[58]

All the same, the picture remains incomplete. Just as the absence of MI5's records on the Krivitsky's dossier distorted the history, so the continued classification of the Cambridge Five's MI5 and SIS files distort it that much more. Without access to these files, it is impossible to say if and to what extent Krivitsky's clues led MI5 to the identification of Maclean or Philby. One of the most frequently cited accounts of Krivitsky's clues about Philby is the latter's memoir, which was designed in part to make MI5 and SIS look foolish. For those tempted to argue that Krivitsky's clues about the Imperial Source represent gross incompetence on the part of MI5 and SIS, they do so partly uninformed, and possibly misinformed. Any conclusions must remain speculative until the MI5, and perhaps the SIS, files on the Cambridge Five are released.

Krivitsky's Departure(s)

By the time Krivitsky departed, his relationship with Archer and others had changed to one in which he actively gave advice. He stressed two threats in particular. First, as mentioned, were the lengths he believed Stalin would go to appease Hitler in order to destroy the British Empire. We now know what Krivitsky did not know then: Hitler's Operation Barbarossa would ignite the fiercest fighting of the Second World War, and the Eastern Front would bury more bodies than any other field of battle. But Krivitsky grasped that Stalin's long-term strategic intentions firmly set the Soviet Union in opposition to Great Britain, rather than establishing the alliance that temporary circumstances soon compelled them to create.

Second, Krivitsky stressed the severity of the threat posed by the CPGB. He conceded that a 'healthy democracy' in a time of peace could hold the revolutionary left at the fringes, but in a time of war with the Soviet Union (which de facto existed following the Nazi-Soviet Pact, at least in the intelligence sense), Krivitsky was 'most emphatic that the existence of the Communist Party organisation is very real danger'. Part of his alarm stemmed from what he perceived to be the public's failure to comprehend the threat. As the summary report on his debriefing states: 'KRIVITSKY is genuinely astonished that he cannot in our press, or periodicals, or in the speeches of ministers, find any indication that the British people realise the gravity of the existence of such an organisation as the Communist Party of Great Britain in time of war'.[59] As he had described, the CPGB amounted to an enemy encampment within Britain's borders. Although subsequent literature has shown that King Street did not operate in complete subservience to Moscow, and that the members of the CPGB did not share a monolithic outlook, neither is there evidence that the CPGB actively worked against Soviet intelligence during the interwar period – quite the contrary.[60] Those years are replete with examples of CPGB succour to hostile Soviet intentions.

In Krivitsky's opinion, there were two ways to meet the Soviet threat in Britain. The first, he said, was to 'grow up agents from the inside', and he specifically cited Olga Grey's penetration of the CPGB. The time-lag necessary to achieve results, if indeed results were to be achieved at all, constituted the obvious drawback to this approach. Nonetheless, it was common practice for Soviet intelligence abroad. Krivitsky said,

> [The] Fourth Department was prepared in some instances to wait for ten or fifteen years for results and in some cases paid the expenses of a university education for promising young men in the hope that they might eventually obtain diplomatic posts or other key positions in the service of the country of which they were nationals.[61]

The exposure of the Cambridge Five would bring home the success of Soviet strategy with unmistakable clarity. In 1940 Krivitsky urged British intelligence to confront the Soviet strategy directly, using its own principles against it.

Krivitsky suggested that simple bribery provided the second most effective means of countering Soviet espionage in the UK. He noted, quite rightly, that most of the original ideologues, 'those who held the old Bolshevik faith', had been or soon would be eliminated from important positions of power as a result of the purges. In their wake arrived petty technocrats and apparatchiks with 'no strong political faith' who were far more susceptible to bribery and corruption. Underpinning this malleable loyalty was 'the ever present idea of fear'. Although particular bribes would have to be considered on a case-by-case basis, Krivitsky insisted that fear united all Soviet civil servants. He believed that 'the only way to approach a Russian working for the Soviet Government is to present him with a plan to eliminate this fear. Such a plan would necessarily involve providing him with protection and a means to live outside Russia.'[62] Unfortunately this was not something provided for Krivitsky himself.

Krivitsky clearly understood the interplay of motivation and persuasion in tradecraft. His analysis also sprang from his own situation – he was afraid and financially susceptible. Just before Krivitsky's departure, Liddell noted in his diary, 'There has been a slight hitch with Walter Krivitsky.' Arrangements had been made to pay Krivitsky £1,000 (over £46,000 in today's terms) plus all expenses for his time in London. Liddell wrote that on finalising these arrangements with Harker, Krivitsky was 'apparently in a good mood', but nonetheless requested a private audience with Alley, the Russian-speaking officer present throughout the debriefing. Liddell relates how Krivitsky explained to Alley that 'he did not wish it to be thought that there any lack of faith as between himself and the British government or that he had not given us information for other than ideological reasons', but, he insisted, one result of his trip to London was his losing a newspaper contract in the United States worth the considerable sum of $6,500. As a result, 'He therefore thought that if we were going to give a little nest-egg which would be used by his wife, £5000 would be a more proper figure.' It was not the first time that Harker had bargained with an informant. The two finally settled on £2,000, to be transferred to Krivitsky in Canada. 'All parties seemed satisfied,' Liddell noted.[63]

Krivitsky left London on 16 February 1940. In remarkable contrast to later practices, there was no notion of supervised resettlement or protection for a defector whose occupational hazards included assassination. One later study of interrogation noted that after 'breaking' a source, the interrogator's 'old job of interrogation is now one of agent testing and agent handling and protection of an agent's life. Interrogation has become counterespionage.'[64] Krivitsky's handlers were not similarly responsible. Over the next year, SIS and MI5 attempted to keep track of his whereabouts as he shifted from one residence to another in the United States, but eventually they apparently lost trace of him altogether. They would not have another opportunity to question Krivitsky.

Nor would anyone else for much longer. Almost a year to the day after he left London, Krivitsky was found dead by gun shot in a hotel room in Washington, DC (10 February 1941). Officially ruled a suicide, many believe he was 'suicided' or died directly at the hand of a Soviet assassin.[65] The killing of defectors, like Ignace Reiss and possibly Krivitsky, laid bare the stakes of secret warfare and demonstrated the primacy of protective security for intelligence sources.

Before Krivitsky came to London, Archer wrote, 'I am convinced . . . that if we wish to get to the bottom of Soviet military espionage activities in this country, we must contact KRIVITSKY.' It is appropriate to ask, therefore, if MI5 got to the bottom of Soviet military intelligence activities. Was Archer's goal achieved? The verdict is mixed. On the one hand, the Imperial Source, and by extension the Cambridge Five – clearly the most successful Soviet penetration agents in British history – were not revealed until much later, and only as the indirect result of Krivitsky's information. One could argue, however, that it is unreasonable to expect MI5 and SIS to have identified the Five at that point as they had only just begun their careers in government – although it also highlights vetting as another great security weakness of the interwar period in Britain. Furthermore, Krivitsky's composite description of the Imperial Source made him exceeding difficult to identify. Perhaps expectations of what information Krivitsky could provide were inflated. However, through Krivitsky, MI5 gained a more complete picture of Soviet tradecraft, operations, personnel, and structure than arguably any other security service did at that time – which, by any account, was a great success.[66]

Some have dubbed the period from 1914 to 1945 the 'long war'. It can equally be said that the period from 1917 to 1989 amounted to a much longer war (with a nominal interlude from 1941 to 1945). Much of the long war against communism was fought in the shadows, but in 1940 Krivitsky delivered to the West the blueprint upon which the Soviets fought their underground battles. It was the achievement of MI5 and SIS to recognise Krivitsky's potential value when few others did. In addition to operational details, he brought with him insight into the strategic intent and mind-set of one of the most closed societies in modern history. From that, MI5 was able to draw out advice on how to combat the communists in Britain and abroad. Though circumstance would necessarily shift British security intelligence priorities towards the Nazi menace during the Second World War, Britain's security and intelligence apparatus would later return to Krivitsky's debriefing. The intelligence that Krivitsky provided prefigured the terms by which the world powers would conduct their underground battle for the remainder of the twentieth century.

Conclusion

A LTHOUGH Britain may boast the world's longest continuously operating intelligence services, they were only three decades old at the onset of the Second World War. Having learned by doing, their handlers and operatives had laid the tracks for the great challenges that lay ahead. That new expertise, however, was typically not the sort depicted in action films and sensational fiction. The real nature of intelligence work was by and large not the world of swashbuckling escapades it is often portrayed to be.

It should be apparent that despite the images conjured by popular media, agent running was dominated by unrelenting paperwork. An in-house summary of MI5's First World War operations concluded that 'one law emerges: success in investigation depends upon mastery of detail.'[1] Or as John Curry's official history evokes the slogging reality of MI5's watchers, it was difficult to find, train, and keep 'suitable staff for this very difficult and usually very dull work.'[2] Surveillance reports, such as those of Ottaway and Hunter on trailing Macartney, the FPA and others, illustrate the degree to which such surveillance, a core component of agent operations, is nothing short of drudgery.

As the preceding chapters show, political dividends can flow from good intelligence, itself born of good tradecraft. In revealing opponents' intentions and operating methods, well-practised human intelligence and the high quality of what it produces can give policymakers an advantage in making decisions. Knowing what one is up against can allow better strategic and tactical calculations. At the extremes, it can change the course of the major rivers of history. Whether policymakers use intelligence wisely, or even at all, is another matter altogether.

It remains to be answered, for example, what intelligence – if any – would have convinced Chamberlain to take a different track in the run-up to the Munich Crisis. SIS at times provided sound tactical intelligence, but what little of their strategic assessments exists in the public domain situates SIS squarely in the camp of endorsing Chamberlain's position. From some quarters, such as

MI5, the message was consistent and clear: reports that did attempt to counsel policymakers on Germany's determined expansionism went unheeded.[3]

During the interwar years, MI5 built an institutional memory centred on the accretion of knowledge about and skill in tradecraft and agent operations. It began by looking to its own wartime past, not only to have 'a record of what was done but as a means of studying and learning the various points that may be useful in the future when the bureau is confronted with similar problems'.[4] Nonetheless, its early histories were largely descriptive, not prescriptive. They provide a foundational contrast to later documents, such as Maxwell Knight's 'M. Section Report', written after the Second World War, which details his interwar experience with penetration agents. Knight explicitly identifies 'lessons learned' from cases in which he was involved.[5]

With the powerful benefit of hindsight, it is clear that interwar intelligence officers – at least not those at MI5 and almost certainly not from other services either – did not explicitly recognise a craft of espionage as we do today. The self-consciousness of craft came with the Second World War, at a time when the near collapse of MI5 forced it to address its agent operations in a more systematic fashion. Although the essence of tradecraft itself might not have changed, its management did, and so did reflection on issues of the art and science of espionage.

Just as the transition from the First World War to peacetime did not treat MI5 kindly, neither did the transition from peacetime back to war. If, after the First World War, MI5 had been like a deflated balloon, it nearly burst from its hasty re-inflation in the transition to the next war. 'In June 1940, the organisation of the Service had all but broken down,' a postwar report found, blaming the rapid development of the war and the burgeoning of the Service in response.[6]

Disorganisation in the suddenly overloaded Registry lay at the heart of the collapse. Although 'it is axiomatic that efficient intelligence work depends primarily on good records, the Registry had been allowed to lapse into a most lamentable position' in the build-up to the war.[7] From September 1939 to May 1940, the Registry nearly quadrupled in size.[8] MI5 was beset by the same panic about the existence of a fifth column that it had experienced at the outset of the First World War – the likelihood that such fears were exaggerated was one lesson it had failed to learn. The scale of paperwork and investigations practically paralysed the Service. MI5 expended scarce resources and valuable hours on futile searches for non-existent agents – money and time that could have been spent investigating the nature of the German secret service (the *Abwehr*) and its head (Wilhelm Canaris), the names of which had, amazingly, only just been learned at the beginning of 1939.[9]

MI5's ranks swelled to cope with the war's demands. This in itself caused problems. Spurred by the Munich crisis of September 1938, MI5's officer count almost trebled from thirty-three to eighty-eight during 1939 – a number that nearly trebled again to 234 by January 1941.[10] Even that increase in personnel was still not sufficient, however, to offset the number of investigations demanded of the Service. Also, because there was no provision for training the influx of recruits, there was often confusion.

Prior to Munich, when the organisation was small, recruitment had been 'haphazard', and 'training took place under the eye of a responsible officer and was acquired in the school of experience'. But such casual arrangements were inadequate to meet a national emergency. Once war was declared, 'Each officer "tore around" to rope in likely people'. But whereas new recruits had been 'placed under old hands' in the past, the sheer number of newcomers meant that 'they were just "thrown into it", no previous training being possible'. As such, 'With increased numbers, training has naturally been curtailed and lack of experience has produced some awkward results'.[11]

Such was the analysis in 1941 of David Petrie, a former police officer in India and the incoming DG of MI5. In the course of his inquiry, Petrie frequently heard 'that the fundamental weakness of the Service was want of control and direction from above'.[12] Nearly a year earlier, Churchill, who had assumed the Premiership in May 1940, had similarly attributed MI5's unpreparedness for war to a failure of leadership. Only a month after moving into 10 Downing Street, he forced the retirements of Kell and his deputy, Holt-Wilson. With war at hand, the timing was terrible, even if perhaps necessary. But on 11 June 1940, Kell wrote in his diary, 'I get the sack', and the tenure of MI5's founding director came to an end.[13]

In the interwar period, intelligence – both as organisation and practice – was highly personalised. Vernon Kell had built MI5 from a staff of one, and tradecraft and agent operations reflected this personal, pragmatic and historically amateur culture; recruitment was informal, and training was on-the-job. Yet the sheer number of recruits entering the service in wartime required an industrial solution to training. External crisis forced the craftsmen of the prewar period to enter the modern age. The maelstrom of war forced a systematic approach to intelligence collection and agent operations. It resulted, for example, in the production of SOE syllabi and the development of training courses on the principles of tradecraft.[14] The days of the journeymen were largely over;

the apprenticeships that had created intelligence professionals from amateurs in the first half of the twentieth century had given way to the training manual.

Epilogue

MI5's tattered image at the outbreak of hostilities with Germany improved during the course of the war. Between September 1940 and June 1941, effective counter-espionage against Germany began to take shape as, 'in an embryonic form', its critical pieces 'began to fit into place'. The three key components consisted of Camp 020 (the agent interrogation centre), the Double-Cross System, and the Registry for indexing ISOS (the decrypted German radio messages).[15] Camp 020's success was in turn also attributed to three sources: ISOS, 'because it was completely reliable and gave concrete facts', 'traces' from MI5 records and SIS agents' reports, though they were more difficult to assess, and Camp 020's own internal card-indexing system for the records of its interrogations.[16] It was not so new, after all. The sources and methods used in the Second World War built on the architecture put in place during the First World War and the interwar years. The Service used human and signals intelligence to complement one another and relied on a registry of information.

The Double-Cross System, too, had been used on a very small scale in the First World War, but its use in the Second World War was of an altogether different magnitude.[17] Through a 'double agent system' run throughout most of the war, MI5 'did much more than practise a large-scale deception through double agents'. J. C. Masterman, chairman of the Double-Cross Committee, did not exaggerate when he later wrote, '*We actively ran and controlled the German espionage system in this country*'.[18] The cardinal principle of Double-Cross was coordination. No significant action was taken or piece of information passed on without the express permission of the various war departments.[19] This protected the interests of the war effort as a whole and maximised the impact of the double agents. R. G. W. 'Tin Eye' Stephens noted that Camp 020, where captured spies were broken, 'became recognised as one of the two most important sources of information in the war, comparable in accuracy indeed to the other, which was ISOS itself'.[20] ISOS provided hard facts, and human intelligence provided insight, judgement and intuition. Difficult to achieve in peacetime, this kind of unity became not even more necessary but also more possible in an era of full-scale war. It also points to the perceived importance of information sharing and the centralised control of agents, much as Maxwell

Knight had insisted upon in a less trying period.[21] In times of limited resources, which most times were, centralised control of agents maximised the efficiency of operations.

As Knight wrote, 'The prime necessity for anyone who is to operate agents is that he shall be, or shall learn to be a man of very wide understanding of human nature; one who can get on with and understand all types and all classes.'[22] T. A. 'Tar' Robertson, who ran the 'Special Agents' section of MI5 (B1a) that handled the turned German agents, possessed a similarly crucial quality: good judgement. According to Masterman, Robertson was 'in no sense an intellectual', but was 'a born leader gifted with independent judgment' who had 'extraordinary flair'. Most important, 'Time and again he would prove to be right in his judgements when others, following their intellectual assessments, proved to be wrong.'[23] Although intellect was certainly an asset, judgement and intuition appeared to be more valuable in agent running.

By Masterman's account, the tradecraft required of the Double-Cross System demanded an immense amount of energy, time and meticulous attention to detail. So although Masterman praised Robertson's 'flair', he pointed out, 'It is a commonplace of counter-espionage work that successes come and spies are caught not through the exercise of genius or even the detective's flair for obscure clues, but by means of patient and laborious study of records.'[24] Yet it was also the officers' insight and 'flair' that enabled them to write the 'careful psychological studies' essential for monitoring the agents' motivations and dispositions, and therefore the stability of the system. Masterman insisted:

> The case officer had to identify himself with his case; he had to see with the eyes and hear with the ears of his agent . . . suffer himself the nervous prostration which might follow an unusually dangerous piece of espionage . . . rejoice with his whole heart at the praise bestowed by the Germans for a successful stroke. . . . [T]he most profitable cases were those in which the case officer had introduced himself most completely into the skin of the agent.[25]

Likewise Stephens wrote of interrogations, 'Personality, above all, is the quality that counts. Then comes experienced direction . . . the right man must be chosen.'[26] The example of Double-Cross, albeit an extreme one, shows that the effective use of an agent must take account not only of the agent's psychology, but also of the character of the intelligence officer handling him.

Double-Cross arguably amounted to the most successful deception in the history of warfare.[27] Numerous agent operations fed into a broader security strategy. Those agent operations were sustained by sophisticated tradecraft that succeeded in large part because of its officers' psychological insights, attention to detail and strategic awareness. It thus connected individual agent runners to wider strategic considerations of historic proportion. The Double-Cross System, therefore, highlights in many ways the primary themes of this study. Ultimately, the finest hour of British intelligence was made possible by the finest tradecraft.

The Second World War challenged the intelligence services by the rapid changes it engendered in both context and the presumed rules of the game. When the Soviet Union became a British ally in June 1941, the Foreign Office laid down 'rigid rules restricting action permissible by the Security Service to the barest minimum'.[28] Cases emerged during the war demonstrating that the Soviets forewent similar restraint, and we now know that Soviet penetration of the British government was pervasive.[29]

As the war ended, however, relationships between nations and the role of intelligence services shifted once again. With the onset (or rebirth) of the Cold War, the USSR re-emerged as Britain's primary strategic opponent. But given the lifting of emergency regulations, MI5 once again faced the difficulties of maintaining security in peacetime, or as John Curry put it, 'Under peace conditions espionage is easy and counter-espionage is difficult, while in war the reverse holds good as a result of war-time controls and the enhanced powers of the Security Service and other authorities'.[30] In a more alarmist vein, he wrote to Liddell (then DDG of MI5), 'It seems to me, we are now in a position vis-à-vis Russia similar to that we had vis-à-vis Germany in 1939/1940 in the sense that we have little positive knowledge of the basic structure of the organisation which we have to counter'.[31] Consequently, the early Cold War saw a flurry of summaries on the history of the Comintern and the reopening of MI5's interwar investigations, Krivitsky's among them.[32] These investigations, often carried out in close concert with American intelligence services, eventually revealed Maclean as a Soviet agent and led to the exposure of Philby and the unravelling of the Cambridge Five.

In revisiting interwar cases, it is clear the extent to which Britain's experience of early Anglo-Soviet relations inherently influenced its counter-intelligence conduct in the Cold War. The apprehension felt by the British government towards communism in the interwar period is illuminated when viewed through the lens of early Bolshevik intentions and operations. When George Kennan, after serving as US American ambassador to the USSR in the early Cold War, reflected upon 'how you deal with a power which openly avows its total enmity towards you but professes an intention to carry it forward not on the plane of direct military warfare but on the plane of limited political and economic competition', he expressed a problem that Britain had faced long before the Cold War proper began. In the end, 'deal with the Devil we must', Kennan wrote, advising that whatever kind of relationship with the devil is formed, the worst course of action would be 'the absence of any relations at all'.[33] This has consistently been the approach of British intelligence since its founding. More often than not, 'dealing with the devil' seems to be a necessary aspect of intelligence work, for only contact with the enemy – often through clandestine tradecraft – will reveal its true intentions.

The Evolution of British Security Studies

Nearly thirty years ago, one trailblazing study of intelligence history cast intelligence as the 'missing dimension' of the history of international relations.[1] Although privately many historians resisted the advent of intelligence history, that sentiment now appears as parochial as when Oxbridge academics did not teach history beyond the nineteenth century.[2] Although some academics still privately dismiss intelligence history as lightweight scholarship, from the episodic furore surrounding the Cambridge Five revelations over the past fifty years and the parliamentary inquiry to the more recent publication of *The Mitrokhin Archive* (1999), the intense governmental concern with intelligence suggests that it is relevance rather than mere popularity driving the rapid expansion of the field as a focus of academic study.[3] In the early twenty-first century, the importance of intelligence policy and the study of the methods, politics and ramifications of intelligence operations have all gained renewed importance in the wake of the 9/11 terrorist attacks and the wars in Afghanistan and Iraq. Earlier eras present similar issues now drawing scholarly attention.

Insider accounts and memoirs comprise most of the literature on intelligence published in the twentieth century. Despite the strict government policy regarding classification, they have been very revealing.[4] Milestone studies include J. C. Masterman's *The Double-Cross System* (1973), which recounted his work as head of the Twenty Committee (so named for the roman numerals representing 'double-cross', 'XX') and told of British success at doubling *Abwehr* agents during the Second World War, and Frederick Winterbotham's *The Ultra Secret* (1974), which revealed the story of the British success breaking of German codes during the Second World War. The government itself opened further chinks in the armour of secrecy, first with the publication of Professor M. R. D. Foot's officially-sanctioned *SOE in France* (1966) and then with the multi-volume official history *British Intelligence in the Second World War* (1979–1990) by Sir F. H. Hinsley et al.[5] Many assumed that the continued classification of the intelligence services' files kept it a closed subject, but Professor Christopher Andrew's *Secret Service* (1985) showed that despite the continued classification of the intelligence archives, a rigorous, scholarly approach to intelligence history was not only possible through the investigation of alternative depositories but also necessary to understand twentieth-century international relations.[6] Yet even with its publication, many historians continued to neglect the history of intelligence. In Piers Brendon's 848-page study of the 1930s, for example, MI5 and SIS receive only one mention apiece.[7] Roy Hattersley's recent account of interwar Britain even tells the story of the Zinoviev Letter and the General Strike without so much as mentioning the intelligence services.[8] But the tide may be changing. Histories by Zara Steiner and Keith Neilson, for example, incorporate intelligence into the fabric or their narrative, showing how intelligence history is integral to our understanding of interwar history.[9]

The study of British intelligence has benefited enormously from the declassification of intelligence files. Following the enactment of the Security Service Act of 1989 and the Intelligence Services Act of 1994, which finally gave the security and intelligence services statutory footing, MI5 and Government Communications Headquarters (GCHQ) began to release files from their archives. By 2012, MI5 had declassified over 4,000 files dating from before 1957, and GCHQ had transferred nearly all of its files covering the years up to the end of the Second World War to the National Archives, Kew.[10] SIS, however, has refused to release any of its documents, contending that the secrecy of its past sources and methods remains crucial to its current ethos and operational success. It argues, for example, that it must uphold its promise of confidentiality to former agents so as not to undermine its credibility with potential agents today. It has, however, followed the MI5's lead in authorising an official history.[11]

Intelligence history is one of the most rapidly developing subfields of historical research. Yet tradecraft – how it was done – remains one of the most secret parts of the secret state and is still conspicuously understudied. In part this is due to the unavailability of source materials, as MI5 keeps secret many files that reveal sensitive operational tradecraft.[12] Although numerous studies have addressed signals intelligence, next to none has given human intelligence, let alone tradecraft, similar attention.[13] To develop a full appreciation of intelligence in any period, one must account for all the *INTs*, including HUMINT.[14]

Memoirs shed some light on tradecraft that is telling, albeit anecdotal. As far back as 1915, Robert Baden-Powell emphasised the importance of an effective disguise – from all angles: 'A man may effect a wonderful disguise in front, yet be instantly recognised by a keen eye from behind.' A man's gait was instantly recognisable from behind, he insisted, so altering it was an important part of a deception.[15] Similarly Paul Dukes observed of his clandestine work in

Revolutionary Russia, 'The one article of clothing which I frequently changed was headgear. It is astonishing how headdress can impart character (or the lack of it) to one's appearance.'[16] His account even included pictures. Baden-Powell's advice is comical in retrospect, and Dukes's tales of derring-do regale us, but they both also provide descriptions of valuable antecedents to more sophisticated recent accounts such as Antonio Mendez's *The Master of Disguise: My Secret Life in the CIA* (1999), which appears on the CIA's recommended reading list.[17] Memoirs such as John Whitwell's *British Agent* (1966) also capture the amateur nature of early espionage while providing sorely missed insight into the tradecraft of the interwar period, for early operatives, like early MI5 itself, only worked out how to do intelligence by doing it. There was no model intelligence system or standard operating manual to fall back on as the British intelligence community created itself as it went along.

Given existing classification policies, historians cannot typically corroborate what they glean from memoirs, especially regarding operational history. Moreover, in a culture of such closely guarded secrecy, the motivations for the writing of memoirs can be suspect. Peter Wright's *Spycatcher* (1987), for example, although in some respects valuable for its descriptions of MI5 operational methods in the 1930s, is undermined by its paranoid conspiracy theory that one of MI5's postwar Directors-General (DG), Sir Roger Hollis, was a Soviet mole. Happily, however, the original files are now becoming far more accessible.

The first reference to espionage tradecraft appears in John le Carré's *Call for Dead* (1961).[18] Its second appearance in public print is in Allen Dulles's *The Craft of Intelligence* (1963). It took forty-five years, however, for a book on tradecraft to appear – that study, *Spycraft* (2008), like much of the available literature on agent operations, relates to the CIA during the Cold War.[19] Nothing of the sort has been written on tradecraft before the Cold War, and nothing has been penned on British operations. Even the term 'tradecraft' did not appear until the early 1960s; it was likely coined sometime in the late 1940s or early 1950s, following the Second World War's professionalisation of intelligence.[20] Declassified SOE syllabi, for example, show that the notion of tradecraft was fully extant before the 1950s, if only by another name.[21] An observer familiar with SIS archives has commented that the postwar SIS adopted SOE tradecraft 'lock, stock, and barrel'.[22] So from a later identification of tradecraft it is possible to analyse retrospectively MI5 operations and those of its adversaries in similar terms. Tradecraft, while not holding nearly as public a profile as it does today, was still a vital contributor to security and intelligence and, by extension, to the information Whitehall used in its decision-making process in the interwar period. Despite new forays into the field, however, tradecraft remains for the moment the missing dimension of the missing dimension.

Record Keeping

History has shown that intelligence can be ineffective or misunderstood without proper collation and organisation. Hence, administration and record keeping form the nucleus of an intelligence organisation. Recent studies of intelligence debacles, such as the failure to prevent the 9/11 terrorist attacks, have revealed the terrible consequences that can result from a nucleus divided.[1]

MI5's own nucleus was its Registry (which ran the file and indexing system). Devised in the immediate pre-First World War period, it did not fundamentally change in peacetime.[2] Even after the Registry overloaded MI5 in June 1940, virtually collapsing, Sir David Petrie, who was about to become the DG of MI5, concluded that B Division merely needed 'manipulation rather than surgery'. It remained fundamentally intact.[3]

The basic organisational structure consisted of file groups. The 'Personal File' (PF) formed the central pillar of the system. One PF per suspect included all reports on that individual, including press clippings in which the suspect's name appeared.[4] Those reports that did not fit neatly into a PF were mostly filed in the place-card index. Known as Official Files (OF), these documents related to certain government departments or offices. Any remaining files not classified as PF or OF were indexed as Subject Files (SF). Although these miscellaneous subject files constituted the dregs of intelligence before the war, their usefulness grew over time. The importance of the OFs, by contrast, waned.[5] All of the names and subjects contained in the files were further cross-referenced in a general card index so that 'particulars regarding the association of any of the names with other given names, places, or subjects could be quickly traced when required with any enquiry'.[6] Covers added to files shortly after the beginning of the First World War, creating space for noting a file's contents, its usage, and notes made by different branches.[7]

Not only were targets, whether individuals or organisations, therefore made part of a web, so was the investigation process within MI5, important because 'experience showed that not only in the filiation of cases, but also as a means of obtaining proof against agents, their "contacts" were of immense value'.[8] Though a case constituted an entity in its own right, it was also 'only one link in a long chain'. Thus 'one law emerges: success in investigation depends upon mastery of detail; and the corollary of these is that one can foretell what detail will not prove to be of primary importance either in the case itself of in some later one'.[9] The value to effective counter-espionage of accurate reporting and record keeping generally was immense.[10]

Secret Inks

The Testing Department (MI9c) devised increasingly cunning tradecraft in its work on postal censorship. As German spymasters grew ever-more sophisticated in their attempts to communicate with their agents in Britain, and as German prisoners in Britain and their officers abroad also developed more inventive ways to interact, the Testing Department kept pace. In addition to experimenting with secret ink, it also investigated ways that civilian correspondence might wittingly or unwittingly reveal strategically sensitive information such as evaluations of public morale or the availability of foodstuffs.[1] Ink, however, accounted for a great deal of its work. The earliest inks exploited the chemical qualities of everyday organic substances. Fruit and vegetable juices, milk, saliva and urine all featured regularly. Not only were they easily available, they were easy to transport without raising suspicion and were similarly easy to make visible, to develop as one would a photograph. The application of heat, as with an iron, quickly reveals these organic compounds.[2] Another technique consisted of dusting paper with graphite, ashes and other pigmented powders, such as cupric oxide. The key to the choice of substance is its ability to adhere to greasy or sticky inks. MI9c documents note that milk, for example, can easily be made perceptible in this manner.[3]

Paper also determines the degree of an ink's invisibility. MI9c categorised paper as being of three basic textures (glazed, thin and tissue) and four basic surfaces (smooth, vellum, rough and linen-faced).[4] Frequently, letters or postcards held at oblique angles to the light revealed the indentations and scratches from an applicator's point, showing the presence of a message or, with careful examination, the message itself.[5] Highly glazed paper, for example, was the most revealing, so special 'prisoner of war paper' was issued to German prisoners to help censors quickly sift through their correspondence.[6] In 1916, the government considered introducing a similar scheme for use by the general public. A paper was developed so that the application of any liquids caused permanent damage to the integrity of the surface, revealing any attempts to write with secret ink. Because it consisted of several layers, dry impressions were also revealed. It was proposed that if the public used this paper, which would be available at the Post Office, their letters would not be delayed due to postal censorship inspections, as letters written on regular paper often were.[7] In the end, the proposal was rejected, but it does show how much postal censorship affected daily life and what an extensive undertaking it had become.

As inks became more sophisticated, searching foreigners entering Britain came to include looking for them and their ingredients. MI9c aided Port Control (E Branch) officers in screening the persons and belongings of travellers coming into the country to identify chemical reagents used for secret ink. Perfume atomisers were a favourite disguise. More innovative methods included saturating clothing such as handkerchiefs, collars, gloves, scarves and sponges with the ink, which was released upon soaking the articles in water.[8] The idea behind the shoe heel, tube, shaving can and cigarette lighter compartments of the Second World War and Cold War had conceptual ancestors in the methods of concealment developed during the First World War.[9]

After the Armistice, MI9 all but disappeared. DORA was repealed, and the OSA of 1911 was superseded by the OSA of 1920 (though much of the 1911 Act remained in place until 1989). Mass censorship ended, and the HOW system re-emerged. As in the prewar period, MI5's relationship with the General Post Office (GPO) again assumed great importance, indispensable as it was to the interception of correspondence.[10] And although MI9 itself was basically defunct, MI9c's work with steganography (the art of secret writing) would prove just as pertinent to postal interception in the interwar period as it had earlier. The three MI9c staff members who remained in December 1918 were tasked 'to carry on the simple testing of prisoners [sic] letters and the special testing of any letters submitted to the Department by M.I.5.g. and other Sections of the Military Intelligence'.[11] MI5g was the Detective Branch. By 1929 at the latest (though almost certainly earlier), this important liaison between the Detective Branch and the GPO was formalised with a permanent MI5 attachment to that office. Captain Frederick B. Booth, having joined MI5 in 1913, was one of its most senior officers, and he was in charge of Special Censorship. The 1931 intelligence reorganisation also incorporated Special Censorship into a Security Research section (S.12), the duties of which included 'scientific and photographic research and censorship'.[12] So the discovery of secret writing and the art of surreptitious letter-opening in no way ended with MI9's demise after the war. Indeed, a former head of a British intelligence service only recently declared that, 'Secret inks are back in.'[13]

Notes

Preface

1 Scott Shane and Charlie Savage, 'In Ordinary Lives, U.S. Sees the Work of Russian Agents', *New York Times*, 28 June 2010, http://www.nytimes.com/2010/06/29/world/europe/29spy.html?pagewanted=all (last accessed 24 June 2012). A version of this article appeared on 29 June 2010 on p. A1 of the New York edition of the newspaper.

2 Scott Shane and Benjamin Weiser, 'Spying Suspects Seemed Short on Secrets', *New York Times*, 29 June 2010, http://www.nytimes.com/2010/06/30/world/europe/30spy.html?hp= &pagewanted=all (last accessed 24 June 2012) added to the rare coincidence of appearances and talents to June 2012. A version of this article appeared on 30 June 2010 on p. A1 of the New York edition of the newspaper.

3 Norman Imler, 'Espionage in an Age of Change: Optimizing Strategic Intelligence Services for the Future', in *Intelligence and the National Security Strategist*, ed. Roger Z. George and Robert D. Kline (Lanham, MD: Rowman & Littlefield, 2006), pp. 217–35 (p. 220).

4 University of Cambridge Intelligence Seminar, information obtained under the Chatham House Rule.

5 University of Cambridge Intelligence Seminar, information obtained under the Chatham House Rule.

6 Victor Cherkashin and Gregory Feifer, *Spy Handler: Memoir of a KGB Officer: The True Story of the Man Who Recruited Robert Hanssen and Aldrich Ames* (New York: Basic Books, 2005), p. 255.

7 See further discussion on definition of tradecraft below, and Robert Wallace and Keith Melton, *Spycraft: The Secret History of the CIA's Spytechs from Communism to Al-Qaeda* (London: Dutton, 2008); James M. Olson, *Fair Play: The Moral Dilemmas of Spying* (Washington, DC: Potomac Books, 2007); Henry A. Crumpton, *The Art of Intelligence: Lessons from a Life in the CIA's Clandestine Service* (New York: Penguin, 2012); Michael Herman, *Intelligence Power in Peace and War* (Cambridge: Cambridge University Press in association with RIIA, 1996); Abram N. Shulsky and Gary J. Schmitt, *Silent Warfare: Understanding the World of Intelligence* (Washington, DC: Brassey's, 2002); Burton Gerber, 'Managing HUMINT: The Need for a New Approach', in *Transforming U.S. Intelligence*, ed. Jennifer E. Sims and Burton Gerber (Washington, DC: Georgetown University Press, 2005), 180–97; Allen Dulles, *The Craft of Intelligence* (London: Weidenfeld and Nicolson, 1963).

8 The term *HUMINT* encompasses intelligence collected by all human sources, overt and covert. In this book, however, HUMINT refers more specifically to clandestine human intelligence. Tradecraft here refers to HUMINT tradecraft; the book does not address analytic tradecraft.

9 Christopher Andrew and Vasili Mitrokhin, *The Mitrokhin Archive: The KGB in Europe and the West* (London: Penguin, 2000), pp. 168–77.

10 See Jerrold Schecter and Peter Deriabin, *The Spy Who Saved the World: How a Soviet Colonel Changed the Course of the Cold War* (Washington, DC: Brassey's, 1995).

11 In Britain, this is partly because its intelligence services only gained statutory footing relatively recently. BBC radio interviews with serving officers and public recruitment advertisements and websites were all unthinkable twenty years ago when these agencies were not publicly acknowledged to exist. 'Security Services Speak to BBC', BBC Radio One and BBC Asia, aired 26 November 2007; see 'Asian MI5 and MI6 Officers Speak', http://news.bbc.co.uk/1/hi/uk/7112190.stm (last accessed 3 April 2008); Seb Ramsay, 'MI5 Uses M.E.N. [Manchester Evening News] for Recruitment Drive', *Manchester Evening News*, 11 January 2007,

http://www.manchestereveningnews.co.uk/
news/s/232/232886_mi5_uses _men_for_
recruitment_ drive.html (last accessed 3
April 2008); Mark Sweney, "'Become a Spy"
Ad Target Gamers', http://www.guardian.
co.uk/media/2007/oct/18/digitalmedia.
advertising (last accessed 3 April 2008); The
Security Service (MI5) website: http://www.
mi5.gov.uk; SIS website: http://www.sis.gov.
uk; GCHQ website: http://www.gchq.gov.
uk. In the United States, too, recent repeated
appearances of a serving CIA director on
television talk shows were unprecedented.
Michael Hayden on 'FOX News Sunday',
FOXNews, aired Sunday 5 February 2006,
partial transcript available at http://www.
foxnews.com/story/0,2933,183844,00.
html (last accessed 3 April 2008); Michael
Hayden on 'Charlie Rose', PBS, aired Tuesday
23 October 2007, available at http://www.
charlierose.com/shows/2007/10/22/1/an-
hour-with-gen-michael-hayden-director-of-
the-cia (last accessed 3 April 2008); Michael
Hayden on 'Meet the Press', MSNBC, aired
Sunday 30 March 2008, transcript available
at http://www.msnbc.msn.com/id/23866794/
(last accessed 3 April 2008).

12 *The 9/11 Commission Report: Final Report
of the National Commission on Terrorist
Attacks Upon the United States* (New York:
W. W. Norton, 2004); Commission on the
Intelligence Capabilities of the United States
Regarding Weapons of Mass Destruction,
Report to the President of the United States
(n.p.: March 2005) ['Silberman-Robb Report'],
available at http://www.whitehouse.gov/
wmd (last accessed 3 April 2008); Rt Hon.
Lord Butler of Brockwell et al., *Review of
Intelligence on Weapons of Mass Destruction:
Report of a Committee of Privy Counsellors*
(London: The Stationery Office, July 2004)
['Butler Report'], available at http://www.
archive2.official-documents.co.uk/document/
deps/hc/hc898/898.pdf (last accessed 3
April 2008). It should be noted that *some*
WMD *were* found (munitions containing
mustard and Sarin nerve agent), but these
were in 'small numbers' and in 'generally
in poor condition', not able 'to be used as
designed', according to a US Army Report
('Officials Discuss Report on Munitions', *New
York Times*, 23 June 2006; Richard K. Betts,
*Enemies of Intelligence: Knowledge and Power
in American National Security* (New York:
Columbia University Press, 2007), p. 215, fn.
30).

13 Christopher Andrew, 'Historical Attention
Span Deficit Disorder: Why Intelligence
Analysis Needs to Look Back Before Looking

Forward', presented at the New Frontiers
Rome Conference, 2004.

14 James W. Harris, 'Building Leverage in the
Long War: Ensuring Intelligence Community
Creativity in the Fight Against Terrorism',
Policy Analysis, 439, 16 May 2002, p. 5, http://
www.cato.org/pubs/pas/pa-439es.html, last
accessed 1 May 2008; reproduced in Loch
K. Johnson and James J. Wirtz, *Strategic
Intelligence: Windows into a Secret World: An
Anthology* (Los Angeles, CA: Roxbury Pub.
Co., 2004), pp. 242-252; Roger Z. George
and Robert D. Kline, *Intelligence and the
National Security Strategist: Enduring Issues
and Challenges* (Lanham, MD: Rowman &
Littlefield Publishers, Inc., 2006), pp. 341-356.

15 Hennessy, 'From Secret State to Protective
State', pp. 15–16.

16 David McKnight, *Espionage and the Roots
of the Cold War: The Conspiratorial Heritage*
(London: Frank Cass, 2002); Franco Venturi,
*Roots of Revolution: A History of the Populist
and Socialist Movements in Nineteenth-
Century Russia* (London: Weidenfeld and
Nicolson, 1960).

17 Term coined by Christopher Andrew and
Oleg Gordievsky, *KGB: The Inside Story of its
Foreign Operations from Lenin to Gorbachev*
(London: Hodder & Stoughton, 1990), p. 145.

18 Fredric Scott Zuckerman, *The Tsarist
Secret Police Abroad: Policing Europe in a
Modernising World* (Basingstoke: Palgrave
Macmillan, 2003), p. 114.

19 Ray Bearse and Anthony Read,
*Conspirator: The Untold Story of Churchill,
Roosevelt and Tyler Kent, Spy* (London:
Macmillan, 1991), p. 108.

20 Christopher Andrew, *For the President's
Eyes Only: Secret Intelligence and the
American Presidency from Washington to Bush*
(New York: HarperPerennial, 1996), p. 164.

21 Allen Dulles, *The Craft of Intelligence*
(London: Weidenfeld and Nicolson, 1963),
pp. 58–9.

22 Michael Herman, *Intelligence Power in
Peace and War* (Cambridge: Cambridge
University Press in association with RIIA,
1996), p. 64; Abram N. Shulsky and Gary
J. Schmitt, *Silent Warfare: Understanding
the World of Intelligence* (Washington, DC:
Brassey's, 2002), p. 19. Cf. Burton Gerber,
'Managing HUMINT: The Need for a New
Approach', in *Transforming U.S. Intelligence*,
ed. Jennifer E. Sims and Burton Gerber
(Washington, DC: Georgetown University
Press, 2005), 180–97: 'A working definition
of HUMINT case officers' tradecraft might
be knowing operations and the operational

situation in detail; integrating that knowledge into physical, political, cultural, and security environments in which they operate; practicing how to conduct themselves in that context with appropriate technology and thinking through and preparing for potential consequences' (p. 183).

Introduction

1 Nick Collins and Duncan Gardham, 'Russian Spy Rock was Real, Former Chief of Staff Admits', *Daily Telegraph*, 19 January 2012, www.dailytelegraph.co.uk (last accessed 15 July 2012).

2 In some documents, the SSB is also referred to as the Special Intelligence Bureau (SIB).

3 NA KV1/46 G Branch: Investigation of Espionage 1915–1919: Appendixes and Annexures, Appendix A, 'Detective Intelligence Work', p. 6.

4 A. C. Wasemiller, 'The Anatomy of Counterintelligence', *Studies in Intelligence*, Winter (1969), 9–24, p. 10.

5 The Detective Branch was referred to as G Branch during the First World War and B Branch in the interwar period. The Security Branch and legislative structure was F Branch and then A Branch, and record keeping was H, D and then O Branch. This is an abbreviated account of MI5's various designations, which were actually more complicated. The domestic section of the SSB was at first incorporated into the Directorate of Military Operations (DMO) as Military Operations Section 5, subsection (g) – MO5(g), run by Vernon Kell. MO5 as a whole also dealt with aliens, the press, censorship and legal questions. In January 1916 the Directorate of Military Intelligence (DMI) was formed, at which point the counter-intelligence service became Military Intelligence, Section 5 (MI5). There were various restructurings of the MI5 subsections, as well. The three essential components remained under various titles and ended the war as MI5(g), MI5(f) and MI5(h). An account of these organisational changes can be found at NA WO 32/10776 History of the Military Intelligence Directorate, pp. 21–2, and John Curry, *The Security Service 1908–1945: The Official History [With an Introduction by Christopher Andrew]* (Kew: Public Record Office, 1999), pp. 70–2. For MI5's wartime organisation at its fullest extent, see NA KV1/57 I.P Book 9, *MI5 Distribution of Duties*.

These 'legislative procedures' will be elaborated below. To be clear, however,

'legislative procedures' did not mean Parliamentary legislation. As has been noted, MI5 had no statutory existence until the Security Service Act 1989 (see http://www.opsi.gov.uk/acts/ acts1989/Ukpga_19890005_en_1.htm (last accessed 22 August 2008).

6 See Appendix II, 'Record-keeping'.

7 The domestic department was incorporated into the Directorate of Military Operations (DMO) in August 1914 as M.o.5, and shortly after as M.o.5(g). In 1916 it became Military Intelligence, Section Five, or M.I.5, and it finally became the 'Security Service' in 1931. The foreign department became MI1(c) in 1916 and the Secret Intelligence Service (SIS) in 1921. As is customary, they will be referred to as MI5 or the Security Service and MI6 or SIS, respectively. See Curry, *Security Service*, pp. 70–2, 100–02.

8 Home Office Identity and Passport Service, 'The History of Passports', http://www.ips.gov.uk/passport/about-history-modern.asp (last accessed 7 April 2008).

9 Quoted in David Stafford, *Churchill and Secret Service* (London: Abacus, 2001), p. 44.

10 NA KV1/38 F Branch: Prevention of Espionage 1909–1916: Summary, p. 8; cf. Curry, *Security Service*, pp. 72–3.

11 NA KV1/38 F Branch: Prevention of Espionage 1909–1916: Summary, p. 11, 59.

12 The use of the term 'fifth column' here is anachronistic; the term was actually coined during the Spanish Civil War. For background on the Anglo-German rivalry, see Paul M. Kennedy, *The Rise of the Anglo-German Antagonism 1860–1914* (London: Allen & Unwin, 1980); Christopher Andrew, *Her Majesty's Secret Service: The Making of the British Intelligence Community* (New York: Viking, 1986), chapter 2.

13 NA KV1/38 F Branch: Prevention of Espionage 1909–1916: Summary, p. 10; cf. KV1/49 H Branch: Organisation and Administration: 1900–1919, p. 12.

14 NA KV1/38 F Branch: Prevention of Espionage 1909–1916: Summary, p. 19.

15 This standard account has been challenged in Nicholas Hiley, 'Entering the Lists: MI5's Great Spy Round-Up of August 1914', *Intelligence and National Security* (February 2006), 46–76. See also Thomas Boghardt, *Spies of the Kaiser: German Covert Operations in Great Britain during the First World War Era* (Basingstoke: Palgrave Macmillan in association with St Antony's College, Oxford, 2004), which questions the commonly held belief that MI5's security proved generally

superior to German foreign intelligence during the war.

16 NA KV1/38 F Branch: Prevention of Espionage 1909–1916: Summary, p. 41. This MI9 is to be distinguished from the MI9 of the Second World War, which ran missions in support of resistance movements and extracted allied soldiers from behind enemy lines.

17 NA WO 32/10776 *Historical Sketch of the Directorate of Military Intelligence during the Great War 1914–1919*, p. 20/29 [this file is double-paginated]. For more on censorship, see Appendix III, 'Secret Inks'.

18 Security Service, 'Who We Are', http://www.mi5.gov.uk/output/Page51.html (last accessed 28 March 2008).

19 Stafford, *Churchill and Secret Service* , p. 45.

20 Her file is available at NA KV2/1570.

21 Albert Inkpin's MI5 files are available at NA KV2/1532–1537 and cover the years 1916–1953 (Inkpin died in 1944). He served as General Secretary from 1920 to 1922 and again from 1923 to 1929. The first HOW was imposed on him on 30 April 1921 (KV2/1533, s.26) and included his among a list of other 'names of communists, among whom are the leaders of the movement in Great Britain. It is desired to obtain, by means of this check, information concerning the roots and ramifications of the movement and to establish the identity of certain important conspirators who employ pseudonyms'.

22 MI5's 'founder member' files include: Robert Bailey (NA KV2/1990–1992): first HOW imposed 12 April 1927 (KV2/1990, s.2a); Thomas Bell (KV2/1538–1539): first HOW imposed 12 July 1922 (KV2/1538, s.3); Reginald T. Bishop (KV2/1599–1602): first HOW imposed 10 March 1922 (KV2/1599, s.2a); William Gallagher (KV2/1753–1755): first HOW imposed 12 April 1922 (KV2/1753, s.14); James Gardner (KV2/1797–1798): first HOW imposed 7 September 1922 (KV2/1797, s.1a); Percy Glading (KV2/1020–23): first HOW imposed 7 December 1922 (KV2/1020, s.1a); Arthur Horner (KV2/1525–1529): first HOW imposed 30 April 1921 (KV2/1525, s.1); Robert Page-Arnot (KV2/1783–1784): first HOW imposed 21 December 1921(KV2/1783, Precautionary Index); David Ramsey (KV2/1867–1870): first HOW imposed 14 December 1921 (KV2/1867, s.31); Douglas Springhall (KV2/1594–1598): first HOW imposed 5 November 1920 (KV2/1594, s.4); and Robert Stewart (KV2/1180–1183, 2787–2792): first HOW imposed 30 April 1921 (KV2/1180, s.3a).

Other notable files set up in the early 1920s include Emile Burns (KV2/1760–63): first HOW imposed 30 April 1921 (KV2/1760, s.5a); John Campbell (KV2/1186–1189): first HOW imposed 19 April 1921 (KV2/1186, s.3a); Ernest Cant (KV2/1051–53): first HOW imposed 30 April 1921 (KV2/1053, s.12a); Thomas Clark (KV2/584): first HOW imposed 19 April 1921 (KV2/584, s.1a); George Hardy (KV2/1027–29): first HOW imposed 7 February 1923 (KV2/1027, s.15a); Peter Kerrigan (KV2/1030–32): first HOW imposed 25 January 1923 (KV2/1030, s.1a); Harry Pollitt (KV2/1034–1047): first HOW imposed 30 April 1921 (KV2/1034, s.1a); William Rust (KV2/1048–1050): first HOW imposed 30 April 1921 (KV2/1048, s.1a); and William Thomson (KV2/1378–79): first HOW imposed 30 April 1921 (KV2/1378, s.2b).

23 Cf. Nicholas Hiley, 'Internal Security in Wartime: The Rise and Fall of P.M.S.2, 1915–1917', *Intelligence and National Security*, 1 (1986), 395–415 (p. 403).

24 Gill Bennett, *Churchill's Man of Mystery: Desmond Morton and the World of Intelligence* (London: Routledge, 2006), p. 71.

25 John G. Hope, 'Surveillance or Collusion? Maxwell Knight, MI5 and the British Fascisti', *Intelligence and National Security*, 9 (1994), 651–75 (p. 658).

26 NA WO 32/10776 History of the Military Intelligence Directorate, p. 17/26.

27 Michael Howard, *War in European History* (Oxford: Oxford University Press, 1976), p. 127; Herman, *Intelligence Power in Peace and War*, p. 23.

28 Until recently, the history of early British cryptanalysis was generally limited to the study of Room 40, the naval bureau of cryptanalysis. See Beesly, *Room 40*; Andrew, *Her Majesty's Secret Service*, chapter 3; and Denniston, *Thirty Secret Years*. Relatively little has been written on the military's contributions to First World War and interwar SIGINT. Historian John Ferris has noted that MI1(b) is 'the worst documented of British intelligence agencies between 1900 and 1945': John Ferris, 'The Road to Bletchley Park: The British Experience with Signals Intelligence, 1892–1945', *Intelligence and National Security*, 17 (2002), 53–84 (p. 55). Recent literature, however, has begun to highlight the importance of MI8 (cable censorship) and MI1(b) (military codebreaking and cryptanalysis). Peter Freeman, the late historian of GCHQ, has shown that military SIGINT played just as significant a role in the formation of GC&CS as the Admiralty's Room 40 did. Peter Freeman, 'MI1(b) and the

Origins of British Diplomatic Cryptanalysis',
Intelligence and National Security, 22 (2007),
206–28; Ralph Erskine and Peter Freeman,
'Brigadier John Tiltman: One of Britain's
Finest Cryptologists', *Cryptologia* 27 (2003),
289–318, available at findarticles.com/p/
articles/mi_qa3926/is_200310/ai_n9311691/
print (last accessed 10 March 2008).

29 NA HW 43/1 The History of British
SIGINT, 1914–1945, Vol. I, 'British SIGINT,
1914–1942' (by Frank Birch), p. 17. Room 40
has received more scholarly attention, but
MI1(b) 'brought the larger dowry in staff and
technical experience' to GC&CS, contributing
a larger proportion of both senior and junior
officers.

30 Freeman, 'MI1(b) and the Origins of
British Diplomatic Cryptanalysis', pp. 221–2.

31 Denniston, *Thirty Secret Years*, p. 101;
Andrew, *Her Majesty's Secret Service*, p. 261;
Victor Madeira, '"Because I Don't Trust Him,
We Are Friends": Signals Intelligence and the
Reluctant Anglo-Soviet Embrace, 1917–24',
Intelligence and National Security 19 (2004),
29–51 (pp. 32–3). See also Victor Madeira,
*Britannia and the Bear: Anglo-Russian
Intelligence Wars, 1917–1929* (Woodbridge:
Boydell Press, 2014).

32 Andrew, *Her Majesty's Secret Service* ,
p. 262.

33 Andrew, *Her Majesty's Secret Service*,
pp. 331–2. This was not the first time the
government tipped its hand, and it had earlier
caused difficulties for GC&CS by doing
so. The one-time pad (OTP), or Vernam-
cypher, is encryption using plaintext and a
random key that when employed properly is
impossible to break.

34 Erskine and Freeman, 'Brigadier John
Tiltman'. MASK intercepts can be found
in the NA HW17 series (Moscow–London
exchanges at HW17/16-22).

35 Denniston, *Thirty Secret Years*, p. 69.
National Security Service/Central Security
Service (NSA/CSS), 'Hall of Honor', Brigadier
John Tiltman, http://www.nsa.gov/honor/
honor00030.cfm (last accessed 18 March
2008).

36 Denniston, *Thirty Secret Years*, p. 88 (cf.
Robin Denniston, 'Diplomatic Eavesdropping,
1922–1944: A New Source Discovered',
Intelligence and National Security 10 (1995),
423–48).

37 Ferris, 'The Road to Bletchley Park', p. 67;
Kevin Quinlan and Calder Walton, 'Missed
Opportunities? British Intelligence and the
Road to War', in *The Origins of the Second
World War: An International Perspective*, ed.

Frank McDonough (London: Continuum,
2011), 205–22.

38 See Chapter 1.

39 NA KV1/39 G Branch: Investigation of
Espionage 1909–1911: German Espionage,
p. 13; cf. KV1/46 G Branch: Investigation
of Espionage 1915–1919: Appendixes and
Annexures, pp. 10.

40 Curry, *Security Service*, p. 75.

41 NA KV1/39 G Branch: Investigation of
Espionage 1909–1911: German Espionage,
p. 12.

42 NA KV1/38 F Branch: Prevention of
Espionage 1909–1916: Summary, p. 49. F
Branch's history describes the application of
these principles as follows: 'INFORMATION
is obtained by a British S.I. [secret intelligence]
agent in enemy or neutral territory that
an enemy agent, vaguely identified as to
name, description and probably mission, is
setting out for some British area. Immediate
COMMUNICATION to the proper S.I. officer
in the British Area enables him to consult the
S.I. RECORDS and to prepare for suitable S.I.
COUNTER-ACTION. On passing through
the first S.I. EXAMINATION post, the
stranger, owing to his correspondence of the
particulars of his personal IDENTIFICATION
with the reported description of the enemy
agent, receives an S.I. CLASSIFICATION
leading to his selection for a degree of S.I.
CONTROL and supervision supplementary
to that applicable to the general public, or
persons of certain categories, such as aliens.
Unaware that his actions or movements
are of special interest to S.I. he despatches
disguised messages to the enemy by post,
telegraph or messenger or intercepted by the
S.I. CENSORSHIP discloses that, although
personally he has done no mischief to date,
he appears to be organising mischief directed
against specified vulnerable objectives, and
involving the services of other persons not
yet identified, some of whom appear to be his
superiors in the enemy intelligence system.
The Military and Civil measures for route
standing PROTECTION . . . or all vulnerable
objectives of the nature specified are then
tuned up at the instance of S.I. In due course
some person is arrested. . . .' (NA KV1/35 F
Branch: Prevention of Espionage 1914–1918:
Volume I, p. 100; KV1/38 F Branch: Prevention
of Espionage 1909–1916: Summary, p. 50).

43 Quoted in Alan Judd, *The Quest for C:
Mansfield Cumming and the Founding of the
Secret Service* (London: HarperCollins, 2000),
p. 470.

44 NA KV1/39 G Branch: Investigation of Espionage 1909–1911: German Espionage, p. 11.

45 Bennett, *Churchill's Man of Mystery*, pp. 33–4.

46 NA KV1/38 F Branch: Prevention of Espionage 1909–1916: Summary, p. 46.

47 NA KV1/38 F Branch: Prevention of Espionage 1909–1916: Summary, pp. 45–6.

48 The Secret Service Committee met in 1919, 1921, 1922, 1925, 1927 and 1931. The first SSC meeting consisted of ministers, but civil servants made up the attendees thereafter. Sir Warren Fisher (permanent secretary of the Treasury and first head of the Civil Service) and Sir Maurice Hankey (secretary to the Cabinet) attended all meetings (leading the group to be sometimes referred to as the Fisher Committee), as did a changing cast of Foreign Office Permanent Under-Secretaries: Lord Hardinge (1916–1920), Sir Eyre Crowe (1920–1925), Sir William Tyrell (1925–1928), Sir Ronald Lindsay (1928–1930) and Sir Robert Vansittart (1930–1938). Permanent Secretary to the Home Office, Sir John Anderson, was also part of the 1925 Committee. Gill Bennett, 'The Secret Service Committee, 1919–1931', in *The Records of the Permanent Undersecretary's Department: Liaison between the Foreign Office and British Secret Intelligence, 1873–1939* (London: FCO, 2005), p. 42.

49 NA KV4/151 SSC 1919–1923, s.[none], War Cabinet 519, draft minutes of meeting of 24 January 1919 (with reference to GT-6665 & 6690).

50 NA KV4/151 Secret Service Organisation 1919–1939: Secret Service Committee 1919–1923 ['SSC 1919–1923'], s.[none] (GT-6665), memorandum for the War Cabinet by the First Lord of the Admiralty (Walter Long), 16 January 1919. It is not made clear why the Scotland Yard's Special Branch, under the Home Office, did not operate to satisfaction.

51 F. H. Hinsley and C. A. G. Simkins, *British Intelligence in the Second World War: Volume IV: Security and Counter-Intelligence* (London: HMSO, 1990), p. 5.

52 Cf. NA KV4/151 SSC 1919–1923, s.[none], 'The Home Office Secret Service: Historical Note', circular of the Home Secretary (E. Shortt), 30 November 1921.

53 See Hiley, 'Internal Security in Wartime'.

54 NA KV4/151 SSC 1919-1923, s.31 (GT-6965), 'Report of the Secret Service Committee', Home Office, February 1919, p. 4.

55 Bennett, 'The Secret Service Committee, 1919–1931', p. 44.

56 Bennett, *Churchill's Man of Mystery*, p. 39; Judd, *The Quest for C*, p. 434. Agreement reached 8 April.

57 Andrew, *Her Majesty's Secret Service*, p. 233 (fn. 36); Lawrence H. Officer and Samuel H. Williamson, 'Purchasing Power of British Pounds from 1245 to Present', MeasuringWorth.com, 2014 (calculated in terms of retail price index at 2012 rates). Throughout the book, these currency values from the interwar period should serve as an indicator of magnitude rather than an exact translation of worth because of various measures of inflation. For the sake of comparison Richard Overy has noted that in the interwar period an average worker made roughly £2–3 per week and a journalist earned roughly £10–15 per week. Anyone making over £1,000 per year might be considered upper middle class or wealthy. See 'Note on currency' in Richard Overy, *The Twilight Years: The Paradox of Britain between the Wars* (London: Penguin 2009).

58 The £8,000 peak was described as 'abnormal' due to a non-recurring disbursement of £1,500. NA KV4/151 SSC 1919–1923, s.[none], 'Secret Service', Note by War Office, 3 February 1919. 'Contre-Espionage'.

59 Curry, *Security Service*, p. 99, Introduction by Andrew, p. 5. In the 'fourth year' of war (presumably 1918), the War Office gives the number of officers as 141 (NA KV4/151 SSC 1919-1923, s.[none], 'Secret Service', Note by War Office, 3 February 1919, 'Contre-Espionage').

60 Classic accounts include Paul Dukes, *The Story of "ST 25": Adventure and Romance in the Secret Intelligence Service in Red Russia* and Augustus Agar, *Baltic Episode: A Classic of Secret Service in Russian Waters* (London: Hodder and Stoughton, 1963).

61 NA KV4/151 SSC 1919-1923, s.[none], 'Secret Service Committee', 22 March 1921, p. 7.

62 Victor Madeira, '"No Wishful Thinking Allowed": Secret Service Committee and Intelligence Reform in Great Britain, 1919–23', *Intelligence and National Security* 18 (2003), 1–20 (p. 7); Andrew, *Her Majesty's Secret Service*, pp. 191–2, 229–30.

63 Andrew, *Her Majesty's Secret Service*, chapter 9; Madeira, 'No Wishful Thinking Allowed'.

64 Madeira, 'No Wishful Thinking Allowed', p. 10; Andrew, *Her Majesty's Secret Service*, pp. 279–82. See also Madeira, *Britannia and the Bear*.

65 This is not to say that there had been no intelligence coordination. The Committee of Imperial Defence (CID), formed in 1902 in response to weaknesses revealed by the Boer War, advised the Prime Minister on military and strategic affairs related to the security of the Empire, but it was not a part of the Cabinet. Nonetheless, it exercised considerable influence on policy due to the prominent officials who served on it, including the heads of armed services, and, important for this analysis, Prince Louis of Battenburg (Director of Naval Intelligence) and General Sir William Nicholson (Director of Military Intelligence). Thus intelligence had been incorporated into broader security strategy before the JIC, but the JIC specifically and primarily concerned itself with the coordination and assessment of intelligence gathered by various Departments. See Franklyn Arthur Johnson, *Defence by Committee: The British Committee of Imperial Defence, 1885–1959* (Oxford: Oxford University Press, 1960).

66 Edward Thomas, 'The Evolution of the JIC System Up to and During World War II', in *Intelligence and International Relations 1900–1945*, ed. Christopher Andrew and Jeremy Noakes (Exeter: University of Exeter, 1987), 219–34 (p. 220).

67 Betts, *Enemies of Intelligence*, p. 31.

68 See Chapter 1.

69 The term 'intelligence community', however, did not emerge until the Cold War. Herman, *Intelligence Power in Peace and War*, p. 27.

70 NA KV4/151 SSC 1919–1923, s.[none], 'Secret Service', circular by Secretary for War (L. Worthington-Evans), January 1922.

71 Quoted in Andrew's introduction to Curry, *Security Service*, p. 4.

72 Curry, *Security Service*, p. 92.

73 See Chapter 2.

74 The debate can be followed in NA KV4/182 Notes on Reorganisation and Future Status of Defence Security Intelligence Service (M.I.5.) including Proposed Amalgamation with other Intelligence Services, 1925.

75 Curry, *Security Service*, p. 99.

76 Hinsley and Simkins, *British Intelligence in the Second World War: Volume IV*, p. 8.

77 Richard A. Posner, *Preventing Surprise Attacks: Intelligence Reform in the Wake of 9/11* (Lanham, MD: Rowman & Littlefield in co-operation with the Hoover Institution, 2005), p. 133.

78 Curry, *Security Service*, p. 102; Hinsley and Simkins, *British Intelligence in the Second World War: Volume IV*, p. 8.

79 Hinsley and Simkins, *British Intelligence in the Second World War: Volume IV*, p. 10. Hugh Trevor-Roper writes, 'How does anyone come to be in any Secret Service? Such a service cannot recruit by open means. Patronage and accident are the only ways in': Lord Dacre of Glanton, 'Sideways into S.I.S.', in *In the Name of Intelligence: Essays in Honor of Walter Pforzheimer*, ed. Hayden B. Peake and Samuel Halpern (Washington, DC: NIBC Press, 1994), pp. 251–60 (p. 251).

80 See John Whitwell, *British Agent* (London: Frank Cass, 1996).

81 NA KV4/88 Director General's Report on the Security Service, February 1941, Prepared for the Security Executive, s.2a, 'Report prepared by Sir David Petrie', 13 February 1941, p. 5.

82 Quoted in Tom Bower, *The Perfect English Spy: Sir Dick White and the Secret War, 1935–90* (London: Heinemann, 1995), pp. 26–7.

83 Posner, *Preventing Surprise Attacks*, p. 133.

84 The SIS archive holds a manual on tradecraft drafted after the First World War, but the nature of the file is unclear. Most indications point to on-the-job training until at least the Second World War (University of Cambridge Intelligence Seminar, information obtained under the Chatham House Rule).

CHAPTER 1

Official Cover

1 Richard H. Ullman, *Anglo-Soviet Relations: Vol. III The Anglo-Soviet Accord* (London: Oxford University Press, 1973); Christopher Andrew, 'The British Secret Service and Anglo-Soviet Relations in the 1920s Part I: From the Trade Negotiations to the Zinoviev Letter', *The Historical Journal* 20 (1977), 673–706; Andrew, *Her Majesty's Secret Service*, chapter 9; (and most recently) Madeira, 'Because I Don't Trust Him, We Are Friends'. See also, Madeira, *Britannia and the Bear*.

2 Three other publications have so far exploited MI5's Klishko files: Victor Madeira, 'Moscow's Interwar Infiltration of British Intelligence, 1919–1929', *The Historical Journal* 46 (2003), 915–33 and Madeira, *Britannia and the Bear*; Kevin Morgan, *Labour Legends and Russian Gold* (London: Lawrence & Wishart, 2006). See also Andrew and Gordievsky, *KGB*, p. 51.

3 Madeira, *Britannia and the Bear*, p. 42.

4 The INO was the Foreign Intelligence Department of the KGB's forerunner. The 'The All-Russian Extraordinary Commission for Combating Counter-Revolution and Sabotage', or *Cheka* as it is commonly known, was founded on 20 December 1917. Technically speaking, the notion of 'residents' likely did not arise until after the formation of the INO in December 1920, whereas Klishko arrived in London in May 1920. Long after Cheka changed names and was subsumed into an increasingly complex security apparatus (first as GPU under the NKVD in February 1922, under the OGPU in July 1923; as GUGB under the NKVD in July 1934, etc.), intelligence officers still referred to themselves as *Chekisty* (Andrew and Mitrokhin, *The Mitrokhin Archive* , p. 30). The standard reference on the Cheka itself remains George Leggett, *The Cheka: Lenin's Political Police* (Oxford: Clarendon, 1981).

5 Quoted in Steiner, *The Lights That Failed*, p. 131.

6 NA KV2/1411 'KLISHKO, Nicolas Clementievich', s.[none], P.P.421. 'Nicholas KLISHKO', Summary made in H.1. from papers filed between 1 September 1915 and 9 September 1918, ref 124891. On the development of Russian revolutionary political thought, see the seminal Venturi, *Roots of Revolution: A History of the Populist and Socialist Movements in Nineteenth-Century Russia*. See also Isaiah Berlin, *Russian Thinkers* (London: Penguin, 1979), esp. pp. 198–237; and Alexander Herzen, *My Past and Thoughts: The Memoirs of Alexander Herzen* (London: University of California Press, 1992).

7 NA KV2/1411 KLISHKO, s.[none], P.P.421., 'Nicholas KLISHKO', Summary made in H.1. from papers filed between 1 September 1915. and 9 September 1918, ref 24654, 88898.

8 See NA KV2/585-87 LENIN, Nikolai, alias Vladimir Ilitch ULYANOV; cf. NA KV2/1575 ROTHSTEYN, Andrey Fedorovich / ROTHSTEYN, Teodor Aronovich, s.[none], P.F. 323/52 'The Brothers Theodore, Albert and Samuel ROTHESTEIN. Precis made in H.1. for reference only from papers filed from 25.7.11. to 8.10.18', precis made by Capt Holyroyd, p. 1.

9 NA KV2/1411 KLISHKO, s.[none], P.P.421., 'Nicholas KLISHKO', Summary made in H.1. from papers filed between 1 September 1915 and 9 September 1918, ref 2322.

10 NA KV2/1410 KLISHKO, s.[none], I.P. No. 295848, letter to J.F. Moylan (HO), enclosing memo 'NICHOLAS KLYSHKO' [*sic*], by M.W. Bray (MI5G4), 11 July 1918.

11 Andrew, *Her Majesty's Secret Service*, chapter 6; Andrew Cook, *Ace of Spies: The True Story of Sidney Reilly* (Stroud: Tempus, 2004); Robert Bruce Lockhart, *Memoirs of a British Agent: Being an Account of the Author's Early Life in Many Lands and of his Official Mission to Moscow in 1918* (London: Macmillan, 1932); Judd, *The Quest for C*, chapter 18. Reilly was lured back to Russia in 1925 and executed as part of Operation TREST, an elaborate Soviet sting.

12 Keith Neilson, '"Joy Rides"? British Intelligence and Propaganda in Russia, 1914–1917', *The Historical Journal* 24 (1981), 885–906. Ransome went on to marry Trotsky's secretary and maintained close links with the Bolshevik leadership, including Lenin. His files also suggest he passed information to SIS (KV2/1903 RANSOME, Arthur Mitchell, s.8, from MI1c, 29 October 1918; ref CX.050167 12.9.18., s.6[b]). Ransome evidently also knew Klishko. An SIS circular listed both of them as being among a party of Bolsheviks in Stockholm considered likely to be expelled by the Swedish government in 1919 (KV2/1903 RANSOME, s.14a, extract from MI1c report, 6 January 1919). Further, Klishko's name is among the few to be found amongst in Ransome's slim list of contacts recorded at the beginning of 1924 (Andrew and Gordievsky, *KGB*, p. 579, fn. 34).

13 The stories of many of the ensuing exploits, including those recounted in Paul Dukes and others' tales, were published as memoirs. It has been noted that there are probably more published first-hand accounts of British intelligence operations at the end of and following the First World War than for any other period between 1909 and the present (Judd, *The Quest for C*, p. 423).

14 NA KV2/1411 KLISHKO, s.[none], P.P.421., 'Nicholas KLISHKO', Summary made in H.1. from papers filed between 1 September 1915. and 9 September 1918, ref Vol.2 (2).

15 The case files are today held by MI5.

16 Quoted in Andrew, *Her Majesty's Secret Service*, p. 245.

17 Andrew, *Her Majesty's Secret Service*, p. 244; Lawrence H. Officer and Samuel H. Williamson, 'Purchasing Power of British Pounds from 1245 to Present', MeasuringWorth.com, 2014 (calculated in terms of retail price index at 2012 rates).

18 NA KV2/1576 ROTHSTEYN, s. 68a, 'Theodore Arnovitch Rothstein', 21 September 1920, p. 2.

19 'The "Daily Herald"', *The Times*, Thursday 19 August 1920, p. 10.

20 'The "Daily Herald"', *The Times*, Thursday 19 August 1920, p. 10. Although the source must be treated with caution, the same figures are given in Basil Thomson, 'Scotland Yard from Within', *The Times*, Tuesday 6 December 1921, p. 11. Lansbury's autobiography largely skirts the issue, but he does deny accepting money that came from jewel smuggling (see below). George Lansbury, *My Life* (London: Constable and Co., 1928), p. 194.

21 Quoted in Andrew, *Her Majesty's Secret Service*, p. 267.

22 Andrew, *Her Majesty's Secret Service*, p. 269; M. V. Glenny, 'The Anglo-Soviet Trade Agreement, March 1921', *Journal of Contemporary History* 5 (1970), 63–82 (p. 72).

23 Exchange in Madeira, 'Because I Don't Trust Him, We Are Friends', pp. 39–40.

24 See decrypt listings in Madeira, 'Because I Don't Trust Him, We Are Friends', p. 50 (fn. 63). See also Madeira, *Britannia and the Bear*.

25 Quoted in Ullman, *The Anglo-Soviet Accord*, p. 308; cf. Andrew and Gordievsky, *KGB*, p. 55.

26 Quoted in Ullman, *The Anglo-Soviet Accord*, p. 309.

27 NA KV2/1392 The Russian Trade Delegation and Revolutionary Organizations in the United Kingdom. KIRCHENSTEIN, Jacob. [hereafter: 'KIRCHENSTEIN'], s.[none], 'The Russian Trade Delegation and Revolutionary Organisations in the United Kingdom' [hereafter: 'The Russian Trade Delegation'], report by Scotland Yard, 7 December 1925, p. 1; Curry, *Security Service*, p. 96. For other network members, see Karl Bahn (KV2/645), called Kirchenstein's 'first lieutenant', Jacob Jilinsky (KV2/799), and Robert Koling (KV2/806-7).

28 NA KV2/1392 KIRCHENSTEIN, s.[none], 'The Russian Trade Delegation', pp. 1–2.

29 NA KV2/1392 KIRCHENSTEIN, s.[none], 'The Russian Trade Delegation', p. 2.

30 Andrew, *Her Majesty's Secret Service*, pp. 280–82.

31 NA KV2/1392 KIRCHENSTEIN, s.[none], 'The Russian Trade Delegation', p. 2.

32 NA KV2/1392 KIRCHENSTEIN, s.[none], 'The Russian Trade Delegation', p. 3. MI5's LRD files available at NA KV5/75–79.

33 Robin Page Arnot's file available at NA KV2/1783–84; C. Palme Dutt's file available at NA KV2/2504–05.

34 R. Palme Dutt's file available at NA KV2/1807–1809.

35 NA KV2/1392 KIRCHENSTEIN, s.[none], 'The Russian Trade Delegation', p. 2.

36 Metropolitan Police Synopsis, 'Siege of Sydney Street', available at http://www.met.police.uk/ history/sidney_street.htm (last accessed 14 April 2008).

37 NA KV2/797 Miller, Anton/Miller, Peter Anjeivitch, s.18., HOW for Peter Miller, 13 December 1923.

38 Morgan, *Labour Legends and Russian Gold*, p. 34.

39 See biographical précis at NA KV2/1576 ROTHSTEYN, s. 68a, 'Theodore Arnovitch Rothstein', 21 September 1920. Walter Kendall, *Revolutionary Movement in Britain, 1900–21: The Origins of British Communism* (London: Weidenfeld & Nicolson, 1969) (esp. p. 241); Morgan, *Labour Legends and Russian Gold*, chapter 2 (esp. p. 35); and David Burke, 'Theodore Rothstein and Russian Political Émigré Influence on the British Labour Movement, 1884–1920' (unpublished doctoral dissertation, University of Greenwich, 1997) (e.g., p. 221, 233).

40 Morgan, *Labour Legends and Russian Gold*, p. 38.

41 NA KV2/1576 ROTHSTEYN, s.68, 'Theodore Arnovitch Rothstein', 21 September 1920, p. 2.

42 NA KV2/1414 KLISHKO, s.246a, 'Activities of Nikolai Klishko', SIS to Captain Miller (Scotland Yard), ref. CX/1205/Ib), 27 November 1924; Morgan, *Labour Legends and Russian Gold*, p. 40.

43 NA KV2/1214 KLISHKO, file summary.

44 Quoted in Morgan, *Labour Legends and Russian Gold*, p. 40.

45 NA KV2/1414 KLISHKO, s.209b, Scotland House papers re Klishko, n.d. (30 November 1921).

46 According to Aino Kuusinen, whose then-husband Otto was one of the Comintern's leading triumvirate, the OMS (Comintern International Liaison Department) provided the link between the Comintern and the Fourth Department, but it is unclear how much this connection led to actual cooperation (Aino Kuusinen, *Before and after Stalin: A Personal Account of Soviet Russia from the 1920s to the 1960s* (London: Joseph, 1974), p. 40).

47 Cf. Andrew and Gordievsky, *KGB*, chapter 3; Kuusinen, *Before and After Stalin*, chapter 2; Kevin McDermott and Jeremy Agnew, *The Comintern: A History of International Communism from Lenin to Stalin* (Basingstoke: Macmillan Press, 1996).

48 NA KV2/1392 KIRCHENSTEIN, s.[none], 'The Russian Trade Delegation', p. 2, 4.

49 NA KV2/804 'KRIVITSKY, Walter J.,
s.25a (T), 2.2.40 (B.4), 'Information re Fourth
Department and the Ogpu', 2 February 1940,
p 2. Cf. Bob Reinalda, ed., *The International
Transportworkers Federation, 1914–1945:
The Edo Fimmen Era* (Amsterdam: Stichting
beheer IISG, 1997).

50 NA KV2/805 KRIVITSKY, s.55x,
'Information obtained from General Krivitsky
during his visit to this country, January–
February, 1940', (Jane Archer), p. 18.

51 NA KV2/1392 KIRCHENSTEIN, s.[none],
'The Russian Trade Delegation', p. 7, letter no.
40.

52 NA KV2/1392 KIRCHENSTEIN, s.[none],
'The Russian Trade Delegation', p. 8, letter no.
56.

53 Literature on surreptitious letter opening
is difficult to come by, and none seems to exist
from the period, but it seems self-evident that
'carefulness' is integral to the enterprise. John
M. Harrison, ed., *CIA Flaps and Seals Manual*
(Boulder, CO: Paladin Press, 1975), p. 1.

54 NA KV2/1412 KLISHKO, s.125, 'Extract'
(MI5. B3. Source:- 'E.R.'), 30 September 1920
(extracted from 31 May report).

55 'Soviet Chief's Visit', *The Times*, Wednesday
26 May 1920, p. 12; 'Krassin [sic] in London',
The Times, Friday 28 May 1920, p. 12.

56 Quoted in Basil Thomson, 'Scotland
Yard from Within', *The Times*, Thursday 8
December 1921, p. 11.

57 Basil Thomson, 'Scotland Yard from
Within', *The Times*, Tuesday 6 December 1921,
p. 11.

58 Lawrence H. Officer and Samuel
H. Williamson, 'Purchasing Power of
British Pounds from 1245 to Present',
MeasuringWorth.com, 2014 (calculated in
terms of retail price index at 2012 rates)

59 *Sic*: The different currencies are as given in
documents.

60 NA KV2/1414 KLISHKO, s.209E, 'G.P
Group', 26 October 1922; NA KV2/1414
KLISHKO, s.209Q, SIS report 'Northern
Summary: Russia', No. 1014, 20 December 1922
(in reference to s.209P, SIS Counter-Bolshevik
Report, 02 December 1922 (CX/1174/1b.),
'Poland: Soviet Agents and Jewel Smuggling').

61 NA KV2/1414 KLISHKO, s.209Q, SIS
report 'Northern Summary: Russia', No. 1014,
20 December 1922, in reference to s.209P,
SIS Counter-Bolshevik Report, 02 December
1922 (CX/1174/1b.), 'Poland: Soviet Agents and
Jewel Smuggling'.

62 NA KV2/1414 KLISHKO, s.209Q, SIS
report 'Northern Summary: Russia', No. 1014,
20 December 1922, 'Note by SIS'.

63 NA KV2/1414 KLISHKO, s.209E, 'G.P
Group', 26 October 1922.

64 'Bolshevist Gold', *The Times*, Wednesday 15
September 1920, p. 10.

65 'Bolshevist Gold', *The Times*, Wednesday
15 September 1920, p. 10; Jane Degras, ed.,
*Soviet Documents on Foreign Policy. Volume I:
1917–1924* (London: Oxford University Press,
1951), 'Wireless Telegram from Chicherin
to Lord Curzon on Interruption of Anglo-
Russian Negotiations', 24 September 1920,
pp. 212: 'As for the interruption the Prime
Minister cited the sale of diamonds and the
subsidising of the *Daily Herald*, with which
the Russian delegation . . . had absolutely no
connexion [sic]'.

66 Quoted in Andrew, *Her Majesty's Secret
Service*, p. 263.

67 Andrew, *Her Majesty's Secret Service*,
p. 264.

68 'Russian Crown Jewels to be Sold', *The
Times*, Monday 22 January 1923, p. 9.

69 See, for example, 'The Platform of
the Communist International', in *Theses
Resolutions and Manifestos of the First
Four Congress of the Third International*,
available at http://www. marxists.org/history/
international/comintern/1st-congress/
platform.htm; cf. V. I. Lenin, 'Theses on the
Fundamental Tasks of the The Second
Congress of the Communist International',
first published July 1920, in his *Collected
Works*, vol. 31, pp. 184–201, available at http://
www. marxists.org/archive/lenin/works/1920/
jul/04.htm#fw02 (last accessed 6 January
2008).

70 Zinoviev did not stop there but went
on to say, 'Now we must say that the hour
has sounded when the workers of the whole
world can arouse and raise up tens and
hundreds of millions of peasants, can form
a Red Army in the East as well, can arm and
organise a revolt in the rear of the British,
can hurl fire against the bandits, can poison
the existence of every insolent British officer
who is lording it in Turkey, Persia, India and
China. . . . May this declaration made today
be heard in London, in Paris, and in all the
cities where the capitalists are still in power.
May they heed this solemn oath sworn by
the representatives of tens of millions of
toilers of the East, that the rule of the British
oppressors shall be no more in the East, that
the oppression of the toilers of the East by the
capitalists shall cease!' ('Baku Congress of the

Peoples of the East', First Session, 1 September 1920, stenographic report available at http://www.marxists.org/history/international/comintern/baku/cho1.htm (last accessed 6 January 2008); Stephen White, 'Communism and the East: The Baku Congress, 1920', *Slavic Review* 33 (1974), 492–514 (p. 500)).

71 'British Note to Soviet. Full Text', *The Times*, Wednesday 9 May 1923, p. 11 (note submitted 8 May).

72 Richard J. Popplewell, *Intelligence and Imperial Defence: British Intelligence and the Defence of the Indian Empire, 1904–1924* (London: Frank Cass, 1995), p. 312.

73 NA KV2/1414 KLISHKO, s.209b, Scotland House Papers re Klishko, n.d., notes for 30 November 1921, 10 April 1923; cf. NA KV2/797 Miller, Anton Anjeivitch/Miller, Peter Anjeivitch, s.18, Home Office Warrant, 13 December 1923.

74 'British Note to Soviet. Full Text', *The Times*, Wednesday 9 May 1923, p. 11.

75 Klishko's NA KV2/1416 file is almost wholly dedicated to tracing the bank notes.

76 NA KV2/1414, s.245y, 'Extract', 28 November 1923, newspaper cutting, 'Morning Post', 'Comrade Klyshko [*sic*]: News of Vanished Bolshevik'; NA KV2/1414 KLISHKO, s.209b, Scotland House papers re Klishko, n.d., note for 5 October 1925.

77 Andrew, *Her Majesty's Secret Service* , p. 296.

78 Held 20 November 1922–4 February 1923, 23 April–24 July 1923. Keith Jeffery and Alan Sharp, 'Lord Curzon and Secret Intelligence', in *Intelligence and International Relations 1900–1945*, ed. Christopher M. Andrew and Jeremy Noakes (Exeter: University of Exeter, 1987), 103–26; Steiner, *The Lights That Failed*, pp. 109–23.

79 NA KV2/1414 KLISHKO, s.246a, SIS report, CX dated 27 November 1924, 'Activities of Nicolai Klishko'.

80 A similar story transpired involving Theodore Rothstein. Denied re-entry to Britain in 1920, he was later posted as Ambassador to Persia. Thus two of Soviet Russia's great organisers and operators were expelled from Britain and ended up in South Asia where their activities were much more difficult to track.

CHAPTER 2

Counter-subversion

1 Foreign Office Historian Gill Bennett's research, which included access to SIS's archives, concludes the letter was a forgery, but that it was indeed representative of the communiqués regularly sent between Moscow and King Street. Gillian Bennett, 'A *Most Extraordinary and Mysterious Business': The Zinoviev Letter of 1924* (London: FCO, 1999). On the 1924 election results, see Peter Clarke, *Hope and Glory: Britain 1900–2000* (London: Penguin, 2004), p. 127 and Appendix, p. 446.

2 A useful overview is provided by Gill Bennett, 'The Secret Service Committee, 1919–1931', in *The Records of the Permanent Undersecretary's Department: Liaison between the Foreign Office and British Secret Intelligence, 1873–1939* (London: FCO, 2005), pp. 42–53.

3 NA CAB 27/260 Supply and Transport Committee meeting (12 & 13), 1 May 1927; quoted in Keith Jeffery and Peter Hennessy, *States of Emergency: British Governments and Strikebreaking since 1919* (London: Routledge & Kegan Paul, 1983), p. 108; James Klugmann, 'Marxism, Reformism, and the General Strike', in *The General Strike, 1926*, ed. Jeffrey Skelley (London: Lawrence & Wishart, 1976), pp. 58–107 (p. 75).

4 NA CAB 27/260 Supply and Transport Committee meeting (12 & 13), 1 May 1927; quoted in Jeffery and Hennessy, *States of Emergency*, p. 108.

5 Clarke, *Hope and Glory*, p. 140.

6 Jeffery and Hennessy, *States of Emergency*, p. 9.

7 MI5 monitored unrest through agent reports. An analysis of a sample of operational reports submitted by regional agents during the General Strike demonstrates in specific terms what has been discussed more broadly, namely the contribution of human intelligence to MI5's understanding of how the General Strike unfolded. In the absence of polling, those agents who penetrated target populations gave intelligence and government officials important insights into public sentiment, troop morale and subversive activity. Although there have been numerous histories written about the General Strike, few have approached it from an intelligence perspective, no doubt in part because MI5's documents have been classified. The pioneering *States of Emergency* by Jeffery and Hennessy is a notable exception, but even it was limited by the unavailability of valuable MI5 files at the time of its writing. Many recently released files offer new insight into MI5's activity during the industrial unrest of the early 1920s and the General Strike of 1926. The more recently published Anne Perkins, *A Very British Strike: 3 May–12 May 1926* (London: Macmillan, 2006) is a general

history that uses MI5 files buts does not specifically focus on MI5's role.

8 A. J. P. Taylor, *English History, 1914–1945* (Oxford: Oxford University Press, 1966), p. 242.

9 NA FO 1093/68 Secret Service Committee 1925, minutes of June 15, p. 10.

10 NA FO 1093/68 Secret Service Committee 1925, minutes of June 15, p. 11.

11 John Bruce Lockhart, 'Intelligence: A British View', in *British and American Approaches to Intelligence*, ed. A. Robertson and K. G. Robertson (London: Macmillan, 1987), 37–52 (p. 45).

12 NA FO 1093/68 Secret Service Committee 1925, minutes of 10 March, p. 2.

13 NA FO 1093/68 Secret Service Committee 1925, minutes of 10 March, p. 2; see also Curry, *Security Service*, pp. 42–50. It has been noted that Kell likely exaggerated the differences between the kind of work he and SIS did to justify MI5's position (Bennett, *Churchill's Man of Mystery*, p. 90).

14 NA FO 1093/68 Secret Service Committee 1925, minutes of 10 March, pp. 3–4.

15 On the reorganisation of the Security Service, SIS and Scotland Yard, see Curry, *Security Service*, pp. 101–04.

16 NA FO 1093/68 Secret Service Committee 1925, minutes of March 2, p. 3; quoted in Bennett, 'The Secret Service Committee, 1919–1931', p. 47; Bennett, *Churchill's Man of Mystery*, p. 88.

17 NA FO 1093/68 Secret Service Committee 1925, minutes of March 2, p. 5. Kell had served as Director since MI5's creation, and Holt-Wilson as his deputy since 1912.

18 NA FO 1093/68 Secret Service Committee 1925, minutes of March 2, p. 6.

19 NA FO 1093/68 Secret Service Committee 1925, minutes of March 2, p. 9.

20 NA FO 1093/68 Secret Service Committee 1925, minutes of March 10, p. 5.

21 NA FO 1093/68 Secret Service Committee 1925, minutes of March 10, p. 7.

22 NA FO 1093/68 Secret Service Committee 1925, minutes of March 10, p. 8.

23 NA FO 1093/68 Secret Service Committee 1925, minutes of March 10, p. 4.

24 Even today, SIS's own central computer index (CCI), a database holding information on all contacts made by its officers on duty since the Second World War, appears to rely on the same principle (Richard Tomlinson, *The Big Breach: From Top Secret to Maximum Security* (Moscow: Narodny Variant

Publishers, 2000), p. 48). However, SIS's files, at least historically, appear to have been less centralised, with relevant records maintained by the different regional controllerates (University of Cambridge Intelligence Seminar, information obtained under the Chatham House Rule).

25 NA FO 1093/68 Secret Service Committee 1925, minutes of March 10, p. 11, minutes of March 2, p. 6. A handwritten emendation to the text also inserts, '. . . and a very large registry of records'.

26 NA FO 1093/68 Secret Service Committee 1925, minutes of March 31, pp. 3–4. As he explained: 'It fell to [MPSB] to carry out any enquiries in this country, other than purely criminal investigations, which might be referred to them by other departments. [Carter] had his own secret service, and it was his duty to keep the Commissions informed of probable developments in revolutionary movements, the activities of the unemployed and similar matters, so that the uniform men might be ready to meet any emergencies which might arise in these quarters. He had his regularly paid agents and informants, and he also received a quantity of information volunteered by the general public.'

27 NA FO 1093/68 Secret Service Committee 1935, minutes of March 31, p 2.

28 NA FO 1093/67, 'Secret Service Committee 1924–1927 Miscellaneous Papers', Report of Sir Russell Scott on investigation into Scotland Yard; FO 1093/68 'Secret Service. Committee 1925', Report of Sir Russell Scott on investigation into Scotland Yard.

29 Quoted in Robert Taylor, *The TUC: From the General Strike to New Unionism* (Basingstoke: Palgrave, 2000), p. 23.

30 MacDonald quoted in George Kennan, *Russia and the West under Lenin and Stalin* (London: Hutchinson, 1961), p. 235.

31 Representatives included Herbert Smith (president of the Miners' Federation), Ben Tillett (founder of Dockers' Union and member of General Council), John Turner (member of the General Council), John Bromley (MP and long-time pro-union activist), Alan Findlay (United Patternmakers' Association), A. A. Purcell as chairman, and Fred Bramley (then-Secretary of General Council) as secretary. See J. Klugmann, *History of Communist Party of Great Britain. Volume II: 1925–1927: The General Strike* (London: Lawrence and Wishart, 1969), p. 14.

32 NA FO 1093/72 'Secret Service Committee 1927 Spare Copies of Minutes and Memoranda' [hereafter—'SSC 1927'], s.[none],

'Review of the Communist Movement', February–October 1925, p. 6.

33 Quoted in NA FO 1093/72 SSC 1927, s.[none], 'Review of the Communist Movement', February–October 1925, p. 9.

34 Klugmann, *History of Communist Party of Great Britain. Volume II*, p. 20. The Anglo-Russian Joint Advisory Council (ARJAC) was established during an International Federation of Trades Union (IFTU) meeting in February 1925 and first convened the following September.

35 NA FO 1093/72 SSC 1927, s.[none], 'Review of the Communist Movement', February–October 1925, p. 7.

36 'Twenty-one Points', NA CAB 24/116, no. 2284, Special Report by Directorate of Intelligence No. 19, November 1920, pp. 10–13; *Second Congress of the Communist International. Minutes of the Proceedings, Vol. I and II* (Publishing House of the Communist International, 1921), minutes of the Seventh Session, 20 July 1920 reproduced at http://www.marxists.org/history/ international/ comintern/2nd-congress/ch07.htm (last accessed 11 January 2008).

37 NA KV4/282 Publication entitled 'Aspects of the General Strike', s.1a, by Scotland Yard, June 1926, Part I, 'Communism and the General Strike', p. 3.

38 NA FO 1093/72 SSC 1927, s.[none], 'Review of the Communist Movement', February–October 1925, p. 8.

39 NA FO 1093/72 SSC 1927, s.[none], 'Review of the Communist Movement', February–October 1925, p. 8.

40 Quoted in Keith Flett, 'An Attempt to Win the Majority of Workers', *Socialist Worker*, 21 May 2005, http://www.socialistworker.co.uk/ article.php?article_id=6524 (last accessed 30 March 2006); Roderick Martin, *Communism and the British Trade Unions, 1924–1933: A Study of the National Minority Movement* (Oxford: Clarendon Press, 1969), p. 37.

41 NA KV4/282 Aspects of the General Strike, s.1a, Part I, 'Communism and the General Strike', p. 8.

42 Quoted in Andrew, *Her Majesty's Secret Service*, p. 318.

43 *Report of the National Minority Conference, 1924*, p. 3; *1925*, p. 31; *March 1926*, p. 34, in Martin, *Communism and the British Trade Unions*, pp. 56–57.

44 Quoted in NA FO 1093/72 SSC 1927, s.[none], 'Review of the Communist Movement', February–October 1925, pp. 19–20, letter from the Anglo-American section of the Executive Committee of the Comintern

(IKKI) to the Central Committee of the CPGB, July 1925 [bold in original].

45 See, for example, Gordon A. Phillips, *The General Strike: The Politics of Industrial Conflict* (London: Weidenfeld and Nicolson, 1976), pp. 43–44.

46 As illuminated in Zinoviev's *Thesis on Tactics*, presented at the Fifth Congress of the Third International in June–July 1924. First published in *Inprekor*, iv, 119, p. 1577, 16 September 1924, and extracts reproduced at http://marx.org/history/international/ comintern/5th-congress/trade-unions.htm [last accessed 16 January 2008]; McDermott and Agnew, *The Comintern* , p. 47.

47 NA FO 1093/72 SSC 1927, s.[none], 'Review of the Communist Movement', February-October 1925, p. 10.

48 NA FO 1093/72 SSC 1927, s.[none], 'Review of the Communist Movement', February–October 1925, p. 10.

49 Quoted in Andrew, *Her Majesty's Secret Service*, p. 319.

50 Klugmann, *History of Communist Party of Great Britain. Volume II*, p. 67. Those arrested on 14–16 October 1925 were: Tom Bell (Editor of *Communist Review*), Ernie Cant (Secretary of the London District of CPGB), Albert Inkpin (CPGB Secretary), Harry Pollitt (then-Secretary of the National Minority Movement), Bill Rust (Secretary of the Young Communist League), Tome Wintringham (Assistant Editor of the *Workers' Weekly*), Wally Hannington (head of the N.U.W.C.M., an organisation of the unemployed) and William Gallacher, J.R. Campbell, Arthur MacManus, J. T. Murphy and Robin Page Arnot (founding members of the CPGB). 'Documents Seized in Police Raid on Communist Party Headquarters in 1925' at NA KV3/18-KV3/32.

51 Andrew Thorpe, *The British Communist Party and Moscow, 1920–43* (Manchester: Manchester University Press, 2000), p. 72.

52 NA KV4/158 Brief Notes on the Security Services and Its Work Prepared for Permanent Under-Secretaries, Service Intelligence Depts., C.I.G.S., Courses, etc., s.13b, 'A short note on the Security Service and its responsibilities', John Curry, p. 14.

53 The Emergency Powers Act 1920 allowed the Government to declare a State of Emergency in the event that there occurred or threatened to occur a disruption to the 'supply and distribution of food, water, fuel or light, or with the means of locomotion, to deprive the community, or any substantial portion of the community, of the essentials of life' (Revised

Statue from the UK Statute Law Database, 'Emergency Powers Act 1920 (c.55)', available at http://www.opsi.gov.uk/ RevisedStatutes/ Acts/ukpga/1920/ cukpga_19200055_en_1 (last accessed 19 August 2008)).

54 The personnel for MI(B), the Military Security and Secret Service Section, came mainly from MI5 through temporary or permanent transfers, but also 'by the employment of selected officers of the regular army reserve with previous war service with M.I.5'. NA KV4/246, 'Summary of events and action taken by Military Security Intelligence and MI5 and its Emergency Section, known as MI(B), during the 1926 General Strike' (hereafter, 'Summary of General Strike'), s.[?], report of 18 April 1921, 'Summary of Military Security Intelligence Action in connection with the Civil Emergency, 1st to 18th April, 1921', Section 5.

55 NA KV4/246, Summary of General Strike, s.[?], report of 18 April 1921, 'Summary of Military Security Intelligence Action in connection with the Civil Emergency, 1st to 18th April, 1921', Section 5.

56 NA KV4/246, Summary of General Strike, s.[?], report of 18 April 1921, 'Summary of Military Security Intelligence Action in connection with the Civil Emergency, 1st to 18th April, 1921', Section 6.

57 NA KV4/246, Summary of General Strike, s.[?], report of 18 April 1921, 'Summary of Military Security Intelligence Action in connection with the Civil Emergency, 1st to 18th April, 1921', Appendix 1.

58 NA KV4/246, Summary of General Strike, s.[?], Appendix 1, 'Proposed Organisation of the intelligence personnel and duties at headquarters of each command', Section 3.

59 Quoted in Jeffery and Hennessy, *States of Emergency*, p. 96.

60 Quoted in Klugmann, *History of Communist Party of Great Britain. Volume II*, p. 37.

61 The British Fascisti, founded in 1923, had offered to contribute. The Government said it would accept their offer only if they expunged 'Fascist' from their name. The debate over the issue split the party and caused an exodus from its ranks. In the end, the Government rejected the offer (Thomas P. Linehan, *British Fascism, 1918–39: Parties, Ideology and Culture* (Manchester: Manchester University Press, 2000), pp. 65–6).

62 Hope, 'Surveillance or Collusion? Maxwell Knight, MI5 and the British Fascisti', p. 657.

63 On IUC and STC, see Ralph H. Desmarais, 'The British Government's Strikebreaking

Organization and Black Friday', *Journal of Contemporary History* 6 (1971), 112–17.

64 NA WO 32/5314 'Duties in Aid of the Civil Power', no.23A, 6 July 1925; quoted in Jeffery and Hennessy, *States of Emergency*, p. 89.

65 NA WO 32/5314 'Duties in Aid of the Civil Power', no.23A, 6 July 1925; quoted in Jeffery and Hennessy, *States of Emergency*, p. 90.

66 NA CAB 24/178 CP 81(26), Report by the Home Secretary, 22 February 1926; quoted in Jeffery and Hennessy, *States of Emergency*, p. 101.

67 A report that day noted, 'Section M.I(B) instituted', 'List of names of past staff prepared for mobilisation as necessary'. NA KV4/246, Summary of General Strike, minutes of 1 May 1926.

68 The number of Special Constables surged from 3,035 on 4 May to 51,807 by 11 May in London alone. Phillips, *The General Strike: The Politics of Industrial Conflict*, p. 152, 161.

69 To monitor the progress of the strike MI5 had to ensure that its own house ran smoothly. Minutes from the first day of the Strike note, 'Volunteer cars took up duties. These included cars and services of: Miss S. Allen, Dame Adelaide Livingstone, Lady Wilson, Lady Dorothy Hope Morely, Captain Hope Morely and Admiral Hugh Lindsay Heard.' They ensured officers' mobility and that 'there was no delay occasioned by the strike in the receipt and delivery of urgent letters'. MI5 made extensive use of women clerks, and in at least one case, the wife or sister of an officer. The minutes of 4 May also note, 'Arrangements made for installation of Wireless Receiving Set and news bulletins circulated in office.' The way MI5 cobbled together its resources brings the amateur nature of the intelligence services at the time into relief (NA KV4/246, Summary of General Strike, minutes of 4 May 1926).

70 University of Cambridge Intelligence Seminar, information obtained under the Chatham House Rule.

71 NA KV4/246 Summary of General Strike, s.[?], Appendix 2, P. Report No. 2, 6 May 1926.

72 Harry Ferguson, *Spy: A Handbook* (London: Bloomsbury, 2004), p. 48.

73 See SOE lecture on 'Cover' given in 1942, in Rigdan, ed., *SOE Syllabus*, pp. 46–58; NA KV4/172 SOE Course at Beaulieu, s.93b, 'Beaulieu Notes', pp. A.3–A.8; KV4/171 General Policy on Liaison with SOE, s.95a, 'Note by T.A.R. on S.o.2. lectures and covering letter to Commander Senter, 21 January 1942.

74 NA KV4/282 Aspects of the General Strike, 1926, s.1a, 'Communist Effort to

Undermine Loyalty and Discipline in H.M. Forces During the General Strike, May 1926', Part III, p. 7.

75 This entire section is based on NA KV4/246, Summary of General Strike, s.[?], Appendix 2, P. Report No. 6, 10 May 1926.

76 No discernible relation to left-wing politician Sydney Webb.

77 University of Cambridge Intelligence Seminar, information obtained under the Chatham House Rule.

78 This entire section is based on NA KV4/246 Summary of General Strike, s.[?], Appendix 3, 'Report sent to M.I(B) 15 May 1926', 'Strike News and Communist News, May 13th, 1926'.

79 Joint control ended in 1927, when ownership passed to the TUC. The *Daily Herald* was subsequently run by Ernest Bevin, Secretary General of the Transport and General Workers' Union and future Foreign Secretary. Taylor, *English History*, p. 141, 251.

80 Phillips, *General Strike*, p. 156.

81 NA KV4/282 Aspects of the General Strike, 1926, s.1a, Part II, 'Summaries of Information Regarding the General Strike Furnished by Chief Constables in England, Scotland and Wales'.

82 Andrew, *Her Majesty's Secret Service*, p. 322.

83 Quoted in Martin, *Communism and the British Trade Unions*, p. 71.

84 NA KV4/246 Summary of General Strike, s.[?], Appendix 4, letter from Kell, 16 May 1926.

85 Philip Williamson, *Stanley Baldwin: Conservative Leadership and National Values* (Cambridge: Cambridge University Press, 1999), p. 202.

86 Martin Gilbert, *Winston S. Churchill, Vol. V: 1922–1939* (London: Heinemann, 1976), p. 159.

87 Jeffery and Hennessy, *States of Emergency*, pp. 117–18.

88 Alastair J. Reid, *United We Stand: A History of Britain's Trade Unions* (London: Allen Lane, Penguin Books, 2004), p. 315.

89 Quoted in Martin, *Communism and the British Trade Unions*, p. 71.

90 NA KV4/282 Aspects of the General Strike, 1926, s.1a, Part I, 'Communism and the General Strike', p. 12; Part III, 'Communist Efforts to Undermine Loyalty and Discipline in H. M. Forces During the General Strike, May 1926', p. 6.

91 NA KV4/282 Aspects of the General Strike, s.1a, Part 3, 'Communist Efforts to Undermine Loyalty and Discipline in H. M. Forces During the General Strike, May 1926', p. 6.

92 NA KV4/282 Aspects of the General Strike, s.1a, Part I, 'Communism and the General Strike', p. 23.

93 NA KV4/282 Aspects of the General Strike, s.1a, Part I, 'Communism and the General Strike', p. 3; Lawrence H. Officer and Samuel H. Williamson, 'Purchasing Power of British Pounds from 1245 to Present', MeasuringWorth.com, 2014 (calculated in terms of retail price index at 2012 rates).

94 NA KV2/989 LAKEY, Arthur Francis, s. 77A, 'document', 11 September 1928.

95 NA HO144/22372 Disturbances: Communist Propaganda to Incite His Majesty's Forces to Mutiny. Sedition Charge Against John Gollan, in Perkins, *A Very British Strike: 3 May–12 May, 1926*, p. 62.

96 W. G. Krivitsky, *In Stalin's Secret Service* (New York: Enigma Books, 2000), p. 46.

97 Martin, *Communism and the British Trade Unions*, p.44; NA KV4/282 Aspects of the General Strike, s.1a, Part I, 'Communism and the General Strike', p. 3, which puts NMM revenue from British sources at 'slightly over £1,000' for 1925.

98 NA FO 1093/68 The Secret Service Committee 1925, minutes of 17 March, p. 4; HO 144/7985 493438 Disturbances: Payments from Russia in Aid of the General Strike, letter to Miller, 11 May 1926, summary report, 15 June 1926.

99 NA CAB 24/180 CP 236(26) 'Russian Money' (by Home Secretary), 11 June 1926; CP 244(26) 'Russian Money' (by Home Secretary), 15 June 1926; quoted in Andrew, *Her Majesty's Secret Service*, pp. 322–3.

100 NA KV4/282 Aspects of the General Strike, s.1a, Part V, 'Foreign Influences on the Strike', p. 9.

101 NA KV4/246 Summary of General Strike, s.[?], Appendix 3, Interview with Maiski, Report sent to MI(B) 10 May 1926.

102 Taylor, *TUC*, pp. 20–37.

103 Quoted in Taylor, *TUC*, p. viii.

104 Rajani Palme Dutt, 'The Meaning of the General Strike', *The Communist International*, no. 21, June 1926, reproduced at http://www.marxists.org/archive/dutt/pamphlets/strike.htm (last accessed 15 April 2008).

105 Richard Sakwa, *Soviet Politics: An Introduction* (London: Routledge, 1989),

pp. 41–2; McDermott and Agnew, *The Comintern*, p. 51.

106 Leon Trotsky, *The Revolution Betrayed* (Mineola, NY: Dover Publications, 2004), p. 69.

CHAPTER 3
Recruitment and Handling

1 Gerber, 'Managing HUMINT', p. 188.

2 James Olson, *Fair Play: The Moral Dilemmas of Spying* (Washington, DC: Potomac Books, 2007), p. 236.

3 Unfortunately, the particulars of Macartney's development, the critical phase when a potential agent is courted by an intelligence officer or agent, are limited by the unavailability of files. MI5's records suggest that much of Macartney's cultivation occurred overseas, the preserve of SIS. But these records were destroyed, weeded, or his development passed unobserved because no record exists in the SIS archives (personal correspondence with Gill Bennett, who had access to relevant SIS files when researching her biography of Desmond Morton, 25 October 2006. See Bennett, *Churchill's Man of Mystery*).

4 See, *inter alia*, Andrew and Gordievsky, *KGB*; Andrew and Mitrokhin, *The Mitrokhin Archive*; Miranda Carter, *Anthony Blunt: His Lives* (London: Macmillan, 2001); Robert Cecil, *Divided Life: A Biography of Donald Maclean* (London: Bodley Head, 1988); John Costello and Oleg Tsarev, *Deadly Illusions* (London: Century, 1993); Phillip Knightley, *Philby: The Life and Views of the K.G.B. Masterspy* (London: Andre Deutsch, 2003); Nigel West and Oleg Tsarev, *The Crown Jewels: The British Secrets at the Heart of the KGB Archives* (London: HarperCollins, 1998). Biographical summaries for Maclean and Burgess also available at NA PREM 8/1542, ref. PM/51/39, 13 June 1951. Relatively little emphasis, however, has been given to the role of tradecraft in the Cambridge Five's penetration of British intelligence, which is surprising considering that the far greater success of Soviet intelligence in penetrating Britain in the 1930s compared to the 1920s was due largely to a dramatic improvement in tradecraft, in part spurred on the fallout from the ARCOS raid and Macartney and Ewer cases. A distinct change in Soviet strategy led to the recruitment of the Cambridge Five, in the process providing a necessary subtext to British counter-espionage.

5 In an anti-establishment rant, he decried the propaganda campaign carried out by the 'governors and jailers, priest and parsons' of Wormwood Scrubs prison, where Macartney was serving a nine-month stint for his part in a jewel raid in London's West End. Macartney's recent conversion to communism meant that he saw the strikers as brothers-in-arms rather than criminals, as he believed the authorities did (NA KV2/647 'MACARTNEY, Wilfred Francis, Remington', s.2a, 'The Monocle Man', 'Boss Propaganda in the Scrubs', *Sunday Worker*, 3 October 1926).

6 See Wilfred Macartney, *Walls Have Mouths: A Record of Ten Years' Penal Servitude* (London: V. Gollancz, 1936), and especially the introduction by his wartime boss Compton Mackenzie. Ball later became the founding head of the Conservative Research Department, from where he successfully ran secret agents against the Labour Party (Robert Blake, 'Ball, Sir (George) Joseph (1885–1961)', *ODNB*, http://www.oxforddnb.com/ view/article/30564 (last accessed 5 May 2008)). NA KV2/647 MACARTNEY, s.1a, 'CX.12650. MI1c [SIS] report re W.F.R MACARTNEY', letter from Menzies to Ball (CX [...] 1151), 15 October 1926. See Overy, *The Twilight Years*. Lawrence H. Officer and Samuel H. Williamson, 'Purchasing Power of British Pounds from 1245 to Present', MeasuringWorth.com, 2014 (calculated in terms of consumer price index at 2012 rates); in the interwar period an average worker made roughly £2–3 per week, and a journalist earned roughly £10–15 per week. Anyone with an income of over £1,000 per year might be considered wealthy. See 'Note on currency' in Overy, *The Twilight Years*.

7 Liddell worked for Section S.S.1., the liaison section.

8 NA KV2/647 MACARTNEY, s.7a, Liddell to Ball, 19 October 1926; s.9a, Liddell to Ball, 25 October 1926.

9 NA KV2/647 MACARTNEY, s.9a, Liddell to Ball, 25 October 1926; KV 2/770 MESSER, s.16A, 'extract' (made by BHSC), Liddell to Ball, 25 October 1927.

10 NA KV2/770 MESSER, s.1., 'Order Prohibiting a Person from Entering Specified Areas', 25 March 1916.

11 NA KV2/770 MESSER, s.11a, Home Office Warrant request, 20 September 1926; KV2/799 'JILINKSKY, Jacob Georgievitch', s.17b, 'Copy of a report on Russ. espionage in UK in connection with meeting bet. Col Carter Capt Butler Capt Liddell and Insp. Clancy [sic]', 4 April 1928.

12 Into the late 1920s, counter-revolutionaries out-ranked Britain as the OGPU's main

security threat and intelligence target. Andrew and Gordievsky, *KGB*, pp. 67–78.

13 NA KV2/647 MACARTNEY, s.16a, Liddell to Ball, 12 November 1926; KV2/770 MESSER, s.16a, 'extract', Liddell to Ball, 12 November 1926.

14 Wilfred Macartney, *Zigzag. [An autobiography.]* (London: 1937), pp. 33–4.

15 Macartney, *Zigzag*, p. 155.

16 Macartney, *Zigzag*, p. 156. The identity of 'Hope-Johnstone' is unknown. Macartney describes him as a mathematician in the process of walking from Paris to Tehran when the war broke out.

17 NA KV2/647 MACARTNEY, s.17a, Liddell to Ball forwarding report re Macartney, 13 November 1926; Macartney, *Zigzag*, pp. 192–217.

18 Macartney, *Zigzag*, pp. 261–2.

19 Macartney, *Zigzag*, p. 62.

20 Macartney, *Zigzag*, p. 260.

21 Acronym used by the US Federal Bureau of Investigation, Professor Christopher Andrew, lecture on 'Secrets v. Mysteries', 'Secret World' Tripos, Cambridge University, 29 November 2004; similar motivations (which MICE subsumes) have been enumerated by General Alexandr Orlov, who devised the NKVD manual on tradecraft in 1936: '1) Idealistic purposes 2) Money, career, and other motives of personal gain 3) Romantic entanglements 4) Love of adventure 5) To conceal a committed crime and escape responsibility 6) Homosexual deviations and other vices.' Aleksandr Orlov, *Handbook of Intelligence and Guerrilla Warfare* (Ann Arbor: University of Michigan Press, 1963), pp. 93–4.

22 Macartney, *Zigzag*, pp. 322–3.

23 Macartney, *Zigzag*, p. 355.

24 Bennett, *Churchill's Man of Mystery*, p. 107.

25 In 1924 SIS obtained an informative document from a German source on the organisation and tradecraft of Soviet military intelligence (Fourth Department). The document reads like a manual, enumerating principles and procedures guiding the establishment of overseas 'departments' and the recruitment of agents. Among other regulations, a department was 'bound' to 'find and enrol resident agents, provide a camouflage [*sic*] for their work and instruct them'; 'find the addresses to which their reports may be sent without arousing suspicion'; and 'create a permanent and safe liaison between the bearers of reports and the Department'. NA KV3/11 Russian Intelligence

Organisation (General), 1924–1931, s.3a, 'Extracts from an instruction concerning the Organisation of the Military Intelligence Agency Services of the Intelligence Administration of the Revolutionary War Council attached to the Plenipotentiary Delegation of the S.S.S.R.' [hereafter, 'Instruction concerning the organisation of Military Intelligence'], forwarded from Lt-Colonel, G.S. [Menzies] (MI1c [SIS]) to MI5, 17 December 1924 (SIS ref. CX.6550), p. 1. The qualities of an officer were thought of as much the opposite: integrity, force of character, honesty and loyalty.

26 NA KV3/11 Russian Intelligence Organisation (General), 1924–1931, s.3a, 'Instruction concerning the organisation of Military Intelligence', p. 3.

27 NA KV2/647 MACARTNEY, s.20a, Letter from Ball to Liddell, 22 November 1926.

28 NA DPP 1/84 REX v MACARTNEY and HANSEN, 'Statement by Major Desmond John Falkiner Morton', 22 November 1927, p. 5.

29 Macartney, *Zigzag*, p. 338.

30 NA KV3/11 Russian Intelligence Organisation (General), 1924–1931, s.3a, 'Instruction concerning the organisation of Military Intelligence', p. 4.

31 Wilfred Macartney and Compton Mackenzie, *Walls Have Mouths: A Record of Ten Years' Penal Servitude* (London: V. Gollancz, 1936), p. 18.

32 NA DPP 1/84 REX v MACARTNEY and HANSEN, 'Statement by Major Desmond John Falkiner Morton', 22 November 1927, p. 1, cf. DPP 1/84 REX v MACARTNEY and HANSEN, 'Statement of Admiral Sir W.R. Hall', p. 1 , n.d. Cf. Bennett, *Churchill's Man of Mystery*, p. 107.

33 NA KV2/647 MACARTNEY, s.23a, Letter from Desmond Morton to O. A. Harker, 2 May 1927. Morton was repeating to Harker the report by 'Biffy' Dunderdale, SIS Chief of Station in Paris (Bennett, *Churchill's Man of Mystery*, pp. 111–12).

34 NA KV2/647 MACARTNEY, s.23a, Desmond Morton to O.A. Harker, 2 May 1927; warrants noted in minutes of 3 May 1927 found on pages KV2/647, s.26a (Monkland), KV2/647, s.27b (Macartney).

35 NA KV2/647 MACARTNEY, minutes of 3 May 1927, by B. (Harker).

36 NA KV2/647 MACARTNEY, s.43a, 'Note by Miss Sissmore on telephone check', 4–8 May 1927.

37 NA KV2/647 MACARTNEY, s.45a, Letter from Morton to Harker, 9 May 1927.

38 NA DPP 1/84 REX v MACARTNEY and HANSEN, 'Statement by Major Desmond John Falkiner Morton', 22 November 1927, p. 2. Quoted in Bennett, *Churchill's Man of Mystery*, p. 109.

39 Raymond W. Leonard, *Secret Soldiers of the Revolution: Soviet Military Intelligence, 1918–1933* (Westport, CT and London: Greenwood Press, 1999), p. 71. The questionnaire method is discussed in the context of the illegal Paris residency headed by Jean Cremet in 1924–1925. See also NA KV3/147 'Russian Espionage Organisation in France', s.45a, press cutting, 'Espionage Plot in France', *The Times*, 16 April 1927; s.160a, press cutting, 'Paris Communist Trial', *The Morning Post*, 26 July 1927.

40 NA KV2/647 MACARTNEY, s.50a, transcript of telephone call to Monkland from Mostyn Hotel, Portland St. W., 7.50pm, 12 May 1927.

41 'X' and 'Y' designations used in NA KV3/15-16 Recovery of British Official Documents by Raids on ARCOS Ltd, May 1927; Bennett, *Churchill's Man of Mystery*, pp. 94–106, is the most authoritative account.

42 W. N. Medlicott et al., *Documents on British Foreign Policy, 1919–1939. Series 1A. Vol. 3* (London: HMSO, 1971), No. 215 [N 2426/209/38], from Chamberlain to Rosengolts, 26 May 1927, pp. 338–40; Gabriel Gorodetsky, *The Precarious Truce: Anglo-Soviet Relations, 1924–27* (Cambridge: Cambridge University Press, 1977), p. 230.

43 W. N. Medlicott et al., *Documents on British Foreign Policy, 1919–1939. Series 1A. Vol. 4* (London: HMSO, 1973), No. 123, letter from Sir A. Chamberlain to Sir W. Erskine [about to take up his post as HM Minister at Warsaw] (London) [FO 800/262] 26 January 1928, p. 233.

44 Steiner, *The Lights That Failed*, p. 538.

45 Jane Degras, ed., *Soviet Documents on Foreign Policy: Volume II 1925–1932* (London: Oxford University Press and RIIA, 1952), 'Statement by Litvinov on Severance of Anglo-Soviet Relations', 26 May 1927, p. 210.

46 Degras, ed., *SDFP: Volume II 1925–1932*, 'Statement by Litvinov on the Severance of Anglo-Soviet Relations', 27 May 1927, pp. 209–12.

47 Medlicott et al., *DBFP, 1919–1939, Series IA, Vol. 3*, No.232, Mr. Preston (Helsingfors) to Sir Austen Chamberlain, No. 7 [N 3016/209/38], 13 June 1927, p. 354. Cf. 'Effect of Soviet War Scare', *The Times*, Wednesday 22 June 1927, p. 15.

48 Gorodetsky, *The Precarious Truce*, pp. 236–7; Macartney and Mackenzie, *Walls Have Mouths*, p. 17.

49 Macartney and Mackenzie, *Walls Have Mouths*, pp. 20–1.

50 Macartney, *Zigzag*, p. 161.

51 NA KV2/647 MACARTNEY, s.78a, 'From Major Morton. CX. [. . .]/C.O.-McCartney [sic] said to have gone to Paris under name of F.W. Hudson', Morton to Harker, 30 May 1927. Cf. Bennett, *Churchill's Man of Mystery*, pp. 100–01.

52 NA KV2/989 'LAKEY, Arthur Francis, "Allen"', s.69a, Allen's statement regarding the activities of the FPA, 20 August 1928, p. 3; s.72A, 'Comparative Statement of information obtained form ALLEN and MI5 records', 29 August 1929, p. 1. Bennett, *Churchill's Man of Mystery*, pp. 100–01. Improbable as it was, the claim is nonetheless intriguing in light of the Ewer case's later exposure of MPSB's Inspector Hubert Ginhoven and Sergeant Charles Jane.

53 NA KV2/647 MACARTNEY, s.86a, 'From Major Morton. CX[...]/[. . .]/C.O. forwarding letters from and to Monkland', Morton to Harker, 1 June 1927.

54 NA KV2/647 MACARTNEY, s.156a, write-up of Morton's interview of Monkland, 21 July 1927. 'Chickenfeed' is relatively low-level intelligence given to the opponent in the service of a more important case, usually involving a double agent or informant and often to prove bona fides to an opposing intelligence service.

55 NA KV2/647 MACARTNEY, s.86b, note from Morton to Monkland, 1 June 1927. Notably, Detective Hubert Ginhoven, one of the Scotland Yard moles later revealed in the course of the Ewer investigation, identified one of Macartney's passports during Macartney's trial (see DPP1/84 Rex v. McCARTNEY [sic] and HANSEN, depositions taken on 26 November 1927, Det. Sergt. Hubert Ginhoven, by Sir Travers Humphreys, p. 3).

56 NA KV2/647 MACARTNEY, s.168a, 'From MI1c [SIS] forwarding further report from Paris re Macartney', 27 July 1927. Dunderdale identified in Andrew, *Her Majesty's Secret Service*, p. 416; Bennett, *Churchill's Man of Mystery*, p. 93. He served SIS in Paris from 1926 to 1940 (John Bruce Lockhart, 'Dunderdale, Wilfred Albert (1899–1990)', rev., *ONDB*, http://www.oxforddnb.com/ view/ article/40173 (last accessed 25 April 2008)).

57 NA KV2/647 MACARTNEY, s.221a, 'From MI1c enclosing further report from the French

re Macartney's movements', Morton to Harker, 18 August 1927.

58 Macartney's lack of tradecraft reflects the fact that he was an informal recruit rather than a trained spy. However, his tradecraft also speaks poorly of his handler, Hansen, who was responsible for training him. NA KV3/11 Russian Intelligence Organisation (General), 1924–1931, s.3a, 'Instruction concerning the organisation of Military Intelligence', p. 1.

59 NA KV2/647 MACARTNEY, s.168a, 'From MI1c [SIS] forwarding further report from Paris re Macartney', 27 July 1927, addressed to 'M. Cartimer, Officier d'Ordonance de S.M. le Roi Carol', reads: 'Monsieur, Je regrette que Sa Majesté ne puisse utiliser mes service et je vous remercie beaucoup pour votre bonne lettre. Si a quelque moment que ce soit il y a une difficulté dans le pays de France pour le pays de Sa Majesté, un télégramme au 32 York Street W.1. Londres me rejoindra. Je vous assure que la chose et tout a fait simple pour mai arranger. J'ai l'honneur d'etre votre obéissant serviteur, (Signé) W. MacCartney [sic].'

60 NA KV2/647 MACARTNEY, s.198, minute of 12 August 1927, by B. (Harker)

61 The watchers were the former MPSB officers John Ottaway or Henry Hunter. NA KV2/647 MACARTNEY, s.228, minute of 19 August 1927, by KMMS (Kathleen Sissmore).

62 NA KV2/649 'HANSEN, George', s.1b, summary of Morton's interview of Monkland, 23 August 1927; s.2a, letter from Monkland to 'Hamilton', 24 August 1927.

63 NA KV2/647 MACARTNEY, s.444–446, minutes of 8 November 1927, B.7 (Sissmore).

64 NA KV2/647 MACARTNEY, s.466a, intercepted letter to 'Hamilton' (Morton) from Monkland, 15 April 1927 [sic: postal stamp on envelope reads 15 November 1927].

65 See, among others, Nicolas Werth, 'A State Against Its People: Repression and Terror in the Soviet Union', in *The Black Book of Communism: Crimes, Terror, Repression*, ed. Stephane Courtois and Mark Kramer (Cambridge, MA: Harvard University Press, 1999), 33–268 (p. 141); Robert Conquest, *The Great Terror: A Reassessment* (London: Hutchinson, 1990), introduction, especially pp. 7–12; Sheila Fitzpatrick, *The Russian Revolution* (Oxford: Oxford University Press, 1994), chapter 4.

66 NA KV2/649 HANSEN, s.6a, copy of letter from Monkland to 'Hamilton', re meeting of Monkland and Johnson, 15 April 1927 [sic: 15 November 1927, see minutes].

67 NA KV2/649 HANSEN, s.8, letter to Vivian re rendezvous between Johnson and Monkland (from Sissmore, MI5), 14 November 1927.

68 NA KV2/647 MACARTNEY, s.50a, intercepted letter from Macartney to Monkland, 16 July 1927.

69 NA KV2/649 HANSEN, s.10a, report on the observation of Monkland and Johnson, 17 November 1927. Ottaway's report reads: 'Johnson walked into Park Lane and then turned back and entered Hyde Park by the Marble Arch. Having walked some distance in the park he again entered Park Lane and then returned to the Park. On reaching Hyde Park Corner he loitered awhile, apparently testing to see if he was being followed, then walked on towards Knightsbridge when he hailed a passing cab and was driven to South Kensington Station, where he again loitered some time, after which he rode by bus to Redcliffe Gardens, S.W. and there entered No.12.'

70 Orlov, *Handbook of Intelligence and Guerrilla Warfare*, p. 115.

71 Ferguson, *Spy*, chapter 8; AMC IV Security Services, *Secrets of Surveillance: A Professional's Guide to Tailing Subjects by Vehicle, Foot, Airplane, and Public Transportation* (Boulder, CO: Paladin Press, 1993).

72 But see Curry, *Security Service*, p. 302; Peter Wright, *Spycatcher: The Candid Autobiography of a Senior Intelligence Officer* (New York: Viking, 1987), pp. 48–53.

73 Curry, *Security Service*, p. 302.

74 NA KV4/127 Security Service Organisation from 1918 to 1939, s.1b 'MI5 Chronological List of Staff taken to 31 December 1939', December 1939, p. 1. Having begun in 1903, Melville was in one sense senior to Kell. On Melville generally, see Andrew Cook, *M: MI5's First Spymaster* (Stroud: Tempus, 2004).

75 NA DPP1/84 'Rex v. McCARTNEY [sic] and others', Statements, taken by Sir Travers Humphreys, 29 November 1927, John Ottaway, pp. 5–10 (p. 1)

76 NA KV1/8 'Memoir of William Melville, Kell's Senior Detective', p. 3.

77 Curry, *Security Service*, p. 302.

78 NA KV2/649 HANSEN, s.10a, report on the observation of Monkland and Johnson, 17 November 1927.

79 NA KV2/649 HANSEN, s.11a, copy of Home Office Warrant, 17 November 1927.

80 Although the file simply says 'Captain Booth', administration files from 1929 note

that 'Captain F. B. Booth' was in charge of 'Special Censorship'. See KV4/127 Security Service Organisation from 1919 to 1939.

81 NA KV2/647 MACARNTEY, minute of 24 November 1927; NA KV2/649 HANSEN, minute of 24 November 1927 (B.7, Sissmore). At the trial, 'Johnson' was revealed to be Georg Hansen. With Monkland and Morton's testimony (the latter appearing as 'Hamilton' – an SIS officer's court testimony is in itself a rare occasion) and the evidence gathered over months of surveillance, the jury sided with the prosecution, and both Hansen and Macartney were convicted. Eventually Hansen was deported to the USSR. He left, appropriately, aboard the M.V. 'Felix Dzerjinsky' (NA KV2/656 HANSEN, s.832b, Cross reference to I.O. report re departure of HANSEN, 18 August 1935). After Macartney's release from 'ten years' penal servitude', he wrote several articles condemning the prison system and was trailed by various charges of fraud and theft. In the mid-1930s, he fought with the International Brigades in Spain, where he was wounded yet again. He thereafter returned to London, became involved with the CPGB, and briefly earned MI5's attention once more. We last hear of him in a post-Second World War note made by W. J. Skardon (known for taking a statement from Lord Haw Haw, extracting confessions from atom spies Klaus Fuchs and Alan Nunn May, and leading the interrogation of Philby), who wrote that Macartney was 'in negotiations with the Soviet authorities in Stettin [Germany] in connection with the racket in surplus military equipment', involving the 'wholesale bribery of US Army officers . . . using Swiss and Lichtenstein banks'. Macartney's trail finally died in January 1950 with reports that he was working with the Chinese People's Party (NA K2/648 MACARTNEY, s.1403a, note by W.J. Skardon (B2a), 18 November 1948).

82 Macartney and Mackenzie, *Walls Have Mouths*, p. 19.

83 See Chapter 6.

84 Krivitsky, *In Stalin's Secret Service*, p. 213. 'Jósef Unszlicht' (Polish)/ 'Josef Unschlicht' (German)/'Iosif Unshlikht' (Russian) had been referred to in MI5 files as the 'vice-president of the OGPU' and was held to be 'personally in charge of the 1923 uprising in Germany'. He was executed in 1938. See NA KV3/11 Russian Intelligence Organisation (General), 1924–1931, s.50, 'A short statement about the OGPU-SSSR', photostat from MI1c [SIS], 11 January 1927, pp. 16–17; Leggett, *The Cheka*, pp. 271–3; Andrew and Gordievsky, *KGB*,

p. 58. The Fourth Department became the GRU in 1937.

85 NA KV2/656 HANSEN, s.837x, 'Extract from Memorandum of information obtained by General [Walter] Krivitsky. Jan–Feb 1940', July 1940. Cf. KV2/805 'KRIVITSKY, Walter J', s.55x, 'Information obtained from General Krivitsky during his visit to this country, January–February 1940', (Jane Archer) p. 9.

86 Macartney and Mackenzie, *Walls Have Mouths*, p. 27.

87 Curry, *Security Service*, p. 5.

88 Quoted in Andrew, *Her Majesty's Secret Service*, p. 229. This section complements research done by Madeira, 'Moscow's Interwar Infiltration of British Intelligence, 1919–1929'. See also Madeira, *Britannia and the Bear: Anglo-Russian Intelligence Wars, 1917–1929* (Woodbridge: Boydell Press, 2014), pp. 41–3, 129, 137–41.

89 NA KV2/1101 Federated Press of America (FPA), s.1a, 'Extract', 'Daily Herald Article', 21 November 1924.

90 NA KV2/1101 FPA, s.19A, 're Advertisement in Daily Herald', 4 February 1925.

91 Peter Jenkins, *Covert Surveillance Techniques: The Manual of Covert Surveillance Training* (Keighley: Intel, 1998), p. 107.

92 NA KV2/1101 FPA, s.19a, 'Report on observation kept re appointment made in latter at "A" in (18a)', 1 January 1925.

93 Cf. MEPO 4/43 Syllabus of Instruction (1921), p. 12, Lesson no 22 (on observation). A Special Operations Executive (SOE) training manual during the Second World War devoted an entire lesson to learning how to describe someone's appearance. It notes: 'Quick recognition of a person in a crowd depends upon quick elimination of unrequired persons. A person's features should, therefore, be described in the following order and under the following headings: a) Features ALWAYS described: Sex; Apparent Age; Height (measure by your own); Build (slight, large, stocky or medium). b) Features only described if DISTINCTIVE: i) Permanent, e.g. shape of eyes, adams apple, nose; ii) Impermanent, e.g. moustache, spectacles, hair, clothes, effects'. The syllabus goes on to list thirteen aspects of an individual's visage one can describe (its shape, the face, complexion, forehead, eyes, etc.) and an additional nine ways of describing the body (neck, shoulders, arms, gait, etc.) (Rigdan, ed., *SOE Syllabus*, p. 64).

94 NA KV2/1101 FPA, s.23A, 'From Box. 573 Daily Herald in reply to (19a)', 9 January 1925.

95 NA KV2/1101 FPA, s.27A, 'Report on interview by "D"(R)', 3 February 1925.

96 NA KV2/1101 FPA, s.19a, 'Report on observation kept re appointment made in latter at "A" in (18a)', 1 January 1925.

97 NA KV2/1101 FPA, minutes of 7 February 1925, 'HOW on "The Federated Press of America"; KV2/1016 EWER, William Norman, s. 809A, 'History of a Section of the Russian Intelligence Service, operating in this country, under management of William Norman Ewer 1919–1929' [hereafter, 'History of a Section of the RIS'], 8 January 1930, p. 2; KV2/1101 FPA, s.[none], 'Synopsis of Telephone Conversations of the Federated Press of America', n.d.; KV2/1414 KLISHKO, s.209b, Scotland House papers re Klishko, n.d. [29.11.22.]; KV2/1101 FPA, minutes of 6 March 1925, by B. (Harker). Hunter identified in DPP1/84 'Rex v. McCARTNEY [*sic*] and others', Statements, taken by Sir Travers Humphreys, 29 November 1927, Henry Hunter, p. 10.

98 NA KV2/1101 FPA, minutes of 5 February 1925; KV2/1099 FPA, s.48a, letter to Morton, 4 March 1925. C. P. Dutt files available at KV2/2504-05; R. P. Dutt files available at KV2/1807-09. On R. P. Dutt, see also Francis Beckett, *Enemy Within: The Rise and Fall of the British Communist Party* (London: John Murray, 1995), esp. p. 30.

99 NA KV2/485 'SLOCOMBE, George Edward', s.205a, 'memorandum on SLOCOMBE', 29 April 1930, p. 2; KV2/1099 FPA, 'HOW on George Slocombe', minutes of 15 May 1925; KV2/1016 EWER, s. 809A, 'History of a Section of the RIS', 8 January 1930, p. 2.

100 NA KV2/1099 FPA, minutes of 5 March 1925, note by B.

101 NA KV2/989 LAKEY, s.2A, 're Federated Press of America', 27 June 1928, p. 2; KV2/989 LAKEY, s.66A, B. report on interview with Allen, 20 August 1928, p. 1.

102 Samuel H. Williamson, 'Seven Ways to Compute the Relative Value of a U.S. Dollar Amount, 1774 to present', MeasuringWorth, 2014, in terms of purchasing power parity at 2012 rates (cf. Madeira, 'Moscow's Interwar Infiltration of British Intelligence, 1919–1929', p. 923, fn. 31); CPGB's annual allocation according to Allen, NA KV2/989 LAKEY, s.77A, 'Mr. Harker's notes on interview of 2.9.28', 11 September 1928.

103 NA KV2/1016 EWER, s.809A, 'History of a Section of the RIS', 8 January 1930, pp. 3–4.

104 NA KV2/1099 FPA, minutes of 8 April 1925.

105 NA KV2/1099 FPA, minutes of 18 April 1925.

106 NA KV2/989 LAKEY, s.84, Harker note on interview with Allen, 23 October 1928, p. 3; KV2/1016 EWER, s.809B, 'Statements made by A. ALLEN corroborating M.I.5. circumstantial evidence that W.N. EWER is a Soviet Agent', 8 January 1930.

A recently published article by Callaghan and Morgan questions Ewer's covert role in part because he was 'an open communist of international repute'. Citing Ewer's trip Moscow in 1922 and subsequent publication of a Trotsky pamphlet in the *Daily Herald*, the article notes, 'This does not meant that Ewer did not talk about more covert matters [while in Moscow], but it was hardly the most effective cover'. His frequent publications in the communist press meant his 'disguise was rather thin' (John Callaghan and Kevin Morgan, 'The Open Conspiracy of the Communist Party and the Case of W.N. Ewer, Communist and Anti-Communist', *The Historical Journal* 49 (2006), 549–64 (p. 554)). While that may be true, the argument rests on the assumption that poor tradecraft indicates that Ewer was not an agent. This is not true; it simply means his activities did not remain covert.

The recent scholarship of Victor Madeira has pointed out that Callaghan and Morgan's criticism fails to address the Paris documents (Victor Madeira, to Cambridge Intelligence Study Seminar 25 May 2007). Despite Callaghan and Morgan's pains to exonerate Ewer from espionage, Ewer himself implicitly admitted to it. 'EWER went out of his way to emphasise that, with the exception of George SLOCUM's [*sic*] organisation in Paris, they [the FPA] did not touch espionage', it was later recorded. Since Ewer was the conduit for Slocombe's funds and regularly received packages from him containing illicitly acquired documents, it seems undeniable that Ewer was involved in espionage. In Madeira's defence, the authors should also consider that whether or not the documents Slocombe obtained 'added up to much' is irrelevant. The intention and action existed. Furthermore, that the French reports originated from 'relatively low-level infiltrations' hardly indicates low-level value, as Callaghan and Morgan's article implies. As one former SIS officer has said, 'You don't have to have the big name, just the person who is passing the information' (University of Cambridge Intelligence Seminar, information obtained under the Chatham House Rule).

Madeira could also note that the article disregards legendary MI5 agent-runner Maxwell Knight's response to Ewer's later contention that the function of the FPA secret organisation was 'purely counter'. Knight observed, 'It is quite impossible to run a counter-espionage organisation of this kind without performing acts which are to all intents and purposes espionage. Also it seems to me to be almost equally impossible to run an organisation like the F.P.A. without obtaining information which is not purely "counter"' (NA KV2/1100 FPA, s.897a, 'Extract from B4.c. report re interview with Ewer, William Norman ment: FPA', 30 January 1950, p. 2). The FPA's 'purely counter' work included monitoring MI5 officers and their surveillance activities, which was undoubtedly of great interest to Soviet foreign intelligence. Clearly, counter-intelligence can reveal a foreign intelligence service's operational methods just as foreign intelligence can reveal a counter-intelligence service's operational methods.

In attempting to put Ewer's communist sympathies into context, the article reminds us of the ideological struggle that existed during the early 1920s – a time not yet tinged by the Cold War, which 'so massively ... loom[s] over the history of the twentieth century' (Callaghan and Morgan, 'The Open Conspiracy of the Communist Party and the Case of W. N. Ewer, Communist and Anti-Communist', p. 552). So massively, however, does Cold War tradecraft tend to loom over our understanding of espionage that we fail to appreciate how the codified tradecraft of the Cold War took years to develop. During the interwar period we witness the transition from amateur to professional intelligence management. So, unwittingly, the article's analysis is correct when it surmises:

If public figures like Ewer really were entrusted with the organization of Bolshevik intelligence networks in the early 1920s, it suggests a form of indiscriminate revolutionary diplomacy which later receded as the delineation of a distinct Soviet state interest took shape from which the open work of communist parties in the west was kept largely separate. (Callaghan and Morgan, 'The Open Conspiracy of the Communist Party and the Case of W.N. Ewer, Communist and Anti-Communist', pp. 550–1)

Inexplicably, the authors are reluctant to accept their own hypothesis. A series of espionage debacles, such as Ewer's, forced Soviet intelligence to adopt an increasingly

sophisticated recruitment strategy, including a policy not to collaborate with local communist parties in agent operations and the adoption of the legal and illegal resident system, precisely along the lines they describe.

107 NA KV2/989 LAKEY, minute of 21 May 1928, B.7 (KMMS) to B. (Harker).

108 NA KV2/989 LAKEY, minute of 21 May 1928, B (Harker) to CSI (Kell).

109 NA KV2/989 LAKEY, s.41a, Home Office Warrant for Allen, 23 May 1928.

110 NA KV2/989 LAKEY, minute of 12 June 1928, B.7 (Sissmore) to B (Harker).

111 NA KV2/989 LAKEY, minute of 14 June 1928, minute by B (Harker).

112 NA KV2/989 LAKEY, s.54a, B.4 report re Allen, 27 June 1928, pp. 1–4. In return for his anonymity and £1,500, Allen agreed 'to provide information about FPA, Arcos, and Russian "intrigues" during his whole tenure (1919–1927)'. For simply information on the 'personnel of the FPA, the nature of its business here, and the reason of its closure', he asked for £100. Ottaway noted, 'I am still of the opinion that Allen can give valuable information and that he believes it is worth the amount he is asking. He, however, is inclined to exaggerate, and I think somewhat overestimate his ability.'

113 NA KV2/989 LAKEY, s.1A (57a), B.4 report re Allen, 25 June 1928, p. 4.

114 Cherkashin and Feifer, *Spy Handler*, p. 63.

115 NA KV2/989 LAKEY, s.2A, 're Federated Press of America', 27 June 1928, p. 1.

116 NA KV2/989 LAKEY, s.63A, note by Harker on his interview with Allen, Harker to C.S.I. (Kell), 24 July 1928, pp. 1–2.

117 NA KV2/1016 EWER, s.809B, 'Statements made by ALLEN', 8 January 1930, p. 1.

118 NA KV2/989 LAKEY, s. 63A, note by Harker on his interview with Allen, Harker to C.S.I. (Kell), 24 July 1928, p. 3.

119 NA KV2/1016 EWER, s.809A, 'History of a Section of the RIS', 8 January 1930, p. 3.

120 John Beavan, 'William Norman Ewer', in *ODNB*, www.oxforddnb.com (last accessed 30 November 2007); Callaghan and Morgan, 'The Open Conspiracy of the Communist Party and the Case of W. N. Ewer, Communist and Anti-Communist', pp. 151–2.

121 NA KV2/989, LAKEY, s.66A, note by Harker on his interview with Allen, Harker to C.S.I. (Kell), 1 August 1928, p. 2.

122 NA KV2/1016 EWER, s.1101a, 'Clandestine Activities of William Norman Ewer 1919–1929' [hereafter, 'Clandestine

Activities'], by Ann Glass (B2b), September 1949, p. 1.

123 NA KV2/989, LAKEY, s.66A, note by Harker on his interview with Allen, Harker to C.S.I. (Kell), 1 August 1928, p. 7.

124 This kind of belated discovery was common. Other agents, such as Olga Gray, had the same experience. See Chapter 4.

125 NA KV2/1016 EWER, s.809B, 'Statements made by ALLEN', 8 January 1930, p. 1; KV2/1016 EWER, s. 1101a, 'Clandestine Activities', September 1949, p. 1.

126 NA KV2/1016 EWER, s.809B, 'Statements made by ALLEN', 8 January 1930, p. 1.

127 NA KV2/1016 EWER, s.1101a, 'Clandestine Activities', September 1949, p. 1. Ewer later insisted that the FPA, a large and reputable news agency, had no knowledge of his covert activities (KV2/1100 FPA, s.897a, 'Extract from B4.c. report re interview with Ewer, William Norman ment: FPA', 30 January 1950, p. 3).

128 NA KV2/989, LAKEY, s.77A, 'Mr. Harker's notes on interview of 2.9.28', 11 September 1928, p. 1.

129 That, indeed, is the assessment of John Curry (author of MI5's official post-Second World War history). Curry, *Security Service*, pp. 97–8.

130 NA KV2/1100 FPA, s.897a, 'Extract from B4.c. report re interview with Ewer, William Norman ment: FPA', 30 January 1950, p. 1; cf. s. 898a, 'Extract from B4.c. report re interview with Ewer, William Norman ment: FPA', 24 April 1950 (Ewer's claim that the advertisement was inserted by an MP 'writing a book connected with matters under discussion' falls flat).

131 NA KV2/1016 EWER, s. 1101a, 'Clandestine Activities', September 1949, p. 2.

132 Andrew and Mitrokhin, *The Mitrokhin Archive*, p. 41.

133 NA KV2/1100 FPA, s.897a, 'Extract from B4.c. report re interview with Ewer, William Norman ment: FPA', 30 January 1950.

134 Harker recorded Allen's comment that 'Ewer was in the habit of dictating every week or ten days a list of addresses on which it was known that H.O.W.s had been taken out. These lists were typed in triplicate, one copy was sent to Chesham House, one copy was submitted through Chesham House direct to Moscow, and the third copy was sent to some individual in the C.P.G.B.' (NA KV2/989 LAKEY, s.69A, Allen's statement regarding the activities of the FPA, 20 August 1928, p. 1).

135 NA KV2/989 LAKEY, s.69A, Allen's statement regarding the activities of the FPA, 20 August 1928, p. 3; KV2/1016 EWER, s.809A, 'History of a Section of the RIS', 8 January 1930, p. 8.

136 NA KV2/989 LAKEY, s.69A, Allen's statement regarding the activities of the FPA, 20 August 1928, p. 3; KV2/989 LAKEY, s.72A, 'Comparative Statement of information obtained from ALLEN and MI5 records', 29 August 1928, p. 1.

137 NA KV2/989 LAKEY, s.69A, Allen's statement regarding the activities of the FPA, 20 August 1928, p. 2.

138 The minute from 6 March 1925 on the interception of mail from Paris reads: 'Major Morton informed me [Harker] . . . that "C" had decided that, on no account, would he circulate any information received from this source to Scotland House [i.e. Scotland Yard], and would take full responsibility for their not being informed of the matter. In discussing this Major Morton agreed with me that, in this case, although some of the suspects were known to be Communists, the information obtained relates to their espionage activities and not to their ordinary activities as Communists, so that there has been nothing which required to be passed to S.H. [Scotland House]; the sole exception of espionage has been the Indian information which has been duly passed to I.P.I.' NA KV2/1099 FPA, minute of 6 March 1925.

139 NA KV2/989 LAKEY, s.66A, note by Harker on his interview with Allen, 20 August 1928, p. 8; cf. KV2/989 LAKEY, s.1A (57a), 'B.4 note re Federated Press of America', 27 June 1928, p. 2.

140 NA KV2/989 LAKEY, s.69A, Allen's statement regarding the activities of the FPA, 20 August 1928, p. 4.

141 NA KV2/989 LAKEY, s. 71A, 'Note by Mr. Harker on interview with ALLEN and questionnaire', 28 August 1928, p. 1, and KV2/989 LAKEY, s.69A, Allen's statement regarding the activities of the FPA, 20 August 1928, p. 4.

142 NA KV2/989 LAKEY, s.69A, Allen's statement regarding the activities of the FPA, 20 August 1928, p. 4. See 'Note on currency' in Overy, *The Twilight Years*.

143 In 1921 Curzon told the Cabinet, for example, 'The Russian menace in the East is incomparably greater than anything else that has happened in any time to the British Empire.' Quoted in Andrew, *Her Majesty's Secret Service*, p. 277.

144 Popplewell, *Intelligence and Imperial Defence: British Intelligence and the Defence of the Indian Empire, 1904–1924*, p. 308; see also Peter Hopkirk, *Setting the East Ablaze: On Secret Service in Bolshevik Asia* (Oxford: Oxford University Press, 2001), pp. 94–122.

145 NA KV2/1016 EWER, s. 809A, 'History of a Section of the RIS', 8 January 1930, p. 8; s.573A, Precis on EWER, 20 April 1929, p. 3.

146 NA KV2/989 LAKEY, s.83a, Harker note on interview with Allen, 15 October 1928.

147 NA KV2/1016 EWER, s.809A, 'History of a Section of the RIS', 8 January 1930, p. 9.

148 NA KV2/1016 EWER, s.809A, 'History of a Section of the RIS', 8 January 1930, p. 9.

149 KV2/1016 EWER, s. 809A, 'History of a Section of the RIS', 8 January 1930, p. 10; Madeira, 'Moscow's Interwar Infiltration of British Intelligence, 1919–1929', p. 927. See also Madeira, *Britannia and the Bear*.

150 KV2/1016 EWER, s. 809A, 'History of a Section of the RIS', 8 January 1930, pp. 12–13.

151 See, for example, Gorodetsky, *The Precarious Truce*, p. 238; by contrast, see Steiner, *The Lights That Failed*, pp. 539–40.

152 Orlov, *Handbook of Intelligence and Guerrilla Warfare*, pp. 39–40; Leonard, *Secret Soldiers of the Revolution*, p. 88.

153 Andrew and Mitrokhin, *The Mitrokhin Archive*, p. 55.

154 NA KV3/12 Russian Intelligence Organisation (General) 1924–1931, s.118a, letter from Vivian (SIS) to Harker (MI5), 'Activities of the G.P.U.', 15 May 1930, p. 2.

155 A notion technically applied to US policy during the Cold War.

156 Steiner, *The Lights That Failed*, p. 134.

157 Bruce Lockhart, 'Dunderdale, Wilfred Albert (1899–1990)', *ONDB*.

158 Chantal Aubin, 'French Counterintelligence and British Secret Intelligence in the Netherlands, 1920–1940', in *Battleground Western Europe. Intelligence Operations in Germany and the Netherlands in the Twentieth Century*, ed. Beatrice de Graf, Ben de Jong and Weis Platje (Amsterdam: Het Spinhuis, 2008), pp. 17–48; J. C. Masterman, *The Double-Cross System: The Incredible True Story of How Nazi Spies Were Turned into Double Agents* (New York: The Lyons Press, 2000), p. 36; Wilson, 'War in the Dark', pp. 117–18; David de Young de la Marck, 'Free French and British Intelligence Relations, 1940–1944' (unpublished doctoral dissertation, University of Cambridge, 2002), introduction, pp. 157–72. Jedburghs were three-men multinational teams parachuted

behind Nazi lines to liaise with resistance groups during the invasion of the Continent. They played an especially prominent part in SOE plans for D-Day in France.

159 Stephen Lander, 'International Intelligence Co-Operation: An Inside Perspective', *Cambridge Review of International Affairs* 17, no. 3 (2004), 481–93.

160 Quoted in Andrew and Mitrokhin, *The Mitrokhin Archive*, p. 75.

161 MI5's first interwar Oxbridge male recruit was Dick White, who joined in 1935. Sir Dick White later served as head of both MI5 and then SIS, a unique occurrence in those organisations' histories. See Bower, *The Perfect English Spy*.

162 Quoted in Knightley, *Philby*, p. 97.

163 IWM Payne Best MSS 79/57/1, Dansey to Payne Best, 14 December 1945; quoted in Andrew, *Her Majesty's Secret Service*, p. 357. See generally Anthony Read and David Fisher, *Colonel Z: The Life and Times of a Master of Spies* (London: Hodder and Stoughton, 1984).

164 Kim Philby, *My Silent War: The Autobiography of a Spy* (London: Arrow Books, 2003), p. 109.

CHAPTER 4

Penetration Agents (I)

1 Ernest R. May, ed., *Knowing One's Enemies: Intelligence Assessment before the Two World Wars* (Princeton, NJ: Princeton University Press, 1984).

2 Robert Gates (former head of the CIA and US Secretary of Defense), quoted in Herman, *Intelligence Power in Peace and War*, p. 103.

3 For clarity, this chapter will refer to Knight's agent-running section as 'M. Section', as it was casually known through the 1930s, though it was technically named B5b. It only formally became 'M. Section' in 1942. On these organisational changes, see Curry, *Security Service*, p. 393. Following the Second World War, Maxwell Knight (1900–1968) became better known as 'Uncle Max', the popular naturalist and BBC radio presenter.

4 NA KV4/227 'Report on the Work of M.S. (Agents) during the War, 1939–1945', by Maxwell Knight (M.), 4 April 1945 [hereafter, 'M.S. Report'], p. 1.

5 This was true even though it became clear that the CPGB had been taken completely unaware by the Mutiny, although it did seek to capitalise on it after the fact (Curry, *Security Service*, p. 107; Hinsley and Simkins, *British Intelligence in the Second World War: Volume IV*, p. 18). After the sailors' largely respectful

protest, the government hastily made amends to placate the Atlantic Fleet's riled hands (Taylor, *English History*, p. 296).

6 NA KV4/227 'M.S. Report', p. 33.

7 NA KV4/227 'M.S. Report', p. 16.

8 Herman, *Intelligence Power in Peace and War*, p. 65.

9 NA KV2/1020 'GLADING, Percy Eded', s.52a, 'note re Glading', 16 March 1932.

10 NA KV2/1020 GLADING, s.5b, 'Extract from SY [Scotland Yard] report', 16 May 1927; s. 5a, HOW on Elisabeth and Percy GLADING, 5 January 1927; s. 21a, 'Resume for Percy E. Glading' (by Captain Boddington), 17 December 1928.

11 NA KV2/1020 GLADING, s.16a, 'press cutting', 24 October 1928; 'The dismissal of a Communist', *The Times*, Wednesday 24 October 1928.

12 NA KV2/1020 GLADING, s. [illegible], 'note re Glading', attachment to letter from IPI (DVW[allinger]) to MI5 (Miss Sissmore, B.4a), 29 February 1932. [*N.B.: Many of the Glading files are badly damaged. The photostats available often do not have reference or page numbers.*]

13 NA KV3/311–12, 'Communist Activities in Portsmouth Dockyard'; see also the file on John Harold Salisbury, dismissed for his part in the sabotage of naval vessels, NA KV2/2497-2501, especially KV2/2499, s. 279a, 'note re J.H. SALISBURY', 19 January 1936. The file includes investigations into the sabotage of machinery by noted and suspected communists to slow the production of British vessels. Similar sabotage occurred at other dockyards. The period of Salisbury's dismissal coincides with a dramatic increase in the surveillance of Glading. His files contain multiple pages of surveillance operations and the identification of his contacts. See KV2/1020 GLADING, s.192-209, April–May 1936.

14 MI5 intercepted a letter in November 1937 from the Executive Committee of the CPGB asking him to reconsider his decision of 'now over a year ago' to leave the Party (NA KV2/1022 GLADING, s. [illegible], 12 November 1937. Yet in MI5's in-house history, Curry writes that Glading 'severed all connection' with the CPGB and the League Against Imperialism, of which he had been a paid official, in March 1937. Curry, *Security Service*, p. 108. His behaviour was similar to that of others (like the Cambridge Five), who severed links with the Party before going to work for Soviet intelligence.

15 Richard C. Thurlow, 'Soviet Spies and British Counter-Intelligence in the 1930s: Espionage in the Woolwich Arsenal and the Foreign Office Communications Department', *Intelligence and National Security* 19 (2004), 610–31 (p. 613).

16 See Joan Miller, *One Girl's War: Personal Exploits in MI5's Most Secret Station* (Dingle, Co. Kerry: Brandon, 1986), p. 50, 65; Eric Homberger, 'Knight, (Charles Henry) Maxwell (1900–1968)', *ODNB*, http://www.oxforddnb.com/view/article/67489 (last accessed 29 April 2008).

17 Anthony Masters, *The Man Who Was M: The Life of Maxwell Knight* (Oxford: Basil Blackwell, 1984). Masters's account must be treated carefully, as there is little to corroborate some of his claims, and because some of his statements are incorrect. However, the work remains important if only for the interviews he conducted. While recognising the methodological deficiencies, this analysis uses the character descriptions he has given as they are the only ones available.

18 Masters, *The Man Who Was M*, p. 30.

19 NA KV2/1023 'GLADING, Percy Eded', s.871a, 'The Woolwich Arsenal Case' (by B2b), 13 February 1950, p. 13.

20 NA KV4/227 'M.S. Report', p. 25.

21 University of Cambridge Intelligence Seminar, information obtained under the Chatham House Rule.

22 See Chapter 5. They were ostensibly lovers but Miller claimed their relationship was never consummated. Miller claims Knight was homosexual and devotes part of her memoir to detailing that charge. All we can say for certain is that they lived together under romantic but evidently troubled circumstances.

23 NA KV4/227 'M.S. Report', p. 17.

24 NA KV4/227 'M.S. Report', p. 25.

25 NA KV4/227 'M.S. Report', p. 19. At that time, all of MI5's officers, save the redoubtable Kathleen Sissmore/Jane Archer, were male.

26 See Howard Gardner, *Frames of Mind: The Theory of Multiple Intelligences* (New York: Basic Books, 1983); Daniel Goleman, *Emotional Intelligence* (New York: Bantam Books, 1995), *Social Intelligence: The New Science of Relationships* (New York: Bantam Books, 2006); cf. Steven M. Kleinman, 'KUBARK Counterintelligence Interrogation Review: Observations of an Interrogator: Lessons Learned and Avenues for Further Research', in NDIC Intelligence Science Board, *Educing Information: Interrogation: Science and Art. Foundations for the Future*

(Washington, DC: National Defense Intelligence College [NDIC] Press, 2006), 95–140.

27 NA KV4/227 'M.S. Report', p. 25.

28 NA KV4/227 'M.S. Report', p. 19.

29 NA KV4/227 'M.S. Report', p. 20.

30 The Dutch-born Margaretha Geertruida Zelle, a.k.a. Mata-Hari, was an exotic dancer hired by German intelligence during the First World War. She was thought have had slept with senior French and Belgian officials in order to gather information. French intercepts eventually led to her arrest and execution in 1917. She was interrogated by MI5 in late 1915 on suspicion of spying for the Germans, but no charges were brought against her. The records of her interrogation can be found at NA KV2/1-2. The literature on Mata-Hari is extensive, the latest account at the time of this book's going to press being Pat Shipman's *Femme Fatale: A Biography of Mata Hari* (London: Weidenfeld & Nicolson, 2007).

31 NA KV4/227 'M.S. Report', p. 20.

32 University of Cambridge Intelligence Seminar, information obtained under the Chatham House Rule.

33 Soviet recruits such as the CIA's Aldrich Ames and the FBI's Robert Hanssen come to mind. They spied for money and ego. Among other accounts highlighting their recruitment and handling, see Cherkashin and Feifer, *Spy Handler*.

34 NA KV4/227 'M.S. Report', p. 17.

35 Masterman, *The Double-Cross System*, p. 32.

36 NA KV4/227 'M.S. Report', p. 21.

37 NA KV4/227 'M.S. Report', p. 33.

38 Herman, *Intelligence Power in Peace and War*, p. 65.

39 'The Spy Who Came in From the Co-op' was the title of the *Times* article (11 September 1999) that first revealed Norwood's identity to the British public, as disclosed in Andrew and Mitrokhin, *The Mitrokhin Archive*. See also David Burke, *The Spy Who Came In from the Co-op: Melita Norwood and the Ending of Cold War Espionage* (Woodbridge: Boydell Press, 2009).

40 Andrew and Mitrokhin, *The Mitrokhin Archive*, p. 153. Some of the most recent research on the Soviet penetration of the British atomic project using newly-declassified MI5 files can be found in Calder Walton, 'British Intelligence and Threats to National Security, c.1941–1951' (unpublished doctoral dissertation, University of Cambridge, 2006).

41 NA KV4/227 'M.S. Report', p. 18.

42 NA KV4/227 'M.S. Report', p. 17.

43 NA KV4/227 'M.S. Report', p. 18.

44 NA KV4/227 'M.S. Report', p. 17.

45 NA KV2/1023 GLADING, s.871a, 'The Woolwich Arsenal Case' (by B2b), 13 February 1950, p. 13.

46 Louis Nemzer, 'The Soviet Friendship Societies', *The Public Opinion Quarterly* 13 (1949), 265–84. Cf. NA KV3/301 International Organisation of the Communist Party – Most Secret Information, s.15, 'F.2b History of the Soviet Union and Communist International, 1917–1943', 7 July 1945, p. 3. When Gray began attending the meetings in the autumn of 1931, the organisation was still called 'The Friends of Soviet Russia', but shortly afterward changed its name to 'The Friends of the Soviet Union'. The head of the International Bureau of the Friends of the Soviet Union was Albert Inkpin, former Secretary of the CPGB. The headquarters of the International Secretariat was based in Germany until 1933, when it relocated to Amsterdam.

47 Andrew, *Her Majesty's Secret Service*, p. 326.

48 NA KV4/227 'M.S. Report', pp. 33–4; NA KV2/1023 GLADING, s.871a, 'The Woolwich Arsenal Case' (by B2b), 13 February 1950, p. 13.

49 NA KV2/1022 GLADING, s.[illegible], 'Statement of "X" the informant in this case', 25 January 1938, p. 1.

50 NA KV4/227 'M.S. Report', p. 34.

51 NA KV2/1034 'POLLITT, Harry', s.235a, 'Harry POLLITT', February 1934.NA KV2/1034.

52 NA KV2/1036 POLLITT, s.149a, Investigation Branch, General Post Office, to Harker, 1 December 1931; KV2/1035 POLLITT, s.51a, Liddell (MI5) to Vivian (SIS), 2 April 1931; KV2/1036 POLLITT, s.60a, Harker (MI5) to Vivian (SIS), 28 April 1931; s.62a, SIS to Carter (MI5), 11 May 1931 (CX 8862); KV2/1035 POLLITT, s.56a, Special Branch to MI5, 17 April 1931.

53 NA KV4/227 'M.S. Report', pp. 34–5.

54 The LAI was originally based in Berlin after its founding in 1927. The Harrow-educated Labour politician Reginald Bridgeman remained secretary of the British section until he became General Secretary upon the LAI's relocation to London in 1933. Its last conference was held in 1937 (John D. Hargreaves, 'The Comintern and Anti-Colonialism: New Research Opportunities', *African Affairs* 92 (1993), 255–61). Münzenberg was the General Secretary of the Workers' International Relief (WIR) and was responsible for the formation of the

'Innocents' Clubs', which tried to 'organise the intellectuals' of front organisations like the World Committee for the Relief of the Victims of German Fascism, which he founded after the German Reichstag Fire in 1933 (Andrew and Gordievsky, *KGB*, pp. 146–52; Krivitsky, *In Stalin's Secret Service*, pp. 23–64; Stephen Koch, *Double Lives: Stalin, Willi Munzenberg and the Seduction of the Intellectuals* (London: HarperCollins, 1995)).

55 NA KV2/1022 GLADING, s.243a, 'Notes re GLADING', [illegible – 3?] May 1938; Irfan Habib, 'Civil Disobedience 1930–31', *Social Scientist* 25 (1997), 43–66.

56 Percy Glading, *The Meerut Conspiracy Case* (London: Communist Party of Great Britain, 1933). This was a follow-up to his subtly titled *India Under British Terror* (London: Percy Glading (Secretary), Meerut Trade Union Defence Committee, 1931).

57 NA KV2/804 KRIVITSKY, s.20a (P), 'Information re the Fourth Department, its work and methods', 31 January 1940, ('Colonial Work of the Fourth Department'), p. 13.

58 As explained by Krivitsky, 'The Lenin School was founded in 1926 to train foreign communists politically and practically in the work of revolution and at the same time to produce a body of propagandists from foreign countries to organise and educate Communist Parties abroad.' NA KV2/805 KRIVITSKY, s. 55x, 'Information obtained from General Krivitsky during his visit to this country, January-February, 1940', (Jane Archer) p. 58.

59 NA KV2/1022 GLADING, s. [illegible], 'Statement of "X" the informant in this case', 25 January 1938, p. 1.

60 NA KV4/227 'M.S. Report', p. 35.

61 Masters, *The Man Who Was M*, p. 33.

62 NA KV2/1022 GLADING, s. [illegible], 'Statement of "X" the informant in this case', 25 January 1938, p. 1; KV4/227 'M.S. Report', p. 36.

63 NA KV4/227 'M.S. Report', p. 35.

64 NA KV4/227 'M.S. Report', p. 36.

65 Masters, *The Man Who Was M*, pp. 33-34.

66 NA KV4/227 'M.S. Report', p. 37.

67 Masters, *The Man Who Was M*, p. 35.

68 NA KV4/227 'M.S. Report', p. 37.

69 NA KV2/1022 GLADING, s. [illegible], 'Statement of "X" the informant in this case', 25 January 1938, p. 1.

70 NA KV4/227 'M.S. Report', p. 37.

71 NA KV2/1020 GLADING, s.129a, note on Percy Glading, headed 'Personal M/3', 16 May 1934; s.192a, 'M report re GLADING', 6 May 1936; s.209, 're Percy GLADING', M/3 report, 30 May 1936. Files also express an increasing interest in British counter-espionage capabilities.

72 Taylor, *English History*, p. 386.

73 NA KV2/1022 GLADING, s. [illegible], 'Statement of "X" the informant in this case', 25 January 1938, p. 2; KV4/227 'M.S. Report', p. 37.

74 NA KV4/22 'M.S. Report', p. 38.

75 NA KV2/1022 GLADING, s.[illegible], 'Statement of "X" the informant in this case', 25 January 1938, p. 2.

76 In the interwar period an average worker made roughly £2–3 per week, and a journalist earned roughly £10–15 per week. Anyone with an income of over £1,000 per year might be considered wealthy. See 'Note on currency' in Overy, *The Twilight Years*.

77 NA KV2/1022 GLADING, s.[illegible], 'Statement of "X" the informant in this case', 25 January 1938, pp. 2-3.

78 KV4/227 'M.S. Report', p. 38.

79 NA KV2/1022 GLADING, s. [illegible], 'Statement of "X" the informant in this case', 25 January 1938, p. 3; KV2/1023 GLADING, s.871a, 'The Woolwich Arsenal Case' (by B2b), 13 February 1950, p. 6.

80 Gray recalled that Glading referred to the Austrian as 'a small man and rather bumptious in manner' (NA KV2/1022 GLADING, s. [illegible], 'Statement of "X" the informant in this case', 25 January 1938, p. 3). Clearly Glading and Maly had discussed Deutsch, because Maly also described Deutsch as 'bumptious' to Walter Krivitsky. (NA KV2/804 KRIVITSKY, s.2b (C), 'note re information from KRIVITSKY', 23 January 1940, p. 8; s.4a (E), 'B.3.c. notes re interview with KRIVITSKY', 25 January 1940, p. 2. Cf. Andrew and Mitrokhin, *The Mitrokhin Archive*, chapter 4. The Brandes files can be seen at NA KV2/1004-1007, though they offer little that cannot be found in the Glading files.

81 NA KV2/1023 GLADING, s.871a, 'The Woolwich Arsenal Case' (by B2b), 13 February 1950, p. 6.

82 NA KV2/815-816, KING, John Herbert; KV2/814 PIECK, Hans Christian, s.375a, 'Report on the Interrogation of HANS CHRISTIAN PIECK, 12–16th April 1950', 1 May 1950; NA KV2/804 KRIVITSKY, s.5a, 'B.4. report re interview with KRIVITSKY (re DAWIDOWICZ and GADA)', 25 January 1940.

83 NA KV4/227 'M.S. Report', p. 39.

84 NA KV2/1023 GLADING, s.871a, 'The Woolwich Arsenal Case' (by B2b), 13 February 1950, p. 1; NA KV2/1022 GLADING, s. [illegible], 'Statement of "X" the informant in this case', 25 January 1938, p. 3. Training in photography may have been given by Austrian-born Edith Tudor-Hart, née Suschitsky. She was one of the Soviet agents, who also included Arnold Deutsch, living at the Lawn Road flats. Tudor-Hart was also acquainted with Kim Philby; his first wife was a friend from her Comintern days in Austria. It was later found that Glading had given Gray invoices from Tudor-Hart's photography shop. NA KV2/1012 TUDOR-HART, Edith, s.34a, circular from Special Branch to MI5, 2 March 1938.

85 This seems to have been a tactic of the early 1930s; young, ideologically motivated activists were drawn into OGPU work after first working for or under the pretence of working for the Comintern.

86 Cf. Ferguson, *Spy*, pp. 109–12.

87 NA KV4/227 'M.S. Report', p.39.

88 NA KV2/1022 GLADING, s. [illegible], 'Statement of "X" the informant in this case', 25 January 1938, p. 4.

89 NA KV2/1022 GLADING, s. [illegible], 'Statement of "X" the informant in this case', 25 January 1938, p. 5; KV2/1023 GLADING, s.871a, 'The Woolwich Arsenal Case' (by B2b), 13 February 1950, p. 2; NA KV2/804 KRIVITSKY, s.20a (P), 'Information re the Fourth Department, its work and methods' (B.4), pp. 4–5 ('Methods of Work'); KV2/805 KRIVITSKY, s.55x, 'Information obtained from Krivitsky', pp. 15–16.

90 NA KV2/1023 GLADING, s.871a, 'The Woolwich Arsenal Case' (by B2b), 13 February 1950, p. 2.

91 The George Whomack files can be seen at NA KV2/1237–38; NA KV2/1022 GLADING, s. [illegible], 'Statement of "X" the informant in this case', 25 January 1938, p. 6; KV2/1023 GLADING, s.871a, 'The Woolwich Arsenal Case' (by B2b), 13 February 1950, p. 2.

92 NA KV4/227 'M.S. Report', p. 40; KV2/1023 GLADING, s.871a, 'The Woolwich Arsenal Case' (by B2b), 13 February 1950, p. 3.

93 NA KV2/1023 GLADING, s.871a, 'The Woolwich Arsenal Case' (by B2b), 13 February 1950, p. 3; KV2/1022 GLADING, s. [illegible], 'Statement of "X" the informant in this case', 25 January 1938, pp. 5–6.

94 NA KV2/1022 GLADING, s. [illegible], 'Statement of "X" the informant in this case', 25 January 1938, p. 6.

95 One report states the book is two hundred pages, a later report, four hundred. NA KV2/1022 GLADING, s. [illegible], 'Statement of "X" the informant in this case', 25 January 1938, p. 6; KV2/1023 GLADING, s.871a, 'The Woolwich Arsenal Case' (by B2b), 13 February 1950, p. 4.

96 NA KV2/1022 GLADING, s. [illegible], 'Statement of "X" the informant in this case', 25 January 1938, p. 6.

97 NA KV2/1023 GLADING, s.871a, 'The Woolwich Arsenal Case' (by B5b), 13 February 1950, p. 4; KV2/1022 GLADING, s. [illegible], 'Statement of "X" the informant in this case', 25 January 1938, p. 7.

98 NA KV4/227 'M.S. Report', p. 40.

99 Albert Williams's files can be seen at NA KV2/1003.

100 NA KV2/1023 GLADING, s.871a, 'The Woolwich Arsenal Case' (by B5b), 13 February 1950, p. 4.

101 NA KV2/1023 GLADING, s.871a, 'The Woolwich Arsenal Case' (by B5b), 13 February 1950, p. 4.

102 NA KV2/1023 GLADING, s.871a, 'The Woolwich Arsenal Case' (by B5b), 13 February 1950, p. 5. For a record of the hearing, see 'Rex v Percy Glading and Others', NA CRIM 1/1003, under violation of the 1911 Official Secrets Act.

103 NA HO 45/25520 'Disturbances', record of Glading's conviction. Andrew, *Her Majesty's Secret Service*, p. 371.

104 Quoted in Masters, *The Man Who Was M*, p. 51.

105 This may, in fact, be the first instance of agent repatriation.

106 Masters, *The Man Who Was M*, p. 54.

107 Masters, *The Man Who Was M*, p. 53.

108 Thurlow, 'Soviet Spies and British Counter-Intelligence in the 1930s', p. 617.

109 Thurlow, 'Soviet Spies and British Counter-Intelligence in the 1930s', p. 612, 613.

110 See NA KV2/777 'KAPITZA, Dr Pierre [sic]' and KV2/1758-59 'DOBB, Maurice Herbert'. Thanks go to Calder Walton for the Kapitza reference.

111 Blunt joined MI5 in 1940. From this position he was able to pass information to the Soviets regarding Driberg's penetration of the CPGB (Miller, *One Girl's War*, pp. 50, 65; Richard Davenport-Hines, 'Driberg, Thomas Edward Neil, Baron Bradwell (1905–1976)', *ODNB*, http://www.oxforddnb.com/view/article/31047, (last accessed 21 August 2008)). *The Mitrokhin Archive* reveals that the KGB later blackmailed Driberg into serving

as an agent (1956–1968), using sexually compromising photographs taken in Moscow (although Driberg's homosexuality was anything but secret (Andrew and Mitrokhin, *The Mitrokhin Archive*, pp. 522–6). Curiously, Driberg's biographer readily accepts Miller's account that Knight was 'sexually besotted' by Driberg, yet simultaneously rejects the possibility that Driberg acted as his agent. That this account lacks reference to Driberg's later involvement with Soviet espionage shows it to be incomplete (Francis Wheen, *The Soul of Indiscretion: Tom Driberg: Poet, Philanderer, Legislator and Outlaw* (London: Fourth Estate, 2001), pp. 158–68). Perhaps unsurprisingly, Driberg's autobiography makes no mention of either work for MI5 or the KGB (Tom Driberg, *Ruling Passions* (London: Quartet Books, 1978)).

112 Eric Homberger, 'Knight, (Charles Henry) Maxwell (1900–1968)', *ODNB*, http://www.oxforddnb.com/view/article/67489 (last accessed 29 April 2008).

113 NA KV4/227 'M.S. Report', p. 41.

114 NA KV2/1023 GLADING, s.871a, 'The Woolwich Arsenal Case' (by B5b), 13 February 1950, p. 7.

115 Curry, *Security Service*, p. 361.

116 NA KV4/127 'Security Service Organisation from 1918–1939', s.2a, 'Chart of activities of B. and S. branches', (n.d.). B.4a (Civil Security—Home) run by Jane Archer (Sissmore) and Bill Younger; B.4b (Civil Security—Foreign) by Dick White; B.5b ('M Organization') by Maxwell Knight. Two other departments (accounting for two more officers) dealt generally with subversion in the armed forces.

117 NA KV4/127 'Security Service Organisation from 1918–1939', s.4a, Director's circular No. 99 of 1937, 'Re-arrangement of peace organisation to facilitate rapid mobilisation for war'.

118 University of Cambridge Intelligence Seminar, information obtained under the Chatham House Rule.

119 NA KV4/228 Report on the Operations of F.2.c. in connection with Russian Intelligence during War 1939–1945, s.1a, self-titled report, May 1945, pp. 2–3; Walton, 'British Intelligence and Threats to National Security, c.1941–1951', chapter 1.

120 Andrew and Mitrokhin, *The Mitrokhin Archive*, p. 153.

121 NA KV4/227 'M.S. Report', p. 41; cf. Curry, *Security Service*, p. 394.

122 NA KV4/227 'M.S. Report', p. 4.

123 Private information; Andrew, *Her Majesty's Secret Service*, p. 370.

124 James M. Olson, 'The Ten Commandments of Counterintelligence', in *Intelligence and the National Security Strategist: Enduring Issues and Challenges*, ed. Roger Z. George and Robert D. Kline (Lanham, MD: Rowman & Littlefield Publishers, 2006), 251–8 (p. 253). (Endnotes)

CHAPTER 5
Penetration Agents (II)

1 See Bennett, *Churchill's Man of Mystery*, pp. 71–9; Hope, 'Surveillance or Collusion? Maxwell Knight, MI5 and the British Fascisti'.

2 In 1923, twenty-eight-year-old Rotha Linthorn-Orman had launched the BF into the rapidly populating field of extreme right-wing politics, and even though the BF's activities had few long-term consequences, some of British fascism's most infamous characters began their political careers with the organisation. Arnold Leese (who founded the violently anti-Semitic Imperial Fascist League) and William Joyce ('Lord Haw-Haw') both got their political feet wet as members of the BF. Linehan, *British Fascism*, p. 69. For MI5's personal files on Leese, see NA KV2/1635–1637 (see also KV3/37–38, 60–63 for MI5 investigations into Leese's part in organising escape routes for Nazi fugitives); personal files on Joyce, KV2/245–250; Martland, *Lord Haw Haw*.

3 See Bennett, *Churchill's Man of Mystery*, pp. 71–9; Hope, 'Surveillance or Collusion? Maxwell Knight, MI5 and the British Fascisti'.

4 Masters's claim that Knight joined MI5 in 1925 has been frequently repeated. Though he had links with Kell at that time, new research has shown that he was on the SIS payroll in 1929 and joined MI5 in 1931. See Bennett, *Churchill's Man of Mystery*, pp. 71–9, 127–34.

5 NA KV4/331 'Policy Re Study and Investigation of Fascism and other Right Wing or Kindred Movements and Activities, 1933–1945', s.1z, 'Fascism in Great Britain', 22 August 1933, pp. 1–2. Maxwell Knight, who made that assessment in the early 1930s, was describing the behaviour of the fascists during the years from 1923 to 1927, which not coincidentally marked his own tenure as Director of Intelligence for the BF. Even if Knight was rationalising past sins, he was not wrong in arguing that fascism had then supported the British political status quo. It is also the case, however, that despite the discontinuities between groups like the BEU in the period

after the First World War and the BUF of the mid-1930s, there were continuities as well, especially in personnel. The women's side of the BUF, for example, was run by Lady Makgill, the daughter-in-law of the BEU's founder, George Mackgill. NA KV4/331 'Policy Re Study and Investigation of Fascism and other Right Wing or Kindred Movements and Activities, 1933–1945', s. 1z, 'Fascism in Great Britain', 22 August 1933, p. 7. His son was also a BEU member. Stephen Dorril, *Blackshirt: Sir Oswald Mosley and British Fascism* (London: Viking, 2006), p. 195. Given his intimate knowledge of these groups, it is hard to imagine that Knight's earlier connections did not aid his efforts.

6   Quoted in Gilbert, *Winston S. Churchill, Vol. V*, pp. 226, 457.

7   Bennett, *Churchill's Man of Mystery*, p. 127.

8   Bennett, *Churchill's Man of Mystery*, p. 133; Curry, *Security Service*, p. 107.

9   NA KV4/331 'Policy Re Study and Investigation of Fascism and other Right Wing or Kindred Movements and Activities, 1933–1945', s.1z, 'Fascism in Great Britain', 22 August 1933, p. 9.

10   Richard Thurlow, *Fascism in Modern Britain* (Stroud: Sutton Publishing, 2000), p. 62.

11   A 6 September 1937 letter from B Branch requested a HOW on Mosley and his 'principal lieutenants', Robert Gordon-Canning, Ian Hope Dundas and Archibald Garrioch Findlay, all of whom, a reliable source informed MI5, were 'connected with' German and Italian subsidies. The HOW on Gordon-Canning only came on 31 March 1938 and on Findlay on 13 April 1939. The HOW on Dundas was never approved (Curry, *Security Service*, p. 116). The first HOW on a Mosley was for Diana in June 1940, surprisingly late considering her ties to Nazi Germany dated back to 1934 (see note on Grant below).

12   Grant, 'Desperate Measures: Britain's Internment of British Fascists during the Second World War' provides the first detailed explanation of MI5's relations with the Home Office regarding the surveillance of British fascists. This recent research suggests that the Home Office's inertia vis-à-vis British fascism may have been for the domestic appeasement of fascism or the result of inherent biases against the 'working class' in Whitehall.

13   NA KV2/245 'JOYCE, William', s.1b, 21 September 1934, reproduced in Peter Martland, *Lord Haw Haw: The English Voice of Nazi Germany* (Richmond: Public Record Office, 2003), pp. 120–3.

14   NA KV2/245 JOYCE, s.1b, 21 September 1934, reproduced in Martland, *Lord Haw Haw*, pp. 120–3. Knight, a long-time acquaintance of Joyce's brothers, may have been basing his conclusions on personal observation. Martland, *Lord Haw Haw*, p. 26. He may also have received information from among others, the BUF's Chief of Intelligence 'P. G. Taylor' (James McGuirk Hughes), frequently cited as having been an MI5 agent who worked at IIB with Knight. E. G. Hope, 'Surveillance or Collusion? Maxwell Knight, MI5 and the British Fascisti', p. 659. Dorril, *Blackshirt*, p. 197. However, there is no official record of Hughes having been an MI5 agent, and the basis for Hope and Dorril's assertion is questionable (personal correspondence with Jennifer Grant, 20 August 2008). See Grant, 'Desperate Measures: Britain's Internment of British Fascists during the Second World War'. In any case, MI5's files on Joyce reveal the extent of MI5's knowledge of key players in the BUF. The identity of the sources of Knight's information is unknown. Indeed, it may have been Knight himself – he openly recorded his long-time acquaintance with Joyce's brothers, Frank and Quentin. It is possible that some of it also came from, among others, the BUF's Chief of Intelligence 'P. G. Taylor' (né James McGuirk Hughes), frequently cited as having been an MI5 agent who worked at IIB with Knight.

15   Information on how the BUF polled is not available. Given that at its height its membership exceeded 30,000, its results would have registered. But given the lack of data, some have concluded that the BUF did not field a candidate that year (correspondence with Dr Peter Martland, 28 September 2008). This lack of information might be the reason for MI5's July 1936 assessment that the BUF was in 'general decline'. The BUF's funding, some of which was known by MI5 and SIS to come from Mussolini, also decreased (Andrew, *Her Majesty's Secret Service*, p. 374). Thus there was all the more reason for the great shock felt when the 'Battle of Cable Street' erupted on 4 October 1936. The police escorting a BUF march through London's East End became embroiled in a riot with Jews and communists opposing the BUF's demonstration. The authorities responded soon after the riot by imposing the Public Order Act proscribing uniformed demonstrations. Knight observed: 'JOYCE is apparently fed up about the loss of the uniform. From what I was told, I feel certain that JOYCE has turned from the Napoleonic pose to a copy of the Prussian officer. I hear that his manner had steadily

been become more parade ground like and that his head was cropped closer than before. From allusions to a certain irritability of manner I would make a guess that JOYCE feels in his inner man that he ought to be more a leading light that [*sic*] he is' (NA KV2/245 JOYCE, s.24a, Extract, 24 January 1937, reproduced in Martland, *Lord Haw Haw*, p. 148). The source providing the intelligence was obviously close to Joyce. Such assets permitted Knight to keep a finger on the pulse of the BUF leadership.

16 For John Beckett file, see NA KV2/1507–1521; for John Angus MacNab file, see NA KV2/2474–2475.

17 NA KV2/245 JOYCE, s.24a, Extract, 24 January 1937, reproduced in Martland, *Lord Haw Haw*, p. 148.

18 Griffiths, *Patriotism Perverted*, pp. 121–2.

19 Quoted in Griffiths, *Patriotism Perverted*, p. 45.

20 Martland, *Lord Haw Haw*, p. 25.

21 An off-shoot of the Anglo-German Fellowship, The Link promoted Anglo-German cooperation and friendship, anti-Semitism and actively campaigned against war with Germany. The Nordic League fashioned itself more simply as an open 'association, rather than an organisation, of race-conscious Britons'. Quoted in Richard Griffiths, *Patriotism Perverted: Captain Ramsey, The Right Club and English Anti-Semitism, 1930–40* (London: Constable, 1998), p. 45. A desire for racial purity formed the bedrock of these groups, which Ramsay and associates referred to as 'the patriotic societies'. Griffiths, *Patriotism Perverted*, p. 66.

22 Maule Ramsay, *The Nameless War* (Finchampstead: Bear Wood Press, 1992), p. 95.

23 Ramsay, *The Nameless War*, p. 97.

24 Thurlow, *Fascism in Modern Britain*, p. 57.

25 One of many websites carrying online versions of the *Protocols of the Elders of Zion* is the rather ominous www.jewwatch.com (last accessed 20 August 2007).

26 Although the precise origin is uncertain, most scholars date the *Protocols'* first appearance to 1903 when they were partially serialised in a Russian paper, *Znamya*, published by Sergei Nilus. He wrote a book on the *Protocols* in 1905. The book gained a much wider audience after the Russian Revolution as a result of the fact that a number of prominent Bolsheviks were Jews. The UK edition of the *Protocols*, published as *The Jewish Peril*, appeared in 1920. In 1921 the *Times* carried an exposé showing that

Nilus's *Protocols* was nothing but a 'literary forgery' which plagiarised a mid-nineteenth century French book titled *Dialogue aux Enfers entre Machiavel et Montesquieu, ou la Politique de Machiavel au XIX. Siecle. Par un Contemporaine* ('*Dialogue in Hell between Machiavelli and Montesquieu, or the Politics of Machiavelli in the Nineteenth Century. By a Contemporary*'). The target of that text was Napoleon III, not Jews. The *Times* concluded that their inquiry 'finally disposes of the "*Protocols*" as credible evidence of a Jewish plot against civilisation' ('"Jewish World Plot"', *The Times*, Tuesday 16 August 1921, p. 9; '"Jewish Peril" Exposed', *The Times*, Wednesday 17 August 1921, p. 9.) Another notable response to the *Protocols* came from journalist Lucien Wolf in *The Myth of the Jewish Menace in World Affairs, or The Truth About the Forged Protocols of the Elders of Zion* (New York: Macmillan, 1921), which comprised material originally published in the *Manchester Guardian*, the *Spectator* and the *Daily Telegraph*. More recent scholarly analysis can be found in the work of Michael Hagemeister; see, for example, 'The Protocols of the Elders of Zion: Between Fact and Fiction', *New German Critique* 35 (2008), 83–95.

27 The Covenant of the Islamic Resistance Movement (Hamas), is available at http://www.yale. edu/lawweb/avalon/mideast/hamas.htm (last accessed 20 August 2007). Article 32 reads: 'The Islamic Resistance Movement calls on Arab and Islamic nations to take up the line of serious and persevering action to prevent the success of this horrendous plan, to warn the people of the danger emanating from leaving the circle of struggle against Zionism. Today it is Palestine, tomorrow it will be one country or another. The Zionist plan is limitless. After Palestine, the Zionists aspire to expand from the Nile to the Euphrates. When they will have digested the region they overtook, they will aspire to further expansion, and so on. Their plan is embodied in the "Protocols of the Elders of Zion", and their present conduct is the best proof of what we are saying.' Cf. Christopher Andrew, 'Historical Attention Span Deficit Disorder: Why Intelligence Analysis Needs to Look Back Before Looking Forward', New Frontiers Rome Conference 2004.

28 NA KV4/227 'M.S. Report', p. 42.

29 NA KV4/227 'M.S. Report', p. 16.

30 NA KV4/227 'M.S. Report', p. 24.

31 Curry, *Security Service*, p. 393

32 NA KV4/227 'M.S. Report', p. 26.

33 One obvious drawback to the centralised system not addressed by Knight was security. If penetrated, the mole would have had access to the organisation's entire agent apparatus.

34 In most reports, Knight's agents are referred to in the 'M/Y', 'M/I' fashion. This was maintained when statements were taken about Rex Kent, but Mackie was also referred to as 'Miss Amor' (CRIM 1/1230). Joan Miller's memoir suggests that Mackie had yet another pseudonym, 'Mrs. Amos' (see Miller, *One Girl's War*, and Masters, *The Man Who Was M*). In Knight's summary 'M.S. Report' (NA KV4/227), produced after the war, Mackie is called 'Miss A' and de Munck 'Miss Z'. De Munck was also known as 'M/I'. The identities of Helene de Munck and Marjorie Mackie can be pinned down by cross-referencing the descriptions of their activities in Knight's KV4/227 with statements given in Wolkoff's case and Miller's account. For example, Helene de Munck: 'M/I' states that she is 'twenty-six years old, a spinster, and a Belgian subject by birth' (KV2/841 WOLKOFF, s.140c, proof 2); Knight notes that 'Miss Z' is 'a young Belgian girl' (KV4/227, p. 44); and Miller describes 'Helen' as a 'young, convent-educated Belgian girl' (*One Girl's War*, p. 26).

35 Miller, *One Girl's War*, p. 22; NA KV2/841 'WOLKOFF, Anna', s.140c, 'Proofs of statements for the case WOLKOFF', 11 June 1940, Proof 1, statement of [Marjorie Mackie] M/Y, p. 1.

36 NA KV4/227 'M.S. Report', p. 42.

37 NA KV2/841 WOLKOFF, s.140c, 'Proofs of statements for the case WOLKOFF', 11 June 1940, Proof 1, statement of [Marjorie Mackie] M/Y, pp. 1–2.

38 NA KV2/841 WOLKOFF, s.140c, 'Proofs of statements for the case WOLKOFF', 11 June 1940, Proof 1, statement of [Marjorie Mackie] M/Y, pp. 4–5.

39 NA KV2/677 RAMSAY, Archibald Maule, s.141a, 'Summary of M/Y's reports', 32.6.40 (report of 29 September 1939).

40 NA KV2/677 RAMSAY, s.141a, 'Summary of M/Y's reports', 32.6.40 (report of 25 October 1939).

41 Richard Thurlow, *Fascism in Britain: A History, 1918–1985* (Oxford: Basil Blackwell, 1987), p. 202.

42 NA KV2/677 RAMSAY, s.141a, 'Summary of M/Y's reports', 32.6.40 (report of 3 November 1939).

43 NA KV2/677 RAMSAY, s.141a, 'Summary of M/Y's reports', 32.6.40 (report of 4 February 1940).

44 NA KV2/841 WOLKOFF, s.140c, 'Proofs of statements for the case WOLKOFF', 11 June 1940, Proof 1, statement of [Marjorie Mackie] M/Y, p. 3.

45 NA KV4/227 'M.S. Report', pp. 43-44.

46 NA KV2/841 WOLKOFF, s.140c, 'Proofs of statements for the case WOLKOFF', 11 June 1940, Proof 1, statement of [Marjorie Mackie] M/Y, p. 10.

47 Mary Stanford file available at NA KV2/832–833.

48 NA KV2/840 WOLKOFF, s.11x, 'M/Y report on communication between Right Club and Germany', 26 February 1940. At this point it was suspected that 'Jean Neumanhaus', the Second Secretary at the Belgian Embassy in London, received the documents from either Mary Stafford or Wolkoff herself.

49 NA KV2/840 WOLKOFF, minute of 26 February 1940.

50 NA KV4/840 WOLKOFF, s.13a, HOW for Anna Wolkoff, 29 February 1940; s.17a, 13 March 1940; s.22, 23 March 1940.

51 NA KV2/841 WOLKOFF, s.140c, 'Proofs of statements for the case WOLKOFF', 11 June 1940, Proof 2, statement of [Helene de Munck] M/I, p. 1.

52 NA KV2/841 WOLKOFF, s.140c, 'Proofs of statements for the case WOLKOFF', 11 June 1940, Proof 2, statement of [Helene de Munck] M/I, p. 2.

53 NA KV4/227 'M.S. Report', p. 18.

54 'Germans Invade Norway and Denmark', *The Times*, Wednesday 10 April 1940, p. 8.

55 NA KV2/841 WOLKOFF, s.140c, 'Proofs of statements for the case WOLKOFF', 11 June 1940, Proof 2, statement of [Helene de Munck] M/I, pp. 2–3. Mackie independently verified the source of Wolkoff's excitement, that she had 'got a letter through to Joyce'. NA KV2/841 WOLKOFF, s.140c, 'Proofs of statements for the case WOLKOFF', 11 June 1940, Proof 1, statement of [Marjorie Mackie] M/Y, p. 10.

56 He described an office 'lined with trestle tables running the length of the room. Each table carried mail addressed to different destinations. . . . Around twenty Post Office technicians worked at these tables opening pieces of mail. They wore rubber gloves so as not to leave fingerprints, and each man had a strong lamp and a steaming kettle beside him. The traditional slit-bamboo technique was sometimes used. It was ancient, but still one of the most effective. The split bamboo is inserted into the corner of the envelope, which is held up against a strong light. By turning the bamboo inside the envelope, the letter can be rolled up around the slit

and gently pulled out. Where a letter had an ordinary typed address it was sometimes torn open and a new envelope typed in its place. But to the end of my career we were never able to covertly open a letter which had been sealed at each edge with sellotape. In those cases, MI5 took a decision as to whether to open a letter and destroy it, or send it on in an obviously opened state. Pedal-operated microfilming cameras copied the opened mail and prints were then routinely sent by the case officer in charge of the interception to the Registry for filing' (Wright, *Spycatcher*, p. 45. cf. Harrison, ed., *Flaps and Seals*. Also see Hinsley and Simkins, *British Intelligence in the Second World War: Volume IV*, p. 12).

57 NA KV2/841 WOLKOFF, s.140c, 'Proofs of statements for the case WOLKOFF', 11 June 1940, Proof 2, statement of [Helene de Munck] M/I, p. 4.

58 Note reads: 'Bitte wenn Moeglich einmal in der Woche den Vortrag wieder-geben den der Deutsche-Radfunk auf Deutsch vor ungefaehr drei Monaten gehalten hat, naemlich: Die Freimaurersitzung im Grand Orient in Paris, 1931 wo auch Lord Ampthill anwesend war. Sehr wichtig jetzt mehr ueber die Juden und Freimaurer zu hoeren.' NA CRIM 1/1230 Rex v. Kent, Exhibit 7.

59 NA KV4/227 'M.S. Report', p. 45.

60 NA KV2/841 WOLKOFF, s.140c, 'Proofs of statements for the case WOLKOFF', 11 June 1940, Proof 2, statement of [Helene de Munck] M/I, p. 4.

61 NA KV4/227 'M.S. Report', pp. 45–6.

62 NA KV4/227 'M.S. Report', p. 46.

63 NA KV2/841 WOLKOFF, s.140c, 'Proofs of statements for the case WOLKOFF', 11 June 1940, Proof 2, statement of [Helene de Munck] M/I, p. 7. Coincidentally, the 'principal agent', Miermans, knew members of de Munck's family. Their meeting was not nearly as reassuring as the one with the Laubespins. He urged her to give up 'this anti-Jewish work', presciently contending that anti-Jewish work would soon become pro-Nazi work, and the allies, in his view, were too strong for the Germans. (NA KV2/841 WOLKOFF, s.140c, 'Proofs of statements for the case WOLKOFF', 11 June 1940, Proof 2, statement of [Helene de Munck] M/I, pp. 7–8). He did not want to see her on the losing side – a practical rather than ideological stance. Obviously he was unaware that de Munck had already begun working against the anti-Semitic group she represented. In other circumstances, this might have been an opening to cultivate Miermans for MI5 or SIS work. No mention is given of this in declassified MI5 files, and

in any case, it might have blown de Munck's cover.

64 NA KV2/543 KENT, s.3a, 'Note from B.5b. re; Kent, Tyler', 4 May 1940; cf. NA KV2/840 WOLKOFF, s.37b, re Tyler KENT, note by B5b, 4 May 1940; Bearse and Read, *Conspirator*, p. 105.

65 NA KV2/841 WOLKOFF, s.140c, 'Proofs of statements for the case WOLKOFF', 11 June 1940, Proof 1, statement of [Marjorie Mackie] M/Y, p. 6; NA KV2/840 WOLKOFF, s.15a, 'M/Y report re Jean NEUMANHAUS and KENT', 2 March 1940; s.24a, 'M/Y note re Anna WOLKOFF and John [sic] KENT', 29 March 1940; NA KV2/543 KENT, s.3a, 'Note from B.5b. to B.4 re; Kent, Tyler' (Knight to Archer), 4 May 1940.

66 NA KV2/841 WOLKOFF, s.140c, 'Proofs of statements for the case WOLKOFF', 11 June 1940, Proof 1, statement of [Marjorie Mackie] M/Y, p. 7.

67 The interaction between a serving head of MI5 and the target of an investigation appears to be unprecedented.

68 NA KV2/840 WOLKOFF, s.20cd, letter to Kell from Anna Wolkoff, 18 March 1940. Her letter read: 'I have never belonged to any party, and if my natural anti-Jewish hatred and propaganda on this subject in drawing rooms is construed as "anti-government" … it definitely bears out my contention that there is too much Jewish influence in this country. I have lost my former country thanks to this fiendish race; having become a British subject I have always striven to be a good citizen of the country I have adopted and on realising the growing danger of the same disorder which over-took Russia I have done my utmost to warn those whom I know to be good and selfless patriots, and who were troubled by a growing uneasiness that all was not as it should be. . . . In other words it has come to this: if one is anti-Jew, one is branded pro-Nazi! This is a bitter reward for being truly patriotic. The inference that I draw from all this is that I am right in what I say, otherwise "they" would not bother to threaten a penniless woman in this manner.'

69 NA KV2/840 WOLKOFF, s.20e, 'Report of Interview with Wolkoff', 20 March 1940. Knight subsequently reported, 'I told her that I thought the position with regard to propaganda was made perfectly clear in the Defence Regulations, and I pointed out that she knew as well as I did that within the limits of the laws of the land there was complete freedom of speech and expression of opinion in this country, and that the law only took notice of activities which were either criminal

or which could be proved to be detrimental to the Defence of the Realm and the prosecution of the war.'

70 NA KV2/840 WOLKOFF, s.20e, 'Report of Interview with Wolkoff', 20 March 1940; Cf. report by Knight using intelligence submitted by 'M/Y' (Mackie) and 'M/I' (de Munck) supporting this conclusion: NA KV2/840 WOLKOFF, s.26c, 'Copy of report re Right Club', 14 April 1940. Maybe the Right Club's stickyback campaign was merely a smokescreen for more serious activities, as Knight suggested, but it appears Wolkoff nonetheless devoted a considerable amount of time to it. Knight was aware of the campaign before Wolkoff so boldly announced her activities to him in the War Office. De Munck brought it to his attention earlier that month (NA KV2/841 WOLKOFF, s.140c, 'Proofs of statements for the case WOLKOFF', 11 June 1940, Proof 2, statement of [Helene de Munck] M/I, p. 1). Examples of the stickybacks Wolkoff gave her boasted slogans such as, 'Jews don't fight, they take your jobs instead!'; 'Federal Union is the Jewish Super State'; and 'This is a Jews' war!' (NA KV2/840 WOLKOFF, s.26a, 'Cross ref. re Stickybacks given to M/I by A. WOLKOFF', 2 April 1940). Wolkoff even instructed Right Club members on basic tradecraft when going out on posting missions: 'As danger signal talk of the weather, for instance. Colder from the East means that someone is approaching on the right. Read your road indication by torch light and memorise at least two streets in advance.' She told members to 'take turns in sticking, look-out watching and route reading. As we leave this house we do so in pairs at a few seconds interval and are strangers until we meet at midnight at Paradise walk.' As part of counter-surveillance measures she went so far as to prepare routes to be taken on stickyback missions, one example of which read: [Marginal note: if no number of turning is indicated it denotes first turning] S. Kensington Station. W.C. — St. James Park. W.C. — Right Tothill Street. — Right Broadway. — Straight across Victoria Street. — Into Strutton Gardens. — Straight into Horseferry Rd. — Bear Right into Regency St. — 2nd Right into Chapter St. — Turn left into Vauxhall bridge Rd. (it is 2nd turning) — Right on to Embankment. — Right on Embankment. — Along Embankment Grosvenor Rd. — Past the Royal Hospital Rd. Gardens. — Right into Tite Street X Don't stick anymore — Left Dilke Street. — Right Paradise Walk. — Garage down on Right' (NA CRIM 1/1230 Rex v. Tyler Kent and Anna Wolkoff, 15th October Sessions, 1940, copy of exhibits, exhibit 22,

'Eleven sheets—instructions as to posting of adhesive labels', p. 25, Sheets 2, 3, 5). So even if a smoke screen, the stickyback campaign was clearly an elaborate one. Its instructions suggested that the Right Club members were at best paranoid, but at worst it pointed to a conspiracy to undermine the war effort.

71 NA KV2/840 WOLKOFF, s.20e, 'Report of Interview with Wolkoff', 20 March 1940.

72 The fact that the Registry was on the road to collapse does not seem to have unduly hindered this investigation. Because of the overwhelming flood of reports resulting from fifth column hysteria, the Registry was in the process of imploding. Curry, *Security Service*, p. 145; Wilson, 'The War in the Dark' (unpublished, chapter 3). See also Hinsley and Simkins, *British Intelligence in the Second World War: Volume IV*, chapter 3.

73 Joan Miller's account of M. Section's operations against the Right Club, and indeed of Knight himself, has been for a long time one of the few first-hand accounts available. Like Masters's biography of Knight, however, it must be treated with caution. Miller's memoir appears to bear witness to the notion that hell hath no fury like a woman scorned.

74 Miller, *One Girl's War*, p. 16.

75 Miller, *One Girl's War*, p. 18.

76 Masterman, *The Double-Cross System*, chapter 5.

77 Miller, *One Girl's War*, p. 23.

78 NA KV2/841 WOLKOFF, s.140c, 'Proofs of statements for the case WOLKOFF', 11 June 1940, Proof 1, statement of [Marjorie Mackie] M/Y, p. 5. Emphasis added.

79 NA KV2/841 WOLKOFF, s.140c, 'Proofs of statements for the case WOLKOFF', 11 June 1940, Proof 1, statement of [Marjorie Mackie] M/Y, p. 6.

80 Miller, *One Girl's War*, p. 24.

81 NA KV2/841 WOLKOFF, s.140c, 'Proofs of statements for the case WOLKOFF', 11 June 1940, Proof 1, statement of [Marjorie Mackie] M/Y, p. 6.

82 NA KV4/227 'M.S. Report', p. 49.

83 NA KV2/841 WOLKOFF, s.140c, 'Proofs of statements for the case WOLKOFF', 11 June 1940, Proof 2, statement of [Helene de Munck] M/I, p. 1.

84 NA KV4/227 'M.S. Report', p. 49.

85 NA KV2/841 WOLKOFF, s.140c, 'Proofs of statements for the case WOLKOFF', 11 June 1940, Proof 2, statement of [Helene de Munck] M/I, p. 9.

86 NA KV4/227 'M.S. Report', p. 49.

87 NA KV2/841 WOLKOFF, s.140c, 'Proofs of statements for the case WOLKOFF', 11 June 1940, Proof 1, statement of [Marjorie Mackie] M/Y, p. 7. Bearse and Read, *Conspirator*, p. 134. Liddell succeeded Harker as head of B division in June 1940.

88 NA KV2/840 WOLKOFF, s.28a, 'B5b note re WOLKOFF. (Special Source)', 16 April 1940; NA KV2/543 KENT, s.3a, 'Note from B.5b. re; KENT, Tyler', 4 May 1940.

89 NA KV2/841 WOLKOFF, s.140c, 'Proofs of statements for the case WOLKOFF', 11 June 1940, Proof 1, statement of [Marjorie Mackie] M/Y, p. 7.

90 NA KV2/841 WOLKOFF, s.140c, 'Proofs of statements for the case WOLKOFF', 11 June 1940, Proof 1, statement of [Marjorie Mackie] M/Y, p. 8.

91 NA KV2/840 WOLKOFF, s.49a, 'From M/Y re Anna and Kira WOLKOFF', 16 May 1940.

92 NA KV2/840 WOLKOFF, s.85a, 'Report by M.K., B.5.b., re interview with KENT', 29 May 1940. The very slim file on Duca Francesco Marigliano del Monte can be found at NA KV2/1698.

93 NA KV2/841 WOLKOFF, s.140c, 'Proofs of statements for the case WOLKOFF', 11 June 1940, Proof 1, statement of [Marjorie Mackie] M/Y, p. 9.

94 Patrick O. Cohrs, 'The Pivotal Power: The United States and the International System of the Inter-War Period', in *The Origins of the Second World War: An International Perspective*, ed. Frank McDonough (London: Continuum, 2011), 446–65.

95 David Reynolds, *The Creation of the Anglo-American Alliance, 1937–41: A Study in Competitive Co-Operation* (London: Europa, 1981), chapter 3.

96 Reynolds, *The Creation of the Anglo-American Alliance*, chapter 3.

97 James Leutze, 'The Secret of the Churchill-Roosevelt Correspondence: September 1939–May 1940', *Journal of Contemporary History* 10 (1975), 465–91 (p. 469).

98 Malcolm Moos, 'The Navicert in World War II', *The American Journal of International Law* 38 (1944), 115–19 (p. 115).

99 C-5x, London [via US Embassy], 29 January 1940, 7.00pm/TOR 1.20pm, Warren Kimball, ed., *Churchill & Roosevelt: The Complete Correspondence Vol. I* (Princeton, NJ: Princeton University Press, 1984), p. 33; Leutze, 'The Secret of the Churchill-Roosevelt Correspondence', p. 475.

100 R-2x, Washington D.C., 1 February 1940, letter, Kimball, ed., *Churchill & Roosevelt*, pp. 33–4; quoted in Leutze, 'The Secret of the Churchill-Roosevelt Correspondence', p. 475.

101 Bearse and Read, *Conspirator*, p. 61.

102 Cf. NA ADM 116/3958 Pan-American Neutrality Conference (Panama Conference): American Neutrality Zone, letter to W. Malkin (FO), 29 September 1939; letter to C.G. Jarrett, 'Panama Conference, Note of meeting held in Sir W. Malkin's room at F.O. at 3pm on Tuesday 3rd October'; NA ADM 116/4107 'American Neutrality Zone: Interpretation of Panama declaration and infringements by belligerents', ref M.01685639, Department of State Press Release, No.589, Address of Sumner Wells (US Undersecretary of State), 19 November 1939.

103 Leutze, 'The Secret of the Churchill-Roosevelt Correspondence', p. 482; Reynolds, *The Creation of the Anglo-American Alliance*, p. 65.

104 C-1x, London [via US Embassy], 5 October 1939, 4.00pm/TOR 1.00pm, Kimball, ed., *Churchill & Roosevelt*, pp. 26–7; quoted in Leutze, 'The Secret of the Churchill-Roosevelt Correspondence', pp. 471–2.

105 Quoted in Leutze, 'The Secret of the Churchill-Roosevelt Correspondence', p. 472; c.f. C-2x, London [via US Embassy] 16 October 1939, 10.00pm/TOR 5.33pm, Kimball, ed., *Churchill & Roosevelt*, p. 27.

106 NA KV4/227 'M.S. Report', p. 47.

107 KV2/840 Wolkoff, s.59a, 'B5b note re Enid RIDDELL', 22 May 1940.

108 Miller, *One Girl's War*, p. 35.

109 Quoted in Bearse and Read, *Conspirator*, p. 129, letter from Guy Liddell to US Embassy official Herschel Johnson.

110 NA KV4/227 'M.S. Report', p. 47.

111 NA KV2/840 WOLKOFF, s.57a, B5b (Knight) report on call to US Embassy, 19 May 1940. Cf. KV4/186 Liddell Diaries, volume 2, 19 May 1940 (p. 464).

112 Regulation 18b of the Emergency Powers (Defence) Act of 1939 granted authority 'for the detention of persons whose detention appears to the Secretary of State to be necessary or expedient in the interests of the public safety or the defence of the realm' (quoted in Cornelius P. Cotter, 'Emergency Detention in Wartime: The British Experience', *Stanford Law Review* 6 (1954), 238–86 (p. 239)). On Anderson, see John Wheeler-Bennett, *John Anderson, Viscount Waverly* (London: Macmillan, 1962).

113 NA KV2/840 WOLKOFF, s.57a, B5b (Knight) report on call at US Embassy 19 May 1940.

114 Quoted in Bearse and Read, *Conspirator*, p. 162.

115 No mention of this incident appears in the Danischewsky file. See NA KV2/1651-1652 White Sea and Baltic Co.

116 NA KV2/840 WOLKOFF, s.57g (57e) 'To Robert Vansittart enclosing report' ('Case of Anna Wolkoff, Tyler Kent, and Others'), 22 May 1940, p. 4.

117 NA KV2/840 WOLKOFF, s.57g (57e) 'To Robert Vansittart enclosing report' ('Case of Anna Wolkoff, Tyler Kent, and Others'), 22 May 1940, p. 5.

118 KV2/544 KENT, s.86a, 'From Foreign Office enclosing memorandum on Kent case by the United States Government', 29 August 1944 (report dated 17.8.44), p. 2; FO 371/38704 Tyler Kent, s.2, 22[illegible], June 1944; NA KV4/227 'M.S. Report', p. 47; Bearse and Read, *Conspirator*, p. 206.

119 Griffiths, *Patriotism Perverted*, pp. 125–42.

120 Bearse and Read, *Conspirator*, p. 22. He had been part of the first US delegation to Moscow under William Bullitt and had not fared particularly well. Between his Russian posting and his transfer to London he interviewed for the Foreign Officer test in Washington with Loy Henderson, another Moscow veteran, who failed Kent on the oral examination. Henderson reputedly explained later, 'I flunked him on personality.' Kent also had a tendency for extravagant living and philandering. One conquest of his in Russia later told the FBI that Kent had spied for the NKVD while in Moscow (Bearse and Read, *Conspirator*, p. 52, 22, 35–6).

121 Malcolm Muggeridge, *Chronicles of Wasted Time, Vol. 2: The Infernal Grove* (London: Collins, 1973), p. 108.

122 The following account is quoted from a transcript of the interrogation. NA KV2/543 KENT, s.22a, 'B.5b report on interrogation of Tyler KENT, at the American Embassy', 20 May 1940.

123 Kleinman, 'KUBARK Counterintelligence Interrogation Review', p. 126.

124 John Costello, *Ten Days That Saved the West* (London: Bantam, 1991), p. 124. Quote is from NA KV2/840 WOLKOFF, s.80a, 'Report by M.K. re interview with KENT', 28 May 1940.

125 NA KV2/840 WOLKOFF, s.80a, 'Report by M.K. re interview with KENT', 28 May 1940.

126 NA KV2/840 WOLKOFF, s.80a, 'Report by M.K. re interview with KENT', 28 May 1940.

127 NA KV2/840 WOLKOFF, s.80a, 'Report by M.K. re interview with KENT', 28 May 1940.

128 NA KV2/840 WOLKOFF, s.85a 'Report by M.K., B.5.b., re interview with KENT', 29 May 1940.

129 Quoted in Bearse and Read, *Conspirator*, p. 6.

130 Allen Weinstein and Alexander Vassiliev, *The Haunted Wood: Soviet Espionage in America – The Stalin Era* (New York: Random House, 1999), chapters 1–7; John Earl Haynes and Harvey Klehr, *Venona: Decoding Soviet Espionage in America* (London: Yale University Press, 1999), chapter 3, pp. 166–72; Harvey Klehr et al., *The Secret World of American Communism* (London: Yale University Press, 1995), chapter 3; Andrew and Gordievsky, *KGB*, pp. 180–5.

131 Quoted in Bearse and Read, *Conspirator*, p. 164; Leutze, 'The Secret of the Churchill-Roosevelt Correspondence', p. 467.

132 NA KV2/543 KENT, s.37d, 'Letter from Robin CAMPBELL to "Alec" re Tyle[r] KENT', 10 June 1940.

133 NA KV2/543 KENT, s.41a, 'Press Cutting', 15 October 1940, *Daily Sketch*.

134 Quoted in Leutze, 'The Secret of the Churchill-Roosevelt Correspondence', p. 467.

135 'Kent's Mother Files Suit', *New York Times*, Tuesday 12 September 1944, p. 14; 'Kent Denies Intent to Aid Axis', *New York Times*, Wednesday 5 December 1945, p. 17.

136 Wilson, 'The War in the Dark', chapter 4; Griffiths, *Patriotism Perverted*, pp. 265–6; Thurlow, *Fascism in Modern Britain*, p. 105.

137 NA KV4/185 Liddell Diaries, Volume 2, 25 May 1940 (p. 475).

138 NA HO 45/26018 Defence Regulation 18B: history written by Mr Carew Robinson 1949; HO 45/25396 DISTURBANCES: Internment under Defence Regulation 18B of members of British Union of Fascists and other fascist organisations 1940. For the most recent research on MI5 and internment during this period, see Jennifer Grant, 'Desperate Measures: Britain's Internment of British Fascists during the Second World War' (unpublished PhD dissertation, University of Cambridge, 2009). See also Peter Gillman and Leni Gillman, *'Collar the Lot!' How Britain Interned and Expelled Its Wartime Refugees* (London: Quartet Books, 1980).

139 NA KV4/227 'M.S. Report', p. 25.

CHAPTER 6

Defection and Debriefing (I)

1 University of Cambridge Intelligence Seminar, information obtained under the Chatham House Rule.

2 Krivitsky first defected to France in 1937.

3 Cf. Gary Kern, *A Death in Washington: Walter G. Krivitsky and the Stalin Terror* (New York: Enigma, 2004), chapters 19–27.

4 Cf. Randy Borum, 'Approaching Truth: Behavioural Science Lessons on Educing Information from Human Sources', in *Educing Information: Interrogation: Science and Art. Foundations for the Future*, ed. NDIC (Washington, DC: National Defense Intelligence College [NDIC] Press, 2006), 17–43 (p. 19). Available at http://www.fas.org/irp/dni/educing.pdf (last accessed 13 February 2008).

5 John Ankerbrand, 'What to Do with Defectors', *Studies in Intelligence* 5 (Fall 1961), 33–43 (p. 33).

6 William R. Johnson, 'Tricks of the Trade: Counterintelligence Interrogation', *International Journal of Intelligence and Counterintelligence* 1 (1986), 103–13 (p. 113, fn. 9).

7 Steven M. Kleinman, 'KUBARK Counterintelligence Review: Observations of an Interrogator: Lessons Learned and Avenues for Further Research', in *Educing Information*, ed. NDIC, 95–140 (pp. 96–7).

8 '[T]here are known knowns; there are things we know we know. We also know there are known unknowns; that is to say we know there are some things we do not know. But there are also unknown unknowns – the ones we don't know we don't know.' Donald Rumsfeld, 12 February 2002, http://www.defense.gov/transcripts/transcript.aspx?transcriptid=2636.

9 This also speaks to the importance of thorough record keeping for *ex-post facto* cross-referencing. Case histories themselves represented a central part of the intelligence collection effort. Important clues were at times only recognised as such much later in an investigation.

10 Robert H. Thouless, *Straight and Crooked Thinking* ([S.I.]: Hodder and Stoughton, 1930) is one of the earliest British books addressing issues later treated by the field of social psychology. In particular, he discussed the ideas of deception and fallacious argumentation in communication.

11 See Jerrold M. Post, *Leaders and their Followers in a Dangerous World: The Psychology of Political Behavior* (Ithaca, NY: Cornell University Press, 2004).

12 On the principle of reciprocation, see Robert B. Cialdini, *Influence: The Psychology of Persuasion* (New York: Morrow, 1993), chapter 2.

13 C. N. Geschwind, 'Counterintelligence Interrogation', *Studies in Intelligence* Winter (1965), 23–38 (p. 24).

14 NA KV2/805 KRIVITSKY, s. 55x, 'Information obtained from Krivitsky', pp. 77–86.

15 The OGPU ('Unified State Political Directorate'), or Soviet security service, as it was known from 1923 to 1934, was called the GUGB from 1934 to 1941 after its incorporation into the NKVD ('People's Commissariat for Internal Affairs'), although NKVD is the name it was usually called during that period. In the Krivitsky files the appellation OGPU (or 'Ogpu') is generally used. For the sake of consistency and clarity, it is the term that is also used throughout this chapter. Similarly, Soviet military intelligence was known as the Fourth Department (or the Razvedupr or RU) from 1924 to 1937, after which point it became the GRU. MI5 documents during the Krivitsky period typically refer to Soviet military intelligence as the Fourth Department or RU, and this chapter follows suit. The debate about whether MI5 blundered in not recognising the Cambridge Five in light of Krivitsky's information continues. Using declassified MI5 files, we can now see that rather than definitive evidence, the source he 'identified' was a composite – primarily of Maclean and Philby – which made their identification of anyone much more difficult than may appear with hindsight. Even if Krivitsky failed to provide conclusive evidence about the moles, MI5 gained precious insights into the structure of Soviet intelligence in the process of identifying their handlers and other operatives.

16 For Krivitsky's life before his arrival to the US and details of the events leading up to his defection, see: Walter G. Krivitsky, *I Was Stalin's Agent* (London, 1939), published in the United States as Krivitsky, *In Stalin's Secret Service* (originally published in 1939); Gordon Brook-Shepherd, *The Storm Petrels: The First Soviet Defectors, 1928–1938* (London: Collins, 1977); Elisabeth K. Poretsky, *Our Own People: A Memoir of 'Ignace Reiss' and His Friends* (London: Oxford University Press, 1969). Most important, see Kern, *A Death in Washington*,

to which this section on Krivitsky's time in the US is particularly indebted.

17 Board of Special Inquiry stenographic record, Ellis Island, 12 November 1938, US Immigration and Naturalization Service (INS); quoted in Kern, *A Death in Washington*, p. 172.

18 See, for example, NA KV1/22 on 'E Branch' (Port Surveillance) during the First World War.

19 Loy W. Henderson, memorandum of conversation [with General Krivitsky], 15 March 1939, in Robert Louis Benson and Michael Warner, *Venona: Soviet Espionage and the American Response 1939–1957* (Washington, DC: NSA/CIA, 1996), pp. 5–10; also copied to FBI file 'Walter G Krivitsky', #100-11146-84, available at http://www.foia.fbi.gov/krivit.htm, volume 2a. For documents on MI5's early investigations into Soviet intelligence organisation, see, among others, NA KV3/11-13 'Russian Intelligence Organisation (General), 1924–1931', especially, KV3/12, s. 118a, 'Activities of the G.P.U', report forwarded from SIS to MI5, 15 May 1930.

20 These files, only obtained by the FBI during the investigation into the circumstances of Krivitsky's death, supposedly amounted to all the relevant files held by the Department of State pertaining to Krivitsky ('Walter G. Krivitsky', #100-11146-83 (-84). Enclosures of State Department interviews dating from 15 March, 28 June 1939, filed by FBI 29 April 1948, vol. 2a (Krivitsky's FBI files available at http://foia.fbi. gov/foiaindex/krivit.htm (last accessed 23 May 2008)). Critically, FBI Director Hoover had asked George Messersmith, Assistant Secretary of State and intelligence liaison, whether he wanted the FBI to question Krivitsky further about passport fraud; Messersmith declined and the FBI did not pursue the issue. The personal antipathy between Hoover and Messersmith undoubtedly played a role (Raymond J. Batvinis, *The Origins of FBI Counterintelligence* (Lawrence: University Press of Kansas, 2007), p. 143).

21 The question of Stalin's strategic intentions leading up to the Nazi-Soviet Pact (23 August 1939) remains contentious. The debate centres around the extent to which Stalin's alliance with Hitler was premeditated. Because Krivitsky defected in 1937, he could not have known with certainty that the Pact would be signed. See Ingeborg Fleischhauer, 'Soviet Foreign Policy and the Origins of the Hitler-Stalin Pact', in *From Peace to War: Germany, Soviet Russia, and the World, 1939–1941*, ed. Bernd Wegner (Providence, RI: Berghahn

Books, published in association with the Militärgeschichtliches Forschungsamt, Potsdam, 1997), 27–45; Teddy J. Uldricks, 'Soviet Security Policy in the 1930s', in *Soviet Foreign Policy, 1917–1991: A Retrospective*, ed. Gabriel Gorodetsky (London: Frank Cass, 1994), 65–74.

22 Copies of articles can be found in NA KV2/802 KRIVITSKY, s.5a, letter from Commissioner S. T. Wood (Royal Canadian Mounted Police) to Vernon Kell (MI5), 3 May 1939 ('Stalin's Hand in Spain, *The Saturday Evening Post*, 15 April 1939; 'Why Stalin Shot His Generals', *The Saturday Evening Post*, 22 April 1939; 'Stalin Appeases Hitler', *The Saturday Evening Post*, 29 April 1939).

23 The FBI's Krivitsky file contains *one* report on an interview with Krivitsky ('Walter G. Krivitsky', #62-25315-192, 27 July 1939, vol. 4), which revolves around Moishe Stern. There is only one other reference to an interview with Krivitsky (which apparently took place on 6 October 1939), noted in a report submitted after his death, but the original report itself is not present ('Walter G. Krivitsky', #100-11146-16, 14 February 1940, vol.1a). Although three hundred pages of the FBI's Krivitsky file remain classified, all but a handful of those files date from after his death in the 1940s (Gary Kern, ed., *Walter G. Krivitsky: MI5 Debriefing and Other Documents on Soviet Intelligence* (Riverside, CA: Xenos Books, 2004), p. vi).

24 Quoted in Andrew, *For the President's Eyes Only*, p. 89; Ronald Kessler, *The Bureau: The Secret History of the FBI* (New York: St Martin's Press, 2002), p. 53.

25 On Hoover's role in the FBI's expanding jurisdiction, see Curt Gentry, *J. Edgar Hoover: The Man and the Secrets* (London: W. W. Norton, 1991), esp. chapters 14–19.

26 This was in part the legacy of instructions given by Harlan Fiske Stone (US Attorney General) on the day after he appointed Hoover as head of the Bureau of Investigation (BOI, predecessor of the FBI) in 1924. The directive confined BOI investigations 'strictly . . . to violations of federal law', effectively proscribing the collection of preventative security intelligence (quoted in Batvinis, *The Origins of FBI Counterintelligence* , p. 44).

27 Hoover apparently had no faith in Krivitsky's credibility and took an instant dislike to him, which may have contributed to the FBI's lack of interest (Batvinis, *The Origins of FBI Counterintelligence* , p. 142; Verne W. Newton, *The Butcher's Embrace: The Philby Conspirators in Washington* (London:

Macdonald, 1991), p. 9; Kern, *A Death in Washington*, p. 190).

28 Intelligence versus law enforcement mentalities and the structural and cultural problems surrounding the reform of the FBI are discussed in depth in Richard A. Posner, *Remaking Domestic Intelligence* (Stanford, CA: Hoover Institution Press, 2005), esp. pp. 8–34. See also Henry A. Crumpton, 'Intelligence and Homeland Defense', in *Transforming U.S. Intelligence*, ed. Sims and Gerber, pp. 198–219.

29 Benson and Warner, *Venona*, p. xii; Haynes and Klehr, *Venona*, p. 151; Andrew and Mitrokhin, *The Mitrokhin Archive*, pp. 140–1. In fairness to Hoover, in October 1940 he wrote, 'Special Agents of the [FBI] have under constant observation and surveillance a number of known and suspected agents of the German, Russian, French and Italian Secret Services. The FBI is able through its counter espionage efforts to maintain a careful check upon the channels of communication, the sources of information, the method of finance and other data relative to these agents. *Arrest is considered inadvisable except in extraordinary cases because counter espionage methods of observation and surveillance result in a constantly growing reservoir or information concerning not only known but also new agents of these governments'* (Hoover memorandum to Major General Edwin Watson (Secretary of the President), 25 October 1939, reproduced in Benson and Warner, *Venona*, pp. 15–26 (p. 16), emphasis added). Hoover's exposé on the expansiveness of the FBI's counter-espionage operations is considerably undermined, however, by the fact that the Soviet agents continued to occupy important positions in the government throughout the war. And although Hoover's statement that 'close and constant liaison is maintained by representatives of the [FBI] with operatives of the British Intelligence Service' may have been true, Liddell, for one, was frustrated by the FBI's lack of interest in cultivating and running double agents: they 'did not seem to comprehend the value of it', he wrote (4 July 1942). Similarly William Stephenson, head of British Security Co-Ordination (BSC) in New York during the War, noted 'the FBI were devoted to traditional police methods, brought up to date by lavish expenditure on laboratory and other technical equipment'. The William Sebold and 'Tricycle' cases further demonstrated, to MI5 at any rate, that the FBI was incapable of running sustained agent operations (Wilson, 'War in the Dark', pp. 145–7).

30 Andrew, *For the President's Eyes Only*, p. 90; Batvinis, *The Origins of FBI Counterintelligence*, chapter 1.

31 If it is the same Kléber, Krivitsky told MI5 he was 'one of the most brilliant military specialists' attached to the GRU to attend the Lenin School. According to Krivitsky, Kléber was first posted to the Far East and later became leader of the International Brigade in Spain, only to disappear during the Red Army purge (NA KV2/805 KRIVITSKY, s. 55x, 'Information obtained from Krivitsky', p. 60). See also note above regarding Hoover and Messersmith.

32 Quoted in Kern, *A Death in Washington*, p. 213.

33 Cf. Stanley B. Farndon, 'The Interrogation of Defectors', *Studies in Intelligence*, Summer (1960), 9–30 (p. 10). The term is uncommon, but as discussed in a comprehensive new study on the subject, it encompasses elicitation, debriefing and interrogation. See NDIC, ed., *Educing Information*. The *OED* notes that the term 'debriefing' first appeared in print in 1945. The MI5 files refer to Krivitsky's debriefing as 'interviews'.

34 From a letter to the US Attorney General during inquiries into the circumstances of Krivitsky's death in 1941. FBI file on Krivitsky at http://www.foia.fbi.gov/krivit.htm, #100-11146-8, Memorandum for the Attorney General from J. Edgar Hoover, 11 February 1941; Newton, *The Butcher's Embrace*, p. 363 (fn. 24).

35 Allen Weinstein, *Perjury: The Hiss-Chambers Case* (New York: Alfred A. Knopf, 1988), pp. 329–30; Haynes and Klehr, *Venona*, p. 91; Andrew and Mitrokhin, *The Mitrokhin Archive*, p. 141.

36 Kern, *A Death in Washington*, pp. 189–94, 233–4; Haynes and Klehr, *Venona*, pp. 89–92; Andrew, *For the President's Eyes Only*, pp. 166–7, 175–6. Chambers did not testify before Congress until 1948, almost ten years after he gave information on a group of American Soviet spies. Hiss was later convicted for perjury and served a five-year prison sentence as a result of Chambers's testimony.

37 '50 Leaders Listed for a 3-Day Forum', *New York Times*, Sunday 22 October 1939, p. 14; 'Forum Will Open Its Sessions Today', *New York Times*, Tuesday 24 October 1939, p. 26. 'The Challenge to Civilization' forum, sponsored by the *New York Herald Tribune*. Kern, *A Death in Washington*, pp. 219, 229.

38 'Investigation of Un-American Propaganda Activities in the United States', Testimony

of Walter G. Krivitsky before the House of Representatives, Special Committee to Investigate Un-American Activities, 11 October 1939, in Kern, ed., *MI5 Debriefing*, 52–104 (p. 85).

39 Kern, *A Death in Washington*, p. 455, fn. 415 (p. 223).

40 'Clash Over Reds Marks Dies Inquiry', *New York Times*, Wednesday 13 October 1939, p. 15. Kern, *A Death in Washington*, p. 224.

41 Gentry, *J. Edgar Hoover*, p. 240.

42 Quoted in Kern, *A Death in Washington*, p. 223.

43 Ernest Southerland Bates, 'Krivitsky's Story', *The Washington Post*, 19 November 1939.

44 NA FO 371/23697 'Soviet Foreign Policy', in Andrew, *Her Majesty's Secret Service*, p. 423.

45 The first record on file is a memorandum on a *Times* clipping, which published notice of Krivitsky's request for permission to stay in France (before his defection to the United States). NA KV/802 KRIVITSKY, s.1a, 'Cross Reference', memorandum on *Times* article, 8 December 1937.

46 NA KV2/805 KRIVITSKY, s.55x, 'Information obtained from Krivitsky', p. ii. Copies of Krivitsky's files can be found at KV2/802 KRIVITSKY, s.5a (as listed in minutes of 15.4.39).

47 Kern, *A Death in Washington*, p. 235.

48 NA KV2/802 KRIVITSKY, s.7a, unnumbered despatch from Ambassador Lord Lothian (Washington) for Gladwyn Jebb (FO), d. 3 September 1939, r. 4 September 1939 (for 'selling everything'); s.9a, from V. A. L. Mallet (Washington) to Jebb (FO), 3 September 1939. For personal accounts of Soviet intelligence in the Spanish Civil War, see among others Alexander Orlov, *The March of Time: Reminiscences* (London: St Ermin's, 2004); George Orwell, *Homage to Catalonia* (New York: Harvest Books, 1980).

49 NA KV2/802 KRIVITSKY, s.13ax, 'Copy of letter to F.O. re LEVINE etc.' (Harker to Jebb), 8 November 1939.

50 NA KV2/802 KRIVITSKY, s.9a, unnumbered despatch from V. A. L. Mallet (Washington) to Jebb (FO), 3 September 1939.

51 For John Herbert King files, see NA KV2/815-KV2/816, especially KV2/816 KING, s.36, 'Leakage from the Communications Department, Foreign Office', by Vivian (SIS), 30 October 1939 (King makes statement on record of spying from 1935 to 1937, p. 9). Some of the files relating to the criminal investigation are still classified (NA HO

144/22700), but the court proceedings are available at NA CRIM 1/1129. For information obtained during Krivitsky's debriefing on King and his handlers Hans Christian Pieck and Teodor Maly, see NA KV2/805 KRIVITSKY, s.55x, 'Information obtained from Krivitsky', pp. 46–48. On King, also see Donald Cameron Watt, '[John] Herbert King: A Soviet Source in the Foreign Office', *Intelligence and National Security* 4 (1988), 62–82; Richard Thurlow, 'Soviet Spies and British Counter-Intelligence in the 1930s: Espionage in the Woolwich Arsenal and the Foreign Office Communications Department', *Intelligence and National Security* 19 (2004), 610–31; Andrew and Gordievsky, *KGB*, pp. 143–4; and West and Tsarev, *Crown Jewels*, pp. 81–92.

Pieck, a Dutch artist, first came to the attention of SIS in 1930, then again in 1935. In the early 1930s he was based in Geneva, where he lived lavishly and cultivated contacts in the British expatriate community to accomplish his task of recruiting agents in the British Foreign Office. This was how he gained an introduction to King. In 1935, he relocated to London and went into business with a UK national as cover for his activities, but stopped handling King by the end of 1936. According to Pieck, in 1937 he was 'dropped' by the Soviets. He apparently then went to Athens before returning to Holland, disillusioned with the Soviets after the murder of fellow illegal and mentor Ignace Reiss in 1937 (who had recruited him in 1932). After the war (part of which he had spent at Buchenwald concentration camp as a result of involvement with the resistance in Holland), he agreed to MI5's request to come to London for interrogation (April 1950) (see Curry, *Security Service*, pp. 189–90; NA KV2/814 'PIECK, Hans Christian', s.[illegible], 'Report on the Interrogation of Henri [*sic*] Christian PIECK. 12th-16th April, 1950', by B2b, 30 May 1950).

52 King was charged under 'Section 2(1) (aa)' [*sic* – Section 2(1)(a)] of OSA 1911, which prohibited the disclosure of official government information without lawful authority (NA KV2/816 KING, s. s.36, p. 8). OSA 1911 available at http://www.opsi.gov. uk/acts/acts1911/pdf/ukpga_19110028_ en.pdf (last accessed 31 May 2008), Section 2(1)(a), p. 4.

53 NA KV2/802 KRIVITSKY, s. 13A, letter from Archer (KMMA) to Vivian, 10 November 1939.

54 Quoted in Krivitsky, *In Stalin's Secret Service*, p. 220.

55 Krivitsky, *In Stalin's Secret Service*, p. 222.

56 Krivitsky, *In Stalin's Secret Service*, p. 219.

57 Krivitsky, *In Stalin's Secret Service*, p. 26. On Russo-Polish War, John Erickson, *Soviet High Command: A Military-Political History, 1918–1941* (London: Frank Cass, 2001), chapter 4; Steiner, *The Lights That Failed*, pp. 144–52. For a comprehensive study, see Norman Davies, *White Eagle, Red Star: The Polish-Soviet War, 1919–20* (London: Macdonald and Co., 1972).

58 NA KV2/805 KRIVITSKY, s.55x, 'Information obtained from Krivitsky', p. i.

59 Cf. later CIA analysis on the traumatic psychological effects of defection: Ankerbrand, 'What To Do With Defectors'.

60 Cf. Oleg Gordievsky to Pembroke College International Summer School, Cambridge, 13 July 2005.

61 Isaac Don Levine, *Eyewitness to History: Memoirs and Reflections of a Foreign Correspondent for Half a Century* (New York: Hawthorn Books, 1973), p. 197.

62 NA KV2/802 KRIVITSKY, s.15A, telegram received 14 November 1939, from Lord Lothian (Washington) to Lord Halifax (London).

63 NA KV2/802 KRIVITSKY, s.16A, letter from Harker to Gladwyn Jebb (FO), 20 November 1939.

64 A founding member of the CPUSA, Lovestone was expelled from the Party in 1929 along with hundreds of his followers for his support of the 'right-wing opposition' leader Nikolai Bukharin when the latter fell from grace. Lovestone then formed the 'Communist Party (Opposition)' (Haynes and Klehr, *Venona*, p. 165; Ted Morgan, *A Covert Life: Jay Lovestone, Communist, Anti-Communist, and Spymaster* (New York: Random House, 1999)).

65 NA KV2/802 KRIVITSKY, s.28A, letter from Vivian to Archer, 21 December 1939.

66 NA KV2/804 KRIVITSKY, s.8a, note by B3c [Major Alley] re Krivitsky, 26 January 1940.

67 NA KV4/185 Liddell Diaries, Volume 1, 14 February 1940 (pp. 324–5).

68 Brook-Shepherd, *The Storm Petrels*, p. 158; Levine, *Eyewitness to History*, p. 184.

69 Levine, *Eyewitness to History*, p. 184.

70 Kern, *A Death in Washington*, p. 241.

71 NA KV2/805 KRIVITSKY, s.55x, 'Information obtained from Krivitsky', p. iv.

72 Reciprocation and authority have subsequently been identified by Robert Cialdini as two of the six 'weapons of influence' (the others are commitment/consistency, social proof, liking and scarcity). Cialdini, *Influence*, for reciprocation see chapter 2, and authority, chapter 6. On the dynamics of rapport, see Jerry Richardson, *The Magic of Rapport* (Capitola, CA: Meta Publications, 1987).

73 NA KV2/802 KRIVITSKY, s.46a, letter from KMMA (Archer) to Colonel Allen (GPO), 19 January 1940.

74 NA KV2/802 KRIVITSKY, s.49a, letter from Allen to Archer, 24 January 1940.

75 On the question of MI5 and the law, see David Williams, *Not In the Public Interest: The Problem of Security in Democracy* (London: Hutchinson, 1965).

76 NA KV2/802 KRIVITSKY, s.22a, letter from Archer (MI5) to Vivian (SIS), 13 December 1939.

77 NA KV2/802 KRIVITSKY, s.25, letter from Vivian to Archer, 20 December 1939; s. 37a, letter from Vivian to Archer, 11 January 1940; Samuel H. Williamson, 'Seven Ways to Compute the Relative Value of a U.S. Dollar Amount, 1774 to present', MeasuringWorth, 2014, in terms of purchasing power parity at 2012 rates.

78 NA KV2/802 KRIVITSKY, s.30a, letter from Vivian to Archer, 27 December 1939.

79 NA KV2/802 KRIVITSKY, s.37a, letter from Vivian to Archer, 11 January 1940.

80 NA KV2/802 KRIVITSKY, s.42a, letter from Vivian to Harker, 15 January 1940; KV4/185 Liddell Diaries, Volume 1, 20 January 1940 (pp. 278–279). See also Langham Hotel history, at http://www.langhamhotels.com/history.htm (last accessed 21 May 2008).

81 NA KV2/802 KRIVITSKY, s.35a, letter from Archer to Harker, 8 January 1940; s.36a, letter from Harker to Vivian, 12 January 1940. Liddell notes that in addition to Alley, Krivitsky was met by a 'friend'. This person's identity remains a mystery, but it could have been someone from SIS – often referred to by MI5 as the 'friends'. It is also worth noting that Krivitsky, despite MI5's best intentions, was very suspicious about having been greeted by two fluent Russian speakers, according to Liddell. But Krivitsky was suspicious about everything, and in the end, Alley's proficiency in Russian proved of great service because Krivitsky spoke only broken English (NA KV4/185 Liddell Diaries, Volume 1, 20 January 1940 (pp. 278–9)).

82 NA KV2/802 KRIVITSKY, s.35a, letter from Archer to Harker, 8 January 1940.

83 NA KV2/804 KRIVITSKY, s.1a., 'B. [Harker] report re interview with Krivitsky', 23 January 1940 (Captain Small also present); KV2/802 KRIVITSKY, s.44a, letter from Vivian to Archer, 17 January 1940.

84 'Krivitsky Leaves U.S.; Time of Departure and Destination are Kept Secret', *New York Times*, Sunday 30 December 1939, p. 3.

85 NA KV2/802 KRIVITSKY, s.36a, letter from Harker to Vivian, 12 January 1940.

86 See Kleinman, 'KUBARK Counterintelligence Interrogation Review', pp. 118–19, on the substitution of 'interrogation world' for the 'outside world'.

87 NA KV2/802 KRIVITSKY, s.35a, letter from B.4 [Archer] to B. [Harker], 8 January 1940.

88 NA KV4/185 Liddell Diaries, Volume 1, 20 January 1940 (pp. 278–9).

89 On D-Notice System, see the official website of the Defence, Press & Broadcasting Advisory Committee (DPBAC) website: www. dnotice.org.uk (last accessed 8 February 2007); Alasdair Palmer, 'The History of the D-Notice Committee', in Andrew and Dilks, *Missing Dimension*, pp. 227–49.

90 NA KV2/802 KRIVITSKY, minute of 16 January 1940 (no. 43), KMMA.

91 KV4/185 Liddell Diaries, Volume 1, 20 January 1940 (pp. 278–9).

92 NA KV2/802 KRIVITSKY, s.35a, letter from B.4 [Archer] to B. [Harker], 8 January 1940.

93 NA KV2/802 KRIVITSKY, s.36a, letter from Harker to Vivian, 12 January 1940.

94 NA KV2/802 KRIVITSKY, s.35a, letter from B.4 [Archer] to B. [Harker], 8 January 1940.

95 NA KV2/802 KRIVITSKY, s.36a, letter from Harker to Vivian, 12 January 1940.

96 NA KV2/802 KRIVITSKY, s.35a, letter from B.4 [Archer] to B. [Harker], 8 January 1940.

97 NA KV2/802 KRIVITSKY, s.36a, letter from Harker to Vivian, 12 January 1940.

98 NA KV2/802 KRIVITSKY, s.35a, letter from B.4 [Archer] to B. [Harker], 8 January 1940. Archer's note 'Hooper in touch with Pieck', suggests that the Holland agent was Hooper. It is almost certain that Hooper corresponds to 'Agent X' in the MI5 summary report on J.H. King (NA KV2/816 'KING, John Herbert', s.36, 'Leakage from the Communications Department, Foreign Department', 30 October 1939, p. 2), which documents a 'disgruntled former Government official' in the employ of Pieck. When Krivitsky was working in Holland, he had expressed to Pieck his suspicions that Hooper, a former passport officer (likely ex-SIS), had been a British double-agent (see KV2/802 KRIVITSKY, s.51a, 'To S.I.S. enclosing chapter on Ogpu and 4th Department', 13 March 1940). Thus it was likely through 'Hooper' that Pieck 'came to the notice of S.I.S. in 1930', as it is stated in MI5's internal history (see Curry, *Security Service*, p. 189).

99 Kleinman, 'KUBARK Counterintelligence Review', p. 126. Masterman, *The Double-Cross System*; Robert Stephens and Oliver Hoare, *Camp 020: MI5 and the Nazi Spies: The Official History of MI5's Wartime Interrogation Centre* (Richmond: Public Record Office, 2000).

100 NA KV2/802 KRIVITSKY, s.36a, letter from Harker to Vivian, 12 January 1940.

101 Vivian wrote, 'It may be impossible for me to spend many hours at a stretch, or many days at a stretch, over this business' (KV2/802 KRIVITSKY, s.42a [re s.36a], 15.1.40). Considering the high priority given the case and Archer and Harker's belief that Vivian was best suited to do the interrogation, Vivian's (and SIS's) remission is notable and curious. Possibly SIS's absence from the debriefing had something to do with Section V's new head, Felix Cowgill, who succeeded Vivian in 1939. Philby, for example, noted that Cowgill was on 'the worst of terms' with MI5 (and just about every other department) (Philby, *My Silent War*, p. 46). On Archer, see 'Bar Examination', *The Times*, 27 April 1922. Thanks to Dr Calder Walton for this reference.

102 Borum, 'Approaching Truth', p. 19.

103 NA KV2/805 KRIVITSKY, s.55x, 'Information obtained from Krivitsky', p. iv.

104 NA KV2/805 KRIVITSKY, s.55x, 'Information obtained from Krivitsky', pp. iii. Archer wrote, 'It was evident that Ogpu methods of investigation and the Moscow reign of terror during the purge had made such a deep impression on his mind as temporarily to obliterate his fairly comprehensive knowledge of British criminal procedure. He obviously feared lest any admission from him of participation in Soviet espionage activities against the United Kingdom would lead to a 'full examination' as understood by citizens of the U.S.S.R.'

105 Expanded upon in Krivitsky, *In Stalin's Secret Service*, pp. 171–7. Arthur Koestler's *Darkness at Noon* (1940) remains the most vivid literary account of the Soviet interrogation process. For historical approaches, see Marc Jansen and N. V. Petrov, *Stalin's Loyal Executioner: People's Commissar Nikolai Ezhov, 1895–1940* (Stanford, CA: Hoover Institution Press, 2002) and Conquest, *The Great Terror*.

106 Quoted in Kleinman, 'KUBARK Counterintelligence Review', in *Educing Information* (see NDIC Intelligence Science Board above), 95–140 (p. 99).

107 NA KV2/804 KRIVITSKY, s.1a (A), 'Report re interview with Krivitsky' [Harker], 23 January 1940.

108 NA KV2/805 KRIVITSKY, s.55x, 'Information obtained from Krivitsky', pp. iii. MI5's report reads: 'In regard to his assistants and friends, KRIVITSKY was actuated by a genuine sense of loyalty; it was only in the last few interviews that he gained sufficient confidence to talk more freely of them, and that after much time had been spent in explaining that British procedure would not admit of [sic] arrests on uncorroborated word of a single informant. Even so he has definitely "stalled" as regards one or two of his more personal friends, explaining that he did not intend to copy Stalin in destroying those who had served him best'.

109 NA KV2/804 KRIVITSKY, s.1a (A), 'Report re interview with Krivitsky', 23 January 1940.

110 NA KV2/804 KRIVITSKY, s.1a (A), 'Report re interview with Krivitsky', 23 January 1940.

111 NA KV2/804 KRIVITSKY, s.1a (A), 'Report re interview with Krivitsky', 23 January 1940; Alexander Ethan TUDOR-HART files can be seen at NA KV2/1603-1604; Edith TUDOR-HART files can be seen at NA KV2/1012-1014; Willy and Mary Brandes files can be seen at NA KV2/1004-1007. See also, David Burke, *The Spy Who Came In From the Co-op*.

112 Cialdini, *Influence*, chapter 3.

113 NA KV2/804 KRIVITSKY, s.1a (A), 'Report re interview with Krivitsky', 23 January 1940. Underscores in original.

114 NA KV2/804 KRIVITSKY, s.1a (A), 'Report re interview with Krivitsky', 23 January 1940.

115 NA KV2/804 KRIVITSKY, s.9a (F), letter from KMMA [Archer] to Vivian, 26 January 1940.

116 NA KV2/805 KRIVITSKY, s.55x, 'Information obtained from Krivitsky', p. 6.

117 Brook-Shepherd, *The Storm Petrels*, p. 182.

CHAPTER 7
Defection and Debriefing (II)

1 Krivitsky did not mention Alexandr Orlov, who was also one of Five's early handlers and a central figure in the OGPU's operations in Spain during the Civil War. See Orlov, *The*

March of Time; Costello and Tsarev, *Deadly Illusions*.

2 NA KV2/804 KRIVITSKY, s.2b (C), 'note re information from KRIVITSKY', 23 January 1940, p. 8; see also NA KV2/804 KRIVITSKY, s.4a (E), 'B.3.c. notes re interview with KRIVITSKY', 25 January 1940, p. 3; Andrew and Mitrokhin, *The Mitrokhin Archive*, pp. 73–4.

3 NA KV2/804 KRIVITSKY, s.13a (J), 'Information obtained from KRIVITSKY; noted by B.4. re DEUTSCH', 30 January 1940. Andrew and Gordievsky identify resident 'Arnold Schuster' as 'Aron Vaclavovich Shuster'. Andrew and Gordievsky, *KGB*, p. 560, appendix D2.

4 NA KV2/805 KRIVITSKY, s.55x, 'Information obtained from Krivitsky', p. 15.

5 The former Dawidowicz was eventually recalled or fired, but GADA remained a functioning cover for Soviet operatives, such as Dmitri Bystroletov when he was handling Ernest Oldham, the Foreign Office cypher clerk who committed suicide in 1933. NA KV2/804 KRIVITSKY, s.5a, 'B.4. report re interview with KRIVITSKY (re DAWIDOWICZ and GADA)', 25 January 1940. See also NA KV2/2242 'DAWIDOWICZ, Bernhard' and NA KV2/808 'OLDHAM, Ernest Holloway'. Krivitsky appears to have been the first to reveal Oldham's spying to MI5 (NA KV2/805 KRIVITSKY, s.55x, 'Information obtained from Krivitsky', p. 44; Thurlow, 'Soviet Spies and British Counter-Intelligence in the 1930s', p. 618).

6 Dawidowicz's file can be seen at NA KV2/2242.

7 NA KV2/804 KRIVITSKY, s.2b (C) 'note re information from KRIVITSKY', 23 January 1940, p. 8; s.6a 'Information from THOMAS', 25 January 1940 (by B.4), 25 January 1940; see also Andrew and Mitrokhin, *The Mitrokhin Archive*, pp. 73–88.

8 NA KV2/804 KRIVITSKY, s.25a (T), 'Information re Fourth Department and the Ogpu', 2 February 1940.

9 Sir Mansfield Cumming had a similar strategy of encircling Germany with stations in the First World War. See Judd, *The Quest for C*. The records of the debriefing frequently have Krivitsky using the term 'agent' for the legals and illegals. These individuals were actually officers on the staff of Soviet intelligence. The people they recruited were 'agents'.

10 NA KV2/804 KRIVITSKY, s.2a (B), 'notes on interview with Krivitsky', B3c, 10pm, 23

January 1940; cf. s.4a (E), 'B.3.c. report re interview with Krivitsky', 25 January 1940.

11　NA KV2/804 KRIVITSKY, s.2a (B), 'notes on interview with Krivitsky', B3c, 10pm, 23 January 1940.

12　NA KV2/805 KRIVITSKY, s.55x, 'Information obtained from Krivitsky', pp. 6–7, 15–16, 37; KV2/804 KRIVITSKY, s.20a (P), 'Information re the Fourth Department, its work and methods' (B.4), pp. 3–4 ('Methods of Work').

13　The Russian *'spekulyant'*, or speculator, can be translated as 'opportunist', but Archer wrote 'speculant' in the English translation. Kern, ed., *MI5 Debriefing*, p. 120 (fn. 34).

14　See Kendall, *Revolutionary Movement in Britain, 1900–21: The Origins of British Communism*, esp. pp. 182, 245–6; Burke, 'Theodore Rothstein'.

15　NA KV2/805 KRIVITSKY, s.55x, 'Information obtained from Krivitsky', p. 8.

16　Cf. the case of Brian Goold-Verschoyle (NA KV2/817), an Irishman identified by Krivitsky, who acted as a Soviet courier and disappeared in Spain during the Civil War.

17　NA KV2/805 KRIVITSKY, s.55x, 'Information obtained from Krivitsky', pp. 6–7.

18　NA KV2/804 KRIVITSKY, s.20a (P), 'Information re the Fourth Department, its work and methods' (B.4), pp. 4–5 ('Methods of Work').

19　NA KV2/805 KRIVITSKY, s.55x, 'Information obtained from Krivitsky', pp. 15–16.

20　Historical examples of concealments may be found in Melton, *Ultimate Spy* (London: Dorling Kindersley, 2002).

21　NA KV2/804 'Krivitsky', s.17a (N), 'B.4 note re information from K. re "Imperial Council"', 30 January 1940.

22　NA KV2/804 'Krivitsky', s.38b (AJ), 'B.3c note on information from K.', 9 February 1940.

23　Andrew and Mitrokhin, *The Mitrokhin Archive*, pp. 65–9.

24　Born in 1900 in Poltava, in today's Ukraine, he fought in the Red Army in Ukraine, and in the early 1920s began work in the Commissariat for Communications under Dzerzhinsky, whom Helfand contended he knew well. He said that his relations with Dzerzhinsky were also known quite well in the GPU/NKVD, affording him a certain amount of privilege. His wife had attended school with the wife of Yezhov. Helfand believed that these two factors aided his survival of the purge. First stationed in Paris in 1926, he eventually rose to Second Secretary in the Embassy. He

was feared by the personnel there as a GPU man and acquired the moniker the 'Eye of Moscow'. After the Kutepov affair in 1930 (in which the White Russian Army General Alexander Kutepov was thought to have been kidnapped by the OGPU in Paris and later to have died in transit to the USSR), he returned to Moscow but was then stationed in Rome from 1933 to 1940 (July), after which he defected to the US (NA KV2/2681 'HELFAND, Leon Bousivitch [Borisovitch]'.)

25　NA KV2/2681 HELFAND, s.17a, Hoyer Millar (Washington) to Codrington (London), 23 April 1941.

26　For a more thorough treatment of the Rome leaks, see David Dilks, 'Flashes of Intelligence: The Foreign Office, the SIS and Security Before the Second World War', in *Missing Dimension*, ed. Andrew and Dilks, pp. 101–25; also, Andrew, *Her Majesty's Secret Service*, pp. 402–07. Security lapses in both Rome and Berlin prompted investigations by Vivian in 1937.

27　NA KV2/2681 HELFAND, s.17a, Hoyar Millar (Washington) to Codrington (London), 23 April 1941, see attached 'Record of a Conversation with Mr. H. . . .', p. 1.

28　Alistair Denniston, first head of GC&CS, claimed Helfand's information regarding the extent to which the Soviets broke British ciphers was exaggerated (NA KV2/2681 HELFAND, s.22a, 'From S.I.S in reply to 21a' (letter from Vivian), 23 June 1941).

29　NA KV2/2681 HELFAND, s.17a, Hoyar Millar (Washington) to Codrington (London), 23 April 1941, see attached 'Record of a Conversation with Mr. H. . . .', p. 1.

30　Andrew and Mitrokhin, *The Mitrokhin Archive*, p. 66.

31　Andrew and Mitrokhin, *The Mitrokhin Archive*, p. 66.

32　NA KV2/804 KRIVITSKY, s.2a (B), 'notes on interview with Krivitsky', B3c, 10pm, 23 January 1940, p. 2.

33　NA KV2/804 KRIVITSKY, s.17a (N), 'B.4. note re information from K. re "Imperial Council"', 30 January 1940; NA KV2/805 KRIVITSKY, s.55x, 'Information obtained from Krivitsky', p. 50.

34　NA KV2/804 KRIVITSKY, s.17a (N), 'B.4 note re information from K. re "Imperial Council"', 30 January 1940.

35　NA KV2/804 KRIVITSKY, s.9a, 'to S.I.S. re information obtained from Krivitsky' [letter from KMMA to Vivian], 26 January 1940; KV2/804 KRIVITSKY, s.2a (B), 'notes on interview with Krivitsky', B3c, 10pm, 23 January 1940.

36 NA KV2/804 KRIVITSKY, s.29a (X), 'Note to B. re secret document seen in Moscow by K.', 3 February 1940.

37 Christopher Andrew and Vasili Mitrokhin, *The Mitrokhin Archive II: The KGB and the World* (London: Allen Lane, 2005), p. 484.

38 Philby, *My Silent War*, p. 105.

39 NA KV2/804, KRIVITSKY, s.41a (AM), 'B.4 note re F.O. Document', 10 February 1940. Emphasis added.

40 NA KV2/805 KRIVITSKY, s.55x, 'Information obtained from Krivitsky', p. 82.

41 Robert J. Lamphere and Tom Shachtman, *The FBI-KGB War: A Special Agent's Story* (London: W. H. Allen, 1987), pp. 233–4.

42 Kern, *A Death in Washington*, p. 264–5.

43 Quoted in Andrew, *Her Majesty's Secret Service*, p. 441.

44 NA KV2/805 KRIVITSKY, s.55x, 'Information obtained from Krivitsky', p. 50.

45 NA KV2/805 KRIVITSKY, s.55x, 'Information obtained from Krivitsky', p. 50, emphasis added.

46 NA KV2/804 KRIVITSKY, s.17a (N), 'B.4 note re information from K. re "Imperial Council"', 30 January 1940.

47 NA KV2/805 KRIVITSKY, s.94a, Note of conversation with S.I.S. seen by KRIVITSKY in Moscow, 1 May 1951 (B2b, A.S. Martin). The identity of 'Mr. Leigh' is unclear.

48 Ultimately, of course, we know he did. For example, Alexander Orlov's KGB file contains explicit references to Imperial Defence Committee documents provided by Maclean during 1936–1937 (Costello and Tsarev, *Deadly Illusions*, p. 200).

49 Stewart Tendler, 'MI5 Given Clues about Professor Blunt in 1939', *The Times*, Wednesday 28 November 1979, p. 2.

50 NA KV2/802 KRIVITSKY, s.13ax, 'Copy of letter to F.O. re LEVINE etc.' (Harker to Jebb), 8 November 1939.

51 NA KV2/804 KRIVITSKY, s.2a (B), 'Notes on interview with Krivitsky', 10pm, B3c, 23 January 1940.

52 See editorial remarks in Nigel West, ed., *The Guy Liddell Diaries, Vol. I: 1939–1942* (London: Routledge, 2005), pp. 14–15 (4 September 1939), 45 (16 November 1939).

53 Andrew and Gordievsky, *KGB*, p. 210.

54 Andrew and Gordievsky, *KGB*, p. 174.

55 Quoted in Bower, *The Perfect English Spy*, p. 34.

56 NA KV4/228 Report on the Operations of F.2.c. in connection with Russian Intelligence during War 1939–1945, s.1a, self-titled

report, May 1945, pp. 2–3; Walton, 'British Intelligence and Threats to National Security, c.1941–1951', chapter 1.

57 Archer had been fired. Philby tells us, 'Jane was a woman after my own heart, tough-minded and rough-tongued. She had been sacked from MI5 for taking the opportunity at a top-level meeting of grievously insulting Brigadier Harker, who for several years had filled the Deputy Directorship of MI5 with handsome grace and little else' (Philby, *My Silent War*, pp. 105–06).

58 Knightley, *Philby*, p. 176; Philby, *My Silent War*, p. 170.

59 NA KV2/805 KRIVITSKY, s.55x, 'Information obtained from Krivitsky', p. 64.

60 McDermott and Agnew, *The Comintern*; Thorpe, *The British Communist Party and Moscow*.

61 NA KV2/805 KRIVITSKY, s.55x, 'Information obtained from Krivitsky', p. 21.

62 NA KV2/805 KRIVITSKY, s.55x, 'Information obtained from Krivitsky', p. 22.

63 NA KV4/185 Liddell Diaries, Volume 1, 14 February 1940 (pp. 324–5). For further details of Krivitsky's remunerations, see NA KV2/802 KRIVITSKY, s.57a, telegram from B.4 [Archer] to RCMP, 21 February 1940; KV2/802 KRIVITSKY, s.66a, letter from RCMP S.T. Wood (Ottawa) to Vernon Kell (MI5), 18 March 1940. Lawrence H. Officer and Samuel H. Williamson, 'Purchasing Power of British Pounds from 1245 to Present', MeasuringWorth.com, 2014 (calculated in terms of retail price index at 2012 rates).

64 Johnson, 'Tricks of the Trade: Counterintelligence Interrogation', p. 112.

65 It is still unclear whether Krivitsky committed suicide or was assassinated. For the best analysis of contending theories, see Kern, *A Death in Washington*, pp. 338–80.

66 Given the success of the Krivitsky debriefing, it is curious that none of the officers involved took part in the questioning of Tyler Kent three months later (May 1940). Perhaps veteran MI5 agent handler Maxwell Knight's lead role in penetrating the Right Club best equipped him, in the same way that Archer wanted Vivian, because he had 'all the Soviet background in his head', to lead the interrogation of Krivitsky.

Conclusion

1 NA KV1/39 G Branch: Investigation of Espionage 1909–1911: German Espionage, p. 10.

2 Curry, *Security Service*, p. 302.

3 See Kevin Quinlan and Calder Walton, 'Missed Opportunities? Intelligence and the British Road to War', in *The Origins of the Second World War: An International Perspective*, ed. Frank McDonough (London: Continuum, 2011), 205–22.

4 NA KV1/39 G Branch: Investigation of Espionage 1909–1911: German Espionage, p. 52.

5 NA KV4/227 'M.S. Report', p. 48.

6 NA KV4/21 Report on the Operations of the Registry during the War 1939–1945, self-titled report, by DDO, 12 December 1945.

7 KV4/21 Report on the Operations of the Registry during the War 1939–1945, self-titled report, by DDO, 12 December 1945. Reorganisation continued into 1944, at which point the Registry consisted of 1.25 million cards even after 750,000 had been eliminated.

8 NA CAB 127/383 Second Report: Investigation into method of operation and organisation of the Security Service (MI5), 'The Secret Services: Inquiry by Minister without Portfolio', by Maurice Hankey, 11 May 1940 ['Hankey Report'], p. 16.

9 Andrew introduction to Curry, *Security Service*, p. 11; Wilson, 'The War in the Dark', pp. 45–50 (cf. chapter 9). In June 1940, Guy Liddell wrote, 'We have drastically cut down on our vetting, which had practically paralysed the work of the office' (NA KV4/186 Liddell Diaries, volume 2, 24 June 1940 (p. 510)).

10 NA KV4/88 Director General's Report on the Security Service, February 1941, Prepared for the Security Executive, s.2a, 'Report prepared by Sir David Petrie' ['Petrie Report'], 13 February 1941, p. 12.

11 NA KV4/88 'Petrie Report', pp. 5–6.

12 NA KV4/88 'Petrie Report', p. 18.

13 Quoted in Andrew introduction to Curry, *Security Service*, p. 13.

14 For example, NA KV4/172 SOE Course at Beaulieu 1945; HS 7/55-56 Lecture Folder STS 103, parts 1 & 2 (respectively), published as Rigdan, ed., *SOE Syllabus*.

15 Curry, *Security Service*, p. 180. ISOS was named after the head of GC&CS Intelligence Section, Oliver Strachey.

16 Curry, *Security Service*, p. 232.

17 An 1940 government report on intelligence noted, 'During the Great War 1914–1918 . . . gradually the work of the Department broadened out to include, besides counter-espionage, sedition and sabotage, such activities as the impersonation of hostile agents (who had been arrested and in one case even suffered the death penalty without the enemy's knowledge), the feeding of the enemy with more or less correct but innocuous facts, interspersed from time to time with misleading information designed to lead his forces into traps. During the last war I myself was once driven in an official motor car, which M.I.5. had purchased, and maintained for some time, out of remuneration received from the Germans in payment for these simulated services.' CAB 127/383, 'Hankey Report', p. 5; cf. Curry, *Security Service*, p. 76.

18 Masterman, *The Double-Cross System*, p. 3. The Double-Cross Committee was called the Twenty Committee after the roman numerals 'XX', or 'double cross'.

19 Masterman, *The Double-Cross System*, pp. 17.

20 Robert Stephens, *Camp 020: MI5 and the Nazi Spies: The Official History of MI5's Wartime Interrogation Centre [With an introduction by Oliver Hoare]* (Richmond: Public Record Office, 2000), p. 58.

21 NA KV4/227 'M.S. Report', p. 25.

22 NA KV4/227 'M.S. Report', p. 25.

23 Quoted in Andrew, *Her Majesty's Secret Service*, p. 460.

24 Masterman, *The Double-Cross System*, p. 27.

25 Masterman, *The Double-Cross System*, p. 22.

26 Stephens, *Camp 020*, p. 57.

27 Apart from Masterman's *The Double-Cross System* and Stephens's *Camp 020*, the best study of Double-Cross is Emily Wilson's PhD dissertation, 'The War in the Dark'. See also Ben Macintyre, *Double Cross: The True Story of the D Day Spies* (London: Bloomsbury, 2012).

28 NA KV4/228 Report on the Operations of F.2.c. in connection with Russian Intelligence during War 1939–1945, s.1a, self-titled report, May 1945, pp. 2-3; Walton, 'British Intelligence and Threats to National Security, c.1941–1951', chapter 1.

29 See for example, the interrogation of Oliver Green in NA KV2/2203–2206, and the case of Douglass Springhall, KV2/1594–1598. Cf. KV3/301 International Organisation of the Communist Party – Most Secret Material, s.21a, 'Note from D.C. enclosing secret and top secret papers drawn up by MI6 on the Int. Communist movement', 5 October 1951; Curry, *Security Service*, pp. 362–3.

30 NA KV4/158 Brief Notes on the Security Service and Its Work Prepared for Permanent

Under-Secretaries, Service Intelligence Depts., C.I.G.S., Courses, etc., s.13b, 'A short note on the Security Service and its responsibilities', John Curry, p. 5.

31 NA KV4/158 Brief Notes on the Security Service, minute of 1 October 1946, Curry to DDG (Liddell).

32 NA KV3/301 International Organisation of the Communist Party – Most Secret Material, s.21a, 'Note from D.C. enclosing secret and top secret papers drawn up by MI6 on the Int. Communist movement', 5 October 1951; Curry, *Security Service*, pp. 362–3.

33 Kennan, *Russia and the West under Lenin and Stalin*, pp. 239–40.

(Endnotes)

APPENDIX I
The Evolution of British Security Studies

1 Christopher Andrew and David Dilks, *The Missing Dimension: Governments and Intelligence Communities in the Twentieth Century* (London: Macmillan, 1984).

2 As Michael Howard observes, 'The academic snobbery that disdains the history of the recent past precisely because it relates so obviously to the present is as indefensible as the lay impatience with the remote past because on the face of it does not' (Michael Howard, *The Lessons of History* (Oxford: Oxford University Press, 1993), p. 17).

3 See, *inter alia*, 'Foreign Officials' Disappearance: "Maximum Secrecy" Needed in Counter-Espionage', *The Times*, Saturday 24 September 1955, p. 4; 'Cabinet Expected on Tuesday', *The Times*, Saturday 15 October 1955, p. 6; 'Text of Statement Issued by Burgess and Maclean', *The Times*, Monday 13 February 1956; 'Preparing for Security Inquiry', *The Times*, Wednesday 9 November 1955, p. 8 [Philby's famous challenge to repeat 'third man' accusations outside Parliament]; 'Philby "Third Man" Who Warned Maclean', *The Times*, Tuesday 2 July 1963, p. 10; 'Professor Blunt Named as Spy', *The Times*, Friday 16 November 1979, p. 1; 'The Spy Who Came In From the Co-Op', *The Times*, Saturday 11 September 1999, p. 1; Home Secretary Jack Straw, statement to the House of Commons, 'The Mitrokhin Archive', 21 October 1999, http:// www.fas.org/irp/world/uk/ docs/991021.htm (last accessed 1 April 2008) (see also the 16,200 references to Mitrokhin at *Hansard*, http://www.publications.parliament. uk/cgi-bin/search.pl (last accessed 1 April 2008)); Intelligence and Security Committee,

'Mitrokhin Inquiry Report', http://www. archive.official-documents.co.uk/document/ cm47/4764/4764.htm, June 2000 (last accessed 1 April 2008); and, not least, Andrew and Mitrokhin, *The Mitrokhin Archive*.

4 Richard J. Aldrich, 'Policing the Past: Official History, Secrecy and British Intelligence since 1945', *English Historical Review* 119 (2004), 922–53.

5 The fifth volume in the series, *Strategic Deception*, was written by Michael Howard.

6 Cf. Wesley K. Wark, 'In Never-Never Land? The British Archives on Intelligence', *The Historical Journal* 35 (1992), 195–203.

7 Piers Brendon, *The Dark Valley: A Panorama of the 1930s* (London: Pimlico, 2001), p. 612, 619 (respectively).

8 Roy Hattersley, *Borrowed Time: The Story of Britain between the Wars* (London: Little, Brown, 2007).

9 Zara Steiner, *The Lights That Failed: European International History, 1919–1933* (Oxford: Oxford University Press, 2005); Keith Neilson, *Britain, Soviet Russia and the Collapse of the Versailles Order, 1919–1939* (Cambridge: Cambridge University Press, 2006).

10 'History: The Security Service at The National Archives', http://www.mi5.gov.uk/ output/ Page233.html (last accessed 31 March 2008); 'Intelligence Records', http://www. intelligence.gov. uk/intelligence_records.aspx (last accessed 31 March 2008).

11 The Security Service's official history, by Professor Christopher Andrew, was published in 2009 and covers all years, 1909–present; SIS's official history, by Professor Keith Jeffery, was released in 2010 and covers the years 1909–1949.

12 University of Cambridge Intelligence Seminar, information obtained under the Chatham House Rule. Jay Jakub, *Spies and Saboteurs: Anglo-American Collaboration and Rivalry in Human Intelligence Collection and Special Operations, 1940–45* (New York: St Martin's Press, 1999) focuses on the management of operations rather than operational tradecraft.

13 David Kahn, *The Codebreakers: The Story of Secret Writing* (London: Weidenfeld and Nicolson, 1967) remains the standard history. An incomplete list also includes Christopher Andrew, ed., *Codebreaking and Signals Intelligence* (London: Frank Cass, 1986); chapters by Christopher Andrew, David Kahn, Jürgen Rohwer and Jean Stingers, in *Missing Dimension*, ed. Andrew and Dilks; chapters by Ralph Bennett, Jürgen Rohwer and Jean

Stengers in *Intelligence and International Relations 1900–1945*, ed. Christopher M. Andrew and Jeremy Noakes (Exeter: University of Exeter, 1987); Patrick Beesly, *Room 40: British Naval Intelligence 1914–18* (London: Hamilton, 1982); Ralph Bennett, *Ultra and Mediterranean Strategy* (London: Hamish Hamilton, 1989); Ralph Bennett, *Ultra in the West: The Normandy Campaign, 1944–45* (London: Hutchinson, 1979); Stephen Budiansky, *Battle of Wits: The Complete Story of Codebreaking in World War II* (London: Viking, 2000); B. Jack Copeland, ed., *Colossus: The Secrets of Bletchley Park's Codebreaking Computers* (Oxford: Oxford University Press, 2006); Robin Denniston, *Thirty Secret Years: A. G. Denniston's Work in Signals Intelligence 1914–1944* (Clifton-upon-Teme: Polperro Heritage, 2007); Ralph Erskine and Michael Smith, ed., *Action This Day* (London: Bantam Press, 2001); F. H. Hinsely and Alan Stripp, ed., *Codebreakers: The Inside Story of Bletchley Park* (Oxford: Oxford University Press, 1993); Hugh Sebag-Montefiore, *Enigma: The Battle for the Code* (London: Weidenfeld & Nicolson, 2000); Simon Singh, *The Code Book: The Science of Secrecy from Ancient Egypt to Quantum Cryptography* (London: Fourth Estate, 1999). Some recent intelligence collections have begun to address HUMINT *per se*, see chapters by John MacGaffin and Burton Gerber in Jennifer E. Sims and Burton Gerber, *Transforming U.S. Intelligence* (Washington, DC: Georgetown University Press, 2005); chapter by Norman Imler in *Intelligence and the National Security Strategist*, ed. George and Kline; Robert Wallace and H. Keith Melton, *Spycraft: The Secret History of the CIA's Spytechs from Communism to Al-Qaeda* (London: Dutton, 2008).

14 The INTs refer to the kinds of intelligence. Other INTs include IMINT (imagery intelligence), MASINT (measures and signatures intelligence), ELINT (electronic intelligence).

15 Robert Baden-Powell, *My Adventures as a Spy: Illustrated by the Author's Own Sketches* (London: C. Arthur Pearson, 1915), pp. 30–3.

16 Sir Paul Dukes, *The Story of "ST 25": Adventure and Romance in the Secret Intelligence Service in Red Russia* (London: Cassell and Company, 1938), pp. 132–3.

17 'Intelligence Literature: Recommended Reading List', https://www.cia.gov/library/intelligence-literature/index.html (last accessed 1 April 2008).

18 'He was suddenly alert. Something had moved in the drawing-room. A light, a

shadow, a human form; something he was certain. Was it sight or instinct? Was it the latent skill of his own tradecraft which informed him? Some fine sense or nerve, some remote faculty of perception warned him now and he heeded the warning' (John le Carré, *Call for the Dead* (London: Sceptre, 1961), p. 50). The etymology is from the *Oxford English Dictionary*.

19 Robert Wallace and H. Keith Melton, *Spycraft: The Secret History of the CIA's Spytechs from Communism to Al-Qaeda* (London: Dutton, 2008). Other intelligence volumes, while very good, focus almost entirely on the US Intelligence Community when addressing HUMINT, if they address it at all. None addresses tradecraft systematically (see above).

20 Indeed the CIA only came into existence with the National Security Act of 1947.

21 See NA KV4/172 SOE Course at Beaulieu 1945; HS 7/55-56 Lecture Folder STS 103, parts 1 & 2 (respectively), published as Denis Rigdan, ed., *SOE Syllabus: Lessons in Ungentlemanly Warfare, World War II* (Richmond: National Archives, 2004).

22 University of Cambridge Intelligence Seminar, information obtained under the Chatham House Rule.

APPENDIX II
Record Keeping

1 *The 9/11 Commission Report*, pp. 353–7, 416–19.

2 Except for minor adjustments, 'no definite change in principle can be said to have been found necessary', H Branch's postwar history reads. NA KV1/49 H Branch: Organisation and Administration 1900–1919, p. 20.

3 NA KV4/88 Director General's Report on the Security Service, February 1941, Prepared for the Security Executive, s.2a, 'Report prepared by Sir David Petrie', 13 February 1941, p. 4; Emily Jane Wilson, 'The War in the Dark: The Security Service and the Abwehr, 1940–1944' (unpublished doctoral dissertation, University of Cambridge, 2003), p. 96.

4 To this day, PFs remain the largest collection of KV documents.

5 Subsequently, Policy File and Organisational File classifications were also introduced. NA KV1/49 H Branch: Organisation and Administration 1900–1919, pp. 20–1.

6 NA KV1/49 H Branch: Organisation and Administration 1900–1919, p. 21.

7 NA KV1/49 H Branch: Organisation and Administration 1900–1919, pp. 24-25. The

following passage from the history of the Detective Branch explains the system in more depth: 'In dealing with persons, it is of vital importance to be able to form a mental reconstruction (1) of a man's career, so far as known, (2) of the previous course of the investigation, and (3) of similar facts about his friends and connections. These last, of course, can best be secured by requisitioning of files, if any, of such persons mentioned in the files of the principal subject of enquiry; but in many cases the Filing Division of the Registry gives cross-references on the cover of the file to other dossiers which contain documents forming part of the same "case", which . . . may include different persons under a single investigation. Subject files also have cross-references, in the index-sheets placed inside the front cover, to all mentions of related subjects in papers which have been put away in other subject or personal files, with which they are more directly concerned' (NA KV1/46 G Branch: Investigation of Espionage 1915–1919: Appendixes and Annexures, Appendix A, p. 17).

8 NA KV1/42 G Branch: Investigation of Espionage 1916: German Espionage, p. 163.

9 NA KV1/39 G Branch: Investigation of Espionage 1909–1911: German Espionage, p. 10.

10 NA KV1/46 G Branch: Investigation of Espionage 1915–1919: Appendixes and Annexures, p. 18.

APPENDIX III

Secret Inks

1 See for example the case of Alfred Hagn, NA KV1/74 The Testing Department (MI9c), pp. 144–51/50–7 [this file is double-paginated]; WO 141/3/5 Charges of Spying Against Alfred Hagn and Commutation of Sentence.

2 Of course, the organic substance must burn at a lower temperature than the paper; only as much heat should be applied as is necessary to char the substance but not burn the paper and thereby destroy the message.

3 NA KV1/73 The Testing Department (MI9c), p. 14/19. For more sophisticated chemicals, such as 'F' and 'P' inks and reagents, see pp. 35–8/40–3 [this file is double-paginated].

4 NA KV1/73 The Testing Department (MI9c), p. 14/19.

5 NA KV1/73 The Testing Department (MI9c), p. 21/26.

6 Example given in NA KV1/73 The Testing Department (MI9c), p. 49/54.

7 NA KV1/74 The Testing Department (MI9c), pp. 166–8/72–4.

8 NA KV1/73 The Testing Department (MI9c), pp. 11–12/16–17.

9 These are but a few examples as illustrated in H. Keith Melton, *Ultimate Spy* (London: Dorling Kindersley, 2002), pp. 154–9.

10 NA KV1/38 F Branch: Prevention of Espionage 1909–1916: Summary, p. 22.

11 NA KV1/74 The Testing Department (MI9c), p. 106/12.

12 NA KV4/127 Security Service Organisation 1919–1939, Defence Security Intelligence Service organisational chart (May 1929); MI5 Chronological List of Staff up to 31 December, 1919; Security Service organisational chart (October 1931).

13 University of Cambridge Intelligence Seminar, information obtained under the Chatham House Rule.

Bibliography

Archival Sources

The National Archives, Kew, London (NA)

ADM	Records of the Admiralty, Naval Forces, Royal Marines, Coastguard and related bodies
CAB	Records of the Cabinet Office
CRIM	Records of the Central Criminal Court
DPP	Records of the Director of Public Prosecution
FO	Records of the Foreign Office
HO	Records created or inherited by the Home Office, Ministry of Home Security and related bodies
HW	Records created and inherited by Government Communications Headquarters (GCHQ)
KV	Records of the Security Service
PREM	Records of the Prime Minister's Office
WO	Records of the War Office

Conferences/Seminars

Cambridge Study Group on Intelligence, Corpus Christi College, Cambridge, UK, weekly gathering during full academic terms, 2004–2008

Conference on Security, Terrorism, and Business (CIBAM Symposium), Cambridge, UK, 22 February 2007

Global Futures Forum, Cambridge, UK, 27 April 2007

International Terrorism and Intelligence Conference, Eden Intelligence, Seaford House, London, UK, 23–24 June 2006

Joint Meetings of British Study Group on Intelligence, Royal United Services Institute (RUSI), Whitehall, London, UK, tri-annual gathering, 2004–2008

'Keeping Secrets: How Important was Intelligence to the Conduct of International Relations from 1914–1989?', German Historical Institute, London, UK, 17–19 April 2008

'Spooked: Cultures of Intelligence', Warwick University, UK, 12–13 May 2007

Transatlantic Perspectives on the Middle East, The Donner Atlantic Studies Program and the Jean Monnet European Centre of Excellence, Cambridge, UK, 11–12 February 2005

Online Resources

BBC News: www.news.bbc.co.uk
Communist Party of Great Britain: www.cpgb.org.uk
JSTOR
Marxists Internet Archive: www.marxists.org
MeasuringWorth: www.MeasuringWorth.com
The National Security Archive: www.gwu.edu/~nsarchiv/index.html
New York Times: www.nytimes.com
Social Science Research Network: www.ssrn.com
The Times: www.times.co.uk
The Times digital archive
TUC Online: www.unionhistory.info
Washington Post: www.washingtonpost.com
Website of the British Foreign and Commonwealth Office: www.fco.gov.uk
Website of the Central Intelligence Agency: www.cia.gov
Website of the Government Communications Headquarters: www.gchq.gov.uk
Website of the Federal Bureau of Investigation: www.fbi.gov
Website of the National Security Agency: www.nsa.gov
Website of The Secret Intelligence Service: www.sis.gov.uk
Website of the Security Service: www.mi5.gov.uk

Reference

Maney, A. S., and R. L. Smallwood, ed., *MHRA Style Guide*, rev. edn. (London: Modern Humanities Research Association, 2002)
Matthew, H. C. G. and Brian Harrison, ed., *Oxford Dictionary of National Biography* [*ODNB*], new edn, 61 Volumes (Oxford: Oxford University Press, 2004)

Official Inquiries and Reports

The 9/11 Commission Report: Final Report of the National Commission on Terrorist Attacks Upon the United States, authorized edn (New York: W. W. Norton, 2004)
Butler of Brockwell, Lord, *Review of Intelligence on Weapons of Mass Destruction* (London: Her Majesty's Stationery Office, 2004)
Commission on the Intelligence Capabilities of the United States Regarding Weapons of Mass Destruction, *Report to the President of the United States* (Washington, DC: USG, March 2005)
Herbig, Katherine L., and Martin F. Wiskoff, 'Espionage against the United States by American Citizens, 1947–2001' (Monterrey, CA: TRW Systems & Defense Personnel Research Security Center, 2002)

Published Documents and Memoirs

Baden-Powell, Robert, *My Adventures as a Spy: Illustrated by the Author's Own Sketches* (London: C. Arthur Pearson, 1915)
Baer, Robert, *See No Evil: The True Story of a Ground Soldier in the CIA's War on Terrorism* (London: Arrow, 2002)

Cherkashin, Victor, and Gregory Feifer, *Spy Handler: Memoir of a KGB Officer: The True Story of the Man Who Recruited Robert Hanssen and Aldrich Ames* (New York: Basic Books, 2005)

Crumpton, Henry A., *The Art of Intelligence: Lessons from a Life in the CIA's Clandestine Service* (New York: Penguin, 2012)

Curry, John, *The Security Service 1908–1945: The Official History [With an introduction by Christopher Andrew]* (Kew: Public Record Office, 1999)

Degras, Jane, ed., *Soviet Documents on Foreign Policy: Volume II 1925–1932* (London: Oxford University Press and RIIA, 1952)

Driberg, Tom, *Ruling Passions* (London: Quartet Books, 1978)

Dukes, Sir Paul, *The Story of 'ST 25': Adventure and Romance in the Secret Intelligence Service in Red Russia* (London: Cassell and Company, 1938)

Essential Handbook for KGB Agents (London: Industrial Information Index, 1991)

Felix, Christopher, *A Short Course in the Secret War*, 4th edn (London: Madison Books, 2001)

Fitch, Herbert T., *Traitors Within: The Adventures of Detective Inspector Herbert T. Fitch* (London: Hurst & Blackett Ltd, 1933)

Harrison, John M., ed., *CIA Flaps and Seals Manual* (Boulder, CO: Paladin Press, 1975)

Herzen, Alexander, *My Past and Thoughts: The Memoirs of Alexander Herzen* (London: University of California Press, 1992)

Kern, Gary, ed., *Walter G. Krivitsky: MI5 Debriefing and Other Documents on Soviet Intelligence*, trans. Kern, Gary (Riverside, CA: Xenos Books, 2004)

Kimball, Warren, ed., *Churchill & Roosevelt: The Complete Correspondence Vol. I* (Princeton, NJ: Princeton University Press, 1984)

Krivitsky, W. G., *In Stalin's Secret Service* (New York: Enigma Books, 2000)

Kuusinen, Aino, *Before and after Stalin: A Personal Account of Soviet Russia from the 1920s to the 1960s* (London: Joseph, 1974)

Lamphere, Robert J., and Tom Shachtman, *The FBI-KGB War: A Special Agent's Story* (London: W. H. Allen, 1987)

Lansbury, George, *My Life* (London: Constable and Co., 1928)

Levine, Isaac Don, *Eyewitness to History: Memoirs and Reflections of a Foreign Correspondent for Half a Century* (New York: Hawthorn Books, 1973)

Lockhart, Robert Bruce, *Memoirs of a British Agent: Being an Account of the Author's Early Life in Many Lands and his Official Mission to Moscow in 1918* (London: Macmillan, 1932)

Macartney, Wilfred, *Zigzag* (London, 1937)

Macartney, Wilfred, and Compton Mackenzie, *Walls Have Mouths: A Record of Ten Years' Penal Servitude* (London: V. Gollancz, 1936)

Mackenzie, Compton, *Aegean Memories* (London: Chatto and Windus, 1940)

Marks, Leo, *Between Silk and Cyanide: A Codemaker's Story 1941–1945*, corrected edn (London: HarperCollins, 2000)

Medlicott, W. N., Douglas Dakin, and Margaret Esterel Lambert, ed., *Documents on British Foreign Policy, 1919–1939. Series 1A.* Vol. 3 (London: HMSO, 1971)

——, ed., *Documents on British Foreign Policy, 1919–1939. Series 1A.* Vol. 4 (London: HMSO, 1973)

Miller, Joan, *One Girl's War: Personal Exploits in MI5's Most Secret Station* (Dingle, Co. Kerry: Brandon, 1986)

Modin, Yuri, *My Five Cambridge Friends* (London: Headline, 1995)

Muggeridge, Malcolm, *Chronicles of Wasted Time, Vol. 2: The Infernal Grove* (London: Collins, 1973)

Orlov, Alexander, *The March of Time: Reminiscences* (London: St Ermin's, 2004)

Orwell, George, *Homage to Catalonia* (New York: Harcourt, 1980)

Philby, Kim, *My Silent War: The Autobiography of a Spy* (London: Arrow Books, 2003)

Poretsky, Elisabeth K., *Our Own People: A Memoir of 'Ignace Reiss' and His Friends* (London: Oxford University Press, 1969)

Ramsay, Maule, *The Nameless War* (Finchampstead: Bear Wood Press, 1992)

Rigdan, Denis, ed., *SOE Syllabus: Lessons in Ungentlemanly Warfare, World War II* (Richmond: National Archives, 2004)

Steinhauer, Gustav, *Steinhauer, The Kaiser's Master Spy. The Story as Told by Himself. Edited by S. T. Felstead, etc.* (London: John Lane, 1930)

Stephens, Robert, *Camp 020: MI5 and the Nazi Spies: The Official History of MI5's Wartime Interrogation Centre [with an introduction by Oliver Hoare]* (Richmond: Public Record Office, 2000)

Sweeney, John, *At Scotland Yard: Being the Experiences during Twenty-Seven Years' Service*, new edn (London, 1905)

Tomlinson, Richard, *The Big Breach: From Top Secret to Maximum Security* (Moscow: Narodny Variant Publishers, 2000)

Unknown, [US Office of Strategic Services], *Locks, Picks, and Clicks* (unknown: n.p., n.d.)

West, Nigel, ed., *The Guy Liddell Diaries, Vol. I: 1939–1942*, Vol. 1 (London: Routledge, 2005)

Whitwell, John, *British Agent* (London: Frank Cass, 1996)

Wright, Peter, *Spycatcher: The Candid Autobiography of a Senior Intelligence Officer* (New York: Viking, 1987)

Monographs and Edited Collections

Ahmann, R., Adolf M. Birke, and Michael Howard, ed., *The Quest for Stability: Problems of West European Security, 1918–1957* (London: German Historical Institute; Oxford University Press, 1993)

AMC IV Security Service, *Secrets of Surveillance: A Professional's Guide to Tailing Subjects by Vehicle, Foot, Airplane, and Public Transportation* (Boulder, CO: Paladin Press, 1993)

Andrew, Christopher, *For the President's Eyes Only: Secret Intelligence and the American Presidency from Washington to Bush*, pbk edn (New York: HarperPerennial, 1996)

——, *Her Majesty's Secret Service: The Making of the British Intelligence Community* (New York: Viking, 1986)

——, *The Defence of the Realm: The Authorized History of MI5* (London: Allen Lane, 2009)

——, ed., *Codebreaking and Signals Intelligence* (London: Frank Cass, 1986)

——, and David Dilks, ed., *The Missing Dimension: Governments and Intelligence Communities in the Twentieth Century* (London: Macmillan, 1984)

——, and Oleg Gordievsky, *KGB: The Inside Story of its Foreign Operations from Lenin to Gorbachev* (London: Hodder & Stoughton, 1990)

——, and Vasili Mitrokhin, *The Mitrokhin Archive: The KGB in Europe and the West* (London: Penguin, 2000)

——, and ——, *The Mitrokhin Archive II: The KGB and the World* (London: Allen Lane, 2005)

Andrew, Christopher M., and Jeremy Noakes, ed., *Intelligence and International Relations 1900–1945* (Exeter: University of Exeter, 1987)

Bassett, Richard, *Hitler's Spy Chief: The Wilhelm Canaris Mystery* (London: Weidenfeld & Nicolson, 2005)

Batvinis, Raymond J., *The Origins of FBI Counterintelligence* (Lawrence: University Press of Kansas, 2007)

Bearse, Ray, and Anthony Read, *Conspirator: The Untold Story of Churchill, Roosevelt and Tyler Kent, Spy* (London: Macmillan, 1991)

Beckett, Francis, *Enemy Within: The Rise and Fall of the British Communist Party* (London: John Murray, 1995)

Beesly, Patrick, *Room 40: British Naval Intelligence 1914–18* (London: Hamilton, 1982)

Bennett, Gill, *Churchill's Man of Mystery: Desmond Morton and the World of Intelligence* (London: Routledge, 2006)

Bennett, Gillian, '*A Most Extraordinary and Mysterious Business': The Zinoviev Letter of 1924* (London: FCO, 1999)

Bennett, Ralph, *Ultra and Mediterranean Strategy* (London: Hamish Hamilton, 1989)

——, *Ultra in the West: The Normandy Campaign, 1944–1945* (London: Hutchinson, 1979)

Benson, Robert Louis, and Michael Warner, ed., *Venona: Soviet Espionage and the American Response 1939–1957* (Washington, DC: NSA/CIA, 1996)

Berlin, Isaiah, *Russian Thinkers* (London: Penguin, 1979)

Betts, Richard K., *Enemies of Intelligence: Knowledge and Power in American National Security* (New York: Columbia University Press, 2007)

Boghardt, Thomas, *Spies of the Kaiser: German Covert Operations in Great Britain during the First World War Era* (Basingstoke: Palgrave Macmillan in association with St Antony's College, Oxford, 2004)

Borovik, Genrikh, *The Philby Files: The Secret Life of the Master Spy – KGB Archives Revealed*, new edn (London: Warner, 1995)

Bower, Tom, *The Perfect English Spy: Sir Dick White and the Secret War, 1935–90* (London: Heinemann, 1995)

Bozeman, Adda B., *Strategic Intelligence & Statecraft: Selected Essays* (Washington, DC; London: Brassey's (US), 1992)

Brendon, Piers, *The Dark Valley: A Panorama of the 1930s* (London: Pimlico, 2001)

Brook-Shepherd, Gordon, *Iron Maze: The Western Secret Services and the Bolsheviks* (London: Macmillan, 1998)

——, *The Storm Petrels: The First Soviet Defectors, 1928–1938* (London: Collins, 1977)

Budiansky, Stephen, *Battle of Wits: The Complete Story of Codebreaking in World War II* (London: Viking, 2000)

Bullock, Alan, and Brian Brivati, *Ernest Bevin: A Biography* (London: Politico's, 2002)

Burke, David, *The Spy Who Came In From the Co-op: Melita Norwood and the Ending of Cold War Espionage* (Woodbridge: Boydell Press, 2009)

Burke, Jason, *Al-Qaeda: The True Story of Radical Islam* (London: Penguin Books, 2004)

Carter, Miranda, *Anthony Blunt: His Lives* (London: Macmillan, 2001)

Cialdini, Robert B., *Influence: The Psychology of Persuasion*, rev. edn (New York: Morrow, 1993)

Clarke, Peter, *Hope and Glory: Britain 1900–2000*, 2nd edn (London: Penguin, 2004)

Coates, W. P. and Zelda K. Coates, *A History of Anglo-Soviet Relations* (London: Lawrence & Wishart, 1943)

Conquest, Robert, *The Great Terror: A Reassessment* (London: Hutchinson, 1990)

Cook, Andrew, *Ace of Spies: The True Story of Sidney Reilly* (Stroud: Tempus, 2004)

——, *M: MI5's First Spymaster* (Stroud: Tempus, 2004)

Copland, B. Jack, *Colossus: The Secrets of Bletchley Park's Codebreaking Computers* (Oxford: Oxford University Press, 2006)

Costello, John, *Ten Days That Saved the West* (London: Bantam, 1991)

——, and Oleg Tsarev, *Deadly Illusions* (London: Century, 1993)

Courtois, Stephane, and Mark Kramer, ed., *The Black Book of Communism: Crimes, Terror, Repression* (Cambridge, MA: Harvard University Press, 1999)

Davides, Norman, *White Eagle, Red Star: The Polish-Soviet War, 1919–1920* (London: Macdonald and Co., 1972)

Denniston, Robin, *Thirty Secret Years: A.G. Denniston's Work in Signals Intelligence 1914–1944* (Clifton-upon-Teme: Polperro Heritage, 2007)

Dilnot, George, *Great Detectives and Their Methods* (London: G. Bles, 1927)

Dorril, Stephen, *Blackshirt: Sir Oswald Mosley and British Fascism* (London: Viking, 2006)

Dulles, Allen, *The Craft of Intelligence* (London: Weidenfeld and Nicolson, 1963)

Erickson, John, *Soviet High Command: A Military-Political History, 1918–1941*, 3rd edn (London: Frank Cass, 2001)

Ferguson, Harry, *Spy: A Handbook* (London: Bloomsbury, 2004)

Ferris, John, ed., *British Army and Signals Intelligence During the First World War* (Stroud: Alan Sutton, 1992)

Figes, Orlando, *A People's Tragedy: The Russian Revolution, 1891–1924*, pbk edn (London: Pimlico, 1998)

Fisher, John, *Gentlemen Spies: Intelligence in the British Empire and Beyond* (Phoenix Mill: Sutton Publishing Ltd, 2002)

Fitzpatrick, *The Russian Revolution* (Oxford: Oxford University Press, 1994)

Foot, M. R. D., *SOE: The Special Operations Executive 1940–1946* (London: Pimlico, 1999)

Gardner, Howard, *Frames of Mind: The Theory of Multiple Intelligences* (New York: Basic Books, 1983)

Gentry, Curt, *J. Edgar Hoover: The Man and the Secrets* (London: W. W. Norton, 1991)

George, Roger Z., and Robert D. Kline, ed., *Intelligence and the National Security Strategist: Enduring Issues and Challenges* (Lanham, MD: Rowman & Littlefield Publishers, 2006)

Gilbert, Martin, *Winston S. Churchill, Vol. V: 1922–1939* (London: Heinemann, 1976)

Gillman, Peter, and Leni Gillman, '*Collar the Lot!' How Britain Interned and Expelled Its Wartime Refugees* (London: Quartet Books, 1980)

Glading, Percy, *India Under British Terror* (London: Percy Glading (Secretary), Meerut Trade Union Defence Committee, 1931)

——, *The Meerut Conspiracy Case* (London: Communist Party of Great Britain, 1933)

Goleman, Daniel, *Emotional Intelligence* (New York: Bantam Books, 1995)

——, *Social Intelligence: The New Science of Relationships* (New York: Bantam Books, 2006)

Gorodetsky, Gabriel, *The Precarious Truce: Anglo-Soviet Relations 1924–27* (Cambridge: Cambridge University Press, 1977)

——, ed., *Soviet Foreign Policy, 1917–1991: A Retrospective* (London: Frank Cass, 1994)

Greenberg, Karen J, ed., *Al Qaeda Now: Understanding Today's Terrorists* (Cambridge: Cambridge University Press, 2005)

Griffin, Roger, *Nature of Fascism* (London: Routledge, 1993)

Griffiths, Richard, *Fellow Travellers of the Right: British Enthusiasts for Nazi Germany: 1933–39* (London: Constable, 1980)

——, *Patriotism Perverted: Captain Ramsay, The Right Club and English Anti-Semitism, 1939–40* (London: Constable, 1998)

Hart, John Limond, *The CIA's Russians* (Annapolis, MD: Naval Institute Press, 2003)

Hattersley, Roy, *Borrowed Time: The Story of Britain between the Wars* (London: Little, Brown, 2007)

Haynes, John Earl, and Harvey Klehr, *Venona: Decoding Soviet Espionage in America* (London: Yale University Press, 1999)

Hennessy, Peter, *The Secret State: Whitehall and the Cold War*, rev. & updated edn (London: Penguin, 2003)

——, ed., *The New Protective State: Government, Intelligence and Terrorism* (London: Continuum, 2007)

Herman, Michael, *Intelligence Power in Peace and War* (Cambridge: Cambridge University Press in association with RIIA, 1996)

Hinsley, F. H., *British Intelligence in the Second World War, Vols I–III: Its Influence on Strategy and Operations* (London: HMSO, 1979–1988); F. H. Hinsley with C. A. G. Simkins, *British Intelligence in the Second World War, Vol. IV: Security and Counter-Intelligence* (London: HMSO, 1990); Michael Howard, *British Intelligence in the Second World War, Vol. V: Strategic Deception* (London: HMSO, 1992)

——, *British Intelligence in the Second World War*, abridged edn (London, 1993)

——, and Alan Stripp, ed., *Codebreakers: The Inside Story of Bletchley Park* (Oxford: Oxford University Press, 1993)

Hopkirk, Peter, *Setting the East Ablaze: On Secret Service in Bolshevik Asia* (Oxford: Oxford University Press, 2001)

Howard, Michael, *The Lessons of History* (Oxford: Oxford University Press, 1993)

——, *War in European History* (Oxford: Oxford University Press, 1976)

Jakub, Jay, *Spies and Saboteurs: Anglo-American Collaboration and Rivalry in Human Intelligence Collection and Special Operations, 1940–45* (New York: St Martin's Press, 1999)

Jansen, Marc, and N. V. Petrov, *Stalin's Loyal Executioner: People's Commissar Nikolai Ezhov, 1895–1940* (Stanford, CA: Hoover Institution Press, 2002)

Jeffery, Keith, *MI6: The History of the Secret Intelligence Service, 1909–1949* (London: Bloomsbury, 2010)

——, and Peter Hennessy, *States of Emergency: British Governments and Strikebreaking since 1919* (London: Routledge & Kegan Paul, 1983)

Jenkins, Peter, *Covert Surveillance Techniques: The Manual of Covert Surveillance Training* (Keighley: Intel, 1998)

Johnson, Franklyn Arthur, *Defence by Committee: The British Committee of Imperial Defence, 1885–1959* (Oxford University Press: Oxford, 1960)

Johnson, Loch K., and James J. Wirtz, ed., *Strategic Intelligence: Windows into a Secret World: An Anthology* (Los Angeles, CA: Roxbury Pub. Co., 2004)

Johnson, William R., *Thwarting Enemies at Home and Abroad: How to Be a Counterintelligence Officer* (Bethesda, MD: Stone Trail Press, 1987)

Judd, Alan, *The Quest for C: Mansfield Cumming and the Founding of the Secret Service* (London: HarperCollins, 2000)

Kahn, David, *The Codebreakers: The Story of Secret Writing* (London: Wiedenfeld and Nicolson, 1967)

Kendall, Walter, *Revolutionary Movement in Britain, 1900–21: The Origins of British Communism* (London: Weidenfeld & Nicolson, 1969)

Kennan, George, *Russia and the West under Lenin and Stalin* (London: Hutchinson, 1961)

Kennedy, Paul M., *The Rise of the Anglo-German Antagonism 1860–1914* (London: Allen & Unwin, 1980)

Kern, Gary, *A Death in Washington: Walter G. Krivitsky and the Stalin Terror* (New York: Enigma, 2004)

Kesaris, Paul L., ed., *The Rote Kapelle: The CIA's History of Soviet Intelligence Networks in Europe, 1936–1945* (Washington, DC: University Publications of America, 1979)

Kessler, Ronald, *The Bureau: The Secret History of the FBI* (New York: St Martin's Press, 2002)

Kissinger, Henry, *Diplomacy* (New York; London: Simon & Schuster, 1994)

Klehr, Harvey, John Earl Haynes, and Fridrikh Firsov, *The Secret World of American Communism* (London: Yale University Press, 1995)

Klugmann, J., *History of Communist Party of Great Britain. Volume I: Formation and Early Years* (London: Lawrence & Wishart, 1968)

——, *History of Communist Party of Great Britain. Volume II: 1925–1927: The General Strike* (London: Lawrence and Wishart, 1969)

Knightley, Phillip, *Philby: The Life and Views of the K.G.B. Masterspy*, new edn (London: Andre Deutsch, 2003)

Koch, Stephen, *Double Lives: Stalin, Willi Munzenberg and the Seduction of the Intellectuals* (London: HarperCollins, 1995)

Langhorne, Richard, ed., *Diplomacy and Intelligence during the Second World War: Essays in Honour of F.H. Hinsley* (Cambridge: Cambridge University Press, 1985)

Le Carré, John, *Call for the Dead* (London: Sceptre, 1961)

Leggett, George, *The Cheka: Lenin's Political Police* (Oxford: Clarendon, 1981)

Leonard, Raymond W., *Secret Soldiers of the Revolution: Soviet Military Intelligence, 1918–1933* (London: Greenwood Press, 1999)

Linehan, Thomas P., *British Fascism, 1918–39: Parties, Ideology and Culture* (Manchester: Manchester University Press, 2000)

Lunn, Kenneth, and Richard Thurlow, ed., *British Fascism: Essays on the Radical Right in Inter-War Britain* (London: Croom Helm, 1980)

Madeira, Victor, *Britannia and the Bear: The Anglo-Russian Intelligence Wars, 1917–1929* (Woodbridge: Boydell Press, 2014)

Martin, Roderick, *Communism and the British Trade Unions, 1924–1933: A Study of the National Minority Movement* (Oxford: Clarendon Press, 1969)

Martland, Peter, *Lord Haw Haw: The English Voice of Nazi Germany* (Richmond: Public Record Office, 2003)

Masters, Anthony, *The Man Who Was M: The Life of Maxwell Knight* (Oxford: Basil Blackwell, 1984)

May, Ernest R., ed., *Knowing One's Enemies: Intelligence Assessment before the Two World Wars* (Princeton, NJ: Princeton University Press, 1984)

McDermott, Kevin, and Jeremy Agnew, *The Comintern: A History of International Communism from Lenin to Stalin* (Basingstoke: Macmillan Press, 1996)

McDonough, Frank, ed., *The Origins of the Second World War: An International Perspective* (London: Continuum, 2010)

McKnight, David, *Espionage and the Roots of the Cold War: The Conspiratorial Heritage* (London: Frank Cass, 2002)

Melton, H. Keith, *Ultimate Spy*, 2nd edn (London: Dorling Kindersley, 2002)

Morgan, Kevin, *Labour Legends and Russian Gold* (London: Lawrence & Wishart, 2006)

NDIC Intelligence Science Board, ed., *Educing Information: Interrogation: Science and Art. Foundations for the Future* (Washington, DC: National Defense Intelligence College [NDIC] Press, 2006)

Neilson, Keith, *Britain, Soviet Russia and the Collapse of the Versailles Order, 1919–1939* (Cambridge: Cambridge University Press, 2006)

Neuberg, A., *Armed Insurrection*, trans. Hoare, Quintin (London: NLB, 1970)

Newton, Verne W., *The Butcher's Embrace: The Philby Conspirators in Washington* (London: Macdonald, 1991)

O'Connell, Robert L., *Of Arms and Men: A History of War, Weapons, and Aggression*, pbk edn (Oxford: Oxford University Press, 2002)

Olson, James M., *Fair Play: The Moral Dilemmas of Spying* (Washington, DC: Potomac Books, 2007)

Orlov, Aleksandr, *Handbook of Intelligence and Guerrilla Warfare* (Ann Arbor: University of Michigan Press, 1963)

Overy, Richard, *The Twilight Years: The Paradox of Britain between the Wars* (London: Penguin, 2009)

Payne, Stanley G., *A History of Fascism: 1914–1945* (London: Routledge, 1995)

Peake, Hayden B. and Samuel Halpern, *In the Name of Intelligence: Essays in Honor of Walter Pforzheimer* (Washington, DC: NIBC Press, 1994)

Perkins, Anne, *A Very British Strike: 3 May–12 May, 1926* (London: Macmillan, 2006)

Phillips, Gordon A., *The General Strike: The Politics of Industrial Conflict* (London: Weidenfeld and Nicolson, 1976)

Popplewell, Richard J., *Intelligence and Imperial Defence: British Intelligence and the Defence of the Indian Empire, 1904–1924* (London: Frank Cass, 1995)

Porter, Bernard, *The Origins of the Vigilant State: The London Metropolitan Police Special Branch before the First World War* (Woodbridge: Boydell Press, 1991)

——, *Plots and Paranoia: A History of Political Espionage in Britain, 1790–1988*, new edn (London: Routledge, 1992)

Posner, Richard A., *Preventing Surprise Attacks: Intelligence Reform in the Wake of 9/11* (Lanham, MD.: Rowman & Littlefield in co-operation with the Hoover Institution, 2005)

——, *Remaking Domestic Intelligence* (Stanford, CA: Hoover Institution Press, 2005)

——, *Uncertain Shield: The U.S. Intelligence System in the Throes of Reform* (Lanham, MD: Rowman & Littlefield, 2006)

Read, Anthony, and David Fisher, *Colonel Z: The Life and Times of a Master of Spies* (London: Hodder and Stoughton, 1984)

Rees, Tim, and Andrew Thorpe, *International Communism and the Communist International, 1919–1943* (Manchester: Manchester University Press, 1998)

Reid, Alastair J., *United We Stand: A History of Britain's Trade Unions* (London: Allen Lane, 2004)

Reinalda, Bob, ed., *The International Transportworkers Federation, 1914–1945: The Edo Fimmen Era* (Amsterdam: Stichting beheer IISG, 1997)

Reynolds, David, *Britannia Overruled: British Policy and World Power in the Twentieth Century*, 2nd edn (Harlow: Longman, 2000)

——, *The Creation of the Anglo-American Alliance, 1937–41: A Study in Competitive Co-Operation* (London: Europa, 1981)

Richardson, Jerry, *The Magic of Rapport* (Capitola, CA: Meta Publications, 1987)

Robertson, A., and K. G. Robertson, *British and American Approaches to Intelligence* (Basingstoke: Macmillan, 1987)

Rose, Kenneth, *Elusive Rothschild: The Life of Victor, Third Baron* (London: Weidenfeld and Nicolson, 2003)

Sakwa, Richard, *Soviet Politics: An Introduction* (London: Routledge, 1989)

Schecter, Jerrold, and Peter Deriabin, *The Spy Who Saved the World: How a Soviet Colonel Changed the Course of the Cold War* (Washington, DC; London: Brassey's, 1995)

Seaman, Mark, ed., *Secret Agent's Handbook: The WWII Spy Manual of Devices, Disguises, Gadgets, and Concealed Weapons* (Guilford, CT: The Lyons Press, 2001)

Sebag-Montefiore, H., *Enigma: The Battle for the Code* (London: Weidenfeld and Nicolson, 2000)

Shulsky, Abram N., and Gary J. Schmitt, *Silent Warfare: Understanding the World of Intelligence*, 3rd edn (Washington, DC: Brassey's, 2002)

Sims, Jennifer E., and Burton Gerber, ed., *Transforming U.S. Intelligence* (Washington, DC: Georgetown University Press, 2005)

Singh, Simon, *The Code Book: The Science of Secrecy from Ancient Egypt to Quantum Cryptography* (London: Fourth Estate, 1999)

Skelley, Jeffrey, ed., *The General Strike, 1926* (London: Lawrence & Wishart, 1976)

Stafford, David, *Churchill and Secret Service* (London: Abacus, 2001)

——, *Roosevelt and Churchill: Men of Secrets* (London: Abacus, 2000)

Steiner, Zara, *The Lights That Failed: European International History, 1919–1933* (Oxford: Oxford University Press, 2005)

Steiner, Zara, *The Triumph of the Dark: European International History, 1933–1939* (Oxford: Oxford University Press, 2011)

Erskine, Ralph, and Michael Smith, ed., *Action This Day* (London: Bantam Press, 2001)

Taylor, A. J. P., *English History, 1914–1945*, 2nd edn (Oxford: Oxford University Press, 1966)

Taylor, Robert, *The TUC: From the General Strike to New Unionism* (Basingstoke: Palgrave, 2000)

Thorpe, Andrew, *The British Communist Party and Moscow, 1920–43* (Manchester: Manchester University Press, 2000)

Thouless, Robert H., *Straight and Crooked Thinking* ([S.I.]: Hodder and Staughton, 1930)

Thurlow, Richard, *Fascism in Britain: A History, 1918–1985* (Oxford: Basil Blackwell, 1987)

——, *Fascism in Modern Britain* (Stroud: Sutton Publishing, 2000)

Thurlow, Richard C., *The Secret State: British Internal Security in the Twentieth Century* (London: Blackwell Publishers, 1995)

Trotsky, Leon, *The Revolution Betrayed* (Mineola, NY: Dover Publications, 2004)

Ullman, Richard H., *Anglo-Soviet Relations, 1917–1921*, 3 vols (London: Oxford University Press, 1961–1973)

Venturi, Franco, *Roots of Revolution: A History of the Populist and Socialist Movements in Nineteenth-Century Russia* (London: Weidenfeld and Nicolson, 1960)

Wallace, Robert, and H. Keith Melton, *Spycraft: The Secret History of the CIA's Spytechs from Communism to Al-Qaeda* (London: Dutton, 2008)

Wegner, Bernd, ed., *From Peace to War: Germany, Soviet Russia, and the World, 1939–1941* (Providence, RI: Berghahn Books, published in association with the Militärgeschichtliches Forschungsamt, Potsdam, 1997)

Weinstein, Allen, *Perjury: The Hiss-Chambers Case* (New York: Alfred A. Knopf, 1988)

——, and Alexander Vassiliev, *The Haunted Wood: Soviet Espionage in America – The Stalin Era* (New York: Random House, 1999)

West, Nigel, and Oleg Tsarev, *The Crown Jewels: The British Secrets at the Heart of the KGB Archives* (London: HarperCollins, 1998)

Wheeler-Bennett, John, *John Anderson, Viscount Waverly* (London: Macmillan, 1962)

Williams, David, *Not in the Public Interest: The Problem of Security in Democracy* (London: Hutchinson, 1965)

Williamson, Philip, *Stanley Baldwin: Conservative Leadership and National Values* (Cambridge: Cambridge University Press, 1999)

Wolf, Lucien, *The Myth of the Jewish Menace in World Affairs, or The Truth About the Forged Protocols of the Elders of Zion* (New York: Macmillan, 1921)

Wright, Lawrence, *The Looming Tower: Al-Qaeda's Road to 9/11* (London: Penguin Books, 2006)

Dissertations

Burke, David, 'Theodore Rothstein and Russian Political Émigré Influence on the British Labour Movement, 1884–1920' (unpublished doctoral dissertation, University of Greenwich, 1997)

de la Marck, David de Young, 'Free French and British Intelligence Relations, 1940–1944' (unpublished doctoral dissertation, University of Cambridge, 2002)

Quinlan, Kevin, '"Tradecraft" and British Intelligence, 1919–1945' (unpublished MPhil dissertation, University of Cambridge, 2005)

Walton, Calder, 'British Intelligence and Threats to National Security, c.1941–1951' (unpublished doctoral dissertation, University of Cambridge, 2006)

Wilson, Emily Jane, 'The War in the Dark: The Security Service and the Abwehr, 1940–1944' (unpublished doctoral dissertation, University of Cambridge, 2003)

Journal Articles and Book Chapters

Aldrich, Richard J., 'Policing the Past: Official History, Secrecy and British Intelligence since 1945', *English Historical Review* 119 (2004), 922–53

Andrew, Christopher, 'The British Secret Service and Anglo-Soviet Relations in the 1920s Part I: From the Trade Negotiations to the Zinoviev Letter', *The Historical Journal* 20 (1977), 673–706

——, 'F.H. Hinsley and the Cambridge Moles: Two Patterns of Intelligence Recruitment', in *Diplomacy and Intelligence during the Second World War: Essays in Honour of F.H. Hinsley*, ed. Richard Langhorne (Cambridge: Cambridge University Press, 1985), pp. 22–40

Andrew, Christopher, and Julie Elkner, 'Stalin and Foreign Intelligence', in *Redefining Stalinism*, ed. Harold Shukman (London: Frank Cass, 2003), pp. 69–94

Ankerbrand, John, 'What To Do With Defectors', *Studies in Intelligence* Fall (1961), 33–43

Aubin, Chantal, 'French Counterintelligence and British Secret Intelligence in the Netherlands, 1920–1940', in *Battleground Western Europe. Intelligence*

Operations in Germany and the Netherlands in the Twentieth Century, ed. Beatrice de Graf, Ben de Jong and Weis Platje (Amsterdam: Het Spinhuis, 2008), pp. 17–48

Bennett, Gill, 'The Secret Service Committee, 1919–1931' in *The Records of the Permanent Undersecretary's Department: Liaison between the Foreign Office and British Secret Intelligence, 1873–1939* (London: FCO, 2005), pp. 42–53.

Borum, Randy, 'Approaching Truth: Behavioural Science Lessons on Educing Information from Human Sources', in *Educing Information: Interrogation: Science and Art. Foundations for the Future*, ed. NDIC Intelligence Science Board (Washington, DC: National Defense Intelligence College [NDIC] Press, 2006), pp. 17–43

Brabourne, Martin L., 'More on the Recruitment of Soviets', *Studies in Intelligence* Winter (1965), 39–60

Callaghan, John, and Kevin Morgan, 'The Open Conspiracy of the Communist Party and the Case of W.N. Ewer, Communist and Anti-Communist', *The Historical Journal* 49 (2006), 549–64

Callaghan, John, and Mark Phythian, 'State Surveillance of the CPGB Leadership. 1920s–1950s', *Labour History Review* 69 (2004), 13–33

Cecil, Robert, 'The Cambridge Comintern', in *The Missing Dimension: Governments and Intelligence Communities in the Twentieth Century*, ed. Christopher Andrew and David Dilks (London: Macmillan, 1984), pp. 169–98

Cohen, Paul, 'The Police, the Home Office and Surveillance of the British Union of Fascists', *Intelligence and National Security* 1 (1986), 417–34

'Concerning Espionage and Social Courtesy', *Studies in Intelligence* Summer (1966), 77–80

Cotter, Cornelius P., 'Emergency Detention in Wartime: The British Experience', *Stanford Law Review* 6 (1954), 238–86

Crumpton, Henry A., 'Intelligence and Homeland Defense', in *Transforming U.S. Intelligence*, ed. Jennifer E. Sims and Burton Gerber (Washington, DC: Georgetown University Press, 2005), pp. 198–219

Dacre of Glanton, Lord, 'Sideways into S.I.S.', in *In the Name of Intelligence: Essays in Honor of Walter Pforzheimer*, ed. Hayden B. Peake and Samuel Halpern, (Washington, DC: NIBC Press, 1994), pp. 251–60

Desmarais, Ralph H., 'The British Government's Strikebreaking Organization and Black Friday', *Journal of Contemporary History* 6 (1971), 112–27

——, 'Strikebreaking and the Labour Government of 1924', *Journal of Contemporary History* 8 (1974), 165–75

Dilks, David, 'Flashes of Intelligence: The Foreign Office, the SIS and Security before the Second World War', in *The Missing Dimension: Governments and Intelligence Communities in the Twentieth Century*, ed. Christopher Andrew and David Dilks (London: Macmillan, 1984), pp. 101–25

Erskine, Ralph, and Peter Freeman, 'Brigadier John Tiltman: One of Britain's Finest Cryptologists', *Cryptologia*, 27 (2003), 289–318

Farndon, Stanley B., 'The Interrogation of Defectors', *Studies in Intelligence* Summer (1960), 9–30

Ferris, John, 'The Road to Bletchley Park: The British Experience with Signals Intelligence, 1892–1945', *Intelligence and National Security* 17 (2002), 53–84

Fleischhauer, Ingeborg, 'Soviet Foreign Policy and the Origins of the Hitler-Stalin Pact', in *From Peace to War: Germany, Soviet Russia, and the World, 1939–1941*, ed. Bernd

Wegner (Providence, RI: Berghahn Books, published in association with the Militärgeschichtliches Forschungsamt, Potsdam, 1997), pp. 27–45

Freeman, Peter, 'MI1(b) and the Origins of British Diplomatic Cryptanalysis', *Intelligence and National Security* 22 (2007), 206–28

Gerber, Burton, 'Managing HUMINT: The Need for a New Approach', in *Transforming U.S. Intelligence*, ed. Jennifer E. Sims and Burton Gerber (Washington, DC: Georgetown University Press, 2005), pp. 180–97

Geschwind, C. N., 'Counterintelligence Interrogation', *Studies in Intelligence* Winter (1965), 23–38

Glenny, M. V., 'The Anglo-Soviet Trade Agreement, March 1921', *Journal of Contemporary History* 5 (1970), 63–82

Hagemeister, Michael, 'The Protocols of the Elders of Zion: Between Fact and Fiction', *New German Critique* 35 (2008), 83–95

Hargreaves, John D., 'The Comintern and Anti-Colonialism: New Research Opportunities', *African Affairs* 92 (1993), 255–61

Harris, James W., 'Building Leverage in the Long War: Ensuring Intelligence Community Creativity in the Fight against Terrorism', *Policy Analysis* 439, 16 May 2002

Hennessy, Peter, 'From Secret State to Protective State', in *The New Protective State: Government, Intelligence, and Terrorism*, ed. Peter Hennessy (London: Continuum, 2007), pp. 1–41

Hiley, Nicholas, 'Entering the Lists: MI5's Great Spy Round-Up of August 1914', *Intelligence and National Security* 21 (2006), 46–76

——, 'Internal Security in Wartime: The Rise and Fall of P.M.S.2, 1915–1917', *Intelligence and National Security* 1 (1986), 395–415

Holquist, Peter, 'Information is the Alpha and Omega of Our Work', *Journal of Modern History* 69 (1997), 415–50

Hope, John G., 'Surveillance or Collusion? Maxwell Knight, MI5 and the British Fascisti', *Intelligence and National Security* 9 (1994), 651–75

Hulnick, Arthur S., 'What's Wrong with the Intelligence Cycle', *Intelligence and National Security* 21 (2006), 959–79

Imler, Norman, 'Espionage in an Age of Change: Optimizing Strategic Intelligence Services for the Future', in *Intelligence and the National Security Strategist: Enduring Issues and Challenges*, ed. Roger Z. George and Robert D. Kline (Lanham, MD: Rowman & Littlefield Publishers, 2006), pp. 217–35

Jeffery, Keith, and Alan Sharp, 'Lord Curzon and Secret Intelligence', in *The Missing Dimension: Governments and Intelligence Communities in the Twentieth Century*, ed. Christopher Andrew and David Dilks (London: Macmillan, 1984), pp. 103–26

Johnson, William R., 'Tricks of the Trade: Counterintelligence Interrogation', *International Journal of Intelligence and Counterintelligence* 1 (1986), 103–13

Kleinman, Steven M., 'KUBARK Counterintelligence Interrogation Review: Observations of an Interrogator: Lessons Learned and Avenues for Further Research', in *Educing Information: Interrogation: Science and Art. Foundations for the Future*, ed. NDIC Intelligence Science Board (Washington, DC: National Defense Intelligence College [NDIC] Press, 2006), pp. 95–140

Klugmann, James, 'Marxism, Reformism, and the General Strike', in *The General Strike, 1926*, ed. Jeffery Skelley (London: Lawrence & Wishart, 1976), pp. 57–107

Laycock, Keith, 'Handwriting Analysis as an Assessment Aid', *Studies in Intelligence* Summer (1959), 23–43

Leonard, Raymond W., 'Studying the Kremlin's Secret Soldiers: A Historiographical Essay on the GRU, 1918–1945', *The Journal of Military History* 56 (1992), 403–22

Leutze, James, 'The Secret of the Churchill-Roosevelt Correspondence: September 1939–May 1940', *Journal of Contemporary History* 10 (1975), 465–91

Lockhart, John Bruce, 'Intelligence: A British View', in *British and American Approaches to Intelligence*, ed. A. Robertson and K. G. Robertson (London: Macmillan, 1987), pp. 37–52

Madeira, Victor, '"Because I Don't Trust Him, We Are Friends": Signals Intelligence and the Reluctant Anglo-Soviet Embrace, 1917–24', *Intelligence and National Security* 19 (2004), 29–51

——, 'Moscow's Interwar Infiltration of British Intelligence, 1919–1929', *The Historical Journal* 46 (2003), 915–33

——, '"No Wishful Thinking Allowed": Secret Service Committee and Intelligence Reform in Great Britain, 1919–23', *Intelligence and National Security* 18 (2003), 1–20

MacGaffin, John, 'Clandestine Human Intelligence: Spies, Counterspies, and Covert Action', in *Transforming U.S. Intelligence*, ed. Jennifer E. Sims and Burton Gerber (Washington, DC: Georgetown University Press, 2005), pp. 79–95

Manningham-Buller, Eliza, 'The International Terrorist Threat to the United Kingdom', in *The New Protective State: Government, Intelligence and Terrorism*, ed. Peter Hennessy (London: Continuum, 2007), pp. 66–73

McIvor, Arthur, '"A Crusade for Capitalism": The Economic League, 1919–39', *Journal of Contemporary History* 23 (1988), 631–55

Moos, Malcolm, 'The Navicert in World War II', *The American Journal of International Law* 38 (1944), 115–19

Neilson, Keith, '"Joy Rides"? British Intelligence and Propaganda in Russia, 1914–1917', *The Historical Journal* 24 (1981), 885–906

Nemzer, Louis, 'The Soviet Friendship Societies', *The Public Opinion Quarterly* 13 (1949), 265–84

O'Halpin, Eunan, 'Sir Warren Fisher and the Coalition, 1919–1922', *The Historical Journal* 24 (1981), 907–27

Olson, James M., 'The Ten Commandments of Counterintelligence', in *Intelligence and the National Security Strategist: Enduring Issues and Challenges*, ed. Roger Z. George and Robert D. Kline (Lanham, MD: Rowman & Littlefield Publishers, 2006), pp. 251–8

Palmer, Alisdair, 'The History of the D-Notice Committee', in *The Missing Dimension: Governments and Intelligence Communities in the Twentieth Century*, ed. Christopher Andrew and David Dilks (London: Macmillan, 1984), pp. 227–49

Quinlan, Kevin and Calder Walton, 'Missed Opportunities? British Intelligence and the Road to War', in *The Origins of the Second World War: An International Perspective*, ed. Frank McDonough, (London: Continuum, 2010), pp. 205–22

Reynolds, David, '1940: Fulcrum of the Twentieth Century?', *International Affairs (Royal Institute of International Affairs 1944–)* 66 (1990), 325–50

Thomas, Edward, 'The Evolution of the JIC System Up to and During World War II', in *Intelligence and International Relations 1900–1945*, ed. Christopher Andrew and Jeremy Noakes (Exeter: University of Exeter, 1987), pp. 219–34

Thurlow, Richard C., 'British Fascism and State Surveillance, 1934–1945', *Intelligence and National Security* 3 (1988), 77–99

——, 'Soviet Spies and British Counter-Intelligence in the 1930s: Espionage in the Woolwich Arsenal and the Foreign Office Communications Department', *Intelligence and National Security* 19 (2004), 610–31

Uldricks, Teddy J., 'Soviet Security Policy in the 1930s', in *Soviet Foreign Policy, 1917, 1991: A Retrospective*, ed. Gabriel Gorodetsky (London: Frank Cass, 1994), pp. 65–74

Wark, Wesley K., 'In Never-Never Land? The British Archives on Intelligence', *The Historical Journal* 35 (1992), 195–203

Watt, Donald Cameron, '[John] Herbert King: A Soviet Source in the Foreign Office', *Intelligence and National Security* 4 (1988), 62–82

Wasemiller, A. C., 'The Anatomy of Counterintelligence', *Studies in Intelligence* Winter (1969), 9–24

Werth, Nicolas, 'A State Against Its People: Repression and Terror in the Soviet Union', in *The Black Book of Communism: Crimes, Terror, Repression*, ed. Stephane Courtois and Mark Kramer (Cambridge, MA: Harvard University Press, 1999), pp. 33–268

White, Stephen, 'Communism and the East: The Baku Congress, 1920', *Slavic Review* 33 (1974), 492–514

Index